D1551346

The East German State and the Catholic Church, 1945–1989

Studies in German History

Published in Association with the German Historical Institute, Washington, DC

General Editors:

Helmut Berghoff, Director of the German Historical Institute, Washington, DC
Uwe Spiekermann, Deputy Director of the German Historical Institute, Washington, DC

THE EAST GERMAN STATE
AND THE
CATHOLIC CHURCH,
1945–1989

Bernd Schaefer

Translated by Jonathan Skolnik & Patricia C. Sutcliffe

Berghahn Books
NEW YORK • OXFORD

Published in 2010 by
Berghahn Books
www.berghahnbooks.com

German Edition
© 1998 Böhlau
Staat und katholische Kirche in der DDR by Bernd Schaefer

English language edition
© 2010 Berghahn Books

Library of Congress Cataloging-in-Publication Data
Schäfer, Bernd, 1962-
[Staat und katholische Kirche in der DDR. English]
The East German state and the Catholic Church, 1945/1989 / Bernd Schaefer ; translated by Jonathan Skolnik and Patricia C. Sutcliffe.
p. cm. — (Studies in German history ; v. 11)
Includes bibliographical references and index.
ISBN 978-1-84545-737-2 (hardback : alk. paper)
1. Church and state—Germany (East)—History—20th century. 2. Germany (East)—Church history—20th century. 3. Church and state—Catholic Church. I. Title.
BR856.35.S24513 2010

282'.43109045—dc22

British Library Cataloguing in Publication Data
A catalogue record for this book is available from the British Library.

Printed in the United States on acid-free paper

ISBN 978-1-84545-737-2 (hardback)

For Karen, Patrick, Cora, and Bjorn

CONTENTS

Preface and Acknowledgments

Among my many private visits to the former German Democratic Republic, the most memorable was the one to Dresden in July 1987 to attend the first-ever GDR-wide convocation of East German Catholics. About 100,000 people from all over the country gathered in this third-largest GDR city, dominating its appearance for about three days. As Erich Honecker was scheduled to visit West Germany in September that year, East German regional and central authorities had been comparatively tolerant in facilitating the Dresden event. Most remarkable, however, were Catholics' expressions of a new self-confidence in the GDR, on the one hand, and of their ultimate acceptance of the country as imperfect but a home, on the other. Nobody in July 1987 in Dresden, including me, could even faintly imagine that about two years later the GDR was to vanish into history and rush toward a united Germany at warp speed. Until October 1989, East Germans' behavior, attitudes, and actions were essentially dominated by their awareness that they would have to spend their entire lives in the rather sullen GDR.

In 1987, I decided to write my dissertation about the state and the Catholic Church in the GDR. Had it not been for the end of the GDR and the opening of its archives after German unification, this enterprise would have resulted in a superficial and misleading work based on published material and interviews that were anything but frank. Yet after 1990, a wealth of archival records and living witnesses from a very recent history suddenly became available.

With regard to GDR history, the 1990s in Germany were characterized by fierce historiographical and political debates embedded in a public climate where accusations and counter-accusations flew back and forth based on repeated investigative revelations. Shaped and hardly unaffected by this context, I was both fortunate and challenged to complete a dissertation wholly different from the one I had envisaged in 1987. After my doctoral exam at Martin Luther University in Halle, the final product appeared as a book in Germany in two editions in 1998 and 1999.[1] Considered to be a contribution toward "coming to terms" with GDR history, the book was introduced to several dozen highly attentive public audiences in places all over East Germany and, in consequence, to scores of diligent readers. On the whole, reactions to the facts and interpretations presented in the book ranged from stunned to deflated, with regard to both the GDR's policies and to the actions of the Catholic Church.

Ten years later, I am extremely grateful to be able to introduce the slightly abridged English version of this book. Though some footnotes on individual Stasi connections and other details have been omitted (readers interested in fuller documentation should refer to the German version of the book), the book's general structure has been maintained: it follows a periodization based on GDR political history (1945–1953, 1953–1957, 1957–1961, 1961–1972, 1972–1989). Chapters are organized in concentric circles, starting with the general history of the period, followed by various aspects of state policy and interactions with the church, and concluding with actions and patterns emanating from the Catholic Church. In addition to the trajectory of church-state diplomatic history and its various shades of repressiveness, the book also addresses social and economic issues, as well as questions of ideology, theology, and culture. The conclusion summarizes the main features of forty-four years of encounters between the Catholic Church and the East German state.

This conclusion remains unchanged from the German edition. Since the original book's appearance in 1998, further research-based works on the subject have been published without changing the substance of the overall picture. Most of them focused on hierarchy-centered regional documentation and issues, and some of them are not entirely free of apologetic tendencies or individual lionizations.[2] Only one other publication discussed the state-church relationship with a few differing interpretations.[3] Two books added some new perspectives: one discussed the practical impact of Catholic theology during GDR times;[4] the other is an edited volume designed to reflect on the state of research.[5]

I want to thank the former director of the German Historical Institute (GHI) in Washington, D.C., Christof Mauch, for initiating this book's publication and GHI Senior Editor David Lazar for shepherding it through the process. Two anonymous referees provided very kind reviews. I am very grateful to Marion Berghahn of Berghahn Publishers in New York/Oxford for heeding their advice and accepting the book for her series. Jonathan Skolnik from the University of Massachusetts at Amherst and Patricia C. Sutcliffe from the GHI did an admirable job translating the German original and editing the book for publication.

Last but far from least: since it is rather unheard of in German academic publishing but sensibly warranted in the United States, I would like to use this opportunity to personally thank many people from various backgrounds and with widely differing GDR biographies. They all have in common a willingness to share their individual memories of "The Catholic Church and the East German State" with me and to offer, in sum, extremely valuable insights. These individuals are listed in alphabetical order with their residences at the time we met: Manfred Ackermann (Berlin), Jürgen Backhaus (Heiligenstadt), the late Ulrich Berger (Magdeburg), Anton Beer (Friedland), the late Alfred Brockhoff (Hünstetten-Wallrabenstein), Ursula Broghammer (Halle-Dölau), Konrad Feiereis (Erfurt), Georg Diederich (Schwerin), Horst Dohle (Berlin), Karl-Heinz

Ducke (Jena), Heinz-Josef Durstewitz (Berlin), Hans-Friedrich Fischer (Leipzig), Siegfried Foelz (Naundorf), Aloys Funk (Berlin), the late Martin Fritz (Magdeburg), Joachim Garstecki (Teltow), Josef Göbel (Berlin), Dieter Grande (Dresden), the Gremler and Körner families (Dingelstädt), Günter Hanisch (Leipzig), Horst Hartwig (Berlin), the late Claus Herold (Halle), Helmut Hiller (Dessau), Matthias Holluba (Leipzig), Josef Horntrich (Cottbus), the late Bernhard Huhn (Görlitz), Clemens Jaunich (Groß Kölzig), Norbert Kaczmarek (Berlin), Hermann Kalb (Berlin), Rudolf Kilank (Bautzen), Renate Krüger (Schwerin), the late Helmut Langos (Merseburg), Claus-Peter März (Erfurt), Theo Mechtenberg (Bad Oeynhausen), Joachim Meisner (Köln), Josef Michelfeit (Berlin), Martin Montag (Zella-Mehlis), Gerhard Nachtwei (Magdeburg), Leo Nowak (Magdeburg), Gerhard Packenius (Halle), Josef Pilvousek (Erfurt), Martina und Johannes Pohl (Dresden), Eberhard Prause (Dresden), Friedrich Rebbelmund (Leipzig), Jens Reich (Berlin), Joachim Reinelt (Dresden), Peter Roske (Berlin), Horst Rothkegel (Berlin), Clemens Rosner (Leipzig), the late Günter Särchen (Wittichenau), the late Theodor Schmitz (Berlin), Andreas Scholz (Bestensee), Arno Schulz (Berlin), Hans-Joachim Seidowsky (Berlin), Eva Storrer (Güstrow), Peter Stosiek (Görlitz), Peter Paul Straube (Bautzen), Wulf Trende (Erkner), Michael Ulrich (Dresden), Julius Schoenemann (Köln), Siegfried Seifert (Bautzen), Willi Verstege (Nienburg), Matthias Wanitschke (Erfurt), Joachim Wanke (Erfurt), Norbert Werbs (Schwerin), Joachim Wiegand (Berlin), the late Lothar Wiest (Stetten am kalten Markt), Friedhelm Wortmann (Essen), and Hubertus Zomack (Görlitz).

Bernd Schaefer, Summer 2010
Kensington, Maryland/Washington, D.C.

Notes

1. Bernd Schäfer, *Staat und katholische Kirche in der DDR,* 2nd ed. (Cologne and Weimar, 1999).
2. Wolfgang Tischner, *Katholische Kirche in der SBZ/DDR 1945–1951* (Paderborn, 2001); Clemens Brodkorb, *Bruder und Gefährte in der Bedrängnis – Hugo Aufderbeck als Seelsorgeamtsleiter in Magdeburg: Zur pastoralen Grundlegung einer "Kirche in der SBZ/DDR"* (Paderborn, 2002); Ruth Jung, *Ungeteilt im geteilten Berlin? Das Bistum Berlin nach dem Mauerbau* (Berlin, 2003); Birgit Mitzscherlich, *Diktatur und Diaspora: Das Bistum Meißen 1932–1951* (Paderborn, 2005); Thomas Schulte-Umberg, ed., *Akten deutscher Bischöfe seit 1945: DDR 1957–1961* (Paderborn, 2006).
3. Ute Haese, *Katholische Kirche in der DDR: Geschichte einer politischen Abstinenz* (Düsseldorf, 1998).
4. Reinhard Grütz, *Katholizismus in der DDR-Gesellschaft 1960–1990* (Paderborn, 2004).
5. Christoph Kösters and Wolfgang Tischner, eds., *Katholische Kirche in SBZ und DDR* (Paderborn, 2005).

ABBREVIATIONS AND GERMAN TERMS

BBK	Berlin Bishops' Conference (1976–1990), Berliner Bischofskonferenz
BDKJ	Catholic Youth Association, Bund der Katholischen Jugend
BEK	Conference of Protestant Churches, Bund der Evangelischen Kirchen (GDR)
BK	Berlin Conference of Catholic Christians of European States (1964–1978), Berliner Konferenz katholischer Christen aus europäischen Staaten; Berlin Conference of European Catholics (1978–1993), Berliner Konferenz Europäischer Katholiken
BKK	Commercial Coordination Division (of the MfS), Bereich Kommerzielle Koordinierung
BOK	Berlin Conference of Ordinaries (1950–1976), Berliner Ordinarienkonferenz
CDU(D)	Christian Democratic Union, Christlich-Demokratische Union (Deutschlands)
CPSU	Communist Party of the Soviet Union
CSCE	Conference on Security and Cooperation in Europe
CSU	Christian Social Union, Christlich-Soziale Union
DBK	German Bishops' Conference, Deutsche Bischofskonferenz
DCV	German Caritas Association, Deutscher Caritasverband
DVP	German People's Police, Deutsche Volkspolizei
EKD	Protestant Church in Germany, Evangelische Kirche in Deutschland (FRG)
FDJ	Free German Youth, Freie Deutsche Jugend
FDP	Free Democratic Party, Freie Demokratische Partei
FRG	Federal Republic of Germany
GDR	German Democratic Republic
Geschäftsgrundlage	Basis for relations
HA	Main Office, Hauptabteilung
Heimat	Home(land)
HV	Main Office (of the East German People's Police), Hauptverwaltung
IM	Unofficial Collaborator (of MfS; Variants IMF/IMB, IMV/IMS)

Jugendweihe	Youth Dedication, a secular alternative to Catholic confirmation
Junge Gemeinde	Young Community, an organization of Protestant youth
Kirchenpolitik	Politics between the church and state, including state church policy
Kirchenpolitiker	Politicians in charge of church matters
KPD	Communist Party of Germany, Kommunistische Partei Deutschlands
KSG	Catholic Student Community, Katholische Studentengemeinde
Kulturbund	Cultural League
LDP(D)	Liberal Democratic Party, Liberaldemokratische Partei (Deutschlands)
MfS	Ministry of State Security, Ministerium für Staatssicherheit
ND	*Neues Deutschland* (SED newspaper)
NKFD	National Committee Free Germany, Nationalkomitee Freies Deutschland
NRNF	National Council of the National Front, Nationalrat der Nationalen Front
NVA	National People's Army, Nationale Volksarmee
OLZ	Operative Headquarters, Operatives Lagezentrum
OPK	Operative Control of Individuals, Operative Personenkontrolle (by MfS)
OV	Operative Measures against Individuals, Operativer Vorgang (by MfS)
PDS	Party of Democratic Socialism, Partei des Demokratischen Sozialismus
SBZ	Soviet Zone of Occupation, Sowjetische Besatzungszone
SED	Socialist Unity Party of Germany, Sozialistische Einheitspartei Deutschlands
SfS	State Secretariat for State Security, Staatssekretariat für Staatssicherheit
SKK	Soviet Control Commission, Sowjetische Kontrollkommission
SMAD	Soviet Military Administration, Sowjetische Militäradministration
SPD	Social Democratic Party, Sozialdemokratische Partei Deutschlands
VdF	League of Freethinkers, Verband der Freidenker
Volkskammer	Parliament of the German Democratic Republic
Volkssolidarität	People's Solidarity Association
ZdK	Central Committee of German Catholics, Zentralkomitee der deutschen Katholiken (FRG)
ZK	Central Committee of the SED, Zentralkomitee der SED

Chapter 1

1945–1953
New Structures in the Postwar Era

The Kirchenpolitik of the Soviet Military Administration and the Communist Party

As Walter Ulbricht prepared a speech for the first assembly of the German Communist Party (KPD) functionaries in Berlin after Germany's surrender in the Second World War—it was 13 May 1945—he added the following notes to his detailed comments on "the question of the churches":

> In this matter, our comrades must not make mistakes in any direction. Churches must be reopened as soon as possible. But that does not mean that the church organizations are to become operational once again.[1]

Written within days of the defeat of the Nazi regime, these lines reveal the fundamental features of the so-called church policy *(Kirchenpolitik)* of the KPD and, later, the Socialist Unity Party (SED). Its approach to religious institutions was supposed to be gauged to the current situation; it was therefore always considered "tactical." That is why the approach could not commit political or strategic errors "in any direction," as Ulbricht put it. From the ideological perspective of "historical materialism" and "proletarian freethinking," most Communists in 1945 regarded the churches (and religion as such) as they had for decades: they were phenomena doomed to historical extinction, a process that, in their view, could be accelerated through propaganda and administrative measures. But religion was also a significant presence in the life of the people and, therefore, a politically potent force that any party wishing to rule had to reckon with. Worldview did not automatically translate into policy, however, and the imperative to be strategically clever often meant using a tactic that contradicted ideology. Within the Communist Party itself, anti-religious ideology was always invoked—in speeches, declarations, etc. This was both a form of internal reassurance and a way to provide the ideological stamina necessary to pursue politically contradictory strategies while projecting a confident image to the outside world.

The policies of the KPD/SED always struck a balance between two tactical variations that became permanent features of the regime's Kirchenpolitik. On the one hand, there was surveillance and repression through the "security policy" (*Sicherheitspolitik*). On the other hand, there was a conciliatory approach, an attempt to instrumentalize the churches through an "alliance policy" (*Bündnispolitik*). These were intertwined. Surveillance, inspection, and repression were the foundations that allowed the SED room for tactical maneuver in its religious policies, right up to 1989.

Because churches represented an alternative way of life and therefore enjoyed some freedom outside the regime, they were always a "politically negative" factor within socialist society. The SED wanted the churches to abstain from any public criticism of the German Democratic Republic (GDR). By contrast, on certain occasions the regime sought the same kinds of political public declarations from the churches that it did from the "bloc parties" (the non-Communist parties united in the National Front under Communist domination) and from mass organizations such as trade unions, student organizations, and professional associations. Such measures were intended to help legitimize the SED while contributing to the political neutralization of the churches. For a long period, the SED sought to limit the major Christian churches to the unremarkable status of "ritual groups" (*"Kultkirchen"*) in order to marginalize them and thus hasten their decline.

Internally, members of the Communist Party and the SED were confronted with a dilemma from the very beginning. For the most part, this dilemma was expressed in the form of criticism of the lower echelons by the higher ones; starting in the 1950s, party organs referred to this with the contrasting negative terms "sectarianism" and "opportunism." "Sectarianism" was used to designate an action toward the churches that, in itself, was ideologically praiseworthy from a Communist viewpoint, but was overzealous and unwise, bringing the SED more political damage than benefits in specific cases. "Opportunism," by contrast, described a policy relating to the churches that SED higher-ups considered too liberal and that allowed churches to expand their influence.

Thus, in the eyes of the Communists, Kirchenpolitik was a complicated encounter with a form of "institutionalized superstition" fated to become extinct, yet—for the time being—it was also a force with a certain social and political relevance. Kirchenpolitik was a concept defined by its negation of religion and the churches. This holds true for the years of SED rule as well as for the earlier era of the Soviet Zone of Occupation (SBZ, 1945–1949), the Soviet Military Administration (SMAD), and the Soviet Control Commission (SKK), which were still relevant in the years after the GDR was founded in 1949. But Kirchenpolitik was only secondarily a policy to render the churches superfluous. It was primarily the product of the interacting strategies of "security policy" and "alliance policy" of the Soviet occupation powers and the hegemonic Communist Party. What was politically relevant was the attempt to balance these two factors in a given context, in order "not to make mistakes in any direction." It was only during phases when Kirchenpolitik was subordinated to a general policy of aggressively "building socialism" (as was the case from mid 1952 to mid 1953, or after 1957) that the SED pursued a kind of collective "sectarianism." During those phases of ideological zeal, Kirchenpolitik and its tactics temporarily gave way to an approach that the SED later characterized as an "error."

Organizational Structures and Their Political Significance

The Working Group for Church Affairs, created in exile in the Soviet Union in June 1944 at a meeting of the National Committee for a Free Germany (NKFD), can be seen as a precursor to the structures that would later emerge in the SBZ. Clergy from various confessions,[2] all German prisoners of war, belonged to the group. As chairman of the KPD, Wilhelm Pieck made a speech at the meeting and, several months later, asked for reports from both Catholics and Protestants on their confessions' expectations regarding church-state relations. These position papers, not authorized by any church, at most served to inform Pieck and had no long-term political relevance. After the NKFD was dissolved in 1945, the SED continued the working group in the form of advisory structures for church matters, beginning in 1946 without the participation of Catholics.

At first, the responsible officers of the SMAD played the decisive role in church matters in the SBZ. But the propaganda office of the SMAD, with a staff of 150, was only marginally concerned with the churches—the office was also responsible for newspapers, radio, censorship, parties, and unions. It was led by the influential Colonel (later General) Sergei Tulpanov; under him, Captain Yermolayev issued decisions in the church affairs department.[3] Soviet officers intervened in local conflicts between religious groups and German Communists; they were viewed by the churches as the real authorities, and on a number of occasions the churches requested their intervention. After the GDR formally became a sovereign state in October 1949, the weight shifted to the ruling SED, although the churches continued to appeal regularly to the Soviet Control Commission and its church affairs division in Berlin-Karlshorst until 1953. Indeed, the SKK was capable of exercising control over the SED when it considered it opportune to do so.

At the local level, the KPD either established official advisory councils for church matters[4] (it had done so as early as May 1945 in Berlin) or arranged to receive informal "advice." The institutionalization of church affairs structures, however, developed only after the founding of the SED in April 1946. At first, these structures were largely staffed by former Social Democrats and Protestant pastors who saw themselves as "religious socialists."[5] The Culture and Education section of the SED's Central Secretariat was comprised of individuals from these groups. In July 1946, before the fall elections and in the context of an ideological debate between the Communists and the Christian Democrats (CDU) over the question of "Christianity and Marxism," the Culture and Education section issued a memo to all regional party organizations announcing that the Communist leadership intended to set up a Commission for Church Affairs.[6] Then, at the SED's so-called Culture Conference in late January 1947, high-level party officials held talks with the religious socialists. In March 1947 a "Church, Christianity, and Religion" unit was set up within the party apparatus, directed by Hans-Joachim Mund, a Protestant pastor.[7] In the wake of the Stalinist development of "a new type of party" between 1948 and 1950, there were purges in the SED that impacted these circles; the majority withdrew from the SED in disappointment.[8] From then on, high-ranking members of the Politburo set the tone in church affairs, working in tandem with Walter Ulbricht's Small Secretariat.[9]

In the newly founded GDR, the SED party apparatus sought to dominate all government offices, including the church affairs bodies. In the early years, this dominance had to be exercised in a more or less veiled way in consideration of the "not yet politically secured" satellite parties and the conceptions of a greater Germany, so it hardly functioned flawlessly. There were often cases where it was unclear which part of the apparatus had authority in a specific case, and contradictory decisions were not uncommon. In their dealings with the state, church representatives could occasionally perceive nuances and differences within the state apparatus and exploit these to their advantage by engaging in negotiations with a broad range of German and Soviet officials.

Under Ulbricht, the Small Secretariat took on the role of coordinating policies, including religious affairs.[10] Occasionally, the Politburo would form ad hoc committees for church affairs, as was the case on 1 August 1950, when a committee was formed under the leadership of Otto Grotewohl through the "National Front" to prepare for the elections in October 1950.[11] Only a few weeks later, these activities resulted in a detailed document with the telling title "Tactics in Church Affairs."[12] The Secretariat of the Central Committee set up a committee on 27 November 1952 to brief the Politburo on the activities of the Junge Gemeinde (Young Community) and determine "the appropriate measures to be taken." This Junge Gemeinde was a new organization of Protestant religious youth, though the SED often used the term to refer to Catholic groups as well. The committee's work led to a Politburo decision on 27 January 1953 "to expose the Junge Gemeinde as a front organization for war-mongering, sabotage, and espionage, directed by West German and American imperialist forces."[13]

Within the executive party apparatus, alongside the above-mentioned advisory structures for religious socialists, church affairs had been handled since April 1946 by three different departments: Regional and Provincial Policy; Municipal Policy; and Justice. On 3 June 1950 the Central Committee of the SED folded these three departments into the State Administration division (which had existed since October 1949) under the direction of Anton Plenikowski and his assistant, Willi Barth. The State Administration division then created a Churches and Religious Groups section on 27 March 1950. Bruno Wolff, who was later arrested for "opportunism," headed the division until 5 January 1953; his successor was Hans Weise.[14]

The Ministry of State Security (MfS), formed on 8 February 1950, also reported to the SED party apparatus regarding church affairs. At first, the MfS set up a church affairs section (Sachgebiet Kirchen) in its main offices in Berlin, part of Department VI at the regional, district, and municipal levels. On 17 September 1952 Erich Mielke ordered that the MfS sections for the CDU, Liberal Democratic Party (LDP), churches, and religious groups be transferred to Department V, which added a Unit E with detailed instructions on dealing with the churches, and especially on how to recruit informers.[15] But, measured against its ambitions to observe and control life in the GDR, the MfS was still understaffed, despite a considerable increase in personnel in the years leading up to 1953.[16] Thus, in the early phase of the GDR, surveillance of the churches was also shared by the Permits Department of the Central Administration of the East German People's Police (Deutsche Volkspolizei), which was under the auspices of the Ministry of the Interior[17] and—until early 1953—the Information Control Department of the Information Office (a predecessor of the GDR Council of Ministers Press Office).[18] All of these offices compiled detailed reports on church activities and events and on any public statements of a political nature. The reports were also sent on to the MfS, which then began to "process" them in many cases.

Whereas the Politburo, Secretariat, and SED party apparatus sought to steer and to control Kirchenpolitik through the MfS, as well as the NKVD and SKK, the formal government under Minister-President Otto Grotewohl appeared to be responsible to those outside of it, as well as to the church representatives who had to depend on discussion partners within it. The office of the Minister-President and its chancellery (called "presidium" after May 1952) under State Secretary Fritz Geyer corresponded with church offices, responding to appeals and complaints. On certain occasions, Grotewohl himself held top-level talks with church leaders.

Within the government, the Main Office for Church Relations was established in January 1950 under the acting Minister-President and CDU chairman Otto Nuschke. It was intended as a liaison office between state and church offices. In both its personnel and its dealings with the churches, this office essentially carried on an "advisory" function. Its decision-making capacity was limited, and its activities were mistrusted by the SED, the MfS, and their agents inside the CDU, who suspected a pro-church bias.[19] Yet because of the complex and unclear structure of decision-making within the state and party apparatus, Nuschke—who was indeed positively disposed toward the churches—and his assistants could tilt some rulings in the churches' favor. The significance of this office for the SED in its dealings with the West after the uprising of 17 June 1953 guaranteed its survival until Nuschke's death in 1957, despite its increasing loss of authority and de facto disempowerment by spring 1953.[20] If the Soviet Union had not dictated the "New Course" at the beginning of June 1953, the Politburo would certainly have carried out its decision of 17 March 1953 to merge the Main Office for Church Relations with the State Secretariat for the Interior.[21]

The State Secretariat for Internal Affairs, directed by Josef Hegen, was detached from the Ministry of the Interior in February 1953 and given its own assignments. Up until that point (beginning in 1950), the state secretary in the Ministry of the Interior, Hans Warnke, had handled discussions with church representatives, especially concerning various approvals. Within the new State Secretariat for Internal Affairs, alongside departments that had been detached from the Ministry of the Interior, a Department of Administrative Affairs was created with a Main Unit for Social Policy and Population Questions headed by Josef Schwarzer; its mission included "direction and control in district and municipal councils to implement the policies of the party and the government in church matters."[22]

The SED once again took up the administrative division of responsibilities for Kirchenpolitik after 1953, but the matter was not really settled until December 1957, when Nuschke died. The bureaucratic and personnel conflicts in the state and party apparatus in the 1950s were by no means limited to Kirchenpolitik. The majority of individuals and institutions involved with the churches after 1950 worked in the realm of "security policy," that is, in surveillance and control. The churches viewed the expansion of Kirchenpolitik bureaucracy after 1949 as confirmation that the new socialist society now under construction saw them as a negative, potentially hostile presence.

The Role of Ideology

The years 1945–1947 have often been romanticized as a hopeful period of mutual tolerance between the KPD/SED and the churches based in a common anti-fascist agenda rooted in the Communist Party's "Popular Front" phase in the 1930s. According to this myth, it was only the tense international climate of the Cold War and the Stalinization of the SED that disrupted relations between the church and the party. This ahistorical view corresponds to the political aims of SED church affairs officials from a later period, when the GDR had already been consolidated.[23]

It is not instructive for analyzing the period after 1945 to reiterate the rhetorical overtures to the Catholic Church in Communist Party documents from the Popular Front era (1935–1939) or statements by the National Committee for a Free Germany between 1943 and 1945.[24] Such explanations by KPD committees or leading politicians like Pieck or Ulbricht cannot be interpreted as somehow part of a developmental process toward a tolerance of worldviews that supposedly led to a favorable starting position for the churches at the end of the war. Rather, Communist policy up until 1945 consisted entirely of tactical variations on the anti-fascist struggle against the common enemy, National Socialism. After the

National Socialists were defeated, the KPD/SED returned to its traditional view of the churches.

The KPD/SED's conviction that religion was illusory and that the church was an institution doomed to extinction never abated. For the 1945–1947 period, however, we must differentiate between the attempt by some SED functionaries to establish a "German path to socialism" and permanent features of Communist ideology that were not always politically opportune, such as atheism. As a rule, Communists associated religion and the churches with politically reactionary anti-Bolshevism. They could only imagine integrating Christians into the SED and churches into the new social order if these were to be completely subordinated to an ideology that foresaw the long-term demise of religion. It was unthinkable to them that Marxism and Christianity could coexist with equal ideological legitimacy, even when, in the short term, Communists accepted the churches' role "of satisfying still-existing religious needs," as Pieck said on 23 November 1947.[25]

These dominant convictions seemed only to be contradicted by the tactical line promoted by the party between 1945 and 1947. This line was not easy to convey to a party base that, as Ulbricht wrote to Pieck on 17 May 1945, "still had to learn the ABCs of our politics."[26] Ulbricht and other leading functionaries could certainly gauge the power relations and the situation of the general population in 1945. It would have been extremely counterproductive for the Communists to seek a confrontation with the churches at this point, particularly considering that the competing CDU sought to present itself as the representative of Christian interests. Thus, in 1946, Ulbricht made a point of rejecting requests to reestablish Weimar-era Free Thinker Associations: "Why do we need organizations of Free Thinkers? So that they can wage war against the churches, provoke them, and thus drive more toward the reactionary side?"[27] On the other hand, former religious socialists who leaned toward the SED were a marginal force within their churches; the SED sought to use them as "alibi Christians" against the CDU. When the CDU adopted a platform of "Christian socialism" in the SBZ, the SED responded with a public declaration by the Central Secretariat on 27 August 1946 (in anticipation of regional and municipal elections); entitled "the SED and Christianity," it promised tolerance "up to the last consequence."[28] But the difficulties and limits of this tolerance were clear at an SED cultural conference in January 1947, when party functionaries held discussions with religious socialists (all SED).[29]

In early October 1947, another conference of SED cultural functionaries had taken place. Leo Stern and Frieda Rubiner had postulated a philosophical incommensurability between Marxism and religion, and described a belief in God as a relic that SED members had to overcome. In response, Arthur Rackwitz, an SED member and a Protestant pastor from the religious socialist milieu,[30] wrote to Grotewohl, asking if these views were really the party's position. Grotewohl forwarded Rackwitz's note to Pieck, adding comments about "the sharp division between our fundamental consideration of this issue and the way it has been transformed in propaganda and the organizational development of the party," thus clearly acknowledging the SED's tactics.[31] A position paper that Pieck requested in November 1947 as a response to Rackwitz ultimately confirmed Stern and Rubiner's views; it referred to those who "still" believed in God and defined the SED's perspective on the future role of the churches: "The church can, of course, refrain from taking positions in political and economic struggles and limit itself to maintaining a belief in God . . . But if the church takes positions that contradict the duties and goals of the party, that will lead to a serious confrontation between the church and party."[32]

The tolerance of other worldviews proclaimed by the SED between 1945 and 1947 was thus nothing more than "a tactical variant for a specific political situation."[33] As soon as the tactical odds shifted in favor of the SED, this variant could yield to the anti-religious and anti-clerical positions of functionaries and the party base. In December 1947, after its leaders Jakob Kaiser and Ernst Lemmer were deposed, the CDU increasingly lost vitality as a political rival of the SED. Occupied Germany was developing into two separate states, pushing certain all-German considerations into the background. Adapting Stalinist structures, the SED was disciplined with "democratic centralism" and cleaned up to be a "new type of party." The SED demanded a monopoly in the area of education and thus saw the churches as opponents. When it concerned "the molding of youth," the SED did not tolerate competing worldviews. The ruling party once again found it opportune to declare that the churches were historically superseded in the new socialist order.

Strategies for Dealing with the Churches

German Communists saw the shaping of youth through education as a foundation upon which to construct a socialist society; it was an opportunity to employ "anti-fascist instruction" to overcome the results of National Socialist indoctrination. The KPD/SED and the Soviet Union believed in the unlimited power of education: in their view, the future belonged to the party that made the youth obedient. In this context, religious instruction in the schools was considered a long-term obstacle. As early as 20 May 1945, Ulbricht declared to KPD members from Berlin that

> Provisionally, it is our view that religious instruction will not be included in the curriculum and that clergy have no place in school offices. However, church representatives may offer extracurricular religious instruction in schools at the parents' request.[34]

After a conversation with Stalin on 4 June 1945, Pieck noted the basic principles: "No religious instruction in the schools—the youth should not be confused by popes—religious study only outside of school."[35] Agreements among the Allies,[36] combined with the reality of power relations in the SBZ, enabled the KPD/SED to enact the "Law for the Democratization of German Schools" with the support of the Liberal Democratic Party on 31 May 1946; the law prevented religious studies from becoming a regular school subject.[37] The teaching of religion was the responsibility of the various religious communities, which were organizationally separate from the schools but allowed in school buildings in certain circumstances. The churches protested this turn away from what had been the accepted practice during the Weimar Republic because it represented the triumph of "the traditional educational policies sought by the workers' movement."[38]

Except in the realm of education, the SED's strategy of allying with the churches dominated until 1948. The Communists had initial success in creating what were at first cross-party social organizations for youth (the Free German Youth, FDJ), culture (Kulturbund), and social aid for the elderly (Volkssolidarität). The apparent exception of the churches from the land reforms of 1945/46, however, had negative consequences for church finances.[39] The GDR constitution, adopted on 7 October 1949, included aspects of the 1919 Weimar constitution pertaining to the churches; in the years to come, church representatives would often refer to these basic laws in their dealings with the state, especially their limited right "to take positions representative of their views on basic questions concerning the life of the people."[40] For the SED, the constitution merely had the character of a political declaration aimed at the West and at still wavering parties within the SED alliance. As of October 1949 the politically relevant state and party offices acted independently of the text of the constitution, which in fact was a text to which there was no real legal recourse through complaint. In practice, the state administration applied the constitution (or ignored it) as the situation required. Legal reality was determined by internal party decisions and normative precedents.

Beginning on 6 April 1949, the SED's Small Secretariat instituted concrete plans for anti-church propaganda and what was later called a "differentiation policy," whereby the SED schematically labeled church representatives "progressive," "loyal," or "reactionary" and attempted to play them against each other and cause institutional breaks within the churches. The SED sought to enlist the Kulturbund, the film industry, and biology classes in the schools in a campaign of "enlightenment" propaganda to reduce the influence of religion, "especially among women, youth, and German refugees from the East."[41] A Pentecost letter by the Protestant Bishop Dibelius that compared the dictatorial methods in the SBZ with the Nazi period prompted the Small Secretariat and the Politburo to plan a campaign in June 1949 to discredit and "differentiate"[42] which established practices for future actions related to church policy.

The regime tried to neutralize the churches through propaganda, administrative intervention, and political attack. At the same time, the SED developed concrete plans to instrumentalize church representatives through umbrella organizations like the National Front and through the solicitation of public declarations.[43] The "successful realization" of such decrees was usually left to the overburdened local

offices of the SED, CDU, and the National Front. When things appeared critical, state offices at the regional and central levels invited church representatives to
talks in order to formulate their expectations and to respond to church requests
and protests. The first meeting of top Catholic and Protestant officials with
Minister-President Grotewohl and others, including Ulbricht and State Security
Minister Wilhelm Zaisser, took place on 28 April 1950.[44]

In addition, the SED continually used secret agents and strategic internal
party decisions to work against the influence and stature of the churches. But
several considerations mitigated an offensive strategy against the churches in the
short term: Soviet strategies aimed at Germany as a whole; the non-Communist
parties in the SED bloc; the peace campaigns (a propaganda move aimed at the
West) in the relatively conflict-free year 1951;[45] and the nominally high number
of church members in the GDR and in the SED itself.[46]

When the "Stalin note" failed in 1952, tensions over the German question
increased, leading the SED to proclaim the phase of "Building Up Socialism"
in the GDR (with Soviet approval) at the Second Party Congress of the SED in
July 1952. Consequently, state executives, who followed the SED's instructions,
regarded the churches increasingly as a Western-controlled disturbance. Pieck
had already set the parameters at an 1 April 1952 meeting with Stalin and the
Moscow Communist Party leaders: "Secure the democratic rule of law. Increasing enemy activity—large farmers, church, vigilance, arrests, public trials."[47]
On 17 June 1952 the Politburo directed the division "State Administration" to
analyze the "politics of the churches," especially regarding youth. The committee was concerned with whether the churches were actual or potential "tools of
imperialism": "The church leadership pursues comprehensive ideological work
with the goal of stirring up the greatest possible segment of the population
against the GDR, under the protective cover of church doctrine." In contrast
to the Protestant churches, the minority Catholic Church was more adept in
avoiding open conflict, but for that reason was viewed as "an opponent not to
be underestimated": "The Catholic Church addresses the natural needs of youth
by organizing social events, even dances, thus winning over the youth in general
and deepening its influence among Catholic youth, drawing them away from
the FDJ."[48]

Another "Attempt at an Analysis of Political Catholicism,"[49] undertaken
shortly thereafter, described it as "paving the way for German fascism." German
Catholicism was said to "be one with the Vatican." Of the Catholic Church in
the GDR, it said that "[t]he only thing to be said in its favor compared with the
Protestant Church is that it is a better judge of the real political power relations
and that it is apparently more prepared to work within these with the idea that it
can conquer from within what is lost in the short-term." Apart from "a few insignificant Catholic personalities in various parts of the GDR," the report claimed
that "no leading Catholic can be viewed as progressive." Bruno Wolff, the report's
author, therefore noted that "to a great degree the Catholic Church must be con-

sidered as a closed, unified block . . . Despite its flexibility on specific issues, the church must always be considered a base for the class enemy."

The SED strategy to weaken this "enemy base" consisted of targeted measures against religious instruction in schools and foster homes[50] and against young Christians in higher education. After January 1953 these measures developed into a *"Kirchenkampf"* ("struggle over the churches"—a term used by the churches with direct reference to the Nazi era), in which the state had the long-term goal of establishing "state churches" along the lines of Eastern European socialist countries.[51] State contributions, an important part of church budgets in the GDR in the early 1950s, were reduced by 25–30 percent in early 1953 and were soon stopped altogether—at least, that is, for the interim; the New Direction policy resumed payments on 11 June 1953, and they continued into 1989 and beyond.[52]

After June 1952, however, the state and party apparatus undertook efforts to halt the churches' youth work in the parishes and at the universities (which the state lumped together under the rubric of Junge Gemeinde) because it was seen as competition with the FDJ (Freie Deutsche Jugend, Free German Youth). On 5 August 1952 the Politburo banned student chaplains "from institutes of higher learning in the GDR and the democratic sectors of Berlin . . . effective immediately."[53] The state's activities culminated on 27 January 1953, when the Politburo decided to "unmask the Junge Gemeinde" and to ban all church youth work.[54] Detailed "administrative measures" were intended to halt "all admission of active members and officials of the Junge Gemeinde to universities and technical and teachers' colleges." The FDJ organized protest rallies at universities and some advanced secondary schools calling for the dismissal of young Christians of both confessions.[55] A further step toward marginalizing the churches as "ritual groups" was also included in the 27 January decision, which required state approval for all activities outside of church buildings and banned "youth excursions, camps, retreats, lay choruses, Christian academies, etc."[56] In practice, these measures were aimed at both Catholics and Protestants: the regime held a negative view of all church activities, even if its approach was occasionally uneven.

The New Direction policy, however, proclaimed after Stalin's death to an SED delegation in Moscow in early June 1953, included a directive "to cease the persecution of ordinary members of the church youth group '*Junge Gemeinde*' and to make political work among them the main focus."[57] Confiscated church property was to be returned. The "blunt administration of the clergy" was to end, and the "shameful heavy-handed intervention of authorities in church matters" was to stop. Instead, the Soviet party bosses declared that "enlightenment" and "anti-religious propaganda" would be the "chief weapons against the reactionary influence of the church."[58] These new guidelines prompted an SED Politburo decision on 6 June 1953, which led to a 10 June meeting between Minister-President Grotewohl and Protestant church representatives. The meeting produced a joint communiqué, published on 11 June in *Neues Deutschland,* that halted or reversed anti-church measures, including the one against Christian students.

The Function of the CDU

After the Soviet Military Administration (SMAD) authorized the formation of anti-fascist political parties on 10 June 1945, the "Christian-Democratic Union of Germany" (CDUD—later CDU) was formed in Berlin around Andreas Hermes, who had been a politician in the Catholic, Weimar-era Center Party. The new party had cross-confessional and all-German ambitions.[59] The party's first public appeal called for members "to consider the moral and spiritual power of Christianity in the shaping of culture" and demanded "freedom of conscience, the independence of all church communities, and a clear line between church and state."[60] Subsequently, similar calls to found a common Christian party were issued in various cities in the Soviet zone. However, in July 1945 the SMAD ordered that all newly founded parties had to join together in a central "United Front Committee."[61]

The pressing nature of social questions led the CDUD to sympathize with the idea of a centrally organized economy. When the SMAD forced CDUD chairs Hermes and Walter Schreiber to resign in December 1945 after they criticized uncompensated land expropriations, [62] the new chairs Jakob Kaiser and Ernst Lemmer declared that the party's "first concern . . . was the social democratic idea."[63] This "idea" included both the protection of private property and the option to nationalize key industries and introduce a planned economy. Kaiser strove for a non-Marxist "synthesis party," combining Christian and socialist ideals; it was an effective way to mobilize the party base.

Features of the CDU in the SBZ were a centralized steering committee in Berlin, difficulties in communication with the local branches, and numerous obstacles from the SMAD, which favored the KPD/SED. The CDU was underrepresented in trade unions and factory councils, as well as in government administration at the municipal and regional levels. In 1948, 58 percent of government administrators in Saxony were SED members, whereas only 5 percent were CDU; in Thuringia, the ratio was 45 percent to 6 percent.[64] Yet despite these structural disadvantages, the CDU got 18.7 percent of the vote in the September 1946 local elections and 24.5 percent in the following month's regional elections.[65]

Kaiser hoped that a united Germany could remain neutral and thus serve as a bridge between East and West, but this proved to be illusory, leading only to a series of depressing confrontations with CDU and Social Democratic Party (SPD) veterans from the Western zones.[66] In addition, he conceived of a "Christian socialism" that would follow the "end of the bourgeois order" and "break the waves of dogmatic Marxism,"[67] but these ideas seriously overtaxed the CDU's real possibilities in the Soviet zone. Kaiser also resisted CDU participation in an SED-sponsored "People's Congress for Unity and a Just Peace," prompting the SMAD to remove him and Lemmer on 20 December 1947. At the time, the CDU had 218,000 members in Berlin and the SBZ. The SED perceived the CDU as a serious competitor because of its mass-party structure.[68] The new CDU chairman, Otto Nuschke, and his general secretary, Georg Dertinger, had ambitious goals: a neutral, united Germany, friendly with the Soviet Union, and with CDU politicians in leading positions. But beginning in 1948 the CDU was transformed, gradually at first and then ever more obviously, into a hierarchical party of "democratic centralism" led by cadres loyal to the SED. Secret agents infiltrated the party and caused disruption; there were arrests, and CDU leaders were provoked into fleeing to the Western zones.[69]

These developments proceeded in stages, once the Soviet Union found the appearance of an independent CDU useful in its foreign policy concerning Germany; they came to a conclusion of sorts with the CDU's Sixth Party Congress in October 1952. The congress subordinated the CDU to the SED and recognized "the leading role of the working class and its party in the construction of socialism without reservation." When the CDU faced critical situations, Nuschke and others always opted for the continued existence of the threatened party. To do so, they made wide-ranging concessions to the SED bloc, such as retreating from the "Theses on Christian Realism," which were proclaimed in Meißen in 1951 as an independent alternative to the Christian socialism of the CDU's early years.[70] However, some resistance to the Berlin party leadership's course emerged among the CDU base at the local and regional levels, despite purges, controlled admissions, and a considerable reduction in the number of party members, as well as organized efforts to form cadres.[71] The activities of the still understaffed MfS were too unsystematic to hinder dissidence in the CDU, or even to completely monitor it. After the events of June 1953, Günter Wirth, at the time the point man for church matters in the Berlin party headquarters who pursued the policies of the SED Central Committee under the banner of the CDU, remarked that "we need to finally become a party of cadres; only then can we have influence."[72]

The CDU and the Churches

Mass assemblies calling for the formation of a cross-confessional Christian political party took place in many cities in the Soviet Zone of Occupation in July 1945, and Catholic clergy and lay members took an active part. In the Catholic milieu, there was a strong desire for the new CDU to act as the Center Party had in the Weimar Republic—as a political representative of church interests. In principle, Catholic clergy were prohibited from holding political office, but many became members of the CDU in 1945 and encouraged lay Catholics to also become involved. The former regional chairman of the Center Party in Saxony, Ludwig Kirsch from Chemnitz, was the most visible Catholic clergyman in the party. Although the SBZ was more than 80 percent Protestant, Catholics were very well represented in the CDU; they formed the majority in the first CDU regional directorships in Saxony-Anhalt and Thuringia, and in Saxony they comprised half of the party leadership.[73]

Under Kaiser's leadership, the CDU tried to present itself as the representative of the churches and the Christian population, especially in the regional parliament's constitutional advisory panels in 1946 and 1947. After Kaiser was removed and the CDU began to be integrated into the SED bloc, Catholics left the party, in particular. For the few with church connections who remained in leading positions in the CDU, the possibilities were limited and, indeed, politically dangerous, as minutes of the United Front Committee from July 1949 make clear.[74]

After the founding of the GDR, CDU Chairman Nuschke, as acting Minister-President, became the leader of the Main Office for Church Relations. He sought advice from the churches on staffing the department and offered to mediate the churches' interests within the state apparatus. For example, after a conference of East German Catholic bishops in March 1950, the bishops had a voluntary "get acquainted" meeting with two staff members of the Main Office. Wilhelm Weskamm, an auxiliary bishop in Magdeburg, later noted that "the conversation clarified many things, but despite their goodwill, the extremely limited purview of their work was apparent."[75] Because of its limited power, the Main Office increasingly functioned merely as a messenger, sending church requests that met with its approval to other government offices.

When Georg Dertinger became the GDR's first foreign minister in 1949, Gerald Götting succeeded him as CDU general secretary, thus becoming the most powerful person in the party. Götting sought to thoroughly transform the CDU by means of the secretariat in Berlin. In "church matters," the CDU party leadership felt obliged to claim that it had greater expertise and direct relations with church officials and the Christian population than the SED. The SED was suspicious of CDU competition in church matters, looking upon the party in the best case as useful, under its guidance, for instrumentalizing the churches within the framework of the National Front. Beginning in 1950, many CDU members involved in church matters—especially Chairman Nuschke—faced a dilemma: on the one hand, they wanted to demonstrate their political success with the churches to the SED, and on the other hand, they had to accommodate the SED to achieve this, displeasing the churches.

The churches tried as best they could to use Nuschke's Main Office—whose policies in large measure targeted West German public opinion—to advance their own interests.[76] Yet early on they recognized the CDU's limited room for maneuver, becoming increasingly critical of the party because of this. After the CDU—and above all Nuschke—had played a role in the Soviet Union's policy toward Germany up through mid 1952, church considerations were among the many things that fell by the wayside when the Building Up Socialism policy was proclaimed in July 1952.

CDU headquarters took part in dismantling Nuschke and his Main Office. On 19 July 1952 General Secretary Götting and the head of his division, Willi Leisner, submitted several written questions to the director of the Main Office, Kurt Grünbaum, in Nuschke's office. Grünbaum responded on 28 July, defending the claims of the churches: "With the announcement of the 'Building Up Socialism,' measures have been put in place that the churches regard as a transformation of our republic into an omnipresent state." One young official in the CDU secretariat characterized Grünbaum in a 1 August position paper as "against the interests of our state and our people . . . a spokesman and tool of the reactionary churches."[77] Further intimidation within the CDU included the MfS arrest of Foreign Minister Dertinger on 13 January 1953, whereupon he was sentenced to fifteen years in prison for espionage.[78] The Office for Church Affairs established within the Berlin party headquarters in October 1950, called the Main Department for Church Questions after July 1952, lost successive leaders: Leisner was transferred in November 1952, and his successor, Kurt Alisch, was relieved of his duties in January 1953. After Leisner was expelled from the party and arrested in February 1953, Günter Wirth headed the office. Wirth consistently supported SED measures against the "Junge Gemeinde," which led to him temporarily being replaced after June 1953, when a new policy of avoiding conflict with the churches was implemented in reaction to the popular uprising.

The church-political activities of the CDU were limited to dialogues with church officials, who were also invited to participate in "pastoral conferences." These were designed to win "progressive" and "loyal" clergy over to the GDR regime, along the lines of the SED's policy of "differentiation." Ambitious CDU politicians saw their party as predestined to "pressure the church faithful and church organizations to take a stand, because developments are going forward at a rapid pace."[79] However, the SED approach to the churches from mid 1952 to mid 1953 considerably detracted from these attempts at instrumentalizing them.[80]

After July 1952 the CDU tried to position itself in relation to the SED by paving the way for the sort of church-state agreements that had been forced upon other Eastern European countries after 1949. In Czechoslovakia and Hungary, the socialist bureaucracies carried on the late eighteenth-century Habsburg tradition of legal (and unevenly repressive) supervision of the churches. By contrast, the events surrounding Provost Josef Streb, the episcopal commissary in Eichsfeld, demonstrated the ambition and dilettantism of the political actors in relation to the Catholic Church in the GDR. Arnold Bahlmann, the CDU regional chairman from Heiligenstadt, had a conversation with Streb in 1952 in which both speculated about the church-political situation in the GDR. Bahlmann then made a suggestion to Götting, who immediately phoned Bruno Wolff in the State Administration Division of the Central Committee of the SED on 20 August 1952, telling him that "several Catholic personalities in the CDU . . . propose establishing one archdiocese for the entire territory of the GDR, headed by an archbishop . . . who would be able to personally handle all questions connected with a church-state agreement." That same day, Wolff told Minister-President Grotewohl that "the details need to be worked out in conversations with CDU representatives; indeed, Götting has already invited me."[81] After Bahlmann spoke with Götting again the next day, Götting wrote a report detailing the possibilities:

> In agreement with Streb, Bahlmann suggested . . . talks to clarify church-state relations. A central point will be setting up an archdiocese for the territory of the GDR . . . Bahlmann is in favor of putting Bishop Wienken in charge of the archdiocese . . . Bahlmann sees the establishment of a primacy in the GDR as another way to make church administration in the GDR independent of West Germany.[82]

The Vatican, which actually decided on such matters, had no knowledge of this political initiative undertaken by a local CDU leader. Nor did the bishops named know anything about this. Thus, the political success in church affairs that the CDU party leadership had hoped for remained elusive.

A remark Wirth made on 13 December 1952, about a meeting that Nuschke had with Wolff from the SED Central Committee, shows how little influence Nuschke had on the political course his own party would take toward the churches. According to Wirth, Nuschke recommended that "pinprick" pressure campaigns against the churches be avoided. Wirth's summary evaluates his party chairman: "The meeting was friendly; only at two points did Nuschke make remarks against 'my young people in the Jägerstrasse [CDU party offices] who don't understand my Kirchenpolitik.'"[83] The Kirchenpolitik of the SED, as well as the "young people in the Jägerstrasse," nevertheless hardened in 1953. When the SED leadership had already received new guidelines in Moscow but the "New Direction" was not yet publicly known, Wirth outlined a scenario for the "loosening of church-state ties" on 3 June 1953, because the Protestant Church in Germany (Evangelische Kirche in Deutschland) had become closer to the Catholic Church through a "common social-political stance against progress." He wrote, "in Germany . . . the progressive forces must take away from the churches what they had and what they had asked for, namely, political power."[84]

When Nuschke was temporarily kidnapped and taken to West Berlin during the uprising in East Berlin on 17 June 1953, the Catholic prelate Johannes Zinke, delegate of Berlin's Bishop Wilhelm Weskamm for negotiations with GDR government offices, called for his release. Zinke received a letter of thanks for this from none other than CDU General Secretary Götting on behalf of "our party."[85] By contrast, in November 1951 Götting had privately said (according to the reliable testimony of Magnus Dedek, the CDU regional chairman in Saxony), "Nuschke is an old fool; in reality I lead the party."[86]

The Catholic Church in the SBZ and the GDR After 1945

Within the SBZ, Catholics lived in a kind of diaspora—spread out as a small minority. Church activities in this region could only be financed with organized support from Catholic regions in West Germany. Before the Second World War, a little more than one million Catholics lived in the territory that would later comprise the SBZ and the GDR. From 1945 to 1949 this number swelled to 2,772,500 because of the influx of refugees from the German regions in the East and from the Sudetenland. In 1949, the percentage of Catholics in the GDR reached its historical peak—13.9 percent of the total population.[87] With the gradual Stalinization of the GDR and the failed uprising in June 1953, 868,000 Catholics emigrated to the West, although a considerable number of these were refugees who then migrated further.

Despite the very difficult material situation, and a marked shortage of priests before 1948, the postwar stream of Catholics to the SBZ led to a clear increase in new parishes and places of worship. The churches played a very important role in the integration of German refugees from East Prussia, Silesia, the Sudetenland, etc., the subsequent migration of many of them to the West notwithstanding. That these refugees were not allowed to socialize or organize in groups associated with the regions from which they were expelled or fled further accelerated their integration into church congregations.[88]

The territory of the SBZ encompassed seven Catholic jurisdictions. Two of these were discrete dioceses (Berlin and Meißen), and the remaining five belonged to dioceses whose seats lay outside of the SBZ (Breslau, Paderborn, Osnabrück, Fulda, and Würzburg). As a preventive measure to secure the continuity of church jurisdiction, the church undertook several preliminary steps that acknowledged the de facto division of these districts:[89]

- The Diocese of Berlin lost its territories east of the Oder River as a result of the Potsdam Conference and the disputed church law rulings by the Polish primate, Cardinal August Hlond.[90] Konrad Graf von Preysing had been bishop of Berlin since 1935; after the destruction of his official residence in 1943, he lived in a part of the city that was later occupied by the Western Allies. In 1946 Pope Pius XII elevated him to cardinal, above all because of his posture during the Nazi years. After his death in December 1950, the auxiliary bishop of Magdeburg, Wilhelm Weskamm, succeeded him.

- The Diocese of Meißen was located entirely within the SBZ, except for four parishes east of the Neiße River. Petrus Legge had been bishop since 1932; he resided in Bautzen. Meißen was a so-called exempt diocese, reporting to the Holy See in Rome. When Legge passed away in March 1951, Heinrich Wienken became bishop of Meißen and resided in Bautzen.

- Beginning in the summer of 1945, the part of the Archdiocese of Breslau (Wrocław) that was west of the Oder-Neiße line was administered by an office set up in Görlitz. When Cardinal Adolf Bertram died in July 1945, Primate Hlond forced Ferdinand Piontek, who had been elected by the Breslau Cathedral College on 16 July 1945, to renounce his jurisdiction over Polish territories. In early 1947 Piontek was expelled from Poland. Together with the Breslau Cathedral College, Piontek resided in Görlitz and led the Görlitz Archbishop's Office.

- In the eastern part of the Archdiocese of Paderborn, the "Archbishop's Commissary of Magdeburg," the powers of a vicar-at-large had been delegated by the archbishop in Paderborn to Weskamm in February 1945. On 17 October 1949 Weskamm was named the second auxiliary bishop of Paderborn with residence in Magdeburg. When Weskamm became bishop of Berlin in 1951,

Friedrich Maria Rintelen came from Paderborn to Magdeburg in 1952 to replace him as auxiliary bishop and commissary.

· In April 1946 Bernhard Schräder, a priest in Schwerin, was named Commissary of Mecklenburg—the eastern section of the Diocese of Osnabrück. In November 1950 he was delegated powers analogous to those of Weskamm in Magdeburg.

· In October 1946 the bishop of Fulda named Joseph Freusberg vicar for the eastern portions of the diocese. His residence was in Erfurt.

· The South Thuringia section of the Diocese of Würzburg, called the Commissary of Meiningen, was in the SBZ. It was elevated to a Bishop's Deaconship in February 1949. In October 1950 Joseph Schönauer, deacon in Meiningen, received powers equivalent to those established in Magdeburg, Schwerin, and Erfurt.

Meetings of delegates from Catholic administrative districts in the SBZ, as well as representatives of the German Caritas Association (DCV), took place as early as December 1945 in Catholic hospitals in the western part of Berlin. These meetings became more frequent beginning in 1947. After the two German states were founded in 1949 and the contours of SED Kirchenpolitik began to emerge, a regional conference of Catholic bishops in the GDR was established on 12 July 1950 under the leadership of Berlin's Cardinal Konrad von Preysing. It was later called the Berlin Conference of Ordinaries (Berliner Ordinarienkonferenz, BOK).[91] The Vatican officially established it to make "more effective and even church administration in the region" possible.[92]

These conferences grew out of an immediate need to coordinate and secure pastoral duties, as well as from the massive problems of refugees and providing for the basic material requirements of a wrecked, starving country. Yet, beginning in 1947, political considerations began to emerge, and it was necessary to find a consensus on how to approach the Soviet administration and, later, the GDR state offices.

One institutional foundation of these conferences was the diocese structure of the DCV, whose activities were by and large untouched by the establishment of the Allied zones of occupation. Bishop Wienken also played an important role. As leader of the DCV and, since 1937, also of the Fulda Bishops' Conference, Wienken had handled negotiations with various branches of the Nazi state. After 1945 he made an almost seamless transition to handling contacts with the SMAD and the new German government offices.[93] Although Wienken's efforts were theoretically aimed at Germany as a whole, he was soon dealing only with the SMAD and SBZ/GDR officials. He was the ideal coordinator of the East German Bishops' Conference because his office was in Berlin and because he knew about the emerging political structures. Wienken joined the BOK in 1947. The most important spiritual promoter of these conferences was Weskamm, who, as the new bishop of Berlin, became chairman of the conference in 1951 after Cardinal von Preysing passed away.

The work of the Catholic Church in the SBZ/GDR relied upon several basic elements. Alongside the possibility of continuing to bring in material goods from the West, the church needed religious instruction in the schools, priests to care for communities, education and training for future generations of clergy, and the ability to distribute religious literature.

While Soviet authorities increasingly exercised ideological censorship to prevent or limit West German church publications from crossing the border, they could not always stop "illegal importation." Until 1 April 1949, *Petrusblatt*, the Catholic newsletter of the Diocese of Berlin that had been licensed by the Americans in November 1945, was also available (with some limitations) in East Berlin and the rest of the Soviet zone. But aside from religion, the journal's clear anti-Communist politics caused it to be banned in the SBZ.[94] Not until May 1951 did the SED allow the Catholic Church in the GDR to publish its own bi-weekly, *Tag des Herrn* [Day of Our Lord]. Edited and published by the St. Benno Press, it was founded in October 1947 by the East German church districts and based in Leipzig-Lindenau. In 1950 a Sorbian-language Catholic newspaper was licensed, and the dioceses could publish their own journals beginning in 1952.[95] The relatively late approval of Catholic press organs, despite years of effort by Wienken, was also the result of competing strategies within the church. There was a debate about whether to base their presence in West Berlin or in the SBZ, rooted in differing hopes and prognoses about the eventual unification of Germany. It was only when Cardinal von Preysing died in 1950 (and his close advisor, Walter Adolph, thus lost influence) that the strategy of ignoring political reality was laid to rest. Previously, the East German bishops and delegates were reluctant to base church institutions in the Soviet zone and hoped instead to influence the SBZ by working from West Berlin.

In 1945 there were no Catholic theological seminaries in the territory that formed the SBZ. Catholic theology students from the East had to train at West German universities, or West German clergy staffed posts in the East. In time, the new Catholic clergy in the SBZ were increasingly unfamiliar with the region, coming largely from Catholic areas in West Germany or from formerly German areas in Silesia, East Prussia, or the Sudetenland. The task of finding sufficient numbers of priests was fundamental for the future of the church in the GDR. As with the issue of church publishing, the East German bishops' differing strategic notions influenced their thinking on the training of priests.

Bishop Wienken negotiated with the SMAD to try to establish a department of Catholic theology at the University of Leipzig.[96] But a new SED policy accelerated the founding of a new institution of higher learning under the supervision of the state: introduced in October 1951, this policy not only promoted such an institution, but prohibited theology students who had gone to the West from returning to the GDR.[97] Bishop Weskamm had pushed for a decision to found a separate Catholic seminary outside of the state university system, and this proposal was now advanced. In the interim, Weskamm appealed directly to Grotewohl in December 1951 in the name of the East German bishops to allow theology students from the West to enter the GDR, which Grotewohl granted for all of 1952.[98]

Acting Minister-President Walter Ulbricht preliminarily approved the opening of a Catholic college and seminary in Erfurt on 5 June 1952, and Grotewohl then approved it in writing on 13 August. This resulted from dramatic proceedings within the state apparatus and the church leadership.[99] The church had been assured that a college would be opened in Berlin-Biesdorf, but this plan was blocked on 6 May 1952 in favor of a location in the GDR outside of Berlin. The state apparatus, in which Nuschke and his department supported the church, then underwent an internal "housecleaning": several officials had to offer "self-criticisms."[100] But in the end, the establishment of a Catholic college whose curriculum, faculty, and students would be overseen by the church rather than the state (with the provision that "no laws of the GDR would be broken"[101]) was an unusual success for the church and a minor retreat for the GDR state.

All of these institutions—the seminary in Erfurt, St. Benno Press, and the new Catholic journals—were "catalysts of integration"[102] for a mentality that recognized and affirmed the church's existence within the GDR's socialist society. At the same time, a diaspora consciousness began to develop; the church began to perceive itself as "the Catholic Church in East Germany." As German reunification became an ever more distant prospect, this consciousness gave rise to more pragmatic strategies of Kirchenpolitik, oriented to the realities of everyday life in the GDR.

New Strategies of Kirchenpolitik

As far as church law was concerned, Catholic institutions in the SBZ continued to be considered in terms of Germany as a whole. But differing conditions in the various territories, combined with the diverse predispositions of the main figures involved, eventually resulted in competing postures within the Catholic Church and rival strategies regarding *Kirchenpolitik*. However, these internal church struggles went largely unnoticed by the SMAD and the SED, because their surveillance methods were still quite rudimentary and because the Catholic Church was not as great a concern to East German authorities as was the Protestant Church.

Konrad Graf von Preysing had been a pronounced opponent of Nazi policies; he had been greatly depressed by the tendency of the Fulda (later "German") Bishops' Conference, led by Cardinal Adolf Bertram from Breslau, to bend to Hitler and avoid public protests.[103] When von Preysing was elevated to cardinal, he took up residence in the American sector of Berlin because of the wartime destruction to the cathedral and bishop's quarters located in the Soviet sector. There, he developed a clear anti-Bolshevist, pro-Western orientation. Along with his close advisor, Walter Adolph, von Preysing openly lamented the lack of opportunity for effective church activity in the Soviet zone.

By contrast, Bishop Wienken—who had been Cardinal Bertram's representative in Berlin for the Fulda Bishops' Conference and had handled contacts with Nazi officials since 1937—remained in the destroyed, conquered territory of East Berlin. Wienken immediately began to establish contact with the SMAD and local German chargés. He now had to operate under a completely new set of assumptions, but he seamlessly carried forth his pragmatic posture of being loyal to those in office. As a former Center Party representative, Wienken's main political connections were from before 1933. In 1945 he participated behind the scenes in the founding of the CDU in Berlin and continued to expand his network of contacts in the SMAD and the various political parties in the SBZ. Although he continued to function as commissioner for the Fulda Bishops' Conference (for all of Germany), took part in bishops' meetings in both East and West Germany, and was named the representative of the Catholic Church to the Allied Control Council in 1947, Wienken's location in isolated East Berlin meant that his contacts were soon limited in practice to the East. Thus, Wienken and von Preysing symbolize the rapid crystallization of differing positions in the early postwar period, as the division and separate development of the Soviet and Western zones proceeded.[104]

In West Berlin and the Western zones, the first priorities for the Catholic Church were the question of religious instruction in all schools and its wish to reestablish Catholic schools. In this regard, the issue of the validity of the Reich Concordat of 1933 was central. For the church in the Soviet zone, by contrast, the issue of schools was quickly eclipsed by the need to react to overwhelming social changes. The decrees in all church districts in the SBZ prohibiting Catholic clergy from holding political or party positions continued the now depoliticized Reich Concordat.[105] Later, when the GDR began to sign citizens up for the People's Congress movement and the National Front,[106] the prohibition was expanded to include political declarations by Catholic clergy and church workers, with the exception of bishops.[107]

These limitations on public political pronouncements, however, must be distinguished from encouraging lay Catholics or tolerating non-ideological CDU activities, as long as it still seemed possible to work within state structures to establish Catholic bridgeheads or to safeguard the church's own activities. Lay Catholics and clergy were among the founders of the FDJ in 1946 and remained active until they were expelled in June 1949; their participation provided cover for the simultaneous pursuit of autonomous Catholic youth projects at the congregational level. The participation of Wienken and the charity association Caritas in the initial phases of the social welfare and elder care program Volkssolidarität can be seen in a similar light. The SED and CDU were increasingly concerned with the ideological purity of their leading cadres, but quite a few Catholics were still regular SED members; even more had no party affiliation but belonged to one of the mass organizations or had a presence in regional or municipal CDU events. With the approval of their priests and bishops, these Catholics participated as long as it was possible, believing that they were thus able "to prevent worse things from happening" and "to gain something for the church." Heavily Catholic areas such as Eichsfeld and the Sorbian regions near Lausitz developed their own methods in this regard. Wienken, a pragmatist, supported this tendency, which was also widely practiced by Catholics during the Nazi era. This strategy began losing steam only in the mid 1950s, when the SED tried to enforce ideological uniformity by means of materialist propaganda and demands that members renounce their church membership.

A prime example of how Catholics in the SBZ in this period were able to position themselves strategically in relation to declarations of principles is the reaction of the bishops and representatives to the so-called Anti-Communist Decree of the Holy Office, issued by the Vatican on 1 July 1949. The decree was effective worldwide but was primarily aimed at Italy and France, where the Communist Party was relatively strong. It prohibited Catholics from joining the party and promoting its "materialist and anti-Christian teachings" under threat of excommunication. The East German newspaper *Neues Deutschland* reacted by publishing an article attacking the Vatican and the Western powers but not the Catholic Church in the SBZ. On 20 July, Ulbricht personally directed the Protestant minister Hans-Joachim Mund, who at that point was still active in the Central Committee, to draft an internal directive for the party leadership.[108] Alongside rhetorical flourishes claiming that the Vatican decree "served the interests of American capitalism," the directive stated that care would be taken so that "comrades remain members of our party."

The Vatican decree was discussed at a meeting of Catholic bishops in Berlin on 9 August.[109] The bishops did not support the idea that Catholics had to resign from the SED and the mass organization: "Concerning Communism, one has to distinguish between its philosophical, socialist, and political sides. As to the last, the press has exploited the Vatican decree in both the East and the West." Attempting to maintain political equidistance, Weskamm noted the bishops' consensus that "the decree needed to be taken out of the political arena." The decree was not to be seen as an attack on socialism but rather on "the anti-Christian teaching of materialism." The conference therefore decided to issue a pastoral letter "against Godless materialism" to be distributed in all Catholic churches, East and West, in order to "raise consciousness about the absolute incommensurability of capitalism with Christianity, the danger of propagating materialism, and the duty of all Christians to guard against it." Weskamm noted further that Bishop Wienken presented the decree to the SMAD in Berlin-Karlshorst "and offered explanations that reassured them to a certain extent."

These kinds of interpretations reflected what Weskamm called "[Soviet] zone reality": they aimed to distinguish the church from perceived materialist tendencies in the hopes that these tendencies would not increase and that it might protect Catholics from a further politicization of society. However, the founding of the GDR in October 1949 made relations with the new regime a priority, and the planned pastoral letter was postponed until the next year. Wienken made a draft that was reworked by the bishops and approved on 14 December 1949. The

Fulda Bishops' Conference reworked it once more in February, and it was distributed on 23 April 1950 to all German dioceses except Meißen. There, Bishop Legge was against the letter because it might appear "aggressive" and because things appeared "already fundamentally clear."[110] This letter was one of the last pastoral letters for the whole of Germany, and many aspects reveal the "East German" input: "The church refrains from taking sides in the political and economic conflicts between Communist and anti-Communist powers . . . it further wishes that religious decisions by the church not be misused for these political and economic conflicts."[111]

The lines that formed after 1945 between Cardinal von Preysing in West Berlin and those bishops who lived inside the "[Soviet] zone reality" can all be reduced to the latter's recognition of the true relations of power in the emerging East German state. In West Germany, the Catholic Church continued seamlessly after the Nazi period to think in terms of a binding state guarantee of the religious status quo. In the SBZ/GDR, on the other hand, the unpredictability and uncertain legal foundation of SED policies within an ideologically partisan state meant that the church had to undergo a learning process. A few differences notwithstanding, there was a consensus among Wienken and the East German bishops that all their actions must recognize the fact that the SED and the Soviet Union held power. Thus, church life could only be reestablished through contact with the new, centralized SBZ/GDR authorities, which required a coordinated and, if possible, unified approach. The East German bishops had no self-interest in the GDR's quest for political legitimacy and in no way welcomed the formation of a separate state. They pursued an all-German strategy as best they could, maintained close ties with the West (where some of their superiors were based), hoped that German reunification would bring about the end of the GDR, and were also sometimes critical of West German government policy. The bishops of Meißen and Berlin, as well as the chapter vicar of Breslau (based in Görlitz), regularly took part in the Fulda Bishops' Conference in West Germany and were signatories to its pastoral letters. At the same time, "[Soviet] zone reality" fostered their ability to distinguish between wishful thinking and the true state of things.

Cardinal von Preysing saw himself as a resident of West Berlin and not a "Soviet Zone bishop." Although the territory of his diocese was mostly in the SBZ/GDR, he refused to function as a spokesman for the Catholic Church in a state he did not accept. Instead, he concentrated on the church affairs of his district, which he increasingly limited to West Berlin because only there did he have a free hand.

In February 1947 the foundation was laid for a meeting of the East German bishops that would take place regularly, at least once every four years. It was Weskamm who took the initiative; Bishop Wienken functioned as the secretary for the conference. From Weskamm's perspective, the conferences at first seemed rather ineffective due to some reservations on the part of the bishops of Berlin and Meißen, who were occasionally absent.[112] On 10 December 1948, Bernhard Schräder, a priest from Schwerin who was the Bishop's Commissary of Mecklenburg, wrote to Apostolic Inspector Bishop Aloysius Muench, who was based in Kronberg im Taunus (West Germany) and led the Vatican mission there:

> The esteemed cardinal of Berlin has stressed repeatedly that he speaks only for the Diocese of Berlin, although many believe that it is his duty to follow the example of other places where the church is oppressed and to step forward as a representative of Catholics in the Soviet Zone of Occupation. He claims that this is not his mission. It is now clear to all who have eyes that things are rapidly developing in the SBZ just as they have in other Eastern European states, not only politically and economically, but also in questions of culture and religion. Whoever does not recognize this is living with fateful illusions. The Catholic Church in the SBZ lacks the necessary unified leadership. The consequences have so far been depressing, but in the future they will be destructive.[113]

After the formal founding of the two German states in May and October 1949, the Catholic Church now faced the questions of how to approach discussions with the new GDR regime and how to establish church activity on a legal basis, i.e., on the basis of the Reich Concordat or an alternative agreement. While the Protestant Church appointed representatives to both Bonn and East Berlin, the Vatican retained its mission in Kronberg im Taunus. At first, it did not want to upgrade diplomatic relations with either German state. Bishop Wienken continued to negotiate with government offices, Soviet officers, and SED and CDU politicians in East Berlin.

On 6 December 1949 Cardinal von Preysing wrote to the Vatican; his letter showed maximalist aims and little connection to reality:

> Personally, I am of the opinion that we cannot proceed with the actual negotiations until the basic rights of the church are not only promised but actually respected. . . . The representatives of the regime in the Eastern Zone must be made aware that conditions there are unconstitutional. They must first respect the constitution before other points can be discussed.[114]

At their first meeting after the founding of the GDR, the East German ordinaries decided on 18 October 1949 to petition the regime; a draft was presented at the 14 December meeting by the representative of the bishop of Meißen.[115] They agreed on a few concrete points they wanted to address: a church press and newspaper; the increasingly anti-religious school curriculum; and the 1 July regulation requiring that all events be registered with the police. Cardinal von Preysing was asked to emphasize that the petition grew out of close communication with all ordinaries in the Eastern zone. Accordingly, von Preysing sent a memo on 29 December to Acting Minister-President Nuschke and other ministers, entitled "The Right to Life of the Catholic Church and its Prospects in the Territory of the German Democratic Republic."[116] Von Preysing's complaint, which appealed to the GDR constitution, went unanswered; it was the first time he had spoken in the name of the East German ordinaries.

The East German ordinaries at first hoped that such petitions would prod the regime to issue executive orders more favorable to the church, without having to enter into negotiations. By contrast, Cardinal von Preysing began to pursue a more aggressive path, declaring sharp differences with the GDR and its political policies. While the Diocese of Meißen sent a cautiously formulated text to priests on 1 February 1950, urging them to decline to participate in the National Front, Cardinal von Preysing published a biting condemnation of the SED and GDR (with a pronounced Western tone) as "a creeping one-party dictatorship . . . [that] seeks to expand to our entire German Fatherland."[117] The SED press responded with pointed criticisms, and Nuschke wrote a critical article in the CDU paper *Neue Zeit* entitled "A Cardinal Error." This article not only railed propagandistically against von Preysing but also offered advice:

> In my official capacity as legal advisor to the Office of Church Affairs, I try to help the various church communities with their legitimate grievances. Does the cardinal really believe that my work is made easier by his sensational published letter? . . . We happily take into consideration that political questions are not his main occupation and that he leaves the details up to political colleagues. But they have not advised him well, and it is not only his reputation but the reputation of his church that suffers if he attaches his name to such political errors.[118]

To be sure, other East German ordinaries shared the views contained in von Preysing's statements, yet they perceived the declarations as tactically counterproductive because the church needed the GDR state apparatus, which was hardly the monolithic bloc that von Preysing made it out to be. Von Preysing was absent from the 14 March 1950 Conference of Ordinaries; under the leadership of Bishop Wienken, the other extreme of detailed negotiations with the regime dominated. Somewhat depressed, Auxiliary Bishop Weskamm wrote in a file note on the meeting that its purpose was "for the representatives of the individual church districts in our zone to find a unified position and a quick response in an era when the GDR is closing ranks and all church-related questions are becoming 'zone questions.'"[119]

One day before the reading of the pastoral letter on "materialism," on 22 April 1950, the cardinal sent another detailed petition, with the consent of the other ordinaries, to Minister-President Grotewohl with concrete demands to guarantee freedom of conscience and freedom of belief.[120] Upon receipt, Grotewohl hurriedly invited the Catholic Church to join a meeting that had already been arranged for 28 April 1950 between Protestant representatives and several high-ranking GDR ministers. At von Preysing's request, the Catholics were represented not by Wienken, who knew some of the ministers, but rather by Weskamm and Adolph. It was a long meeting that produced no agreements, yet it constituted a detailed and emotional exchange of views. Weskamm was quoted as saying: "Fundamental things are at stake here—things that a Christian cannot remain silent about if he is true to himself. Must a person growing up in the

GDR become a materialist? Mr. Minister-President, you must leave that up to us. According to the materialists, it is not likely that one can be both a materialist and a Christian."[121]

The differences of opinion within the Catholic Church over the appropriate response to the increasingly aggressive regime policies were heightened when von Preysing wanted the petition to Grotewohl to be publicly read in all churches in the GDR. A majority of the ordinaries rejected this, so there was no reading. Instead, all bishops and bishops' commissioners except for von Preysing made their own "declarations of peace" on 25 July 1950, based on the peace rhetoric and petitions of the National Front that sought to instrumentalize the churches. Cardinal von Preysing then joined with Prelate Adolph and Wilhelm Böhler, a prelate in the West German government seat (Bonn) in the service of the Bishops' Conference, to seek the removal of Wienken as head of the commission of the Fulda Bishops' Conference and thus as the contact person for GDR government offices.

After a final conversation in June 1950, relations between von Preysing and Wienken were so strained that the latter considered ending his activities. The combative cardinal resisted the two-pronged strategy of exercising caution regarding public statements while pursuing talks with the regime. Von Preysing wanted his West Berlin views to form the basis for decisions made by the BOK, which was constituted on 12 July 1950. He believed that the church had little practical chance in the GDR without binding legal guarantees in view of the "systematic Bolshevization" there.[122] Because he knew such guarantees were not forthcoming and believed he had right on his side, von Preysing hoped to influence the Soviet zone from West Berlin by means of public protests, preferring not to recognize the official government in the GDR (except in writing). In 1950 he wrote a papal secretary that he was "unwilling to engage in any oral negotiations with [GDR] officials."[123] But von Preysing could not persuade the East German ordinaries. As Weskamm noted of their 18 October 1950 meeting,

> The necessity of a single agent to deal with government agencies was stressed from all quarters. A unanimous vote rejected picking a new man for the job. . . . With the exception of [the] Berlin [representative], all feel that [Wienken], who has done the job so far, is indispensable. Essential questions, fundamental things, and all matters of Kirchenpolitik are the exclusive domain of the BOK.[124]

After the meeting, Weskamm requested that Wienken continue his work for the church districts of the Eastern zone. At the same meeting of the BOK, in the context of developments in Poland and rumors about an "agreement" between the churches and the GDR regime, there was also unanimity: "We agree that no understanding be reached with the regime without the approval of all other responsible church bodies."[125]

The East/West conflict within the church over how to react to the new political reality was the fundamental problem for Catholics in the GDR; it only began to gradually become superfluous after Cardinal von Preysing died on 21 December 1950. Weskamm succeeded him as bishop of Berlin and chairman of the BOK in June 1951. His views on "Soviet Zone reality" could now develop. Adolph's political activities as prelate were now limited to West Germany and the Vatican, and his influence on the new bishop of Berlin was considerably reduced.

When Petrus Legge died in March 1951, Wienken became the new bishop of Meißen and moved to Bautzen. Wienken had filled in for Legge in 1937 when the latter had been condemned by the Nazis. Wienken's successor as leader of the commission of the Fulda Bishops' Conference in Berlin was the prelate Johannes Zinke (Wienken had suggested him), who was simultaneously the leader of the main Berlin office of the DCV, located in West Berlin. Zinke subsequently became one of the most important advisors to Bishop Weskamm and the East German ordinaries. As their representative, Zinke continued Wienken's tradition of talks with GDR government officials. He dealt regularly with the Main Office for Church Relations, the Ministry of the Interior, and occasionally other ministries. In contrast to Wienken, however, who had never had contact with the MfS (founded in 1950), Zinke was confronted with members of the state security services in a January 1953 meeting at the Ministry of the Interior. But after a second meeting, which he attended as an authorized church representative, they broke off contact with him.[126]

Despite the fact that he resided in West Berlin, the ordinaries naturally accepted Bishop Weskamm as BOK chairman and were just as accepting of the basic premise of being able to influence GDR religious policy from the outside. As the church historian Josef Pilvousek remarks,

> With Weskamm, the Catholic Church in the GDR began to see the social and political situation more realistically and to react in original ways . . . understanding the situation of the church in the GDR as a diaspora and theologically embracing it, even seeing it as an opportunity for a "mature" Christianity; this laid the groundwork for it to develop into "the church in the GDR."[127]

Together with his deputy, Zinke, Weskamm played an essential role in the complicated founding of a seminary in Erfurt. In 1952 he presided over a Catholic convention with over 150,000 participants from East and West Germany; the convention finally came together after multiple confrontations with GDR government offices that had acted in unpredictable ways.[128] When GDR officials forcibly evicted people near the border with West Germany, established a restricted zone there, and interrupted religious services, Weskamm organized a BOK protest letter addressed to Minister-President Grotewohl.[129] After this protest and several other petitions, Grotewohl invited Catholic and Protestant leaders to separate talks on 25 July 1952, in order to discuss the new political situation in the GDR in the wake of the Second SED Party Congress. As the Catholic representatives, Weskamm and Zinke discussed the recent measures taken at the border, the Berlin Catholic convention, the Erfurt seminary, and the

political neutrality of the church.[130] But when the GDR officials wanted to influence the Erfurt curriculum—a demand they later backed away from—Bishop
Weskamm became increasingly agitated, claiming that "the regime was trying to
turn the church into a state church, imposing limits found nowhere else in the
world and asking Grotewohl pointedly, 'Are you a dictator?'"[131] As a West Berlin
resident, Weskamm was prohibited from traveling in the GDR with the exception of East Berlin beginning in 1952. Clearly marked by the meeting, he noted
on 29 July 1952, in a report to Cardinal Frings in Cologne, that "the results of
the conversation were negative. Their desire to end every consideration given to
the church and to expose it to the full pressure of administrative and political
measures was clear. The authoritarian state is tightening its grip."[132]

Statements made by leading SED politicians after the Second Party Congress,
where the new "Building Up Socialism" program was proclaimed, led some in
religious circles to expect that they would be placed under state supervision and
subjected to more restrictive laws and to mandatory materialist education in the
schools. The SED measures were perceived as "a plan for liquidation."[133] In an
emotional pastoral letter of 11 January 1953, the bishops singled out the elimina-
tion of religion in the schools as a grave threat to Christian belief, because now
parents and priests would bear sole responsibility for Christian education.[134] The
"Bishops' Words of Greeting to the Youth" of 3 May 1953 was also dramatic;
issued during a campaign against Christian high school and university students,
it offered biblical examples for youth to help bear the disadvantages they must
confront in their careers and personal lives.[135]

In his May 1953 "Remarks on the State of the Church," Bishop Weskamm
noted darkly that

> [t]he attack on religious work with youth is intended to annihilate all circles whose
> worldviews do not match those of the regime. It is widely known that the largest num-
> ber of intellectual and spiritual opponents to Communism are found in the churches.
> . . . In negotiations, the officials still appear to be somewhat loyal [to the constitution],
> but the powers that exist alongside the leaders are so strong that they will also attempt
> with the churches what they are doing in economic and other sectors. The security
> services and the Politburo are the main players.[136]

It was only the new course dictated to the GDR by the Soviets in June 1953 that
spared the churches from this perceived state of siege.

As bishop of Meißen, Wienken now continued utilizing the personal style as
a tactically savvy negotiator that he had displayed when he had chaired the BOK
on a regional level in Saxony. Whereas he could now only meet with leading
government officials and CDU politicians during his rare stays in Berlin, Wienken took advantage of every opportunity to have personal talks with state functionaries and representatives of the National Front in his diocese. At the same
time, after his first experiences with the regime's attempts to use the churches,
he sought to prohibit priests and other church workers from taking on party or

especially targeted Catholics in the Saxon CDU in order to protect church interests and head off interventions by the SED.[137] He tried to have an influence on CDU personnel matters through lay Catholics in Dresden and Bautzen, with whom he occasionally met.[138]

Wienken's style in talks with government and party officials was very friendly, according to their accounts—full of goodwill and obliging statements alongside numerous firm demands regarding church affairs and various individual cases. Beginning in 1952, the MfS took notes on Wienken's talks with representatives of the National Front and the CDU who cooperated with the security services, such as the CDU regional chairman in Saxony, Magnus Dedek (code name "David"). In November 1953 the MfS opened a comprehensive surveillance file to evaluate these conversations as well as Wienken's correspondence (to the extent that they had access to it). They discovered "subversive" statements like the following letter from 1955: "With the help of God, I stand here as a faithful guardian on the Eastern border."[139] The Wienken files contain such headings as "his fight to gain influence for the Catholic Church among the youth, the state, and the prisons in the GDR," "his contacts with GDR officials and his true intentions," and "his attempt to secure the release of political prisoners."[140] A high-level MfS report from 1 February 1957 says of Wienken that

> politically, he is against the course of things in the GDR but presents himself to government officials as loyal—this shows his underhanded approach to our state. He gives the impression of being friendly, accommodating, and astute. He is very familiar with political events and procedures; however, his entire posture reveals him as a true representative of the Catholic Church and the Vatican.[141]

Wienken's letters and statements to GDR officials—with all of their friendly greetings, loyal phrases, and hopes for positive collaboration—were calculated tactical means to ends that were actually transparent. Using secretive diplomacy, he cautiously sought to create as much room for maneuver as possible for the Catholic Church and to help free people from prison in humanitarian cases.

Walter Breitmann, the official responsible for church affairs for the Dresden area, made the following notes in a report about the actions of the churches during the uprising of 17 June 1953:

> On Wednesday, June 17, the Catholic Bishop Wienken made a surprise visit at four in the afternoon; he wanted to discuss several questions with the government. That Wienken showed up on that day is remarkable. He made a number of well considered requests which, in my view, are meant to feel out the authorities here in Dresden. It was clear that he wanted to find out if the local officials are in control of the situation.[142]

Four years later, in another report, Breitmann maintained that

> We should recall that, on June 17 and 18, 1953, Protestant and Catholic GDR defectors who formerly held high positions in the petty-bourgeois parties and in the govern-

ment administration held meetings; the chief rabble-rouser in Dresden was Grothaus, a Catholic and former member of the SED, who was sentenced to fifteen years in prison and who, as head of the Catholic Church's land commission, took responsibility for several properties. After his arrest, it was Dr. Jung, the chairman of the Caritas organization for the Diocese of Meißen, who took care of him.[143]

Notes

1. Gerhard Keiderling, *"Gruppe Ulbricht" in Berlin April bis Juni 1945: Von den Vorbereitungen im Sommer 1944 bis zur Wiedergründung der KPD im Juni 1945* (Berlin, 1993), 335.

2. Cf. Clemens Vollnhals, "Zwischen Kooperation und Konfrontation: Zur Kirchenpolitik von KPD/SED und SMAD in der Sowjetischen Besatzungszone 1945-1949," *Deutschland Archiv* 27 (1994): 478–90. Catholic members included Josef Kayser, Alois Ludwig, and Peter Mohr.

3. To this day, researchers have only had limited and fragmentary access to sources in Moscow relating to the activities of SMAD, SKK, and the Soviet intelligence services in church affairs in the SBZ and GDR.

4. Peter Buchholz, a prison pastor, was the Catholic advisor to the Berlin city government. See Martin Höllen, *Loyale Distanz? Katholizismus und Kirchenpolitik in SBZ und DDR,* 3 vols. (Berlin, 1994–2000), 1:35–43.

5. Cf. Michael Rudloff, "Das Verhältnis der SED zur weltanschaulichen Toleranz in den Jahren 1946 bis 1949," *Internationale wissenschaftliche Korrespondenz zur Geschichte der deutschen Arbeiterbewegung* 29 (1993): 490–505. On the "religious socialists," see Siegfried Heimann and Franz Walter, *Religiöse Sozialisten und Freidenker* (Bonn, 1993).

6. SAPMO-BArch, DY 30, IV 2/14/1. On the possible direct impact of SMAD on church affairs before the 1946 elections, compare Norman Naimark, *The Russians in Germany: A History of the Soviet Zone of Occupation, 1945-1949* (Cambridge, MA: 1995), 290ff.

7. Andreas Beckmann and Regina Kusch, *Gott in Bautzen: Gefangenenseelsorge in der DDR* (Berlin, 1994), 59ff.

8. Rudloff, "Verhältnis der SED," 502ff.

9. Created in early 1949, the Small Secretariat became the Secretariat of the Central Committee in July 1950. Next to the Politburo, it was the most important decision-making body in the GDR until 1989.

10. Cf. Joachim Heise, "Zwischen ideologischem Dogma und politischem Pragmatismus. Kirchenpolitik der SED in den 50er Jahren," *Berliner Dialog-Hefte* (Sonderheft 1993): 5.

11. Minutes of the 1 August 1950, meeting of the Politburo. SAMPO-BArch, DY 30, IV 2/2/102.

12. Minutes of the 22 August 1950 meeting of the Politburo. SAPMO-BArch, DY 30, IV 2/2/105. Cf. Heise, "Kirchenpolitik der SED zwischen ideologischem Dogmatismus und politischem Pragmatismus." *Berliner Dialog-Hefte* (Sonderheft 1993): 344–52.

13. SAPMO-BArch, DY 30, J IV 2/2/259.

14. Thomas Raabe, *SED-Staat und katholische Kirche: Politische Beziehungen 1949-1961* (Paderborn, 1995), 54ff.

15. Gerhard Besier and Stephan Wolf, eds., *"Pfarrer, Christen und Katholiken": Das Ministerium für Staatssicherheit und die Kirchen* (Neukirchen/Vluyn, 1991), 47–54 (document 18) and 154–58 (document 19).

16. In 1951, the MfS had 2,458 employees; by 1952 it had 5,380. In 1953, the main office had 6,655 employees. See Jens Giesecke, "Die hauptamtlichen Mitarbeiter des Ministeriums für Staatssicherheit," in Klaus-Dieter Henke, Siegfried Suckut, Clemens Vollnhals, Walter Süß, and Roger Engelmann, eds., *Anatomie der Staatssicherheit*, 4 vols. (Berlin, 1995), 1:6.
17. The relevant archival holdings for 1950–59 are BAP, MdI, HVDVP, Best.11. See also the numerous reports from Deutsche Volkspolizei stations and from SED municipal officials, BAP, DO-4, 306.
18. On the Catholic Church, see Höllen, *Loyale Distanz*, 1:213ff. and 308ff.
19. Though it may have represented wishful thinking, a note on a conversation with the SKK (dated 7 January 1953) claimed that "all important political decisions have been made by the Ministry of the Interior since the summer of 1950; the Main Office *[Hauptamt]* is more or less a messenger," SAPMO-BArch, NY 90/455.
20. At the time, the MfS exerted massive pressure on the employees of the Main Office for Church Relations. See Stephan Wolf, "Rolle und Funktion des Ministeriums für Staatssicherheit und seiner Vorläufer bei der Umsetzung der SED-Kirchenpolitik für den Zeitraum bis zum ersten Grundsatzgespräch vom 10. Juni 1953" (MA thesis, Kirchliche Hochschule Berlin, 1991).
21. Minutes of the 17 March 1953 meeting of the Politburo, SAPMO-BArch, DY 30, J IV 2/2/70.
22. Raabe, *SED-Staat*, 62.
23. This is confirmed by a quick glance at the titles and publication dates of GDR works that cite documents from 1935–1947. See, for example, *Auf dem Wege zur gemeinsamen humanistischen Verantwortung: Eine Sammlung kirchenpolitischer Dokumente 1945 bis 1966 unter Berücksichtigung von Dokumenten aus dem Zeitraum 1933 bis 1945* (East Berlin, 1967) and Klaus Drobisch, ed., *Christen im Nationalkommitee "Freies Deutschland": Eine Dokumentation* (East Berlin, 1973).
24. Cf. Höllen, *Loyale Distanz*, 1:11–18.
25. In response to a letter from Arthur Rackwitz, SAPMO-BArch, NY 36/756.
26. SAPMO-BArch, NY 182/246.
27. Edgar Dusdal, "Gesellschafts- und kirchenpolitische Positionen innerhalb des Protestantismus und der SED nach 1945," *Evangelisches Bildungswerk* (Berlin, 1993): 21–33, here 27.
28. Rudloff, "Verhältnis der SED," 490ff. See the text of the declaration in Otto Meier, *Partei und Kirche* (East Berlin, 1947), 45ff.
29. Rudloff, "Verhältnis der SED," 500; Meier, *Partei und Kirche*, passim.
30. Rackwitz had been deeply involved in the formulation of the "SED and Christianity" declaration. See Rudloff, "Verhältnis der SED," 491.
31. Ibid., 501.
32. SAPMO-BArch, NY 36/756.
33. Rudloff, "Verhältnis der SED," 498.
34. Keiderling, *"Gruppe Ulbricht,"* 362.
35. Rolf Badstübner and Wilfried Loth, eds., *Wilhelm Pieck: Aufzeichnungen zur Deutschlandpolitik 1945–1953* (Berlin, 1994), 51.
36. Cf. Vollnhals, "Zwischen Kooperation und Konfrontation," 483ff. One unique situation in East Berlin was the reopening in 1945 of the Theresienschule, a Catholic school closed during the Nazi era. Protected by a decision of the Allied Command in February 1946, it was able to survive through the various phases of the GDR. See Annaliese Kirchberg, ed., *Theresienschule zu Berlin: 1894–1994* (Berlin, 1994), 25–29.
37. See Thomas Boese, *Die Entwicklung des Staatskirchenrechts in der DDR von 1945 bis 1989* (Baden-Baden, 1994), 66ff.
38. Ibid., 77
39. See Tim Möhlenbrock, *Kirche und Bodenreform in der Sowjetischen Besatzungszone* (Frankfurt am Main, 1997).

40. On the text of the GDR constitution, see Boese, *Die Entwicklung der Staatskirchenrechts in der DDR*, 121–29.
41. SAPMO-BArch, DY 30, IV 2/14/6.
42. Gerhard Besier, *Der SED-Staat und die Kirche: Der Weg in die Anpassung* (Munich, 1993).
43. The "National Front" was originally an idea of Stalin's to encourage integration with the Western zones of occupation and with former Nazis in the SBZ/GDR. See Badstübner and Loth, eds., *Wilhelm Pieck*, 285, 291, 321; and Rüdiger Henkel, *Im Dienste der Staatspartei. Über Parteien und Organisationen in der DDR* (Baden-Baden, 1994), 97–115.
44. It was the first church-state summit in the GDR that both Catholic and Protestant representatives participated in. See the minutes in SAPMO-BArch, NY 90/452.
45. See Hermann Wentker, "'Kirchenkampf' in der DDR. Der Konflikt um die Junge Gemeinde 1950–1953," *Vierteljahreshefte für Zeitgeschichte* 42 (1994): 95–127, here 99ff.
46. In 1949, some 90 percent of the GDR population belonged to a church or religious community; 12 percent were Catholic. Even into the mid 1950s, over 70 percent of SED members were nominally church members. See Heise, "Zwischen ideologischem Dogma," 3.
47. Badstübner and Loth, *Wilhelm Pieck*, 384.
48. SAPMO-BArch, DY 30, IV 2/14/1.
49. SAPMO-BArch, DY 30, IV 2/14/1.
50. The Catholic foster home in Bad Saarow, for example, was accused of being a "base for American agents" and was taken over by the state in May 1953. A few weeks later, it was back in church hands as a result of the New Direction policy. See Höllen, *Loyale Distanz*, 1:338ff.
51. Dusdal, "Gesellschafts- und kirchenpolitische Positionen," 28ff.
52. At the time, the Catholic Church received 1.2 million (Eastern) marks to distribute among its six districts.
53. SAPMO-BArch, DY 30, J IV 2/2/224.
54. SAPMO-BArch, DY 30, J IV 2/2/259.
55. See Peter-Paul Straube, *Katholische Studentengemeinde in der DDR als Ort eines außeruniversitären Studium generale* (Leipzig, 1996), 80–83; Wentker, "Kirchenkampf," 105–22; Raabe, *SED-Staat*, 115–41.
56. SAPMO-BArch, DY 30, J IV 2/2/259.
57. Wentker, "Kirchenkampf," 122; Raabe, *SED-Staat*, 141–46.
58. SAPMO-BArch NY 90/699.
59. Alexander Fischer, "Der Einfluß der SMAD auf das Parteiensystem in der SBZ am Beispiel der CDUD," *Deutschland Archiv* 26 (1997): 265–72; Alexander Fischer, "Andreas Hermes und die gesamtdeutsche Frage der Union," in Manfred Agethen and Alexander Fischer, eds., *Die CDU in der sowjetisch besetzten Zone/DDR 1945–1952* (Sankt Augustin, 1994), 7–20.
60. Siegfried Suckut, "Zum Wandel von Rolle und Funktion der Christlich-Demokratischen Union Deutschlands (CDUD) im Parteiensystem der SBZ/DDR (1945–1952)," in Hermann Weber, ed., *Parteiensystem zwischen Demokratie und Volksdemokratie* (Cologne, 1982), 129–31.
61. See the minutes of their meetings from 1945 to 1949 in Siegfried Suckut, *Blockpolitik in der SBZ/DDR* (Cologne, 1986).
62. Siegfried Suckut, "Der Konflikt um die Bodenreformpolitik in der Ost-CDU 1945," *Deutschland Archiv* 15 (1982): 1080–95.
63. These are Kaiser's words in the CDU party newspaper *Neue Zeit*, 30 December 1945.
64. Christel Dowidat, "Personalpolitik als Mittel der Transformation des Parteiensystems in der SBZ/DDR (1945–1952)," in Weber, *Parteiensystem*, 484ff.
65. Cf. Günter Braun, "Zur Entwicklung der Wahlen in der SBZ/DDR 1946–1950," in Weber, *Parteiensystem*, 545–62.
66. Werner Conze, *Jakob Kaiser: Politiker zwischen Ost und West 1945–1949* (Stuttgart, 1969).
67. See Kaiser's speech of 6 September 1947, ibid., 171, as well as his 12 July 1947 speech in Tilman Mayer, ed., *Jakob Kaiser: Gewerkschafter und Patriot* (Cologne, 1988).

68. Braun, "Zur Entwicklung der Wahlen," 513–17.
69. Cf. Brigite Kaff, ed., *"Gefährliche politische Gegner": Widerstand und Verfolgung in der sowjetischen Zone/DDR* (Düsseldorf, 1995).
70. Siegfried Suckut, "Innenpolitische Aspekte der DDR-Gründung," *Deutschland Archiv* 25 (1992): 370–84.
71. Cf. Martin Rißmann, *Kaderschulung in der Ost-CDU 1949–1971* (Düsseldorf, 1995).
72. Notes in a file from 17 September 1953. ACDP VII-013-1019.
73. Siegfried Suckut, "Christlich-Demokratische Union Deutschlands. CDU(D)," in Martin Broszat and Hermann Weber, eds., *SBZ-Handbuch: Staatliche Verwaltungen, Parteien, gesellschaftliche Organisationen und ihre Führungskräfte in derSowjetischen Besatzungszone Deutschlands* (Munich, 1990), 521.
74. Cf. Suckut, *Blockpolitik*, 434, 443, 452, 460–63.
75. Report on the conference from 14 March 1950 (ABAM).
76. See, for example, Nuschke's 18 August 1951 letter to Minister-President Grotewohl (ACDP VII-013-857): "We must set aside everything that might turn Western public opinion against the GDR. This means a tactically savvy approach to the churches."
77. ACPD VII-013-1801.
78. See Höllen, *Loyale Distanz*, 1:326ff.; Beckmann and Kusch, *Gott in Bautzen*, 97–102.
79. These are Dertinger's comments to the CDU political commission on 16 December 1952 (ACDP VII-01301754).
80. Hermann Wentker, "Ost-CDU und Protestantismus 1949–1958," *Kirchliche Zeitgeschichte* 6 (1993): 349–78; here 365–70.
81. BAP, C-20, 101.
82. ACDP VII-013-1763.
83. ACDP VII-013-3041.
84. ACDP VII-013-1801.
85. ACDP VII-013-1763.
86. BStU, Ast Dresden, AIM 619/55, Part II, Vol. 1, Nr. 160.
87. Cf. Josef Pilvousek, "Flüchtlinge, Flucht und die Frage des Bleibens: Überlegungen zu einem traditionellen Problem der Katholiken im Osten Deutschlands," in Claus-Peter März, ed., *Die ganz alltägliche Freiheit: Christsein zwischen Traum und Wirklichkeit* (Leipzig, 1993), 9–23.
88. Ibid., 14.
89. See Konrad Hartelt, "Die Entwicklung der Jurisdiktionsverhältnisse der katholischen Kirche in der DDR von 1945 bis zur Gegenwart," in Wilhelm Ernst and Konrad Feiereis, eds., *Denkender Glaube in Geschichte und Gegenwart* (Leipzig, 1992), 415–40.
90. Cf. Stanislaw Wilk, "Der Vatikan, die Regierung und die Kirche in Polen in den Jahren 1945–1948," in Institut für vergleichende Staat-Kirche Forschung, ed., *Der Weg der katholischen Kirche in verschiedenen realsozialistischen Ländern in den Jahren 1945 bis 1948/49: ein historischer Vergleich* (Berlin, 1995), 28–37.
91. In ecclesiastical law, this refers to clerics with ordinary jurisdiction in the external forum over a specified territory; from the Latin ordinarius. See http://www.catholicreference.net/index.cfm?id=35302 (accessed 28 March 2009).
92. See Josef Pilvousek, "Gesamtdeutsche Wirklichkeit—Pastorale Notwendigkeit: Zur Vorgeschichte der Ostdeutschen Bischofskonferenz," in Emerich Coreth, Wilhelm Ernst and Eberhard Tiefensee, eds., *Von Gott reden in säkularer Gesellschaft: Festschrift für Konrad Feiereis zum 65. Geburtstag* (Leipzig, 1996), 229–42, here 242.
93. See Martin Höllen, Heinrich Wienken, der 'unpolitische' Kirchenpolitiker (Mainz, 1981).
94. Renate Hackel, Katholische Publizistik in der DDR 1945–1984 (Mainz, 1987).
95. See Hackel, Katholische Publizistik, 32–54.
96. See Erich Kleineidam, "Vorgeschichte, Gründung und Aufbau des Regionalpriesterseminars Erfurt," in Ernst and Feiereis, Denkender Glaube, 97–116; Konrad Feiereis, "Katholische Theologie in der DDR: Chance, Grenze, Selbstverständnis," hochschule ost 4 (1995): 46–55.

97. SAPMO-BArch, DY30, IV 2/14/239.
98. SAPMO-BArch, NY 90/453.
99. SAPMO-BArch, NY 90/457; DAB, Asig 30/39.
100. State Administration Department of the Central Committee of the SED to the Soviet Control Commission, 23 May 1952. SAPMO-BArch, DY 30, J IV 2/14/239.
101. Decision of the Politburo of the Central Committee, 5 August 1952. SAPMO-BArch, DY 30, J IV 2/2/224.
102. Josef Pilvousek, "'Innenansichten': Von der 'Flüchtlingskirche' zur 'katholischen Kirche in der DDR,'" in Deutscher Bundestag, ed., Materialien 6:2, 1134–63.
103. See Antonia Leugers, Gegen eine Mauer bischöflichen Schweigens (Frankfurt am Main, 1996).
104. See Bernd Schäfer, "Katholische Kirche in der DDR," Stimmen der Zeit 213 (1995): 212-14.
105. Cf. the decree circulated by the Diocese of Meißen on 31 August 1945, in Gerhard Lange, Ursula Pruß, Franz Schrader, and Siegfried Seifert, eds., Katholische Kirche—Sozialistischer Staat DDR: Dokumente und öffentliche Äußerungen 1945–1990 (Leipzig, 1993), 11.
106. See the memoranda of 1 February 1950 from the Diocese of Meißen, ibid., 33 and the Diocese of Berlin, ibid., 34. The only Catholic priest who deliberately opposed this policy was Karl Fischer, who joined the National Front as a member of the CDU steering committee and furthermore signed numerous public declarations. See Bernd Schäfer, "Priester in zwei deutschen Diktaturen: Die antifaschistische Legende des Karl Fischer (1900–1972)," Historisch-Politische Mitteilungen 7 (2000): 49–74.
107. Dieter Grande and Bernd Schäfer, "Interne Richtlinien und Bewertungsmaßstäbe zu kirchlichen Kontakten mit dem MfS," in Clemens Vollnhals, ed., Die Kirchenpolitik von SED und Staatssicherheit. Eine Zwischenbilanz, 2nd ed. (Berlin, 1997), 388–95.
108. SAPMO-BArch, DY 30,2/14/1.
109. See Wilhelm Weskamm's minutes, ABAM.
110. See Weskamm's notes on the conference in Berlin on 14 December 1949, ABAM.
111. Lange et al., Katholische Kirche—Sozialistischer Staat DDR, 36.
112. Pilvousek, "Gesamtdeutsche Wirklichkeit," 229-242.
113. ABAS. No locator number. For contrasting views of von Preysing, see Pilvousek, "Gesamtdeutsche Wirklichkeit," Walter Adolph, Kardinal Preysing und zwei Diktaturen (West Berlin, 1971), and Ulrich von Hehl and Wolfgang Tischner, "Die katholische Kirche in der SBZ/BRD 1945–1989," in Deutscher Bundestag, Materialien, 6:2, 875–949.
114. Höllen, Loyale Distanz, 1:195ff.
115. Cf. Weskamm's notes on the conference from 14 December 1949 (ABAM).
116. See the text of the memo in Lange et al., Katholische Kirche—Sozialistischer Staat DDR, 30ff.
117. Ibid., 34.
118. Otto Nuschke, "Der Kardinalfehler," Neue Zeit, 19 February 1950, 1. Nuschke was reacting to a press declaration by von Preysing in which he described an internment camp set up by the SMAD in 1945 as a "concentration camp on GDR territory." See the text of his declaration in Gerhard Lange and Ursula Pruß, eds., An der Nahstelle der Systeme: Dokumente und Texte aus dem Bistum Berlin, vol. 1: 1945–1961 (Leipzig, 1996), 79.
119. ABAM. The term "zone questions" is underlined in the original document.
120. Lange et al., Katholische Kirche—Sozialistischer Staat DDR, 42–45.
121. Government transcripts. SAPMO-BArch, NY 90/452.
122. See his report to the Fulda Bishops' Conference in August 1950, "Zur kirchenpolitische Lage der Ostzone," in Höllen, Loyale Distanz, 1:229ff.
123. Letter of 20 September 1950. DAB, V/16-4.
124. File notes by Weskamm, ABAM.

125. Ibid. Catholic bishops in the GDR adhered to this principle through 1989. See Bernd Schäfer, "Selbstbehauptungsstrategie und (Über)lebensmuster der katholischen Kirche in der Zeit des DDR-Staats," Kirchliche Zeitgeschichte 7 (1994): 264–78.
126. BStU, ZA, AOP 614/59, B1, 28ff., 36ff.
127. Pilvousek, "'Innenansichten,'" 29.
128. Raabe, SED-Staat, 210–17.
129. Inge Bennewitz and Rainer Potratz, Zwangsaussiedlungen an der innerdeutschen Grenze (Berlin, 1994), 65–70, 236–41.
130. State transcripts by State Secretary Geyer, BAP, C-20, 101.
131. Ibid. The church minutes of the meeting, by contrast, describe a more factual exchange of views, DAB, Asig 32/86.
132. DAB, Asig 30/39.
133. See Dusdal, "Gesellschafts- und kirchenpolitische Positionen."
134. See Lange et al., Katholische Kirche—Sozialistischer Staat DDR, 58ff.
135. Ibid., 61.
136. DAB, Asig 30/39.
137. See ACDP III-035-65 and -94.
138. BStU, Ast Dresden, AOP 71/59, Band III, Bl.36ff.
139. Letter of Wienken. Ibid., Bl. 218.
140. Ibid., not numbered.
141. Ibid., Bl. 5.
142. SAPMO-BArch, DY 30, IV 2/14/31.
143. SAMPO-BArch, DY 30, IV 2/14/64. Dr. Paul Jung, as the Caritas director in Meißen, was a close associate of Wienken. See Peter Russig, Wilhelm Grothaus—Dresdener Antifaschist und Aufstandsführer des 17. Juni (Dresden, 1997).

Chapter 2

1953–1957
Conflict and Stabilization after the Uprising

The GDR after the Uprising of 17 June 1953

The suppression of the June 1953 revolt, which kept the SED in power, was only possible because of Soviet intervention. The hegemonic party and its foreign protector drew closer together than ever. The GDR was able to consolidate itself in the months following the uprising because the SED was able to compensate for its obvious lack of support from the majority of the population using a more aggressive security policy. SED leaders were prepared to take any measure necessary to ensure that the trauma of the 17 June revolt would not recur. They were aware that their future could not only be based on Soviet backing.

Isolated strikes and problems with the trade unions that the party could not always contain continued through the fall of 1953, and the SED remained nervous. Internal conflicts emerged in the party leadership. The Politburo heavily criticized Ulbricht for authoritarian methods, for building a "cult of personality," and for a heavy-handed style of administration. The main spokesmen for Ulbricht's critics within the party were Rudolf Herrnstadt, the editor-in-chief of *Neues Deutschland,* and State Security Minister Wilhelm Zaisser. In the Politburo session of 8 July 1953, a majority was against Ulbricht continuing as first secretary of the SED Central Committee (ZK). Zaisser said: "He must be distanced from the party apparatus. The apparatus in [Ulbricht's] hands would be a disaster for the new direction."[1] During the crisis of the revolt, however, Zaisser and Herrnstadt had behaved no differently from the rest of the Politburo, including Ulbricht. Their attempt to climb to the top of the SED ranks, with Soviet cover, failed when Beria fell from power and the Soviet high commissioner in Berlin, Vladimir Semyonov, played a two-sided game. At the Fifteenth SED Central Committee Congress on 24–25 July 1953, Herrnstadt and Zaisser were removed from office, accused of forming a "faction" after the uprising and committing an array of political crimes including "capitulation to the enemy." Ulbricht was unanimously reelected first party secretary. Once the imaginary "Herrnstadt-Zaisser faction" was "uncovered" and Minister of Justice Max Fechner was arrested, the highest-ranking scapegoats had been taken care of.[2]

SED efforts to safeguard its power were directed both internally—against the SED membership itself, its allied bloc parties, and ordinary GDR citizens who had taken part in the revolt—and externally, against "foreign agents" and "provocateurs" who had directed the "attempted fascist putsch" with helpers inside the GDR, allegedly to execute a Western plan called "X-Day." But, at the same time, the amnesty of prisoners that had begun with the "New Direction" on 9 June 1953 continued through early 1954; some 30,000 of the 66,000 people arrested before June 1953 were released.[3] There was a significant change of cadres within the SED due to numerous ejections and resignations (about 26,000 in 1953), which new members made up for.[4] New measures to discipline the SED party base were carried out in the spirit of a speech in August 1953 to the party leadership of the new State Secretariat for Security (SfS, so named for a time after the MfS was temporarily incorporated into the Ministry of the Interior):

> A certain group of party members succumbed to a spirit of atonement. They believed that, because we had made some mistakes, we should now kneel down before the cross. The Fifteenth Congress of the Central Committee has given the appropriate answer to such comrades. There is no basis for this sort of spirit of contrition.[5]

Unwilling to submit to self-criticism, the SED had to search for conspiracies, foreign agents, and saboteurs. SfS Director Ernst Wollweber gave the SfS—strengthened by its own espionage in foreign countries—the task of supplying "evidence" for this conspiracy theory in the form of arrests.[6] From December 1952 to the end of 1955, the number of employees in the State Security Main Office doubled to at least 10,286.[7]

The Politburo had little patience, noting on 23 September 1953 that "despite the fact that three months have passed since the events of June 17, the state security agencies have not yet uncovered the responsible organizations."[8] Politburo member Hermann Matern attempted to motivate SfS staff in an internal speech on 11 November 1953: "Within the ranks of the security services, there can be no liberalism in regard to the enemies of our republic. We must strike ruthlessly. There is no place here for weak-kneed pacifists or stargazers. Comrade Walter Ulbricht once said at a ZK meeting, 'We have to make the GDR hell for foreign agents.'"[9]

GDR citizens who had contact with groups in West Berlin and whom authorities considered to be "acting against our zone" were especially targeted. In January 1954 Operation Vermin *[Ungeziefer]* rounded up contact people in the GDR and kidnapped others from West Berlin. In June, the GDR's highest court held a show trial that lasted several days, declaring: "The case before us has proved the intensity with which the warmongers planned their fascist coup attempt of June 17 and their 'X-Day.'"[10]

By the end of January 1954, a total of 1,526 people had been sentenced to prison for participating in the uprising, and two were executed.[11] Under Wollweber, the SfS strengthened its anti-Western operations, as he had called for in an internal speech on 5 August 1955: "From now on, the regional chiefs must devote at least half of their efforts to investigative work in the political centers and to penetrating groups of enemy agents in the West. Again, I emphasize, fifty per cent attention to the West."[12]

Germany's division grew deeper following the failure of the conference of the foreign ministers of the four Allied powers in Berlin from 25 January to 18 February 1954. After the FRG ratified the Paris Treaty in October 1954, which took effect in May 1955 and brought West Germany (with its own military) into NATO and the European Community, the GDR took part in founding the Warsaw Pact on 14 May 1955. The Geneva summit meeting of the Second World War Allies in July 1955, with representatives from the FRG and the GDR present as observers, also failed to bridge the divide. Returning from this conference, Khrushchev spoke in East Berlin for the first time (publicly) about the "two state theory." The result was the treaty of 20 September 1955 between the Soviet Union and the GDR recognizing the latter's "sovereignty" and dissolving the Office of the Soviet High Commissioner in East Berlin. Another Allied foreign ministers' conference in Geneva failed in October-November 1955. In December 1955 the FRG raised its claim to be the sole representative of Germany according to international law and proclaimed the Hallstein Doctrine, which threatened to break off diplomatic relations with any third country that recognized the GDR; the Soviet Union was the only exception because it was one of the four Allied victors.

De-Stalinization and the Fear of "A New June 17"

On 25 February 1956 Khrushchev gave a sensational, secret nighttime speech at the Twentieth Party Congress in Moscow in which he came to terms with the legacy of the deceased Stalin: the "cult of personality," his personal qualifications, and his political errors. De-Stalinization in the Soviet Union had an impact on other socialist countries, too, and the Soviets implicitly gave each of these countries a free hand to develop their own version. The new Soviet style was a considerable problem for Ulbricht, who dominated the GDR Politburo in a Stalinist fashion.[13] Ulbricht denied that de-Stalinization had any relevance to him or to the GDR, claiming that the "Stalin problem" was purely an internal Soviet matter: "When Stalin placed himself above the party and launched his cult of personality, the Soviet state and its Communist Party suffered considerable damage; Stalin can no longer be counted as one of the leading figures of Marxism."[14]

GDR Politburo member Karl Schirdewan read Khrushchev's speech to delegates at the Twenty-Sixth Congress of the Central Committee on 22 March 1956 and at the SED's Third Party Congress a few days later. At the same time, reports of Khrushchev's speech, and eventually the entire text, filtered into the West, eventually finding their way back to the GDR. Ordinary GDR citizens could learn about things their government did not mention from the West Berlin radio station RIAS—or the open border in Berlin, for that matter. De-Stalinization became a serious credibility problem for the SED as a whole. The party leadership did not do much beyond making a Politburo statement on "the collective nature of leadership" (distancing itself from Stalin's "personality cult"), rehabilitating some Communists who had been discredited during their Nazi-era exile in the USSR and overturning some GDR-era party censures and criminal convictions. The SED was cautious to avoid anything that might push the GDR population toward a "new June 17" in the face of additional social and economic hardships. About 35,000 prisoners were released, out of a total that had again risen to 60,000.[15] However, when the wave of de-Stalinization began to take a national-Communist turn in Poland and Hungary, intellectuals at GDR universities engaged in discussions that appeared threatening to the SED leadership.

On 28 June 1956 the Polish military put down a workers' uprising in Poznan with considerable violence. In the GDR, too, there were strikes and protests; the MfS counted forty-four between 1 July and 7 October 1956.[16] Hungary drifted the furthest away from the Soviet Union after the fall of its Stalinist party secretary, Matyás Rakosi. On 22 October demonstrations began in Budapest, calling for free elections, the release of political prisoners, and the withdrawal of Soviet troops. Soviet forces attacked and then withdrew on 28 October when Hungarian soldiers joined in the rebellion. The new Hungarian leader Imre Nagy announced that his country would pull out of the Warsaw Pact. On 4 November Soviet troops intervened again and fought until the revolt was crushed on 15 November. During the Hungarian uprising, SED officials feared "a new June 17" in the GDR. MfS reports from late October considered a widespread workers' revolt a serious possibility.[17]

On 8 November 1956 the Politburo issued a decision on "Measures to Suppress Counterrevolutionary Operations."[18] The GDR, they said, "has a duty to use its own powers to maintain calm and order on its territory and to suppress and destroy all counterrevolutionary offensives." The Politburo statement detailed the organization of the armed forces, the chain of command, and the guidelines for the use of force: "If and when it comes to military intervention, there will be no negotiations."

GDR leaders would be much better prepared in the event of "a new June 17." There were no protests that seriously threatened the East German regime in the fall of 1956 because in the aftermath of the 1953 revolt, which was traumatic for all sides, the general population's fear of the SED and the Soviet army was just as great as the regime's fear of the general population. In contrast to citizens in Poland or Hungary, those who were dissatisfied in the GDR already had the experience of a failed revolt behind them, and the suppression in Hungary only confirmed their belief in the futility of an uprising. In 1956 as in 1953, Ulbricht was about to fall from power, but in both cases he was paradoxically saved by the uprisings: when the Soviet Union began to feel nervous it preferred a tough response over new experiments, and it needed an Ulbricht more than ever as head of the SED. Just as in 1953, the GDR leadership "had proof" that the 1956 disturbances were not the result of repressive SED policies but rather were engineered by "the imperialist enemy" and its agents. This rigid thought matrix, nurtured and validated by the MfS and its conspiracy theories, remained a persistent feature of the Politburo up through 1989.

SED Kirchenpolitik and Its Organization

Beginning in 1954, the SED tried to simplify the administration of its Kirchenpolitik. The regime sought to subordinate all offices to the party apparatus in order to systematize its church policies.[19] The Politburo formed an ad hoc working group on 2 March 1954 "to formulate our line on the churches." The group was comprised of its leader, Politburo member and ZK Secretary for Culture and Education Paul Wandel, and four other officials, including the SfS state secretary, Erich Mielke.[20] They quickly produced a strategic document—"Party Policy in Church Affairs"—for the 14 March Politburo session, which the highest SED board adopted with some amendments.[21] The document called the churches in the GDR "the strongest legal base for the imperialist powers," which the West German church leaders used "to execute their criminal intentions"; therefore, "the party, the mass organizations, and the state have the duty to systematically investigate and enlighten the entire Christian population."

The SED decided to create a new Department of Church Affairs within the ZK. It was formed on 24 November 1954 under the leadership of Willi Barth[22] and his deputy, Rudi Bellmann; it replaced the Section for Churches and Religious Groups within the ZK Department of State Administration. Within the new department, Hans Weise was named head of the Section for Protestantism, Catholicism, and other Religious Communities. The department was housed within the ZK apparatus and functioned like its other departments. It was soon referred to as the Working Group for Church Affairs; the semantic shift was intended to assign a lesser significance to "church affairs," because the SED saw them as a provisional concern. On 4 January 1955 the Politburo reiterated that the department/working group would be subject to "the direction and control of the party leaders" and the "leadership, coordination, [and] control of the work of the comrades in the state apparatus." It further determined that within each regional government council a department of the interior would address church matters. SED plans for a "church affairs advisory council comprised of progressive theologians and scholarly experts" to advise the Department of Church Affairs were never realized.[23]

On 21 December 1954 Wollweber ordered that the SfS also set up its own church affairs division, called V/6 (V/4 starting in 1955), within Main Department V, because its "operative work . . . to counter adversarial activity by churches and religious groups" was insufficient. The new central department was split into three sections: Protestant (Lutheran), Catholic, and other Protestant denominations. The larger regional governments (*Bezirke*, henceforth translated as "districts") were to set up a unit to "work on" church affairs, and the smaller ones (*Kreise*, henceforth translated as "counties") were to dedicate an employee to the task.[24]

A further reorganization of the Politburo, decided on 19 June 1956, was to improve the efficiency of the new central state apparatus with the formation of a new Office for Church Affairs.[25] The office was to unite functions carried out by several different ministries. With this administrative act, Nuschke's Main Office was dissolved; it had been barely noticeable in the shadows, having lost its power in 1953. In a detailed analysis from 4 October 1955, Barth had characterized the Main Office as "the church hierarchy's agency within the GDR state apparatus . . . this Main Office has been an obstacle to the improvement of church-state relations; there are people working there who are indifferent or negative toward the German Democratic Republic."[26]

On 21 February 1957 the Council of Ministers called a State Secretary for Church Affairs into being to head the Office for Church Affairs. They informed the Press Office on 7 March that Werner Eggerath, the GDR ambassador to Romania, would fill the position. The office began its work on 1 April, staffed by workers transferred from the ZK, the Ministry of the Interior, and the Main Office for Church Relations. The regulations required that the state secretary be an SED member and his second-in-command come from the CDU, and the main department head—who maintained close contact with the ZK and the security agencies—also had to belong to the SED. Max Hartwig (CDU) was tapped to fill the number two job; he had previously been an advisor to Nuschke. The ZK staffer Hans Weise was named as main department head. Nuschke himself was permitted to continue to represent church affairs within the Council of Ministers as a deputy to the Minister-President; he held this ceremonial position, without any real significance, until his death in December 1957.

Thus, 1957 saw the establishment of the administrative contours of GDR Kirchenpolitik that would remain intact until 1989. The party (ZK, SED, and regional and local leaders), working in close cooperation with the MfS (at the central and district levels), was to direct and monitor the state apparatus (state secretariats and interior affairs departments at the district and county levels). In practice, this meant that the regime was increasingly capable of surveying matters and minimizing contradictory or uncoordinated policies. It became more difficult, but not completely impossible, for the churches to use the new government dynamics to their advantage.

"Security Policy" and "Alliance Policy"

The Central Committee's Department of State Administration, having issued a joint communiqué with the Protestant Church on 10 June 1953 and then experienced the June 17 uprising, declared in a report that "the state is now on the defensive against the reactionary attacks and demands of the churches."[27] The regime sought new strategies in its Kirchenpolitik that would impact both Catholics and Protestants but, as a rule, keyed them to the Protestant majority—which was of greater importance in matters involving the two Germanys. At this point in time, the SED considered the small Catholic Church in the GDR merely an extension of the Vatican, part of the "reactionary" political camp, and a partner to Konrad Adenauer's government in West Germany.

SED Kirchenpolitik from 1954 to 1957 consisted of these main elements:
- A systematic encroachment upon the churches' ability to exercise their autonomy by pushing "foreign bodies" out of public life under the rubric of building a socialist society.
- Strengthening "scientific propaganda," directed especially at youth and at church members within the SED.
- The systematic surveillance of church officials, organizations, and institutions by the SfS/MfS.
- Application of the "differentiation policy" to the Protestant churches with the goal of fomenting divisions.
- Taking steps to sever church connections across the FRG/GDR border, including pressuring individuals and organizations to make "declarations of loyalty" to the GDR.

The Politburo decision of 14 March 1954 systematized Kirchenpolitik. It included a method for differentiating between "progressive" and "reactionary" forces in the churches—the so-called differentiation policy. It also detailed a long list of "pinprick" measures to hinder church activities, called for more "popular scholarly information campaigns within the party and among the masses," and planned to promote the *Jugendweihe* (Youth Dedication)—a militantly secular, GDR alternative to religious confirmation—in 1955.[28]

Another Politburo decision on 4 January 1955 defined the mission of the new Department of Church Affairs as "the defeat of the provocations and hostile ideologies spread by the church hierarchies of both confessions."[29] To support the "differentiation policy," it allocated financial resources to "encouraging" progressive views: "The State Secretariat for Internal Affairs shall be given DM 1 million to support needy or underpaid clergy, or those who have been reprimanded or punished by the church, or forced to retire against their will; it may also be used for miscellaneous costs in the context of talks between clergy and state officials." The same day, the Politburo also passed a measure to control and censor religious printing licenses, "in order to influence and control church literature and journals in the GDR and to defend against reactionary attacks . . . approval [can] only occur in close connection with the total context of the political-ideological struggle." The Politburo forbade the publication of "any literature which openly or surreptitiously attacked the GDR constitution and the policies of our government."

On 15 February 1955 the SED mounted its first internal party meeting of all regional secretaries on church matters. Wandel gave a lecture on SED church policies that was later circulated within the party.[30] Wandel pointed out that over-coming religion would be a long and arduous process and that the SED risked "sinking in the swamp of opportunism and strengthening the hand of political reactionaries if we do not do everything to reduce the church's base and its influ-ence upon the masses." Kirchenpolitik was supposed to simultaneously weaken the churches, strengthen the party, create "progressive" circles within the church, and encourage these to work with the party. Wandel's paper outlined the Jugend-weihe and its relation to SED membership, and also questioned—in the context of "the separation of church and state"—the legal framework by which the state still collected taxes for the churches.[31] Most importantly, he warned against "mis-takes": "We have to be clear: when dealing with an organized force such as the church apparatus, any error we make in the smallest area becomes enormous capital for the reactionary powers within the church. They understand—this we must grant to them—how to profit 'biblically' from this filthy lucre."

After the 17 June uprising, the SED continued to view the CDU with mistrust as a competitor; this attitude extended to its Kirchenpolitik as well. Some CDU officials attempted to raise the party's and their own profile using their church connections, encouraging the churches to fall in line with the GDR's Kirchen-politik and demonstrate loyalty to the state; yet the SED considered this elevated role of the CDU as politically dangerous.[32] In strategic questions relating to Kirchenpolitik, the SED viewed the CDU as merely a conduit, and it disempow-ered Nuschke's Main Office. At the regional level, however, the CDU was still largely autonomous in its responses to church requests. Officials in the CDU's Berlin headquarters who cooperated with the SED Central Committee, such as Götting and Wirth, could do little to change this. As the formal chairman of the CDU, Nuschke continued to make his compromises and declarations of loyalty to the SED. However, he permitted a lot to go on within the CDU and could approve church requests more easily because he could usually assume that the SED—which was ultimately responsible—would reject them anyway. At times, Nuschke spoke more honestly, as he apparently did in a lecture he gave to the Protestant student congregation at Humboldt University on 10 December 1956 entitled "The CDU between Church and State." In an account of this event for the SED Central Committee, a theology student and SED member reported,

> As a political party, the CDU has the right to take positions from the church's point of view . . . the churches, however, are not free from exaggerations and Dr. Nuschke rejects these. Thus, he is always "hit from both sides" but has developed a "thick skin" . . . Dr. Nuschke says that he could go to the West and is sure that he could make a political career there, but he would consider

this a cowardly retreat . . . Finally, Dr. Nuschke remarked that socialism will prove what it can do, and that this will demonstrate which system is better.[33]

An integral component of SED Kirchenpolitik was the activity of the security services, who provided the decision makers with information acquired in various ways. Deeply marked by a perception of the churches as "enemies," they carried out the party leadership's doctrinaire "security policy" with intrigue and police methods. In the summer of 1953 the SfS/MfS began to systematically conduct surveillance of the Catholic Church in its search for proof of espionage. On 25 November 1953 it began an operation called "The Old Man" (*Der Alte*) against Wienken and the leading members of the ordinaries' office in Bautzen: "Bishop Wienken is sufficiently suspected . . . of spying on behalf of Western capitalist states."[34] After 1955, Wienken's successor, Otto Spülbeck, was also subjected to surveillance; security agents opened his mail. During this phase, they tried to do without electronic bugging, opting instead to use secret informers and other means. The limited "insights" thus gained were formulaic— for example: "Because the Diocese of Meißen is the only one in the GDR that is directly under the pope, the conditions are right for it to become a center of espionage against the GDR as well as the other people's republics and the Soviet Union."[35]

State Secretary Wollweber's order of 21 December 1954 also contained directives for concrete "processing" of the information obtained by the security agencies. These were so all-inclusive that they could hardly be put into practice by underqualified local officials and agents:

> Examination procedures are to be developed for investigating the enemy activities of suspicious clergy, church employees, and fanatic followers of Catholic and Protestant reactionary leaders. These procedures are to be quickly developed into operations . . . Files are to be prepared on monasteries, seminaries, theology departments, hospitals, orphanages, and old age homes, Protestant academies, young men's fellowships, the Kolping Association, etc. Operations are to be carried out in all of these targets. Our work in Protestant and Catholic student groups, young men's fellowships, and the Young Community is to be strengthened.[36]

On 18 October 1955 a "monitoring operation" was launched against the Catholic Church negotiator Johannes Zinke. He was watched personally, as were the offices of the Caritas Association in Berlin and the Fulda Bishops' Conference. According to a government report:

> Interrogations of arrested persons have revealed that Zinke has carried out espionage and anti-democratic agitation . . . The Caritas Association is one of the Catholic Church's largest legal organizations in Germany, which carries on its hostility to the GDR and to the peace camp under the guise of love for one's fellow man.[37]

On 1 March 1955 the MfS regional administration in Magdeburg opened a surveillance file on the Catholic commissary for "enemy activity and agitation against the SED and the state." The code name was Operation Rosary [*Rosenkranz*], and there was another file called Operation Sacrament [*Sakrament*].[38]

The Kolping Association became active in the SBZ in 1945 under the umbrella of the church communities after talks with the SMAD. It maintained good contacts with the main office in Cologne in West Germany. Around 1953, it aroused the attention of the police and the MfS because almost all of its male members were active workers suspected of "economic espionage." After the MfS recruited a Kolping Association member as an informer and made some temporary arrests and interrogations, it came to dramatic conclusions.[39] An August 1956 MfS report described the association as "hostile" and "illegal," but recommended that, instead of arrests, secret informers should be used:

> In the search for leading officials of the Kolping Association [that we could recruit], we need to pay attention to persons with debts and those who are often looking for work on the side, as well as to drinkers, and others with moral or criminal baggage . . . All Kolping groups must be registered. We are to open files on all leaders and officeholders and to prepare lists of all members. These measures are necessary because we are dealing here with illegal groups, in which each member is capable of every sort of hostile activity because of his fanatic beliefs.[40]

In his 15 February 1955 speech to SED officials, Paul Wandel indicated that in political matters, the National Front and the SED should speak directly with the clergy: "As a rule, the state apparatus must handle other questions; this includes delicate matters, both pleasant and otherwise."[41] It was the SfS/MfS, as part of the state apparatus and "the party's sword and shield," that was especially involved in "delicate matters," such as blackmailing clergy or congregants with compromising information in order to "recruit" them as collaborators, or planting provocateurs in the church milieu. In March 1954, for example, the SfS employed a schizophrenic former prison inmate to work against Catholic priests in the Dioceses of Meißen and Berlin; he caused spectacular disruptions that even had repercussions in West Germany.[42] The security agencies had no scruples in their methods: they put targets "under pressure" by sexually baiting them or engaging in outright criminal activity—though their success in using such tactics was extremely meager. The church registered numerous attempts by the SfS/MfS to recruit informants as early as 1954–1955 because the targets declined to collaborate and reported the incidents to church authorities.

The Introduction of the Jugendweihe

The Jugendweihe—a secular alternative to religious confirmation—had its roots in the Enlightenment and in late nineteenth-century efforts to develop unique proletarian traditions. During the Weimar Republic, the ritual was common in the Communist Party and in unions and Free Thinker Associations close to it.[43] In the GDR, the SED attached itself to the custom relatively late. Because the SED anticipated that the introduction of the Jugendweihe would lead to conflict with the churches, it was not emphasized in the early phase, when SED power was not yet secure.[44] In 1954 the SED changed its position, choosing to abandon a defensive stance in its Kirchenpolitik and to promote "clear worldviews" in its own party ranks through secular cultural offerings.[45]

In its comprehensive statement on Kirchenpolitik of 14 March 1954, the Politburo remarked,

> Today, many parents who have no inner connection to the church send their children to confirmation and communion classes because there is no other option for celebrating this transition into a new phase of their lives after they graduate from elementary school. To end this state of affairs and to strengthen civic education, we shall begin now to prepare and institute the Jugendweihe ceremony beginning in 1955.[46]

On 6 July the Politburo took action, forming a committee to prepare for the Jugendweihe. It was decided that teachers would receive training, and registration for the Jugendweihe would begin on 30 November. On 2 November, Ulbricht sent a note to all regional SED first secretaries alerting them that a call to the Jugendweihe would be published. In his note, Ulbricht emphasized that the Jugendweihe, "admired throughout Germany," addressed a "general need from parents and students" and would be introduced in the GDR on an annual basis. The regional SED leaders were to see to it that "influential and informed comrades" join the committees without the party "run[ning] the Jugendweihe in practice. Only when a broad framework is visible can it be successful." Ulbricht emphasized that "we need to convince our own comrades to have their children take part."[47] The call was published on 9 November; signers included the writers Johannes R. Becher, Stephan Hermlin, and Anna Seghers, the "hero worker" Adolf Hennecke, and Paul Wandel.

The churches soon began to protest publicly, and the Jugendweihe campaign became a problem for the CDU in the GDR. General Secretary Götting told a meeting of the CDU steering committee on 14 December that he had not been informed "about any of this business" and recommended that CDU members not join the Jugendweihe committees.[48]

Nor was the Jugendweihe campaign uncontroversial in the SED. In a speech to regional SED secretaries on 15 February 1955, Wandel addressed this point directly.[49] Across the various regions, participation in the Jugendweihe ranged from 2 to 80 percent. The goal of the Jugendweihe, said Wandel, was to "bring in" as many youths as possible, "to make it more difficult for the reactionary church leadership to force their torturous 'either/or' policy on thousands of citizens," referring to the Protestant Church's original stance that confirmation and Jugendweihe were mutually exclusive. It was "self-evident" that SED members' children would take part. Wandel also articulated a key motivation for the SED Jugendweihe campaign:

> It is clear . . . that alongside our goals for the entire GDR, the Jugendweihe also aims to clarify things within our own ranks. A discussion about whether to have children participate in the Jugendweihe is a first step in finally putting some impossible ideological compromises in matters of religion up for debate within the party. We have not yet raised the question of religious instruction in the schools, marriage, church membership, although all of these questions must be posed sooner or later by all comrades.

Wandel emphasized that he was against threatening parents whose children did not participate in the Jugendweihe, or teachers and officials who did not join the committees. It would be wrong, he said, "to establish quotas for participation."

By mid May 1955 Wandel's office in the ZK found that out of 283,951 graduates, only 18.9 percent had taken part in the Jugendweihe in its first year. Participation was lowest in regions with a Catholic majority.[50] A report to the ZK by the Department of Church Affairs on 24 June 1955 concluded that in the future preparations would have to be better: "scientific-atheist propaganda must be strengthened among our comrades, as well as the general population."[51]

CDU General Secretary Götting advanced the issue beginning in January 1956 by suggesting modifications to the Jugendweihe to Wandel and Barth, and then directly to Ulbricht on 25 October.[52] Above all, he emphasized the extraordinary difficulties for the CDU in the matter. He remarked, for example, that the ceremonial book presented to participants, *Weltall, Erde, Mensch* [Universe, Earth, Man], contained statements that made it "impossible for youths who had been raised as Christians to participate with honesty," and that they could not undertake "two consecrations."

In 1956, according to the Central Commission for the Jugendweihe, the participation rate was 23.7 percent.[53] After two years of the Jugendweihe, the SED faced a dilemma as the "leading party": it wanted to raise the participation rate, but doing so would require a break with previous practice, which the general populace would perceive as party weakness in the face of criticism from the churches and the CDU. On the other hand, the SED could pressure people into participating. This approach was ruled out, however, in light of all the other difficulties the party faced in 1956. For the time being, "ideological clarity" appeared beyond reach within the SED. To prevent people from resigning from the party, the SED had to expressly state that party membership was not contingent upon renouncing church membership.[54] Although the Politburo did not adopt the changes to the Jugendweihe that the CDU proposed in October, it did decide on 27 November to "soften . . . atheist activity in connection with the Jugendweihe."

The Catholic Church's Reaction: A Policy of Flexibility

No public actions or statements by the Catholic Church or its representatives are known that directly relate to the June 1953 uprising. The church's tactics consisted of conveying an image of passivity and cautious waiting. However, noting contacts between Protestant representatives and the SKK starting on 19 June 1953, Catholic leaders, too, hoped that they could bring about a reorientation in the GDR by appealing to the Soviet Union as the real authority. Zinke prepared confidential notes dated 23 June as preparation for "conversations with the occupying power."[55] He referred to the sections of the GDR constitution on freedom of belief, conscience, and science, which the establishment of "the Marxist-Leninist worldview as the official basis" of the GDR violated. Zinke wrote:

> The church feels bound by religious responsibility to approach the occupying power in a decisive moment for the world and for world peace. . . . The measures now threatened against or imposed upon the participants in the events of June 16–17 are painful. This will be a source of further dissatisfaction and mistrust of the integrity of the . . . New Direction.

In this instance, Catholic leaders expressed their interests as representative of the whole population of the GDR for the first time and appealed to the regulatory force of the Soviet Union against the SED. But events of the next few days led them to conclude that the GDR regime could not be bypassed. On 3 July, Zinke spoke with State Secretary Geyer from the Minister-President's office. Afterwards, Zinke requested that Minister-President Grotewohl prepare to discuss "the fundamental questions causing worry for the bishops."[56] What Zinke had originally conceived as a memorandum to the SKK evolved into "Thoughts on the Church-Political Situation in July 1953 in Reference to the Normalization of Church-State Relations."[57] This document was the basis for Bishop Weskamm's letter to Grotewohl on 11 July,[58] which detailed numerous church grievances. At the end of this letter, Weskamm referred to "the great worry over the spiritual foundations of our people and about the preservation of public order and welfare" and listed seven points for a joint discussion. Finally, Weskamm demanded "freedom from compulsion regarding one's worldview in schools, universities, for teachers and all public service workers" and "legal security, as should be expected in a state of laws." The state never responded to Weskamm's memorandum. No talks with the SED came about, either, as by July 1953 the party had already begun to feel secure enough to continue to follow its own direction without considering the churches' claims.

The June 1953 uprising and its suppression led to an increase in the number of Catholics fleeing to the West. The church counted 868,364 Catholics leaving the GDR between 1949 and 1954, which reduced its entire membership by 30 percent.[59] In the period that followed, church statements regarding SED measures took the form of petitions to the Minister-President. The Berlin Conference of Ordinaries first petitioned against a planned revision of family law on 28 August 1954, and massive protests against the Jugendweihe followed, beginning in December 1954.[60]

The state's strategy of avoiding conflict in church matters by negotiating individual questions went hand in hand with its policy of using "pinprick" measures to repress opposition. SED efforts to "scientifically enlighten" the youth led repeatedly to concrete measures, the most visible being the Jugendweihe. In May 1955, on the occasion of a youth pilgrimage in Erfurt, "police turned away thirteen buses with approximately 450 passengers with the warning that this event violated church-state agreements."[61] The church sent a letter of protest to the Ministry of the Interior but received no response. In January 1956 the Politburo tightened the guidelines for religious instruction in schools, at first just in Berlin. In middle and high schools, religion classes were cut entirely; in other schools, they were limited to two hours after school. The state reserved the right to reject certain clergymen as instructors because of their political profile. In addition, in February 1956 the state ceased to collect church taxes, obstructed West German clergy who sought to move to the GDR, once again, and made it more difficult for churches to obtain building permits and virtually impossible for them to acquire land. On top of all of these measures, the MfS/SfS had been working intensively since 1955 to recruit church employees as secret informers. The Berlin Conference of Ordinaries took this up repeatedly at its meetings, noting on 13–14 April 1955, for example, that

> We need to continually emphasize at priests' conferences that individual priests or church employees should never give out information about church affairs, that only the Bishops' Office should control [such communications]. We should consider whether in individual cases letters of protest to the State Secretariat of the Ministry of the Interior are in order.[62]

Against this background, the main Catholic offices in Berlin were not alone in trying to do something—for example, undertaking mediation through Nuschke and the CDU. The auxiliary bishop of Erfurt, Joseph Freusberg, one of the founders of the CDU in 1945 who resigned from the party in 1953, gave sermons at the CDU party congresses in Weimar in 1954 and 1956.[63] The bishops' commissioner for Eichsfeld, Provost Josef Streb, took notable steps to willingly cooperate with the CDU. He helped found the CDU in Heiligenstadt in 1945 and remained a member. His proximity to the CDU officials and his occasional public statements and articles went too far even for Freusberg, his auxiliary bishop in Erfurt. In an address to a CDU assembly in Heiligenstadt on 26 April 1956,

Streb spoke of "the duty to join hands with one another to say 'yesterday's routines have been overcome, replaced by the responsibilities of the present.'"[64]

Another who acted independently was Franz Westermann, a Catholic priest from Hundeshagen in Eichsfeld, who was elected to the CDU steering committee at the September 1956 party congress in Weimar. Before this, he had made a notable speech—more or less claiming to speak for the church—on church-state relations, offering the church's cooperation under certain conditions: "The church would see a concordat as an effective way to guarantee genuine coexistence—one that would grant it legal security and the necessary independence for its mission. A concordat would avoid continued conflict over basic questions."[65] Westermann's speech caused great uncertainty among state administrators and the party. The ZK Working Group for Church Affairs issued two statements on this issue—one to the Protestant CDU official Herbert Trebs, and the other to Emil Fuchs, a former religious socialist and Protestant professor of theology in Leipzig. These statements assumed that the Catholic leadership had naturally endorsed Westermann's "foray" and recommended a "wait and see" response. On the one hand, a concordat would secure the certified rights of the churches; on the other hand, such an agreement would increase the legitimacy of the GDR. Trebs even went so far as to make the following comparison: "Because the Vatican has weight in international law, a concordat would raise the international recognition of the GDR. With very different intentions, Hitler used a concordat to gain international respectability in his day."[66] In the end, the state did not react further to Westermann's ideas because the Catholic Church—which had not authorized his initiative at all—did nothing.

Because Bishop Wienken of Meißen remained in unstable health, Otto Spülbeck, the provost of Leipzig, was made auxiliary bishop in July 1955 with the right to succeed Wienken.[67] Spülbeck was not only a theologian but had also studied math and physics and had already published work on the relation of religion to the natural sciences. The district government in Dresden therefore thought it had discovered the "real reason" for his nomination:

> From conversations with Catholic Christians and theologians, we have ascertained that Dr. Spülbeck is the leading scientist in Germany and was only named auxiliary bishop because it was already known during the summer that the professorship for nuclear science and the circle of German nuclear scientists who were in the Soviet Union for the past ten years would continue their work in Dresden.[68]

In 1955 the MfS integrated its surveillance of Spülbeck into its operation against the ordinary's office in Bautzen. In particular, it monitored his contacts with nuclear scientists at a regional event celebrating Wilhelm Pieck's birthday. In addition, the MfS kept watch for suspicious Catholic nuclear physicists.[69]

As Berlin's bishop, Weskamm spent most of 1956 in the hospital before passing away on 21 August and Wienken had retreated to a West Berlin hospital,

Spülbeck became the de facto bishop of Meißen, as well as the most important representative of the Berlin Conference of Ordinaries. Consequently, Spülbeck, together with Prelate Zinke, held talks on 24 February 1956 in Berlin with State Secretary Josef Hegen from the Ministry of the Interior. According to the ministry's file notes, they discussed numerous individual matters, and Spülbeck was said to have even declared: "We are not Marxists but live in a Marxist state and are loyal to it. The constitution provides the basis for this, and loyalty is the foundation for cooperation between church and state."[70] It would be difficult to persuade people in the West of this, he felt, because they would regard him as "a Communist" for it.[71] In November 1955 Spülbeck had traveled to Rome with GDR travel documents and had had an audience with Pope Pius XII. In the February 1956 talks with Hegen, Spülbeck stressed that the pope had told him "to maintain close contact and continue to negotiate with the regime."[72]

Spülbeck found himself in turbulent waters after giving a sermon during the Seventy-Seventh German Catholic Convention in Cologne on 1 September 1956.[73] The sermon caused quite a stir because he reported on a conversation with GDR officials in it:

> The conversation begins stereotypically: Herr Minister, you are a Marxist; I am a Catholic Christian. Our worldviews have nothing in common. There are no bridges between us. We are two separate peoples. But we live together in one house whose foundation we did not build and whose supporting structure we believe is false. And if we now live here together, then our dialogue can only be on the level of—forgive the banality, but I really said it—who is going to clean up? This is not meant to diminish the serious church-state conversations, but it is only to say that basic conversations between the two partners are not possible. We are happy to contribute to this household so that we can live in dignity and as Christians, but we cannot add a whole new floor to the building when we think the foundation is flawed. Marxism's image of man, as well as its concept of society and economics, do not match our own. This house remains an alien, strange house for us. Thus, we live in a diaspora, not only in our church but in our state as well.

Later on in the sermon, Spülbeck qualified his statements somewhat:

> I have often stressed that we are not an underground movement. We are not enemies of the state. We respect the state as the guarantor of public order and, as long as it carries out this function, we are bound to it by conscience.

Finally, he refrained from making a judgment about the Federal Republic of Germany:

In no way should my presentation give the impression that everything is in order over there. I live in the GDR and speak about what I know. I cannot judge how things are in the West.[74]

The first reaction to Spülbeck's sermon in *Neue Zeit*, the CDU's East Berlin publication, was positive.[75] Two days later, the same paper attacked him, remarking that "one should refrain from reckless generalizations . . . one cannot approve of such characterizations, especially coming out of West Germany."[76] In a report on the Catholic convention, Hans Joachim Seidowsky and Helmut Dressler,[77] who were in Cologne as "observers" for the SED Central Committee, wrote: "Spülbeck's speech is a clear rejection of his declaration of loyalty, a refusal to take part in solving state and economic challenges on the plane where they belong, and an affirmation of the West German political system."[78]

In fact, Spülbeck had never made a "declaration of loyalty" of the sort the GDR wished to have, but he also never applauded the Federal Republic's system. He clearly underestimated the political climate in the West, where his words were appropriated—to the detriment of the Catholic Church in the GDR—to be used as a rejection of the GDR and praise of the FRG. "This house is not our house" became a phrase often quoted in the West to describe the alleged position of Catholics in the GDR. Yet Catholics in the GDR did not want to understand Spülbeck's words in this politicized way. The reception of his Cologne speech added to the caution of leading Catholic clergy in the GDR, who already took care not to make public statements that could be interpreted as pro-Western or pro-Communist; it reinforced their intention to keep the church out of politics in the GDR. According to an MfS report from 20 September 1956, "unofficial circles" claimed that Spülbeck "should have expressed himself differently" in Cologne and "wished he had."[79]

At the same time, Spülbeck's speech and the responses to it can be interpreted as a sign that the Catholic Church had accepted the reality of existing and surviving in the GDR despite its fundamental rejection of the Marxist worldview.[80] Contributing most to this were external factors, such as the growing gap in Eastern and Western mentalities arising from completely different social systems. This gap grew despite church gatherings that drew from both Germanys, such as the Catholic conventions in Fulda (1954) and Cologne (1956), the Bonifatius Jubilee in Erfurt (1954), and the Protestant Church convention in Leipzig (1954). Hopes for German reunification were again and again disappointed by the policies of both Bonn and East Berlin, as well as by diplomatic efforts on the part of the four Allied powers.

Within the Catholic Church in the GDR, regional pilgrimage traditions were established, and a "diaspora theology" began to take shape in institutions such as the Leipzig Oratorium, inspired by Bishop Weskamm and other theologians from the Erfurt seminary.[81] In a report on church life in the GDR of August 1955, after enumerating problems caused by the state measures, Weskamm noted that the church milieu had gradually adapted to the GDR environment and that "common Catholic interests ha[d] given rise to a community and church consciousness in the GDR."[82]

The Jugendweihe

After the Jugendweihe was introduced, Catholic ordinaries used it consciously, if selectively, to distance themselves from the politics of the SED. The pseudo-religious consecration was seen as a provocative, sacrilegious "ersatz ritual" and thus as "irreconcilable" with the Catholic faith. This confrontation between the Catholic Church and the GDR state became a matter of deep principle, carried out more publicly than any other. Though both sides varied their stance some over the years, neither ever abandoned their basic positions. Neither side wanted to be seen as "giving in" in an ongoing conflict that was often a test of power. Beyond the substantive issue at hand, the conflict took on a representative character. For the church, there were several reasons for this:

- The Jugendweihe touched on church teachings and theology in a direct way. The SED's use of the term "Weihe" (consecration) and the materialist character of the oath aimed directly at undermining the Christian understanding of creation.
- The church wanted any protest on its part to appear genuine and not be dismissed as politics or mere tactics. At the same time, the church could use its stance on the Jugendweihe to implicitly show its rejection of Marxist ideology. The Jugendweihe issue provided an excellent opportunity for the church to demonstrate its own "clarity of worldview" to the SED.
- Officially, the state always declared that the Jugendweihe was voluntary, but in practice it proved otherwise. This gave the church an irrefutable point of protest.
- Church protests against the Jugendweihe did not touch upon the core identity of the SED or the state, so the political risk involved in undertaking such protests was measured. The later oath required of draftees doing military service, by contrast, was more closely tied to the core identity of the state and Communist Party, so the church purposefully and rather unconvincingly determined that it was not "irreconcilable" with the Catholic faith, even though it was similar in content to the Jugendweihe.
- Because the Jugendweihe was introduced in 1954, relatively early in GDR history, it could become a symbolic focus for distancing oneself from the SED, before the party introduced further compulsory rituals associated with civic life.

After the Jugendweihe was publicly proclaimed in November 1954, the BOK took up the issue in its meetings on 9–10 December. The minutes record that the Jugendweihe was "fundamentally rejected in the sharpest terms."[83] Participants clearly agreed that each ordinary should issue a pastoral letter on the Jugendweihe in his district before Christmas 1954.[84]

Before the first Jugendweihe was celebrated in spring 1955, a number of declarations were read from the pulpit and instructions were sent to all priests on how to respond. These declarations threatened Catholics who "led their children to the Jugendweihe," or who took part in its preparation, with the possibility of excommunication on the grounds that the secular ritual was "a serious sin." One ordinary who resided in West Berlin made especially rigid demands: "[Those who participate] cannot receive the Holy Sacrament until they truly repent their sin and have made amendments for their bad moral example. They must do this in a written declaration before their pastor and two witnesses."[85] Ordinaries living in the GDR tended to take a more moderate view.

The ordinaries received reports from their parishes about the number of Catholic children who participated in the Jugendweihe, and they came to the conclusion that the "Jugendweihe Year 1955" did not have a relevant impact on the church. The bishops' commissioner in Meiningen, Joseph Schönauer, praised parents and children for "resisting the temptation of the Jugendweihe" on 3 April 1955.[86] The church issued no new declarations before Jugendweihe lessons began in the fall of 1955 in preparation for the next ceremony in the spring. Instead, on 23 October, the ordinaries in the GDR issued a collective pastoral letter that repeated the previous year's stance, though in a condensed form.[87] Bishop Weskamm, in particular, raised the issue of passing on the Catholic faith to the youth as "a matter of life and death" and made the fight against the Jugendweihe a touchstone of the church's work.[88] In a "senior pastoral directive" of 18 October 1955, Weskamm said "the Jugendweihe is more than an isolated episode. It is like a judgment of our ministry, testing its authenticity."[89]

Above all, the church worried about the campaign for the Jugendweihe in the schools. In order to steel young Catholics against this influence, Sunday schools concentrated on refuting the arguments of state educational materials. Government officials made public statements offering assurance that the Jugendweihe posed no problem for religious youth, but GDR newspapers challenged these by collecting quotations that detailed the atheist beliefs of the SED.[90] Children were trained to recite statements rejecting it:

I am Catholic, so the Jugendweihe is out of the question for me. I am consecrated to God through baptism, Holy Communion, and confirmation. Our bishop does not want us to participate in the Jugendweihe, and I am obedient to the bishop.[91]

The number of Jugendweihe participants across the GDR in 1957 was almost as low as in the pervious two years (18.9 percent in 1955, 23.7 percent in 1956, and 26.7 percent in 1957).[92] However, when the SED shifted to a more aggressive strategy on the Jugendweihe question, things became more difficult for the churches.

Notes

1. Handwritten note by Otto Grotewohl, SAPMO-BArch, NY 90/699.
2. Fechner was arrested on 30 June 1953 because of an interview in *Neues Deutschland*. See Falco Werkentin, *Politische Strafjustiz in der Ära Ulbricht* (Berlin, 1995), 143-50.
3. Ibid., 121. The fact that 30,000 were released *after* the 17 June uprising demonstrates the tremendous number of indiscriminate arrests made during the "Building Up Socialism" campaign from July 1952 to June 1953.
4. Ilko-Sascha Kowalczuk, Armin Mitter, and Stefan Wolle, eds., *Der Tag X. 17. Juni 1953: Die "Innere Staatsgründung" der DDR als Ergebnis der Krise 1952/54* (Berlin, 1995), 219-42.
5. Ibid., 241.
6. Jan van Flocken and Michael F. Schulz, *Ernst Wollweber: Saboteur—Minister—Unperson* (Berlin, 1994); Armin Mitter and Stefan Wolle, *Untergang auf Raten: Unbekannte Kapitel der DDR Geschichte* (Munich, 1993), 144–60.
7. Jens Gieseke, *Die Hauptamtlichen 1962: Zur Personalstruktur des Ministeriums für Staatssicherheit* (Berlin, 1994), 6.
8. Mitter and Wolle, *Untergang auf Raten,* 153.
9. Ibid., 154.
10. Karl-Wilhelm Fricke, *Politik und Justiz in der DDR: Zur Geschichte der politischen Verfolgung 1945–1968* (Cologne, 1990).
11. See Werkentin, *Politische Strafjustiz in der Ära Ulbricht,* 158–62.
12. Roger Engelmann and Silke Schumann, "Der Ausbau des Überwachungsstaates: Der Konflikt Ulbricht-Wollweber und die Neuausrichtung des Staatssicherheitdienstes der DDR 1957," *Vierteljahreshefte für Zeitgeschichte* 43 (1995): 341–86, 347.
13. Karl Schirdewan, *Aufstand gegen Ulbricht* (Berlin, 1994), 76–87.
14. *Neues Deutschland,* 4 March 1956.
15. Falco Werkentin, "Zwischen Tauwetter und Nachtfrost (1955–1957): DDR-Justizfunktionäre auf Glatteis," *Deutschland Archiv* 26 (1993): 341–49, here 349.
16. Mitter and Wolle, *Untergang auf Raten,* 251.
17. Ibid., 256.
18. SAPMO-BArch, DY 30/J IV 2/2/511.
19. See Raabe, *SED-Staat und katholische Kirche,* 55–71; Martin Goerner, "Zu den Strukturen und Methoden der SED-Kirchenpolitik in den fünfziger Jahren," in Klaus Schroeder, ed., *Geschichte und Transformation des SED-Staates: Beiträge und Analysen* (Berlin, 1994), 112–29.
20. SAPMO-BArch, DY 30, J IV 2/2/350.
21. SAPMO-BArch, DY 30, J IV 2/2/353.
22. On Barth, who was a member of the Thuringia Association of Free Thinkers before 1933 and became active in the ZK apparatus in 1946, see Raabe, *SED-Staat und katholische Kirche,* 55.
23. SAPMO-BArch, DY 30, J IV 2/2/398.
24. Besier and Wolf, *"Pfarrer, Christen und Katholiken,"* 180–83.
25. SAPMO-BArch, DY 30, J IV 2/2/483.
26. SAPMO-BArch, DY 30, J IV 2/14/2.
27. SAPMO-BArch, DY 30, IV 2/14/1.
28. SAPMO-BArch, DY 30, J IV 2/2/353.
29. SAPMO-BArch, DY 30, J IV 2/2/398.
30. SAPMO-BArch, DY 30, J IV 2/14/43.
31. The state's collection of taxes for the churches ended with a ruling by Minister of Justice Hilde Benjamin on 10 February 1956, which was based upon a 7 February Politburo decision. As early as 1953, the Ministry of Finances had ruled that the churches had to process the tax contribution for churches themselves, although it had previously been done by the government.

See Theodor Schmitz, *Kirchenfinanzen in der SBZ/DDR 1945–1989,* unpublished manuscript, 1996 (author's private archive). The churches now had to finance their own operations using a combination of donations they collected and state allocations, which the SED could easily cut off. Thus financial support from West Germany became much more significant, which served the interests of the GDR regime. See Armin Boyens, "'Den Gegner irgendwo festhalten': 'Transfergeschäfte' der Evangelischen Kirche in Deutschland mit der DDR-Regierung 1957–1990," *Kirchliche Zeitgeschichte* 6 (1993): 379–90.

32. See the 15 December 1953 report by a ZK department in Leo Haupts, "'Die CDU ist die Partei, in der am stärksten der Feind arbeitet,'" in Kowalczuk et al., *Der Tag X. 17. Juni 1953,* 278–310.

33. SAPMO-BArch, DY 30, IV 2/14/68. Hans Wilke wrote this report. He worked in the Office of the State Secretary for Church Affairs from 1958 to 1989, where he headed the section for the Protestant Church, and for the MfS from 1954 to 1970 as a secret informer with the code name "Horst." BStU, ZA, AIM 2968/70, Part 1.

34. BStU, Ast Dresden, AOP 71/59, p. 11.

35. BStU, ZA, AP 20181/92, p. 82.

36. Besier and Wolf, eds., *"Pfarrer, Christen und Katholiken,"* 181ff.

37. BStU, ZA, AOP 614/59, p. 9.

38. BStU, Ast Magdeburg, AOP 272/59 ("Rosenkranz") and AOP 193/59 ("Sacrament").

39. Heinrich Schimetzek from Berlin worked as a secret informer (code name: "Schramm") for thirty-six years after being recruited in September 1953. In his later years, he held a leading position in the Kolping Association, from which he was expelled in 1993. See BStU, ZA, 3716/61, Pt. 2, 9 vols. (1953–1980).

40. SAPMO-BArch, DY 30, IV 2/14/235. Often, investigations and surveillance by regional MfS offices produced no results. See, for example, the file on the "Kolping family" Panschwitz in the Kamenz district, BStU, Ast Dresden, AOP 276/56.

41. SAPMO-BArch, DY 30, IV 2/14/43.

42. BStU, ZA, AIM 208/56, 2 vols. (Secret Informer "Strahlbach"/Hans van Nahl). This file illustrates the dilettantism of the SfS/MfS in its early years, as well as Cold War hysteria on both sides of the border. See Bernd Schäfer, " 'er wollte in Fulda Zeuge sein': Eine deutsch-deutsche Geschichte aus den fünfziger Jahren," in Joachim Köhler and Damian van Melis, eds., *Siegerin in Trümmern: Die Rolle der katholischen Kirche in der deutschen Nachkriegsgesellschaft* (Stuttgart, Berlin, Cologne, 1998), 242–59.

43. Bo Hallberg, *Die Jugendweihe: Zur deutschen Jugendweihetradition,* 2nd ed. (Göttingen, 1979), 135–39.

44. An article appeared in *Neues Deutschland* on 31 March 1950, entitled "Why don't we have the Jugendweihe?"

45. See Raabe, *SED-Staat und katholische Kirche,* 184–209; Hermann Wentker, "Die Einführung der Jugendweihe in der DDR. Hintergründe, Motive und Probleme," in Hartmut Mehringer, ed., *Von der SBZ zur DDR: Studien zum Herrschaftssystem in der Sowjetischen Besatzungszone und in der Deutschen Demokratischen Republik* (Munich, 1995), 139–65; Klemens Richter, "Jugendweihe und katholische Kirche," *Deutschland Archiv* 20 (1987): 168–80; Detlef Urban and Hans Willi Weinzen, *Jugend ohne Bekenntnis? 30 Jahre Konfirmation und Jugendweihe im anderen Deutschland 1954–1984* (West Berlin, 1984).

46. SAPMO-BArch, DY 30, J IV 2/2/353.

47. Höllen, *Loyale Distanz?* 1:376.

48. ACDP VII-013-871. See also Wentker, "Ost-CDU und Protestantismus 1949–1958," 370–78.

49. SAPMO-BArch, DY 30, IV 2/14/43.

50. SAPMO-BArch, DY 30, IV 2/14/26.

51. Ibid.

52. ACDP VII-013-1803.

53. SAPMO-BArch, DY 30, IV 2/14/2.
54. *Neues Deutschland,* 31 August 1956.
55. DAB, Asig 30/39. On 30 June 1953 Zinke added a handwritten note: "material for 'memorandum.'"
56. Note by Zinke, DAB, Asig 30/40.
57. Ibid.
58. Lange et al., *Katholische Kirche—Sozialistischer Staat DDR,* 63–67.
59. Pilvousek, "Innenansichten," 1136.
60. Lange et al., *Katholische Kirche—Sozialistischer Staat DDR,* 69–72. The ordinaries objected to women's equality through work, the education of young children in state-run daycare centers, and the ideological influence of the state on school curricula. The text of the petition was printed in both Catholic newspapers in the GDR.
61. Report by the main office of the Volkspolizei, 26 May 1955, BAP, MdI, HVDVP, Best. 11, 869.
62. DAB, Asig 30/42, p. 628.
63. Josef Pilvousek, ed., *Kirchliches Leben im totalitären Staat. Seelsorge in der SBZ/DDR 1945–1976: Quellentexte aus den Ordinariaten* (Hildesheim, 1994), 222–26; Lange et al., *Katholische Kirche—Sozialistischer Staat DDR,* 103–7.
64. ACDP VII-013-1763.
65. "Katholische Forderungen an die Machthaber der SED," *Herder-Korrespondenz* 11 (1956): 50. See also SAPMO-BArch, DY 30, IV 2/14/68.
66. SAPMO-BArch, DY 30 2/14/68. Herbert Trebs had worked for the MfS as a secret informer (code name: "Anton") since 1950. He later became a professor of Protestant theology at Humboldt University. See BStU, ZA, AIM 10990/68, Pt. 1: Vol. 1, Part II.
67. See the report on Spülbeck's inauguration by Walter Breitmann of the Dresden district government on 23 July 1955 (SAPMO-BArch, DY 30, IV 2/14/64): "Provost Spülbeck is a strong man within the Catholic Church; one has great hopes for him."
68. HStA Dresden, Bt/RdB, 6284.
69. Compare a report by HA V/4 from 20 March 1956 (BStU, ZA, AP 20181/92, p. 116); Spülbeck, however, did not have any such contacts or ambitions.
70. Noted by Ernst Kusch, head of the Department of Religious Questions in the Ministry of the Interior, BStU, ZA, 20181/92, pp. 119–26.
71. Ibid., 123.
72. Ibid., 125.
73. The SED had wanted to limit the number of GDR participants at this event to 5,000, but a coordination error between state entities—the sort of error that was becoming increasingly rare—enabled 25,000 East German Catholics to attend. See Raabe, *SED-Staat und katholische Kirche,* 219.
74. Lange et al., *Katholische Kirche—Sozialistischer Staat DDR,* 101.
75. "Heilige Unruhe gegen unnatürliche Spaltung," *Neue Zeit,* 2 September 1956.
76. *Neue Zeit,* 4 September 1956.
77. At the time, Seidowsky worked in religious affairs in the Ministry of the Interior. From 1957 to 1974, he worked with the MfS as a secret informer (code name: "Jochen," later "Gerhard"), BStU, ZA, AIM 3654/71, Pt. 1: 4 vols., Pt. 2 [through 1971]: 13 vols. Dressler worked from 1950 to 1952 as secret informer "Zange" and from 1959 to 1989 as secret informer "Harry." See BStU, ZA, AIM 3671/71 and attachment 186/85. From 1957 to 1960, he worked in the Office of the State Secretary for Church Affairs, and after 1962, he taught basic Marxism-Leninism courses in the theology department of Humboldt University.
78. SAPMO-BArch, DY 30, IV 2/14/225.
79. BStU, ZA, AP 20181/92, p.90.
80. See Pilvousek, "Innenansichten," 1141. Pilvousek investigates whether the rhetoric of the speech constitutes "the beginning of the 'Catholic Church in the GDR.'"

81. See the speech by Josef Gülden, editor of the church newspaper *Tag des Herrn* and head of the Leipzig Oratorium, at the Seventy-Sixth Catholic Convention in Fulda, "Über Wesen und Aufgabe der Diaspora," in Zentralkomitee der deutschen Katholiken, ed., *Ihr sollt mir Zeugen sein. Der 76. Deutsche Katholikentag in Fulda* (Paderborn, 1954), 311–19.

82. DAB, Asig 32/109-1.

83. DAB, Asig 30/42.

84. This sort of coordinated action, with seven public declarations by the Catholic Church on the same theme, occurred only this once in the SBZ/GDR between 1945 and 1990.

85. Lange et al., *Katholische Kirche—Sozialistischer Staat DDR,* 82.

86. Pilvousek, *Kirchliches Leben,* 226.

87. Lange et al., *Katholische Kirche—Sozialistischer Staat DDR,* 88.

88. See Gülden, "Über Wesen und Aufgabe der Diaspora," 318.

89. DAB, Asig 32/109-1.

90. See the detailed statement by the Diocese of Meißen on 26 November 1956 in Pilvousek, *Kirchliches Leben,* 122–25.

91. Ibid., 125, 471.

92. SAPMO-BArch, DY 30, IV 2/14/28.

Chapter 3

1957–1961

"Building Up Socialism"

Stalinism and "Building Up Socialism"

On the heels of the events of 1956 in Hungary and Poland at the Thirtieth Congress of the Central Committee of the SED, Walter Ulbricht announced an ideological and political offensive to "build up socialism" in the GDR. Without mentioning Stalin, the party returned to his methods and propaganda campaigns, just as the ruling party in the Soviet Union was doing. The SED simplistically attributed its difficulties to hostile actions of "enemies." In his speech at the congress on 30 January 1957, Ulbricht clearly delineated the points that needed to be achieved:

> The ideological, political, and organizational strengthening of the party! The fight within the party against any bourgeois ideological influence, so that the party will really be able to lead the youth, the working class, and the intelligentsia! That students and young teachers are educated to be comrades-in-arms in our party schools as well as in other schools and universities, which is now only partly the case.[1]

Moreover, feeling threatened by its own population, the SED distributed pistols to 8,182 functionaries beginning in December 1956. MfS troops were to protect the offices and homes of state and party leaders.[2]

Not all political cadres survived the first critical year after the turmoil of 1956. In 1957, Ulbricht and his supporters settled accounts at all levels with those who had attempted to de-Stalinize the SED in 1956. In March 1957, the Harich Group show trial saw the primary defendant quickly become a witness for the prosecution; in addition, Walter Janka, the director of the Berlin publishing house Aufbau, was subjected to an especially draconian trial in July.[3] In October, Paul Wandel lost his position in the party apparatus because he lacked "ideological strength." Having been a member of the Politburo, ZK secretary for culture and education, and also having had responsibility for church affairs, he was sent to China as the GDR ambassador. That same month, Minister for State Security Ernst Wollweber lost a power struggle within the MfS and against the Politburo and was forced to retire on the pretext of illness. His deputy Erich Mielke, who had eagerly ingratiated himself with Ulbricht, replaced him.[4] Finally, at the Politburo meeting of 11 January 1958, Ulbricht's last opponent—Karl Schirdewan, the ZK secretary—was removed from office because it was falsely alleged that he and Wollweber had formed a "revisionist faction."[5] Schirdewan later recalled the political atmosphere at that time: "Members of the Central Committee pledged their allegiance to Ulbricht's revenge campaign . . . It was like an Inquisition in the Middle Ages. Political barbarism such as the party had never seen before now grew rampant."[6] After the Thirty-Fifth Plenary of the Central Committee in February 1958, a Politburo "conference" was organized for 2–3 April in Potsdam-Babelsberg at which the entire legal system of the GDR was formally subordinated to the normative principles of the party. The "conclusions" reached at this conference laid the groundwork for the SED's future use of the law as a partisan tool.

At the SED's Fifth Party Congress on 10 July 1958, Ulbricht announced that the "the foundations of socialism" had essentially been created. Although food rationing had just been phased out in May, the SED did not want to fall behind the Communist Party of the Soviet Union (CPSU). Led by the experienced propagandist Nikita Khrushchev, the CPSU had declared that the Soviet Union would soon overtake the United States in industrial and agricultural production. Ulbricht offered the German version of this rhetoric at the Fifth Party Congress: the "main economic task" of the GDR was to surpass West Germany in per capita consumption.

The success of the Soviet space program (Sputnik) drove such rhetoric from Moscow to East Berlin. The slogan directed against the West soon became "Surpass the West without imitating it." Propaganda such as Ulbricht's "Ten Commandments of Socialist Morality" (proclaimed at the Fifth Party Congress) or the call for writers to adopt socialist realism (at the Bitterfeld conference in April 1959) flanked the GDR's economic goals. "Socialist work brigades" were formed in factories and offices in 1959; the catchword of the time was "we shall work, study, and live in the socialist way." Integrated, practical training in schools became mandatory when the "polytechnical high school" was introduced. On 1 October 1959 the Volkskammer, the GDR parliament, suspended the five-year economic plan (1956–1960), replacing it with a seven-year plan that set ambitious goals for 1965. At this very legislative session, Ulbricht could already declare that the future had come. As the leading GDR newspaper described it: "When Walter Ulbricht concluded his speech with the exclamation 'The kingdom of humanity has arrived!' the deputies from all parties rose to their feet in a wave of enthusiasm."[7]

Collectivization of agriculture had begun in 1952 but slowed after June 1953. It had been based more or less on a farmer's free choice to join a collective. In mid 1959, more than half the farmland in the GDR was still privately held. But the SED believed that it could surpass West Germany and reach its economic goals only by means of a comprehensive, Soviet-style collectivization of agriculture. In October 1959, the Council of Ministers decided to use forced expropriations with the aid of the party, the police, and the MfS to accomplish this. In April 1960, the party declared the "triumph of socialist relations of production," glorifying it as "the springtime of socialism in the countryside." However, farmers soon began to quit the collectives. Large numbers of refugees from rural areas began to go to West Germany, and GDR food production dropped increasingly. The GDR did not overtake West Germany, but rather, GDR propaganda overtook GDR reality.

The Road to the Berlin Wall

The number of refugees from the GDR reached its high point in 1956 when 316,028 people fled. After Soviet tanks crushed the Hungarian uprising, 228,658 more East Germans left for the West in the first three months of 1957. Almost 90 percent of them left via the open border in Berlin.[8] In the following years, the numbers dropped considerably because, among other reasons, the supply levels in the GDR improved in 1958–1959. Only 81,073 people left the GDR in 1959.[9]

Not least because of the economic improvement and the euphoric goal of "surpassing" West Germany by 1961, the GDR leadership supported the Soviet aims of demilitarizing the "disruptive presence" of West Berlin "on the territory of the GDR" and loosening its ties with the Federal Republic of Germany. The USSR issued an ultimatum to the three Western powers on 27 November 1958 to withdraw from West Berlin within six months; otherwise the GDR would exercise its sovereignty over all routes of access to the city.[10] The Western powers rejected the Soviet demands in a 31 December letter and offered to participate in talks if the ultimatum was withdrawn. On 10 January 1959 Khrushchev responded by publishing a draft of a "peace treaty" between the two German states, according to which West Berlin should have the status of "a demilitarized free city." If such a treaty did not come to be, he threatened that the USSR would conclude a separate treaty with the GDR. At the same time, the nuclear arms race heated up.

As the collectivization of agriculture in the GDR was completed in April 1960, the plans to overtake the West German economy by 1961 stalled. Even SED leaders had to acknowledge this in light of dwindling supplies and rising numbers of refugees. In 1960, 159,768 people fled the GDR.[11] For "security purposes," Politburo members began to move their place of residence from Berlin to Wandlitz, a rural retreat north of the city. When Wilhelm Pieck died on

7 September 1960, Ulbricht became the chairman of the newly formed State Council. In a programmatic speech in October, Ulbricht struck a more moderate tone and spoke of a "socialist human community" that could "win the hearts . . . of those of goodwill." The State Council pardoned 12,000 prisoners and published a statement on 30 January 1961 on "the further development of our legal system."[12] The number of trials for political crimes such as "propaganda that endangers the state," "agitation," or "slandering the state" decreased.

Measures the regime introduced in September 1960 to limit the number of people traveling between East and West Berlin led the West German government to abrogate the inter-zone trade agreement in August 1960. However, the government in Bonn reinstated it on 1 January 1961. The short interruption in trade had sharpened economic difficulties in the GDR. The Politburo tried in vain to get the Soviet Union to help by reducing the size of deliveries the GDR owed according to various contracts and by increasing food aid from Moscow. Although the GDR wanted to free itself from economic dependence on the West, the Soviet Union pressed it to maintain trade with West Germany because it was in the USSR's national interest. The GDR's total debt to the "capitalist economic zone" was DM 472 million (West) at the end of 1960 and DM 670 million by 31 December 1961. GDR debt equaled 25 percent of its total exports to capitalist countries.[13] Considering the open borders in Berlin, the Politburo viewed this state of affairs as economic extortion and a threat to GDR independence, particularly because neither the USSR nor other socialist countries were in a position to replace the FRG. On 19 January 1961 Ulbricht wrote Khrushchev on behalf of the SED Politburo asking whether a "compromise" could be reached on the West Berlin question in order to ensure the economic and political stability of the GDR: "The great economic growth in West Germany, which is visible to everyone in the GDR, is the main reason approximately 2 million people have left in the past ten years . . . we are not at all able to catch up with West Germany in production levels, investment, or worker productivity."[14] On 17 February 1961 the USSR repeated its ultimatum regarding Berlin. Khrushchev and Kennedy agreed to hold a summit meeting on 2–3 June 1961 in Vienna.

Between January and June 1961, about 17,000 people fled the GDR each month, half of them younger than twenty-five.[15] Typically, the central SED party organs put the blame for the rising numbers of emigrants on lower-ranking officials by assuming that they had misapplied appropriate decisions from above. As a result, increasing numbers of government administrators also fled, especially from the Ministry of Agriculture, which had taken hits from all sides because of the collectivization campaign.[16] During the first half of 1961, regional party leaders and MfS stations reported to the ZK in large numbers that the populace was again discussing a "new June 17 –[style uprising]" a great deal.[17] In May 1961, the State Planning Commission reduced the goals of the seven-year plan. At the 6 June session of Politburo, Ulbricht had to admit "that the plan was not fulfilled regarding many aspects of consumer goods production and agriculture" but that "a complicated situation" had arisen.[18]

The Khrushchev-Kennedy summit meeting in Vienna in June 1961 produced no results on the Berlin question. Meanwhile, the number of refugees from the GDR escalated: 19,168 in June; 30,415 in July; and 47,433 by mid August.[19] The SED, which had failed so spectacularly in its own "main economic task," decided on 13 August 1961, with the agreement of the USSR and the other Warsaw pact countries, to "solve the problem of the open borders and the Berlin question" and preserve the GDR by closing all Berlin border crossings and building a wall. One consequence was a decrease in the threat of war that loomed over the hot-button issue of Berlin, as President Kennedy noted: "Khrushchev would not have built a wall if he really wanted West Berlin . . . A wall is a hell of a lot better than a war."[20] Kennedy's sympathy for East Germans was limited because, in his words, they had had fifteen years during which they could have "left their prison."

The SED celebrated sealing the borders in Berlin as a great success and ridiculed the mayor of West Berlin, Willy Brandt. Party members hardly concealed their attitude in public and expressed it even more dramatically in internal reports, as in this one from Bernhard Quandt, a regional SED leader in Schwerin, to other SED regional secretaries on 26 August 1961:

> By deploying our power on the border with West Berlin, that is, at the Brandenburg Gate, we have demonstrated to the entire world that the plans of the militarists and imperialists in Bonn and in the USA are illusory. The German Democratic Republic took action, confronted the adventurists and brinkmen, and visited a great political defeat upon them . . . Brandt's thick skull never grasped what Kennedy said: that the Americans will aid only if there is a successful uprising in the GDR; otherwise, they will apply the hard lessons learned in Cuba. That means, in effect, that West Berlin has been abandoned.[21]

The Kirchenpolitik of the SED

The aggressive course adopted by the SED in the wake of the Thirtieth Congress of the Central Committee (30 January-1 February 1957) was soon reflected in a sharpened Kirchenpolitik. By 5 February, the Politburo had issued a long document entitled "On the Activities of Religious Communities on the Territory of the German Democratic Republic,"[22] which, at first primarily addressed to the Protestant majority, expanded in detail a kind of "declaration of loyalty to the GDR." It expected the churches to recognize the GDR as a sovereign German state and actively support its policies. Church leaders were "to take note that a new social order is being constructed in the GDR upon a framework of law—socialism." The churches were not to use "differing worldviews and opinions . . . as the basis for struggle against the state."

When leaders of both major Christian churches (including Bishop Otto Dibelius) concluded an agreement with the Bonn government in 1957 establishing their chaplaincy for the West German military, the SED saw a welcome opportunity to force Protestant churches in the GDR to declare their "loyalty" and to uncouple them from the "NATO chaplains." East German government posts no longer accepted Bishop Dibelius and Prior Heinrich Grüber, both residents of West Berlin, as negotiating partners, although they were the representatives of the Protestant Church in Germany (Evangelische Kirche in Deutschland, EKD) authorized to interact with the GDR government. At first, no analogous measures were applied to the Catholic Church, even though both the Catholic Bishop of Berlin and the designated Catholic negotiator Prelate Johannes Zinke were based in West Berlin and the Catholic Church had also joined the FRG's military chaplaincy.

The coordination of GDR Kirchenpolitik was the responsibility of the office of State Secretary for Church Affairs Werner Eggerath, which became operational on 1 April 1957.[23] On 12 April, Eggerath informed regional leaders about his centralized office's mission of leading and undertaking "systematic work": "We will put a stop to the uneven, area-by-area approach that has prevailed up until now. Therefore, the chairmen of the regional councils or a designated deputy will be directly responsible. To aid them, politically qualified, goal-oriented assistants should be carefully selected."[24] The central state organs tended to administer Kirchenpolitik from above, assigning responsibility and blame for political errors or failures to regional subordinates. For example, Eggerath's office compiled a detailed report on errors committed in the community of Neuzelle an der Oder (population 3,000) after a shouting match took place between FDJ groups and Catholic youth during a pilgrimage to a Baroque church there in June 1958.[25] GDR officials regularly accused subordinates of "sectarianism," "opportunism," "pursuing independent regional policies," or "placing praxis above ideology," despite the fact that this last charge could be applied to almost all government activity in the GDR. One internal document shows officials' awareness of this: "If our work in the area of church affairs is improvised, if a new church roof is approved as a reward for a sermon on peace or a signature on a petition against nuclear weapons earns a trip abroad, then it will lead to disdain for the state."[26]

Central and regional officials for church affairs at first pursued a systematic "differentiation policy" aimed to force a split between "progressive," "loyal," and "reactionary" representatives of the Protestant churches. Their methods included open corruption ("special accounts" or "politics with the Mark"),[27] the establishment of pro-regime associations (such as the Union of Protestant Pastors in the GDR, founded in April 1958), and "dialogues" designed to further differentiation. In the early stages, they merely watched the Catholic Church and its representatives closely, because these representatives had early on adopted strict internal guidelines for dialogue with government officials in order to thwart the regime's efforts to work with individual church figures to foster their objective. In 1957, they renewed such efforts.

State Secretary Eggerath developed a Kirchenpolitik with its own ideological and practical rules, which vacillated between ideological rigor, a critique of atheistic propaganda, and unintended curiosity. For example, in his first internal memo to regional church affairs workers of 2–3 December 1957, he offered a simple version of the differentiation policy:

> We not only hold political power in our hands, but we also have considerable means at our disposal. We must get our message across so that clergymen pass the word that it pays to be a friend of the Workers' and Peasants' state and that it does not pay to oppose us. It is not at all forbidden now to send holiday greetings to clergymen who have behaved well and sometimes also a basket of good food or a few bottles of wine. Word gets around, and it therefore should be done consistently.[28]

Willi Barth, the head of the SED Central Committee's Working Group for Church Affairs, marked up Eggerath's memo in red pen. In the following years, there were often fundamental conflicts between Eggerath and Barth, who felt his function in the ZK gave his ideas more authority; often Paul Verner, the Politburo member responsible for church matters, or Ulbricht, had to intervene to break a stalemate.[29]

Skepticism led the party to supervise and watch over State Secretary Eggerath and his deputy Max Hartwig constantly. (Hartwig, a CDU member and former close associate of Otto Nuschke, was fired in March 1960 when it was discovered that he had hidden his SS past.) The few other employees in the Office of the State Secretary not secretly cooperating with the ZK (Ingeborg Vieillard) or the MfS (Helmut Dressler, Hans Wilke, Hans Joachim Seidowsky, Gerhard Quast) were also monitored. The main figures involved in checking up on Eggerath were Seidowsky and Hans Weise, who worked closely with both the ZK and the MfS. They managed to provoke him to resign "for health reasons" on 15 November 1960.

The Office of the State Secretary for Church Affairs had been conceived of as an executive state body, visible to the outside world, that would carry out a Kirchenpolitik directed by the ZK and the Politburo. The MfS, by contrast, had a dual function in serving the SED leadership: on the one hand, it provided an invisible component of state executive power, and on the other, it monitored the churches and other state bodies. Under Eggerath's successor, Hans Seigewasser (State Secretary for Church Affairs beginning in November 1960), the MfS had a strong presence in the office while Seigewasser himself was able to avoid contact with the agency.

From 1957 to 1961, the central government's work concerning the Catholic Church consisted primarily of monitoring and controlling by means of intimidation—because it was hardly succeeding in recruiting "loyal" or "progressive" Catholics. A few regional and individual exceptions aside, the Catholic hierarchy clearly rejected the CDU. The Department of Church Affairs in the CDU Secretariat in Berlin, the working group it formed in 1957, and the Working Group for Christian Circles established in April 1957 by the National Council of the National Front all failed to achieve political success among Catholics with their

publications and agitation. They could not enlist representative Catholic personalities because their efforts occurred in a time of intensified SED Kirchenpolitik,
which they had to represent. At the same time, the CDU often negated its mod-
est inroads with Catholic priests with its overzealous propaganda. CDU functionaries—especially those who approached Catholics in Eichsfeld—encountered
problems in their own party and often fell victim to cadre purges or fled to West
Germany.

The centralized Office of the State Secretary for Church Affairs, combined
with the heightened activities of the MfS, rendered church monitoring more
effective. The pilgrimage on the 750th birthday of Saint Elizabeth of Thuringia
brought 50,000 Catholics to Erfurt in September 1957. For the first time, the
Office of the State Secretary, together with the church affairs desk of the Erfurt
district council, was able to control a large, transregional Catholic event in the
GDR, including the preparation, arrival of West German visitors, and the festivities themselves.[30]

While the papal nuncio and all the other bishops refrained from political commentary, limiting themselves to religious statements, the new bishop of Berlin,
Julius Döpfner, was less diplomatic. In his 22 September 1957 sermon, Döpfner
railed against the "powers of godlessness," speaking of hell and Satan. The very
next day, party reports from Erfurt quoted from his "aggressive" sermon. On 26
September Prelate Zinke tried to assure the State Secretary for Church Affairs
that it was all a misunderstanding that would be cleared up when the full text of
the sermon was printed in the East Berlin church newspaper *Hedwigsblatt*. The
paper's editors toned down the sermon's rhetoric, but West German church newspapers printed the original text.[31] Johannes Klein, who in the Office of the State
Secretary for Church Affairs was responsible for the Catholic Church, noticed
the discrepancy and confronted Zinke with the "lie" at their next meeting. On
21 December 1957 Klein noted that Döpfner's aggressive activity had caused
the Erfurt district council to "seriously weigh whether, in the future, he can be
allowed an internal passport for travel within the GDR."[32] A few months later, it
did prohibit him from traveling freely in the GDR on the basis of statements it
had recorded long before.

Beginning in May 1958, the main office of the regular police (Hauptverwaltung Deutsche Volkspolizei) undertook surprise searches of Catholic lending
libraries and the private libraries of individual priests, confiscating "reactionary,
militarist, and decadent" literature.[33] When the Seventy-Eighth German Catholic
Convention met in West Berlin on 13–17 August 1958, the GDR coordinated
measures to torpedo it, except for two events allowed to take place in East Berlin.[34] Nonetheless, 60,000 East German Catholics took part. In conjunction with
the National Front and the CDU, the GDR government employed surveillance
measures both before and after the event on an unprecedented scale, analyzing sermons and speeches and confiscating materials from many Catholics who
returned to the GDR. The GDR regime had come to the conclusion that the
Catholic Convention was tantamount to "psychological warfare by the Adenauer

government" and "political diversionary tactics," as the ZK's Working Group for Church Affairs reported to the SED Politburo on 25 August:

> Their main concern was to mobilize as many Catholics from the GDR as possible—especially youth, former refugees from Eastern Europe, and Catholic citizens who are members of the various lay orders and organizations—in order to influence them in West Berlin, to undermine their trust in the socialist point of view, and to destroy the moral and political unity of our population in the spirit of clerical-militarist NATO thinking. By activating the Catholic lay organizations and related groups, a core force would be created that would obey the clerics outside the domain of the church in anti-socialist activities.[35]

The first regular government "evaluations" of leading church figures indicate the direction that differentiation policy would later take. The government began to control Catholic ties to West Germany more tightly and to monitor relations with the Vatican and with Protestants. GDR officials judged the Catholic Church to be as "dangerous" as, but "more skillful," than the Protestants,[36] and they perceived collaboration between Catholic and Protestant bishops against the GDR as an especially threatening possibility. State Secretary Eggerath suggested in a 20 February 1958 letter to the ZK that such coordinated efforts could actually be observed.[37] Eggerath viewed a joint appearance by the Catholic and Protestant bishops of Magdeburg as "the development of a common platform" and contact between bishops in Dresden and Görlitz as "an alliance in a struggle of principles."[38] When the new pope, John XXIII, called an "ecumenical council," the Working Group on 9 February 1959 demanded further "exact political analysis" to hinder "coordinated clerical action against the socialist world-system."[39] The state apparatus had fixed its image of the enemy. The MfS provided the basis for this image by supplying the government with information that "proved" the churches were involved "in political campaigns planned with the West German state."[40]

The Ministry of State Security and Its Methods

In 1957, the Politburo, led by Walter Ulbricht, gradually disempowered Minister for State Security Ernst Wollweber and tied the MfS more closely to the SED at the central and regional levels. Erich Mielke's installation as the new minister on 8 October 1957 advanced the changes in MfS work.[41] At an MfS meeting on 26 April 1957, Ulbricht directed the ministry to strengthen itself internally by training its workers, establishing a greater presence in key social sectors, intensifying regional work, and improving the flow of information.[42]

The expansion and more precise definition of the ministry's work with informants was completed with the "1/58" directive issued on 1 October 1958,[43] which bore consequences for the Catholic Church as well. One effect was that numerous files related to individuals or specific events were reviewed and then archived or re-registered in 1959–1960. The directive also introduced a new political tactic that would mark MfS interventions through 1989. This "political-ideological diversion" (so-called to distinguish it from "political underground activities") was first used in a 20 February 1958 meeting of the MfS Collegium.[44]

In 1957, the MfS had a total of 14,442 employees for its main office. This number grew by about 8 percent in 1959 and even more in 1960, reaching 19,130 in 1961.[45] As of 1957, there were twenty-five MfS main office employees working on the "church front" in section HA V/4 in Berlin; together with the regional MfS employees at the district (55) and county (15) levels, there were ninety-five MfS officers in the GDR whose main duty was to "work" with the churches. The number of personnel in this capacity did not change substantially in the following years.[46] At the end of 1957, 32-year-old Hans Ludwig became the leader of the church department in Berlin, replacing Willi Butter. Arno Schulz was in charge of the Catholic Church unit until 1962.

A 1 November 1957 meeting of all unit chiefs for church affairs in section V/4 spelled out the main points of MfS operations for all regional administrations. Listed as targets for surveillance in the Catholic Church were all bishops' seats, Kolping Association groups, student communities, Jesuit institutions, schools, seminaries, and "the church presence among the Sorbs."[47] In practice, however, not all MfS offices were capable of carrying out detailed work on this scale, and they often reported only on public events.[48] They also failed to reach their quantitative objectives for establishing files. Therefore, in 1958, the HA V/4 commissioned eavesdropping operations in various church offices and private residences throughout the GDR. Regional MfS stations coordinated these, enlisting "reliable" postal employees. According to a 23 December 1959 HA V/4 report, these operations spied on "for example, Bishop Spülbeck, Meißen; Bishop Rintelen, Magdeburg; Jesuit institutions in Berlin, Magdeburg, Leipzig, and Weimar; the seat of the council of ordinaries in the democratic sector; Auxiliary Bishop Bengsch."[49] The bugs in Bishop Spülbeck's office in Bautzen (which were operational from 5 September 1958 to 10 September 1959) and in the bishop's office in Magdeburg gave the MfS, and thus the SED regime, a qualitative lead in acquiring the most valuable information about the Catholic Church, which could then be used in drafting policies and tactics.[50]

The HA V/4 section summarized the value of the information collected as follows:

A) learning the goals and aims of the Catholic Church against the GDR and the socialist camp;

B) gaining insight into Catholic money transfers into the GDR via West Berlin;

C) acquiring information about weaknesses and deficits among the Catholic clergy that might make our approaches more effective; the technique allows us to check up on the honesty of the informers already in place;

D) acquiring materials which can offer us deeper insight into the hostile activities of the Catholic Church in general and specifically spying activities, as in the case of the Jesuits in Biesdorf.[51]

The last example refers to a case in which four Jesuits—Robert Frater, Joseph Menzel, Wilhelm Rueter, and Joseph Müldner—were arrested in July 1958 and sentenced to prison terms of one and a half to four years for "espionage; endangering the state by inciting, aiding, and abetting flight from the GDR; and illegal possession of foreign currency." The arrests and trial constituted a draconian spectacle that, an MfS report noted, had fulfilled its purpose: to intimidate the church.[52] The church, on the other hand, could not deny (internally, at least) the conscious affront against dictates of the GDR regime, which it perceived as illegitimate and repressive, and could only hope for mercy.

Another trial accompanied this deliberate intimidation of the Catholic Church in the GDR. In Potsdam, eleven Catholic men from Rathenow were arrested in July 1958 as they attempted to return from an event in West Berlin sponsored by the "Catholic Social Secretariat." There, under the leadership of Heinz Brauweiler, the Catholic Relief Organization for Men in the [Soviet] Zone held lectures and "social seminars" that expounded on Catholic social theory as a theoretical foil to dialectical materialism. The men were convicted of espionage in December 1958 and received prison terms of up to five years.[53] The MfS had prepared for this trial long in advance by infiltrating the "social seminars" with three secret informers—in particular, Secret Informer "Eduard," who became a member of the Kolping Association.[54] The draconian punishments were meant to deter Catholics in the GDR and East Berlin from taking part in future church events in West Berlin.

In another case, on 4 September 1959, Auxiliary Bishop Alfred Bengsch, who lived in East Berlin, thought that the postal employees installing a telephone line in his apartment were behaving strangely. The next day, he asked a friend from West Berlin, who was a telegraph office official, to come by. The friend discovered a bug and cut its wire. A short time later, two repairmen arrived at the apartment. When Bengsch and his friend tried to leave, two MfS agents disguised as regular police officers arrested them and took them in for questioning. According to a 7 September 1959 file report, one of the police officers "told him politely . . . in a private conversation" that the authorities had a file cabinet full of incriminating evidence of illegal Catholic activities in the GDR.[55] Bengsch noted that he was told that the bishops

needed to understand that this state will continue to exist . . . It could be, if I were to remain in my office for a long time, that I would undertake actions that other church officials would think heretical, but which in truth would just be realistic and would in no way entail the surrender of my views and principles. It was Cardinal Döpfner's own fault that he could no longer accomplish anything in the GDR. His last pastoral letter—which, by the way, the official claimed to have known before it was read—showed how disconnected from the facts he really was.[56]

Reports by MfS secret informers based on close contact with Döpfner's and Bengsch's circles reveal how much the church feared that the auxiliary bishop's activities in East Berlin would be limited; they even feared he would be expelled from the GDR and were upset by the dramatic reports of eavesdropping and anti-church persecutions in the West German press.[57] These reports, in turn, led the MfS to fear further discoveries, and for a while it suspended "operational techniques" in all previously penetrated Catholic institutions in the GDR—so much so that a 23 December 1959 report notes "a gap in the monitoring of the Catholic Church."[58] Although the MfS "urgently" needed to restart operations, it was impossible to do so in the near future. Even a nighttime MfS infiltration of Bishop Spülbeck's office in Bautzen on 6–7 January 1961 did not re-install eavesdropping "technology."[59] After Bengsch discovered the listening device, the MfS tried to blame American and British secret agents (the device the MfS used was British-made). The MfS even hid some information from its own government to shift the blame for the failure. Indeed, the heads of the "Catholic" section of the MfS HA V/4 and HA XX/4 kept internal documents about the incident in their own office until 1989.[60]

After September 1959, the MfS had to get its information about the Catholic Church from its few secret informers. As a rule, it "recruited" new operatives by presenting prospects with personal or legal information that would damage them in public or in the church community. More effective than this method in the long term was the practice of targeting and making contact with priests who had made statements somewhat critical of their superiors and who tended to be loners within the clergy. Not all of the MfS measures were ultimately as unsuccessful as Operation Black Plague against the ordinariate in Bautzen.[61] One success was when the MfS managed to recruit at least two priests to work as secret informers. Bengsch told his listeners at a conference of priests in Prenzlau on 3 March 1960, and at a pastoral conference in West Berlin on 24 November 1960, that they should immediately report MfS attempts at contact to their bishop. The MfS, however, received detailed reports of Bengsch's statements from these informers.[62]

One priest from the Meißen diocese was successfully blackmailed by the MfS in 1958 and from then on supplied, to a secret address, memos and pastoral letters he had received from the ordinaries. In the same period, two other priests voluntarily passed similar internal information to the MfS. The letters were secretly intercepted, transcribed by the MfS and sent to Berlin, and then returned.[63] In 1958, the regional government of the Gera district was able to install a secret informer, "(Bernhard) Schüler," into the seminary in Erfurt.[64] Until he left in 1962, he supplied the MfS with valuable reports on the curriculum, individual students, internal conferences, and visits by bishops.

In a January 1960 internal report on MfS activities during the fourth quarter of 1959, agents responsible for the Catholic Church noted "a substantial uptick."[65] In total, the MfS maintained contact in varying degrees with nineteen "lower clergymen" throughout the GDR. In the early years, the MfS referred to this group collectively as an "agency," but its hope of creating an "opposition movement" within the clergy by means of it did not materialize. The main emphasis of MfS activity was to penetrate targets that would be easier for outsiders to get in to, such as Catholic student groups or the Kolping Association (in both parts of Berlin) or the Caritas Association.[66] After the listening device program was suspended, however, the quality of information declined. As the chief Catholic negotiator, Prelate Zinke channeled a portion of the MfS focus in his direction. It was only after 1961 that the "Catholic front" within the MfS enlarged its arsenal of perfidious methods and increasingly targeted specific individuals. It received analytical and pseudo-scientific support from "a so-called evaluation group" within HA V/4. This independent working group, housed in Berlin within the shadowy "Wandlitz Institute" set up by the MfS, worked with multiple unofficial informers (*Inoffizielle Mitarbeiter,* IM) from 1960. Its mission was to systematically evaluate church publications, to maintain extensive files on individuals, to compile reports, and especially in the 1960s, to prepare negative propaganda campaigns.[67]

Atheism, Jugendweihe, and Science as Religion

As in the lead-up to the introduction of the Jugendweihe to compete with Christian confirmation in 1954 (which was relatively late for strategic purposes), voices within the SED agitated for the complete suppression of religion in public schools and of religious holidays and ceremonies in public life. At first, they targeted religious practice within their own ranks that they labeled "inconsequential" behavior. For example, regional SED leaders in Neubrandenburg sent a memo on 2 January 1956 to Barth with detailed suggestions for non-religious weddings and funerals that would end "dependency on the churches."[68]

After the Thirtieth Congress of the Central Committee, the SED had a variety of new administrative and propaganda measures connected with the "Building Up Socialism" drive at its disposal for suppressing religion in GDR society. Beginning in the second half of 1957, the SED directed the most offensive political and atheistic propaganda campaign against the churches in the history of the GDR. These measures, which the SED implemented with unyielding thoroughness in schools and universities, along with the new Jugendweihe, would limit the influence of religion until the end of the GDR, remaining in effect until 1989.

In October 1957, in a lecture at the University of Jena, State Secretary for Universities Wilhelm Girnus declared that "on November 7, 1917 [the date of the October Revolution in Russia], the age of belief in myths was irrevocably assigned to the dustbin of history." Deputy Prime Minister and CDU Chairman Otto Nuschke reacted to this angrily, declaring to Prime Minister Grotewohl: "If Dr. Girnus, a member of our government, holds the opinion that faith has been consigned to history's dustbin, then I count myself as one of those who will also be thrown there."[69] But when Nuschke—the "bourgeois" figurehead—died on

27 December 1957, the last obstacle to the SED and its partners in the CDU leadership was gone.

On 18 December 1957, the Politburo empowered Girnus to issue a decree banning the activities of "so-called student chaplains and student congregations at universities and technical colleges."[70] To carry out atheistic education in the elementary and secondary schools, the "Order to Secure Order and Continuity in the Education Process in Common Schools" was issued on 12 February 1958. Called the Lange Decree after the minister of education, it extended an order the East Berlin magistrate had made on 15 February 1956 to the entire GDR, limiting and controlling religious instruction in the schools, as well as teachers of religious studies. Issued without the approval of the Office of the State Secretary for Church Affairs, the measure soon drove all religious instruction out of schools and into churches, though it happened less quickly in certain areas.[71]

After 1958, the SED refused to engage in substantive discussions of school matters with the churches. On 4 March 1958 the Politburo introduced compulsory atheistic education in all schools: "To study Marxism-Leninism comprehensively and to apply it means . . . to understand its atheistic essence as a starting point for the treatment of any single aspect. That is the only possible way to educate socialist human beings . . . Atheistic education is the foundation of a true humanist education."[72] Following up on this, the Politburo resolved on 1 April 1958 to prepare a "schools conference" that month with a keynote address by the minister of education; its goal was to outline ideological training for teachers. Teachers who were CDU members, without party affiliation, or with Christian ties were targeted to get "convinced," and only "staunch Marxists" were to be allowed to continue as school directors, assistants, or classroom teachers.[73] Ulbricht personally announced the new pedagogical line, the "Ten Commandments of Socialist Morality," at the SED's Fifth Party Congress in July 1958. Responding to appeals, the Ministry of Education unveiled its "socialist, general education, polytechnical school" and new curricula. The formal conclusion to this SED offensive to win the youth over to socialism—predicated upon an unconditional belief in the power of education—was a law for the "Socialist Development of the Schools," ratified by the Volkskammer on 1 December 1959.

After its earlier, rather disappointing experiences, the SED saw the issue of the Jugendweihe as a primary field for testing its strength against the churches. The year 1958 was declared "the year of the Jugendweihe," and Ulbricht wanted it to be a priority.[74] Working against those in the SED who hoped that a more flexible stance would increase the number of participants, Ulbricht made a targeted public appearance on 29 September 1957 in Sonneberg (in Thuringia). He spoke with members of the Jugendweihe committee and, in his speech, called for all youths to take part in the ceremony and for materialist and atheistic propaganda to be strengthened.[75] Following this, the proponents of the "materialist-atheist" line prevailed within the ZK apparatus against those who had instead championed what they called German "socialist patriotism." Paul Wandel was among those who fell, relieved of his party offices as ZK secretary and Politburo member.

Ulbricht had criticized him sharply at the ZK meeting of 16–19 October 1957 for "bending to the pressure from our enemies." Wandel had led a drive to replace *Universe, Earth, Man,* a decidedly atheistic book, with a work glorifying regional pride (entitled *Our Germany*) as the official gift for Jugendweihe participants.

The Politburo approved extensive political guidelines on 22 October 1957 to prepare party organizations for the 1958 Jugendweihe, including a new, materialist oath. On 5 February 1958 the Politburo issued a declaration of state support for the Jugendweihe, through the various branches of government and industry.[76] Thus, with his personal intervention Ulbricht transformed the Jugendweihe from a nominally voluntary ritual (nevertheless widely perceived as obligatory) to a dictate of the SED party leadership under the thin veneer of various other organizations and committees. CDU leaders fell in step with the SED line on the Jugendweihe and suffered a significant loss of confidence among their own ranks and in church circles; many members resigned.[77]

Beginning in mid 1958, Protestant churches took a more moderate stand on the question of participating in both a Christian confirmation and the Jugendweihe. This, combined with massive pressure on teachers, students, and parents, led 44.1 percent of eligible youth across the GDR to participate in the SED ritual (according to SED statistics), more than double the numbers from 1955 to 1957.[78] In 1959, 80.4 percent of GDR youths opted for the Jugendweihe, and after 1960 the figure remained around 90 percent. The SED saw measurable "progress" in the way its own members integrated socialist rituals into their own family celebrations (weddings, funerals, baby namings) to replace Christian sacraments.

The SED did more than take administrative measures to limit the churches. State and party organs viewed the churches as dangerous political enemies, even though they believed the churches were doomed to gradually die out in the face of the "superiority" of "scientific socialism." But to accelerate this decline, the party wanted to analyze the "enemy." The Office of the State Secretary for Church Affairs wrote in late 1958 that "[i]n the GDR, only one main power remains that spreads old, outdated, reactionary thought . . . the church. It is a highly structured organization and tries to disguise its reactionary ambitions as religious ideas."[79] The Catholic Church thus appeared as an obstacle sui generis. Based on its preconceived matrix for interpreting social reality, the SED deduced the specter of a powerful, international Catholic enemy. State Secretary Eggerath said, in a talk to regional church affairs offers in December 1957,

As an international organization, the Catholic Church has extraordinary power. One of its most important means is the iron discipline and unconditional obedience that is taken for granted within its hierarchy. The church possesses a tremendous means of control through its sacraments and confessions, which influence working people throughout the world, keeping them from participating in the struggle for their own interests. They lull the working masses to sleep and push them in a reactionary direction.

The "most effective organization," in Eggerath's opinion, was the Jesuit order: "The Jesuits have unlimited resources; they have fourteen universities of their own, and more than one third of their membership is American."[80] Eggerath considered the Catholic orders in the GDR the "elite troops of political Catholicism" with a "network of bases" that "organize political campaigns" and "uniformly carry out Vatican policies."[81]

The SED took the confrontation between its ideology and social teachings and those of the Catholic Church very seriously. Between 1957 and 1961, the SED fought this campaign with a flood of conferences, popular scholarly and scientific publications, articles in the general GDR press, and contributions to the SED monthly publication *Einheit* and the academic journal *Deutsche Zeitschrift für Philosophie*. Alongside a campaign against "political clericalism," philosophical discourse addressed neo-Thomism, materialism, and Darwinism.[82] But the polemical attack on religious "superstition" in light of "modern science" was uneven. East German philosophers and other authors carried on the debate using Western publications not officially available in the GDR. Opposing viewpoints could not be published, except when they were couched as theology in church newspapers, which were censored. Western literature had to be smuggled in, for the most part, and informally passed around in Catholic circles to counter Communist education. For example, a scientist from Halle named Siegfried Kirschke wrote an article for the April 1959 issue of the *Deutsche Zeitschrift für Philosophie* entitled "Modern Genetics and Clerical Propaganda." Ostensibly, Kirschke was concerned only with short articles in church newspapers in the GDR, but he based much of his discussion on church publications from the West,[83] repeatedly attacking the views of Bishop Spülbeck of Meißen as expressed in his *Christ and the Worldview of the Modern Natural Sciences*. As this work could only be published in West Berlin (in its fourth print-run in 1957), Spülbeck had no chance to reply publicly in the GDR.[84]

Reciprocal "refutations" between West German Jesuits and Marxist philosophers from the GDR characterized this debate. Marxists singled out Jesuits for attack, rendering "Jesuit" synonymous with "underhandedness" and "pedantry." For example, Marxist philosopher Georg Klaus replied to *Dialectical Materialism*, a 1953 book published in West Germany by the Jesuit priest Gustav Wetter, with his 1957 polemic *Jesuits, God, and Matter: The Jesuit Wetter's Revolt Against Reason and Science*. Wetter responded in 1958 with *Dialectical Materialism and the Problem of the Origin of Life*, which GDR authors followed up on with a series of "refutations."[85]

Beginning in 1958, the SED journal *Einheit* promoted the new ideological tone with articles "unmasking political clericalism" in West German politics. The titles of some of these articles say it all: "The Theory of 'Peace Between the Classes' in Catholic Social Thought: Political Catholicism's Demagogic Deception"; "The Justification of the Imperialist Plans for Atomic Warfare through Political Clericalism"; "The Ideology of Political Clericalism: A Tool of German Militarism."[86] With slogans such as "political clericalism" and "clerical fascism," the articles attacked NATO, Adenauer's CDU/CSU (Christian Social Union) government in West Germany, and the churches, which were portrayed as closely aligned with them. These articles clearly intended to make church leaders in the GDR aware that they needed to "separate" from the West and to pledge allegiance to the GDR state and social system. After legal scholars Karl Mollnau and Karl-Heinz Schöneburg published an article in February 1959 on "The Social and Theoretical Foundations of Clerical Fascism,"[87] the ZK formed the Commission for the Struggle against Clerical Fascism on 18 March to coordinate public agitation and propaganda, as well as detailed plans for related publications.[88]

As more people fled the GDR and the "socialist buildup" generated ever greater economic problems, the SED soft-pedaled its atheistic propaganda, though without changing its content. In a programmatic speech as chairman of the newly organized State Council, Ulbricht proclaimed a new "socialist community of mankind." Among other things, Ulbricht criticized the council for failing to reach an agreement with the Catholic Church in the GDR comparable to the "Joint Declaration" of the Protestant churches on 21 July 1958, which declared that there was "no opposition between Christianity and the humanist goals of socialism."[89] Soon thereafter, the CDU and the state apparatus organized a "Meeting of Progressive Christians" with Ulbricht. On 9 February 1961, Ulbricht met with a delegation led by a Protestant professor of theology from Leipzig, Emil Fuchs, who delivered a supportive letter with signatures collected by the CDU.[90] After years of publicly attacking the churches, the SED now, through its first secretary, once again sanctioned Christianity, in so far as it supported socialism and restricted its social role to religious ceremony. The churches, however, rejected these limits on their identity and withdrew religious credentials from those within its ranks who entertained such ideas.[91] A chief goal of Ulbricht's statements in both October 1960 and February 1961 was the full legal division of the Protestant churches in Germany. A binding agreement with the regime would force them to recognize GDR sovereignty. The churches were skeptical of this new approach, which they rightly saw as a new strategy of SED Kirchenpolitik. For the SED, however, it was likewise an acknowledgment that the decline of religion, seen in its worldview as preordained, would take longer than expected.

Catholic Reactions

On 25 March 1957 the 43-year-old bishop of Würzburg, Dr. Julius Döpfner, was installed as the bishop of Berlin, replacing Wilhelm Weskamm, who had died in August 1956. A few days earlier, the Office of the State Secretary for Church Affairs had prepared a "short biography and evaluation" that described Döpfner's installation as "not only a shift but a strengthening of [the Vatican's] hostile activities in the East, on GDR territory."[92] As both a resident of West Berlin and the new chairman of the Berlin Conference of Ordinaries, Döpfner soon made the transition from the West German social system and framework for church-state relations to become a decisive counterpart to GDR officials and their Kirchen-politik. These officials saw him as a Western import with little sense of reality who would steer the political course of the Catholic Church in the GDR on a more confrontational path. Indeed, together with Prelate Walter Adolph, Döpfner pursued an aggressive public campaign through the West Berlin church journal *Petrusblatt* to match the equally aggressive Kirchenpolitik of the GDR.

A few weeks after first officially visiting Prime Minister Grotewohl on 28 March 1957, Döpfner sent Grotewohl a letter complaining of several cases of "unjustifiably" limited church activities and asking "very sincerely" for his help.[93] State Secretary Eggerath's answer on 4 June set the tit-for-tat tone that would prevail over the coming years: "Perhaps you see things differently as someone who is not a citizen of our republic . . . your ideas and conclusions must be rejected because they proceed from false premises."[94] Prelate Zinke, who continued to function under the new bishop as a contact person for GDR government offices, noted on 11 June that Döpfner's letter had "achieved its goal . . . [of] denying the GDR regime the opportunity to claim cheaply that 'there were no problems with the Catholic Church.'"[95]

The Catholic Church would have its share of "problems" in the aftermath of the above exchange, focused on Bishop Döpfner. Based on a study of his sermons and the contents of his pastoral letters, Eggerath wrote on 9 May 1958 to Paul Verner, a member of the Politburo, that the bishop should be denied permission to travel in the GDR outside of East Berlin.[96] On 30 May Eggerath dismissed Zinke's complaint about this with the following words:

> Because you have ignored repeated warnings, I see no reason to reverse the decision made by the other state branches. Bishops Döpfner's statements . . . are only one example of the continued interference in the internal affairs of the GDR, the misuse of churches and related institutions for unconstitutional and partisan political aims, and the support of the Cold War against the Workers' and Peasants' State.[97]

Döpfner's travel ban barred him from visiting the areas of his diocese in Bran-denburg and Pomerania. In this context, and also in view of measures against Protestant representatives, even Prelate Zinke was no longer received by the state secretary for church affairs or by other GDR ministers because he resided in West Berlin. Zinke thus tried various other ways to maintain government contacts.

The trial of the Jesuits gave Zinke the opportunity to establish his first contacts with the MfS in 1958, which he did in agreement with Döpfner. These contacts continued in 1959 and occurred regularly after 1960.[98] In part, the talks could justifiably be called negotiations; until September 1961, they were the only line of communication in Berlin between the Catholic Church and the GDR regime, and they took place without the involvement of the State Secretary for Church Affairs. Both sides seemed aware of the significance of these direct contacts, and the MfS made the extent of their influence clear to the Catholic representatives, remarking: "If church officials tell us something of fundamental importance, we immediately pass it on personally or in writing to the ZK or to the Council of Ministers. Strangely, they never mentioned the Zeughaus [i.e., the Office of the State Secretary for Church Affairs], which may or may not have any significance."[99] Zinke's importance within church circles grew because of these SED-sanctioned contacts. With the "front door" closed, Catholics found that the SED had opened the back door. In an internal report on the situation of the church, Döpfner wrote on 13 July 1960 that "with the regime's current tendencies . . . [Zinke's connections] were more important than ever."[100] However, the GDR did not approve Zinke's move to East Berlin, which Döpfner had tried to bring about. After the Berlin Wall was built, the MfS helped Zinke go back and forth across the border. Sometimes they even picked him up at the Bahnhof Friedrich-straße crossing.

While Catholics were establishing this line of communication through the MfS, they also tried to limit all other contacts with the security services, as with all state organs. In 1957, all church jurisdictions issued internal decrees governing conversations with officials to counter the regime's "differentiation policy." One such decree by Döpfner in Berlin on 26 November acquired symbolic importance for the regime, although there were many others like it across the GDR. This coordinated action by the East German ordinaries authorized only the chairmen of the Berlin Conference of Ordinaries to discuss fundamental issues, and only local ordinaries to negotiate with regional government; it restricted all local conversations to the practical matters at hand, dictated that at least two church representatives be present during talks, and required ordinaries to make written reports. It further stipulated that negotiations be undertaken only with state offices, not with parties or mass organizations. Those approached by the MfS, which the decrees did not mention by name, were to write detailed reports to the ordinaries.[101] These decrees, which were followed very closely, succeeded so well in their defensive intentions that the GDR officials began to attack the church for "denying civil rights" to clergy and church workers when the "talks" (which were meant to politically influence or use the churches) did not go their way. In the Erfurt, Magdeburg, Leipzig, Dresden, and Karl-Marx-Stadt (Chemnitz) districts, discussions took place only with bishops or their deputies; while the state representatives brought up political themes and demands, the Catholic officials limited themselves to concrete practical matters. Thus, the council of the Karl-Marx-Stadt district concluded from a meeting with Bishop Spülbeck that "Catholic leaders are not interested in speaking with the state unless it concerns demands to their advantage."[102]

Under the leadership of Bishop Döpfner, the Berlin Conference of Ordinaries continued to issue complaints and make requests to the state in the form of internal memoranda, public pastoral letters, and articles published in the West. After his one meeting with Eggerath on 10 February 1958, Döpfner said that "the claims of the church must be raised again and again . . . and will succeed from time to time" against the SED plans for education, its push for the Jugendweihe, and its atheist and materialist propaganda.[103] The main thrust of the church's public appeals was to encourage Catholic parents and children to uphold the Christian faith at home and in church in the face of the regime's propaganda and the atheistic school curriculum.

The church feared the wide-ranging consequences of materialism in the schools, which the SED perceived as a confirmation of the legitimacy of its policy. The ordinaries appealed to the 1949 GDR constitution to support their claim of freedom of religion and freedom of conscience. These appeals—soon typical of church statements—became increasingly plaintive, as the GDR state did not engage in any kind of discussion or argumentation regarding education and thoroughly applied the SED political guidelines. The Berlin Conference of Ordinaries issued the pastoral letter "On Schools and Education in Our Times" on 23 October 1957, followed on 4 December 1957 by a detailed "Memorandum on the Situation of Religious Life," which they sent to the GDR prime minister.[104] The prime minister replied on 14 January 1958 with a letter to Döpfner decrying "directives from West Germany": "I must reject your stance against the teaching of exact science in public schools and universities, which is protected in the German Democratic Republic. The leadership of the Catholic Church has no right to meddle in questions of instruction in the public schools."[105] Bishop Döpfner asked the prelates Adolph and Zinke to evaluate the letter and then composed an analysis, concluding that the state had "not made the slightest effort to reach a modus vivendi."[106] A "genuine confrontation," he continued, would not be possible, but "clear offensive moves from the church" would be taken very seriously. As a result, he recommended that they continue writing letters and insisting upon the constitutional principle of freedom of conscience.

Catholic leaders felt obliged to put their protests in writing and to make them public in order not to remain silent and passive. They wanted to signal to the Catholic community that the church did not support the socialist education policies and was doing everything in its power to counteract them. Beginning in 1958, for example, steps to educate Catholic children were intensified across the GDR by means of vacation schools or "illegal" summer camps.[107]

The SED campaign to increase the number of Jugendweihe participants in 1958 and 1959 prompted ordinaries across the GDR to issue statements encouraging Catholic youths to reject it and confirming that sacraments would be withheld as long as they did not comply with the church's steep demands.[108] It was up to Catholic students, parents, and priests to translate this into an effective form of resistance to government pressure. Some priests asked their bishops if the decrees were appropriate and practical. One priest from Magdeburg said to the bishops on 20 September 1958:

> Our hearts are heavy because of the Jugendweihe problem in a way that I have not experienced in almost forty years as a priest. All of the difficulties of the Nazi years pale in comparison because now a large portion of our good congregants can no longer agree with the judgment of our head pastors and shake their heads because they do

not understand . . . parents simply do not agree that participation in the Jugendweihe is a disavowal of faith. For they are all long accustomed to living in two worlds and to thinking differently than they appear to express themselves through votes, essays, public statements, [etc.].[109]

Another priest asked the now-Cardinal Döpfner (who had been elevated by the Vatican on 15 December 1958) on 22 April 1959 if the "heroic willpower" of parents and children would not be overtaxed by this demand. "[T]he common understanding among the people," he remarked, was that the Jugendweihe was not explicitly atheist.

Although the church had been rigid on this question since 1954, it now had difficulty demonstrating to Catholics that the Jugendweihe should be singled out among the numerous declarations of loyalty to the GDR and to socialism. In addition, the church now had to evaluate every version of the Jugendweihe oath and related educational materials. By 1958, the bishops could no longer do this, so the regent of the seminary in Neuzelle, Paul Ramatschi, wrote to Döpfner on 12 May 1959, recommending a regular review of the "official declarations." Noting that the clergy "did not stand united behind the measures taken by the bishops," Ramatschi expressed "serious concerns because the danger has emerged for the first time that the inner solidarity of the clergy might be compromised."[110] The state apparatus was aware of this situation; despite all tactical efforts to soften its appearance, the regime saw the obligatory Jugendweihe as an exemplary test of the power of the churches. An MfS report from 28 March 1959 deduced from a conversation overheard between Döpfner and Spülbeck that the auxiliary bishop of Magdeburg, Rintelen, had gone to Döpfner of his own accord to ask (in vain) the bishops to soften their position regarding the Jugendweihe, citing a statement published in *Neues Deutschland* by the Central Committee for the Jugendweihe, as well as mentioning the critical views of some priests in Magdeburg.[111]

In order to keep track of this confrontation, each parish began to fill out internal questionnaires that were passed on to the ordinaries.[112] At a BOK meeting in July 1958, Döpfner calculated that, in 1958, "as a whole, Catholic parents and children behaved well": throughout the entire GDR, between 11 and 12 percent participated in the Jugendweihe.[113] In 1959, 37.5 percent of Catholic youth took part, and in 1960 the number climbed to 43.58 percent. About a quarter of the Catholic youth who did participate were then "reconciled." Despite the rising numbers of Jugendweihe participants, Catholics remained the sole segment of GDR society that rejected the Communist ritual in significant numbers. The rates of participation in the counties of Heiligenstadt and Worbis were always below average in the GDR because of ongoing Catholic resistance there.

For Catholic leaders, the fight over the Jugendweihe from 1957 to 1961 became a symbol of a comprehensive struggle with an opposing worldview. But the tendency to see it in these terms was stronger in West Berlin and West Germany than for Catholics who lived with the reality of the GDR. A triumphant consciousness that the Christian faith would not be defeated by the atheist environment and its propaganda went together with the "trials of conscience" evoked in pastoral letters with reference to Christ's suffering on the cross and the need to persevere. The SED's ideological offensives showed that the party took religion seriously. This led Catholics to feel empowered as equally worthy opponents and strengthened their belief in the relevance of their positions. Catholic leaders devoted considerable effort to understanding their "atheist enemy," scouring GDR newspapers and journals to decipher its politics and ideology and note subtle changes. At BOK meetings, participants cited set SED phrases, such as "the church is the last organized enemy of the GDR," with a certain sense of pride. This practice echoed the *West* German tendency to overestimate the Catholic Church's power to oppose the SED and to integrate all of Germany. When one lower ZK employee fled to the West, reconnected with the Catholic faith, and "broke with Communism," he became an "advisor" to Cardinal Döpfner.[114] At the 7–8 July 1959 BOK meeting, Döpfner repeated in his report what this advisor had determined:[115]

> The Catholic Church's pastoral letters have a clear format; they are outstanding in orienting the faithful and are on target in every respect. They address the essential questions at hand. Ulbricht thought that the Catholic Church in the SBZ was a most capable enemy. This is a great compliment for us.[116]

During his visit to Rome, Bishop Spülbeck had an audience with Cardinal Domenico Tardini on 11 November 1958. According to Spülbeck's report, the cardinal said

> to persevere and not to despair or give in . . . even if the pressure increases. We will hold on. The Berlin Conference of Ordinaries have informed the Vatican well, and he explained that our posture was correct . . . [he emphasized] strengthening the will to resist on a religious basis when he said to me that we are fulfilling a national duty for all Germany. His exact words were "Votre résistance, c'est d'oevre nationale." He could not offer us any practical aid. We could be assured of blessings and prayers . . . victory is at our doorstep.[117]

But in the GDR itself, the regime's intimidation measures and demonstrations of its power spread fear around the church. The raids on parish libraries and the various trials in 1958 and 1959 had a chilling effect.

In March 1959 Bishop Spülbeck expressed his view—within church circles—that Döpfner should move to East Berlin from the West because fear that the city would be divided and church structures would be compromised had already become severe:

> He has to move to East Berlin, it's useless for him to be there . . . [if he moves,] then he can take care of West Berlin, he can take care of East Berlin, and he can go to the GDR. But if East Berlin is forcibly attached to the GDR, he can only be effective in

West Berlin. That would spell the end of the diocese. We would have no more contact. Then what use would the cardinal be? The situation is bad.[118]

Döpfner had already engaged in negotiations in Rome, "so that things would not continue as they are."[119]

Instead of deliberately transferring the residence of the bishop of Berlin to the East to strengthen church authority in the GDR, the Vatican named 37-year-old Alfred Bengsch the auxiliary bishop of Berlin, with residence in the eastern part of the city, on 4 May 1959. Additionally, during the high point of the Berlin crisis on 20 July 1959, the Vatican gave Cardinal Döpfner special authority in case their communication got cut off.[120] When the bishops of Osnabrück, Paderborn, Würzburg, and Fulda were no longer able travel to the areas of their dioceses in the GDR, additional powers as vicar-general were granted to the ordinaries in Magdeburg (9 March 1958) and Schwerin (1 December 1958). The bishop's commissioner in Meiningen was made a vicar-general on 14 October 1959. The vicar-general of Schwerin, Bernhard Schräder, was additionally made an auxiliary bishop on 22 July 1959, and the chapter-vicar of Görlitz, Ferdinand Piontek was consecrated as titular bishop.

After the pastoral letter for Lent, "The Christian in an Atheist Environment," was read on 20 January 1960, the state organized targeted countermeasures to further intimidate Catholics for the first time. In Erfurt, Auxiliary Bishop Freusberg was asked to come to local government offices for a conversation on 21 February.[121] In Eichsfeld, with little success but considerable visible effort, "public declarations of positions" from Catholics were "organized."[122] In Leipzig, the local government made clear to Bishop Spülbeck on 23 March that construction permits, etc., might very well be linked to the content of pastoral letters. The Dresden regional council temporarily withheld state funds from the Diocese of Meißen. All of this was intended to signal that the state's policies would be linked to any official statements by church leaders. On 3 March 1960 Bengsch pointed out at a conference of priests in Prenzlau that too great a portion of the Lent pastoral letter drafted by the diocese leadership had been removed; further, he wondered how much longer pastoral letters would be possible without being banned by the state.[123] The BOK wrote a petition on 6 April 1960 to the GDR prime minister protesting inhumane methods in the collectivization of agriculture (which was not published) but thereafter wrote no more statements intended for public release until October 1961.[124]

The loss of 235,458 congregants who emigrated to the West between 1954 and 1961 hit Catholic communities hard.[125] At the 3–4 November BOK meeting in 1960, ordinaries discussed three possible recommendations for a Christian "Ethics of Remaining in the GDR" but could not agree on a common declaration.[126] One recommendation noted that although a moral argument could be made for remaining, it could not be designated as "a generally binding moral duty . . . In any case we have no reason to spread the 'prophylactic' fear, even if it is understandable. Nor are we able to say that we trust in a 'change of circumstances in a Western direction."'[127] On 23 March 1959, accepting the political situation of the GDR, Bishop Spülbeck recommended staying:

> Marxism may indeed last 1,000 years . . . we cannot know whether God will free us . . . It is somehow a punishment for us . . . I know exactly how things are in the West. I would not care to change places . . . We have a much happier state of affairs . . . We need to stay the course. That brings a great blessing. Look at the esteem we are held in, not by government officials, but by the people in general. How the people stand by us! . . . When the Marxists have disappeared then the next devil will take his turn and everything will be as before. And we can continue with our work very nicely.[128]

When a BOK joint declaration urging Germans to remain in the GDR failed to appear, Bishop Spülbeck preached about it on New Year's Eve 1960 in the Bautzen Cathedral. In his sermon, he played down the social environment of the church:

> God has willed the church here . . . God wills that the church remain here in the future. It is His will that Catholic people live here. One can live here as a Catholic . . . Do not believe that because the schools are atheistic your children must become non-believers. That depends upon something entirely different, above all upon the example you and your family set . . . Here is where we prove ourselves.[129]

Paradigm Shifts in Kirchenpolitik in 1961

In the Western zones of occupation, and later in the FRG, the Catholic Church tried to exercise political and social influence on Catholics in the CDU/CSU and in lay organizations. The goal was to preserve the substance of canon law from the pre-1934 regional- and Reich-level concordats and to secure church matters in the new state and federal constitutions. Referring to the concordats and the constitution, the bishops sought political influence and protested publicly when the church's claims were not acknowledged. In the SBZ/GDR, by contrast, the church soon faced one-party rule. The ruling SED based its "socialist understanding of law" on ideology and calculated power-politics and denounced attempts to invoke the legal principles of freedom of thought, assembly, and conscience as outdated "bourgeois legal thought." The 1949 GDR constitution was a window display, decorated with freedoms that could be pointed to or ignored as befit the circumstance. When the church petitioned central government offices in the GDR, recalling guarantees of freedom of religion and conscience as it asked for concrete administrative measures and political remedies, the appeals usually fell on deaf ears, except when the SED anticipated that a positive response would bring domestic or international political gain.

Bishop Döpfner and his West Berlin ordinaries had employed strategies of religious protest shaped by Western attitudes, using the public sphere and the media, since 1957. Bishops and ordinaries living in the GDR went along with this as long as they had the common conviction that the church could not "remain silent" regarding state measures that impacted it. However, this consensus began to fall apart when the central state organs of the GDR not only ignored religious protests but continued to sharpen their policies and reacted to critical sermons and pastoral letters with surveillance and organized countermeasures. BOK members thus began to weigh the risks of further petitions or public declarations. Cardinal Döpfner was increasingly alone in the BOK with his opinion—recorded by the MfS on 15 June 1960—that "for more than a year we have received no answer [to our petitions]. That is not a loss, because there are some matters where the church does not want an answer. The church can secure these if I sign on . . . But the Catholic Church does not need to consider tactics if it does not negotiate."[130]

The Lent pastoral letter "Church in Crisis—Church under the Cross" of 8 February 1959 was "not read" in the city of Görlitz, although Ferdinand Piontek, the chapter-vicar who resided there, had co-signed it.[131] On 7 April 1959 at a BOK meeting, Piontek declared himself against the bishops taking a position on Grotewohl's speech of 23 March 1959 because he feared for the continued existence of church institutions in the GDR:

> One result of our response will be applause—applause in the FRG—applause in the whole Western world. In the struggle for the freedom of the church, the West has expended a great deal of applause, but that has done nothing to improve our situation. When faced with an enemy that has all outward power in his hand and knows how to wield it ruthlessly, one must sometimes make the sacrifice of silence, as difficult as it is when one is feeling outrage.[132]

The BOK decided upon "principles for leadership in the office of bishop" in its 7–8 July 1959 session. The episcopate was to "take only unified positions regarding measures taken by the government and the judgment of social policies." It should conclude "no kind of agreement" with the government nor make "any declaration of loyalty" to it. The episcopate was to be concerned with the "unified posture of the clergy . . . to refrain from any kind of public position on political measures taken by the government."[133]

The bishops held to these principles, maintained a unified front, and accepted immobility even to the point of public silence as part of the bargain in cases of internal differences of opinion. The pre-conciliar paternalism remained unquestioned for the time being within the church, even regarding its obvious protective function in the face of the state's attempts to instrumentalize the church. Silence increasingly marked the BOK after the Lent pastoral letter of 1960, especially Cardinal Döpfner, who was limited to his diocese and his sector of Berlin and thus hampered in the exercise of his office. In order to preserve the symbolic value of his presence in West Berlin, he was unwilling to move to the eastern part of the city—something worth considering for pastoral and other internal church reasons. This certainly would have given the GDR a political propaganda success and would have led to sharp criticism of the Catholic Church in West Berlin and West German politics. Döpfner had actually given serious consideration to such a move but decided against it, probably out of political concerns vis-à-vis the government in Bonn.[134]

After Döpfner had an audience with the pope on 6 May 1961, the West German press began to speculate that he was to succeed the deceased archbishop of Munich-Freising.[135] Döpfner's indications that he would be reluctant to move, combined with public discussion in West Berlin about the possibility that the Vatican and the Bavarian government would collude behind the divided city's back, delayed a decision.

In June 1961, the cardinal drafted a detailed letter to Ulbricht as chairman of the State Council, referring to his speeches of 4 October 1960 and 9 February 1961. In the tone of a testament, the letter listed all of the church's complaints over the previous years and sharply rejected a "modus vivendi" between the state and the Catholic Church:

> The conclusion that there is no common basis for the ideas of socialist humanism and Christian humanism cannot be avoided . . . So long as the ship of state is steered exclusively toward dialectical and historical materialism, a normalization of relations between the Catholic Church and the state in the GDR will be impossible. The bishops sincerely regret that they must arrive at such a conclusion, for they are convinced that the current church/state tensions impact not only religious life but the welfare of the people.[136]

Spülbeck received the draft before the BOK meeting and unequivocally rejected it:

> Such a letter would mean a new beginning and cannot, in my opinion, remain without mention of the positive sides of our situation . . . The letter can result in our chairman being treated roughly by the government, such that they will play deaf, even in the future, when something is co-signed by the bishop of Berlin. It can lead to a worsening of the current wavering situation and to decisions being taken that we really do not want to see. The answer that will be spoken, not written, will be "You let yourselves be influenced by a NATO bishop in this letter—break with him!"

Spülbeck further opined that the geographic location of a bishop was decisive for his political relevance: "A bishop whose territory is in the GDR will be taken seriously as the spokesman of the Catholic population and his statements will somehow be received."[137] In a handwritten note after the BOK meeting, Döpfner recorded: "The draft of a letter to Ulbricht was presented to the conference of ordinaries on July 3, 1961, but discussion was postponed because of the political situation (new discussions of the Berlin question!)."[138] Two days later, Pope John XXIII named Julius Döpfner the archbishop of Munich. The Office of the State Secretary for Church Affairs began to strategize about how the naming of a new bishop for Berlin might enable East Germany "to enter into legal contact with the Vatican" in order to secure a treaty-like agreement that included recognition of the GDR.[139]

After the GDR began to build the Berlin Wall on 13 August 1961, the Vatican named a new bishop of Berlin on 16 August; Alfred Bengsch, the auxiliary bishop resident in East Berlin, had been elected, however, by the Berlin Cathedral Chapter on 27 July.[140] Bengsch named a general vicar for the western part of the city and a director of the ordinariat for the eastern part of the bishopric. Because of where he resided, Bengsch could move freely within the GDR, but the new reality cast doubt on him traveling to West Berlin. As early as 18 August, "Prelate Zinke appeared at the MfS" and requested that Döpfner be permitted entry to East Berlin for his departure on 20 August, that Bengsch have access to West Berlin, and that bishops from the GDR continue to participate in the Fulda Bishops' Conference.[141] The GDR was not prepared to make such concessions without political sacrifices from the church, especially concerning the possibility of travel permission for an all-German bishops' conference in the West. Cardinal Döpfner had to hold his last services before his departure in West Berlin.[142]

To keep his diocese unified on the issue of the bishop's access to West Berlin, Bengsch, chairman of the BOK since 21 August 1961, did not issue any church protest against the building of the Berlin Wall or the GDR-wide propaganda campaign to elicit affirmative public statements about it. On 24 August, the Catholic CDU official Alfons Malik sought out Bengsch and signaled to him, allegedly in the name of the GDR State Council, that no permits for Western travel were possible at that time but that "loyal" church responses to the measures begun on 13 August would be rewarded in the future. Bengsch remarked upon this in an internal note: "I could never speak out in approval of [the wall]. But our ministerial efforts aim to calm the community. Toleration from the state would be very welcome from our perspective, but the State Council must know that souls cannot be bought."[143]

The paradigm change under Bishop Bengsch primarily involved emphasizing the "ministering" duty of the church in the GDR and renouncing any kind of public political statement, as well as attempting to achieve a "modus vivendi" with the regime in East Berlin through talks. On 29 August 1961 the Politburo decided to respond to a letter of 21 August to the Council of Ministers and the East Berlin Magistrate from the Ordinary's Office in East Berlin that expressed a wish for "fruitful collaboration." The Politburo recommended that Acting Minister-President Willi Stoph receive Bengsch, as Minister-President Grotewohl was suffering from a lengthy illness.[144] Prior to this, at least two conversations Prelate Zinke had with the MfS on 24 and 28 August touched upon the inaugural visit. These stressed the combination of "loyalty" and "political abstinence" that was to be the fundamental precondition for the bishop to have access to West Berlin.[145] The official meeting between Bengsch and Stoph had originally been planned for 20 September, before the inaugural celebration in West Berlin, but it had to be postponed because the church schedule conflicted with it, and Stoph became ill. In its 12 September session, the Politburo had already approved Bengsch's inauguration in Berlin-Weißensee (East) on 19 September and in Berlin-Schöneberg (West) on 21 September. For the latter, the bishop and his driver received, for the first time, "approval for travel to West Berlin."[146]

After the building of the Berlin Wall, the SED leadership consciously distinguished its treatment of the Catholic Church from that of the Protestant Church. In contrast to Bengsch, Protestant leader Kurt Scharf, who had headed the council of the EKD since February 1961, was not allowed to return to East Berlin (where he resided) after receiving permission to travel to a council meeting in West Berlin.[147] On 15 September 1961 Johannes Klein of the Office of the State Secretariat for Church Affairs noted, "The differentiation between the Catholic and Protestant churches can be increased by provisionally not giving Bishop Scharf permission to visit democratic Berlin but allowing Bishop Bengsch the possibility to travel to West Berlin on a case by case basis."[148] Beginning on 15 September, Bengsch maintained direct contact through his advisor Drews with the State Secretariat for Church Affairs; both sides were interested in renewing contact.[149]

Bengsch's inaugural sermons in both parts of the city dealt with the ministerial duties of a global church; his tone was decidedly religious and apolitical. In East Berlin, the State Secretary for Church Affairs was invited to attend; in West Berlin, on the other hand, guests included the papal nuncio and West German bishops but not city politicians. With his strategy of political abstention along with a modicum of loyalty to the GDR state—in the form of no critical public statements—Bengsch, and thus the Catholic Church in the GDR, was able to maintain contact with the FRG and the Vatican and have access to West Berlin.

On 11 October 1961 Bengsch wrote a detailed report to the BOK entitled "We Are Living after August 13, 1961" with the subheadings "The Changed Situation," "Changes in Kirchenpolitik," "What Has Not Changed," and "The Nevertheless Changed Situation." In it, Bengsch saw continuity in the state's actions:

> The strategy of the atheist state we live in has not changed one millimeter . . .[Its goal is to create] a church that is 'loyal' to the socialist state and that can be used for political goals, as a screen, especially in foreign policy. The time has obviously not yet arrived for the liquidation of religion foreseen in Communism's final stage.

Because the state had not changed, Bengsch argued that the church must also hold the line and not enter into any agreement with the government nor—in the tradition of the 1957 decree—admit any political statements by clergy that might lead to a division within the church. Bengsch diplomatically sanctioned a change in methods that had already been introduced in 1960, a turn from public protest to behind-the-scenes diplomacy:

> The bishops' petitions and complaints to the government still make sense. If we have not yet raised our voice since August 13, it in no way means that we have given up.

It could be that the context of such steps had to be weighed, and it had to be decided when and in what form the public around the world should be addressed.

In addition, Bengsch admitted uncertainty about the future course of the ruling party:

> It is foreseeable that one will not be able to set firm rules about the numerous possibilities that the future may bring. We must wait for the other side to make its move. As difficult as that may be for us, no step of ours would really have any influence. Short of total capitulation, there is no measure that would defend against a blow [from the state].[150]

Once the wall was built, GDR policy actually moved in a direction opposite to what Döpfner had feared—that Bengsch could be "shoved off to the West." Bengsch's assistants Drews and Zinke were soon negotiating with GDR government officials—who showed goodwill in this matter—about the construction of an ordinary's office in East Berlin, for which West German churches had offered DM 1.1 million in financing. The GDR state was trying to keep Bengsch, as both a bishop and chairman of the BOK, in the East to convince him that its political system was superior by means of its supposedly attractive reality, so denying him access to West Berlin would be counterproductive. The Office of the State Secretary for Church Affairs noted in its 31 October 1961 "Evaluation of Dr. Alfred Bengsch": "It can be recognized from the bishop's first actions that he is astute enough, in contrast to the previous policies of the ordinaries, to realistically understand the political situation of the diocese and to behave accordingly."[151] The MfS had prepared a report on 23 September 1961 entitled "An Evaluation of the Personality of Bishop Bengsch," which declared that a change of his "politically negative" posture was especially important: "Because he is a truly strong personality, it will be difficult. He will not be intimidated by threats or danger, nor can he be tripped up by certain tricks we have at our disposal."[152] The report's author was confident that stabilizing the political situation in the GDR would have a positive effect on Bengsch's views in the long run:

> The faithful live in a socialist country and must adapt to the character of their surroundings to one degree or another. Bengsch's judgment is too sober not to take his environment into account, if Rome will allow it. On the other hand, he will also have to reflect whether the dangers of Communism feared by the church do not correspond to reality.

Bengsch's charted course served both the church and the state as a basis for future relations. This course was reinforced on 2 November 1961, when the acting minister-president, Willi Stoph, received Bengsch. The bishop opened the conversation with a wish for "peaceful and fruitful cooperation" between church and state. Pastoral and charitable duties would not take place "in the political sphere," he said, "but I believe that when people are educated toward peace, order, and conscience that it can only serve the common welfare." Stoph replied: "We share your wish for a fruitful and, as you say, peaceful collaboration. Let there be no doubt that we are ready. We are prepared to use all our offices to work together peacefully, fruitfully, and, if you wish, also in a spirit of friendship."[153] For the remainder of the two-hour conversation, the two gentleman discussed politics. Although there was no friendly rapprochement between them, they respected each other. Each tried to persuade the other, and the two discovered that both were born in Berlin-Schöneberg. The state accepted the bishop's request for changes in a press communiqué without objection.[154]

Symptomatic of the church's flexible diplomacy was Bengsch's comment at the end of the meeting regarding clergy and church workers who had been arrested after 13 August: Bengsch characterized their offenses as "stupidities."[155] In contrast to the 1958 trials, the church organized no public protest against these arrests. Instead, it used quiet diplomacy signaling understanding for the state's position but requested that it act with moderation. Two of the defendants were released two days after their conviction in December 1961; the other two were freed after Bengsch interceded personally on their behalf with Ulbricht.[156] These were the last political arrests of Catholic clergy in the history of the GDR.

Those who strove to maintain the existence of the Catholic Church in the GDR soon rationalized the Berlin Wall. Closing the "escape valve" created clarity and would lead the church to concentrate on the actual situation in East Germany rather than remain oriented to the West. This kind of acceptance could lead, as Spülbeck put it in a talk in Erfurt on 25 October 1961, "to a very fruitful period of religious work."[157] He also expressed optimism in December 1961 at the Magdeburg seminary, reasoning that, as the Berlin Wall had ended flight, the Catholic communities would be more stable:

> The situation has not been as dangerous as we may have feared it to be just after August 13, 1961. Nothing has happened to the church in this period, and, as things stand, nothing will happen. If many feared that the state would take the church's independence through a concordat or other means, as was done in the CSSR, the People's Republic of Hungary, or in Poland, this fear has proven to be foolish.[158]

However, Bengsch was notably more skeptical when he spoke at a BOK meeting on 9 January 1962 of "a prophylactic anxiety" that could further the "illusion . . . that responsive moves and promises by the other side and our own caution can keep them from laying their hands on us or protect us from future blows."[159]

Notes

1. Quoted in Dierk Hofmann, Karl-Heinz Schmidt, and Peter Skyba, eds., *Die DDR vor dem Mauerbau: Dokumente zur Geschichte des anderen deutschen Staates 1949–1961* (Munich, 1993), 289.

2. Otto Wenzel, *Kriegsbereit: Der Nationale Verteidigungsrat der DDR 1960 bis 1989* (Cologne, 1995), 19–21; Armin Wagner, *Walter Ulbricht und die geheime Sicherheitspolitik der SED: Der Nationale Verteidigungsrat der DDR und seine Vorgeschichte (1953–1971)* (Berlin, 2002).

3. Walter Janka, *Die Unterwerfung* (Munich and Vienna, 1994).

4. Roger Engelmann and Silke Schumann, "Der Ausbau des Überwachungsstaates. Der Konflikt Ulbricht-Wollweber und die Neuausrichtung des Staatssicherheitsdienstes der DDR 1957," *Vierteljahreshefte für Zeitgeschichte* 43 (1995): 341–78; Jan van Flocken and Michael F. Scholz, *Ernst Wollweber: Saboteur, Minister, Unperson* (Berlin, 1994), 190ff.

5. Karl Schirdewan, *Aufstand gegen Ulbricht* (Berlin, 1994), 211–18.

6. Ibid., 143.

7. *Neues Deutschland*, 1 October 1959, 1.

8. See Hoffmann et al., *Die DDR vor dem Mauerbau*, 306.

9. André Steiner, "Politische Vorstellungen und ökonomische Probleme im Vorfeld der Errichtung der Berliner Mauer. Briefe Walter Ulbrichts an Nikita Chruschtschow," in Hartmut Mehringer, ed., *Von der SBZ zur DDR* (Munich, 1995), 240.

10. Michael Lemke, *Die SED und die Berlinkrise 1958 bis 1963* (Berlin, 1995).

11. Steiner, "Politische Vorstellungen," 240.

12. Falco Werkentin, *Politische Strafjustiz in der Ära Ulbricht* (Berlin, 1995), 243ff.

13. Steiner, "Politische Vorstellungen," 239ff.

14. Ibid., 253.

15. Jürgen Rühle and Günter Holzweißig, *13. August 1961: Die Mauer von Berlin* (Cologne, 1981), 151.

16. Armin Mitter and Stefan Wolle, *Untergang auf Raten: Unbekannte Kapitel der DDR-Geschichte* (Munich, 1993), 344.

17. Werkentin, *Politische Strafjustiz*, 246ff.

18. SAPMO-BArch, DY 30, J IV 2/2/766.

19. Rühle and Holzweißig, *13. August 1961*, 151.

20. Michael Beschloss, *Powergame. Kennedy und Chruschtschow: Die Krisenjahre 1960–1963* (Düsseldorf, 1991), 281, 739.

21. Landtag Mecklenburg-Vorpommern, ed., *Zur Arbeit der Enquête-Kommission "Leben in der DDR, Leben nach 1989: Aufarbeitung und Versöhnung,"* 9 vols. (Schwerin, 1996), 1:103.

22. SAPMO-BArch, DY 30, J IV 2/2/526, Attachment No. 3.

23. Armin Boyens, "Staatssekretariat für Kirchenfragen und Militärseelsorgevertrag. Anmerkungen zur Geschichte eines Amtes," *Kirchliche Zeitgeschichte* 6 (1993): 211–35. See also Thomas Raabe, *SED-Staat und Katholische Kirche* (Paderborn, 1995), 72–76.

24. BAP, DO-4, 354.

25. BAP, DO-4, 2726. This unique, direct confrontation became something of a legend in church circles. See the report by Bernhard Huhn, the youth pastor for the Görlitz disctrict, in Josef Pilvousek, ed., *Kirchliches Leben im totalitären Staat. Seelsorge in der SBZ/DDR 1945–1976* (Hildesheim, 1994), 383ff.

26. "Zu einigen Problemen des Verhältnisses von Staat und Kirche in der DDR," undated document from 1959. BAP, DO-4, 2363, p. 7.

27. Peter Beier, *Die "Sonderkonten Kirchenfragen": Sachleistungen und Geldzuwendungen an Pfarrer und kirchliche Mitarbeiter als Mittel der DDR-Kirchenpolitik (1955–1989/90)* (Göttingen, 1997).

28. SAPMO-BArch, DY 30, IV 2/14/57.

29. See Eggerath's letter of 20 February 1958 to Barth and an undated commentary by Barth. SAPMO-BArch, DY 30, IV, 2/14/58.
30. See the report of the Erfurt district council of 23 September 1959, BAP, DO-4, 2726.
31. Gerhard Lange and Ursula Pruß (eds.): *An der Nahtstelle der Systeme: Dokumente und Texte aus dem Bistum Berlin, 1. Halbband: 1945-1961* (Leipzig, 1996), 242–45.
32. BAP, DO-4, 824.
33. BAP, MdI, HVDVP, Best. 11, 842. These police measures had the desired effect upon the Catholic Church because the ordinaries then issued instructions that "we need to prove to the government that we have taken responsibility for cleansing our libraries of banned literature ourselves." See Pilvousek, *Kirchliches Leben im totalitären Staat*, 529; Lange and Pruß, *An der Nahtstelle der Systeme*, 276ff.
34. Raabe, *SED-Staat und Katholische Kirche*, 224–29.
35. SAPMO-BArch, DY 30, IV 2/14/3.
36. See, for example, the 24 January 1959 analysis by the Dresden district council, SAPMO-BArch, DY 30, IV 2/14/64.
37. SAPMO-BArch, DY 30, IV 2/14/58.
38. SAPMO-BArch, DY 30, IV 2/14/61 and BAP, DO-4, 2557.
39. SAPMO-BArch, DY 30, IV 2/14/4.
40. See the MfS document from 5 May 1959 entitled "Einflußnahme westdeutscher Regierungskreise auf die Entstehung von Dokumenten und Materialien der kath. und ev. Kirche gegen die Regierung der Deutschen Demokratischen Republik," BStU, ZA, AO 20300/92, pp. 125–30.
41. See Engelmann and Schumann, "Der Ausbau des Überwachungsstaates."
42. Ibid., 349. Engelmann and Schumann see this meeting as "a decisive stage in the history of the MfS."
43. Helmut Müller-Enbergs, ed., *Inoffizielle Mitarbeiter des Ministeriums für Staatssicherheit. Richtlinien und Durchführungsbestimmungen*, 2nd ed. (Berlin, 1996), 195–239. On the provisions regarding the church, see Bernd Schäfer, "'Inoffizielle Mitarbeiter' und 'Mitarbeit': Zur Differenzierung von Kategorien des Ministeriums für Staatssicherheit im Bereich der katholischen Kirche," in Klaus-Dietmar Henke and Roger Engelmann, eds., *Aktenlage: Die Bedeutung der Unterlagen des Staatssicherheitsdienstes für die Zeitgeschichtsforschung* (Berlin, 1996), 449ff.
44. Engelmann and Schumann, "Der Ausbau des Überwachungsstaates," 354.
45. Ibid., 355.
46. Clemens Vollnhals, "Die kirchenpolitische Abteilung des Ministeriums für Staatssicherheit," in Clemens Vollnhals, ed., *Die Kirchenpolitik von SED und Staatssicherheit: Eine Zwischenbilanz*, 2nd ed. (Berlin, 1997), 84ff.
47. Gerhard Besier and Stephan Wolf, eds., *Pfarrer, Christen und Katholiken'. Das Ministerium für Staatssicherheit und die Kirchen*, 2nd ed. (Neukirchen and Vluyn, 1992), 190–94.
48. See the HA V/4 surveillance plan of 18 June 1958 (BStU, ZA, BdL 789/58) and the 26-page summary report of 23 August 1958 on the Catholic Congress in Berlin and the related "Catholic Youth Congress" (BStU, ZA, ZAIG, Z 110).
49. BStU, ZA, AP20200/92, p. 14.
50. Compare Spülbeck's detailed report on various conversations he had during his visit to the Vatican in November 1958, which he clearly discussed aloud. BStU, ZA, AP 20201/92, pp. 107–14.
51. BStU, ZA, AP 20200/92, p. 14.
52. BStU, ZA, AP 20200/92, pp. 12ff. See also the detailed report (21 August 1958) on the trial by Erich Mielke to Erich Honecker, BStU, ZA, ZAIG, Z 103, pp. 1–55.
53. BStU, Ast Potsdam, Untersuchungsvorgang 51/58 and AOV 5/59.
54. BStU, ZA, XX/4, 332, p. 25.
55. See Höllen, *Loyale Distanz? Katholizismus und Kirchenpolitik in SBZ und DDR: Ein historischer Überblick in Dokumenten*, Vol. II, 1956 bis 1965 (Berlin, 1997), 2:182ff.

56. DAB, V/5-1-5.
57. See BStU, ZA, AP 12065/92, pp. 12–15 and 25.
58. BStU, ZA, AP 20200/92, p. 18.
59. BStU, ZA, AP 20201/92, pp. 65–68.
60. These included a report describing the MfS installation of the device and Bengsch's discovery of it. BStU, ZA, HA XX/4 3147, pp. 4–10; 27–30.
61. BStU, Ast Dresden, AOP 71/59, Vol. 3, pp. 31–34.
62. BStU, ZA 12065/92, pp. 29–32 and SAPMO-BArch, DY 30, IV 2/14/236.
63. BStU, Ast Chemnitz, AIM 2081/79 ("Gustav"). One priest from Aue (Secret Informer "Wagner") passed information in July 1958 out of a sense of conviction, even typing up sections for the MfS. See BStU, Ast Chemnitz, 593/58 as well as 2592/60 and AIM 1721/69. Because Stasi officers in Berlin boasted to Zinke that they knew the contents of pastoral letters (which the church tried to keep secret using couriers) before they were read, Zinke later began to deliver the final text of the letters to the MfS himself a few days before they were publicly read. The first evidence of this is a handwritten note on a torn-off calendar page—"received from Prelate Z"—on a copy of a 10 February 1963 letter from the BOK (BStU, ZA, AP 11284/92, pp. 108ff.) All of Zinke's successors continued this practice until 1989. Beginning in the mid 1960s, attempts to blackmail priests in order to obtain pastoral letters finally ceased.
64. BStU, Ast Gera, 545/55 and AIM 721/85.
65. BStU, ZA, XX/4, 332, pp. 18–38.
66. BStU, ZA, AOP 614/59 and ZA, HA XX/4, 2694.
67. Vollnhals, "Die kirchenpolitische Abteilung des Ministeriums für Staatssicherheit," 89.
68. SAPMO-BArch, DY 30, IV 2/14/40.
69. ACDP VII-013-857.
70. SAPMO-BArch, DY 30, J IV 2/2/572. Cf. Peter-Paul Straube, *Katholische Studentengemeinde in der DDR als Ort eines außeruniversitären Studium generale* (Leipzig, 1996), 222–39.
71. See Raabe, *SED-Staat und Katholische Kirche,* 166ff., and the detailed directives by the Ministry of Education on 10 June 1958, SAPMO-BArch, DY 30, IV 2/14/8.
72. SAPMO-ABrch, DY 30, J IV 2/2/583.
73. Ibid., J IV 2/2/587.
74. Hermann Wentker, "Die Einführung der Jugendweihe in der DDR: Hintergründe, Motive und Probleme," in Mehringer, *Von der SBZ zur DDR,* 160–64.
75. *Neues Deutschland,* 1 October 1957.
76. SAPMO-BArch, J IV, 2/2/579.
77. See Hermann Wentker, "Ost-CDU und Protestantismus 1949–1958: Die Partei der 'fortschrittlichen Christen' zwischen Repräsentationsanspruch und Transmissionsaufgabe," *Kirchliche Zeitgeschichte* 6 (1993): 374–78.
78. SAPMO-BArch, DY 30, IV 2/14/29.
79. BAP, DO-4, 2363.
80. SAPMO-BArch, IV, 2/14/57.
81. BAP, DO-4, 1918 ("Re: Catholic Orders in the GDR").
82. Norbert Kapferer, *Das Feindbild der marxistisch-leninistischen Philosophie in der DDR 1945–1988* (Darmstadt, 1990), 170–205.
83. Siegfried Kirschke, "Moderne Abstammungslehre und klerikale Propaganda," *Deutsche Zeitschrift für Philosophie* 7 (1959): 603–13.
84. Spülbeck's reply to another article by Kirschke in *Neues Deutschland* in 1958 entitled "The Incompatibility of Science and Faith" was intercepted by the MfS using the "operative technique" in his office in Bautzen. On 12 December 1958 a bug recorded Spülbeck dictating a response that was never published in the GDR. BStU, ZA, AP 20200/92, pp. 204–6.
85. See the work by the SED ZK philosopher Alfred Kosing, "Die 'gesunde Vernunft' des Jesuitenpaters Josef de Vries," *Deutsche Zeitschrift für Philosophie* 7 (1959): 65–85, which also took up a book by Josef de Vries. The polemic endured for quite a while; an East German philosopher

wrote a detailed analysis of the fifth edition of Wetter's *Dialectical Materialism* (1960). See Helmut Metzler, "Pater Wetter kämpft mit stumpfen Waffen," *Deutsche Zeitschrift für Philosophie* 10 (1960): 1554–57.

86. Marlies Oehme, "Die Theorie der katholischen Soziallehre vom 'Klassenfrieden' – ein demagogisches Verwirrungsmanöver des politischen Katholizismus," *Einheit* 13 (1958): 199-210; Willi Barth and Rudi Bellmann, "Die Rechtfertigung der imperialistischen Atomkriegspläne durch den politischen Klerikalismus," *Einheit* 13 (1958): 1564–76; Dieter Bergner and Gernot Preuß, "Differenzierung im politischen Klerikalismus: Zur Enzyklika 'Pacem in Terris,'" *Deutsche Zeitschrift für Philosophie* 11 (1963): 1189–1202.

87. Karl A. Mollnau and Karl-Heinz Schöneburg, "Die sozialtheoretischen Grundlagen des Klerikalfaschismus," *Deutsche Zeitschrift für Philosophie* 7 (1959): 271–89. The theory of "clerical fascism" was first formulated by Walter Ulbricht in the 28 September 1958 issue of *Neues Deutschland*.

88. BAP, DO-4, 2363.

89. Gerhard Besier, *Der SED-Staat und die Kirche: Der Weg in die Anpassung* (Munich, 1993), 261–91.

90. SAPMO-BArch, DY 30, IV 2/14/5.

91. For example, Auxiliary Bishop Schräder from Schwerin suspended Karl Fischer, a Catholic priest and a deputy in the Volkskammer, for participating without authorization in a meeting with Ulbricht as the sole Catholic representative. See Schräder's 24 April 1961 letter to Fischer, ACDP VII-013-452, and Fischer's emotional answer on 30 April, BAP, DO-4, 464.

92. BAP, DO-4, 79.

93. BAP, DO-4, 2441.

94. BAP, DO-4, 362.

95. DAB, 31/43.

96. SAPMO-BArch, DY 30, IV 2/14/58.

97. BAP, DO-4, 362.

98. Dieter Grande and Bernd Schäfer, "Interne Richtlinien und Bewertungsmaßstäbe zu kirchlichen Kontakten mit dem MfS," in Vollnhals, *Die Kirchenpolitik von SED und Staatssicherheit*, 388–404, here 395ff.

99. Zinke's notes on "A Conversation on June 17, 1960," DAB, Asig 31/52, p. 112.

100. DAB, Asig 31/53.

101. See Grande and Schäfer, "Interne Richtlinien," 392ff.

102. BAP, DO-4, 355.

103. DAB, 32/109-2.

104. Lange et al., *Katholische Kirche – Sozialistischer Staat DDR*, 111–20.

105. BAP, DO-4, 362.

106. DAB, Asig 33/133.

107. See the texts in Pilvousek, *Kirchliches Leben im totalitären Staat*, 140, 154ff., 397ff., and 480ff. See also Lange and Pruß, *An der Nahtstelle der Systeme*, 294ff., 337ff., 413ff.

108. See Lange and Pruß, *An der Nahtstelle der Systeme*, 246–49 and 324ff.; Pilvousek, *Kirchliches Leben im totalitären Staat*, 523–27, 535–43, 388–91, 246.

109. DAB, Asig 32/109-2.

110. DAB, Asig 32/109-3. The word "inner" is underlined in the original.

111. BStU, ZA, 20200/91, p. 174ff. Döpfner and Spülbeck categorically rejected Rintelen's position. Döpfner said, "this Rintelen is beginning to waver as a pillar of the church."

112. For an example of one such questionnaire from Görlitz in 1960, see Pilvousek, *Kirchliches Leben im totalitären Staat*, 400.

113. DAB, Asig 32/109-2 and 109-3.

114. See Herbert Prauß, "Doch es war nicht die Wahrheit," *Petrusblatt*, 4 September 1960.

115. DAB, Asig 31/47, p. 392.

116. DAB, Asig 32/109-3.

117. BStU, ZA, AP 20201/92, pp. 109ff.
118. BStU, ZA, AP 20200/92, p. 135.
119. Ibid., 119.
120. Lange and Pruß, *An der Nahtstelle der Systeme*, 426ff.
121   122. See the government's report of 3 March 1960, BAP, DO-4, 828.
122. Ibid.
123. Reported by the MfS, BStU, ZA, AP 12065/62, pp. 29–32.
124. Lange et al., *Katholische Kirche – Sozialistischer Staat DDR*, 180ff.
125. Pilvousek, "Innenansichten," 1136.
126. Ibid., 1140–44.
127. DAB, Asig 31/54, Bl. 571. Alfred Bengsch was the author of this recommendation.
128. BStU, ZA, AP 20200/92, p. 133f.
129. Pilvousek, *Kirchliches Leben im totalitären Staat*, 158–67.
130. BStU, ZA, AP 22533/92, p. 237f.
131. See the report of 24 February 1959 by the Görlitz city council to the Dresden council, HStA Dresden, Bt/RdB, 25078. Auxiliary Bishop Rintelen read it in Magdeburg with an addition that qualified it, for which he was criticized in the BOK. BAP, DO-4, 844.
132. DAB, Asig 31/51.
133. Ibid.
134. Heinrich Krone, *Tagebücher*, vol.1 (Düsseldorf, 1995), 309, 347.
135. Rome considered transferring Döpfner to Munich by April 1961 at the latest. Ibid., 494.
136. DAB, V/5-7-2.
137. ROO, H VIII.
138. DAB, V/5-7-2.
139. BAP, DO-4, 1302.
140. Bengsch was elected on 27 July 1961 by secret ballot, as per the Prussian concordat of 1929. See Theodor Schmitz, "Die Bischofswahlen in Berlin zwischen 1945 und 1989," in Heinrich J. F. Reinhardt, ed., *Theologia et Jus Canonicum: Festgabe für Heribert Heinemann zur Vollendung seines 70. Lebensjahres* (Essen, 1995), 610.
141. MfS report of 19 August 1961, BStU, ZA, ZAIG, Z 457.
142. On Döpfner's departure sermon, see Lange and Pruß, *An der Nahtstelle der Systeme*, 421–25.
143. Höllen, *Loyale Distanz*, 2:276.
144. SAPMO-BArch, DY 30, J IV 2/2/78.
145. Höllen, *Loyale Distanz*, 2:276, 282.
146. SAPMO-BArch, J IV 2/2/790.
147. Besier, *Der SED-Staat und die Kirche: Der Weg in die Anpassung*, 423–31.
148. BAP, DO-4, 2722.
149. File note of 15 September 1961, "On the Visit of Prelate Bernhard Drews," ibid.
150. ROO, A III 15.
151. BAP, DO-4, 824.
152. BStU, ZA, AP 12065/92, p. 98.
153. See the state's transcript of 4 November 1961, BAP, DO-4, 824, and Bengsch's report of 2 November ROO, A VIII 6.
154. *Neues Deutschland*, 3 November 1961.
155. Transcript of 4 November 1961, BAP, DO-4, 824, p. 22. Cf. Lange and Pruß, *An der Nahtstelle der Systeme*, 454; and Friedrich Maria Rintelen, *Erinnerungen ohne Tagebuch*, 3rd edition (Paderborn, 1988), 178.
156. MfS report of 23 May 1962, BStU, HA XX/4, 1134.
157. BStU, ZA, AP 20202/92, p. 59 (Report by Secret Informer "Schüler").
158. Ibid., 57 (Report by Secret Informer "Oberhaus").
159. ROO, A VIII 15.

Chapter 4

1961–1971

The GDR on the Path to International Recognition

SED Attempts to Gain Legitimacy at Home and Abroad

After the Berlin Wall sealed off the exterior, the SED leadership used multifaceted repression to increase its internal "vigilance"—especially in connection with the 17 September municipal elections, which took place without any visible disturbances. With the border closings, the Politburo and National Security Council made detailed decisions on the construction and military security of the blockades.[1] On 24 August 1961 the "Law for the Defense of the GDR" was passed. Another regulation concerned currency exchange between "the GDR, including its capital" and West Germany, requiring that all holdings in West German marks be declared and exchanged at a 1:1 ratio to the Deutsche Notenbank der DDR. On 25 August, a law limiting movement and residency took effect, which included penalties such as work camps for "transients" and "elements averse to employment" and restricting a person's movement to a specific residential area.[2] In late August, the Politburo decreed that "unreliable persons" would be forced to resettle away from restricted areas near the border—the second such comprehensive measure since the 1952 actions—and carried this out after the municipal elections of 3 October 1961.[3]

After the Berlin Wall went up, "order campaigns" by the FDJ (Free German Youth)—some within the framework of the "Aktion Blitz" against "ideological fence-sitting"—forcibly militarized the youth. In numerous locations, FDJ members vandalized antennas on the roofs of private apartments in East Berlin to disrupt the Western radio reception in advance of the 5 and 9 September 1961 municipal elections.[4] After the FDJ had already initiated a campaign for

---

voluntary military service, the SED Politburo, on 29 August 1961, confirmed the National Security Council's proposal to introduce universal compulsory military service. The law took effect on 24 January 1962.

Further revelations by Khrushchev about the crimes of Stalin at the Twelfth Party Congress in October 1961 led to a cosmetic "de-Stalinization" in the GDR; "Stalinstadt," for example, was renamed "Eisenhüttenstadt." Stalinist practices nonetheless prevailed between August and December 1961. Alongside numerous measures within the SED against members charged with "ideological confusion" or "defeatism," the second half of 1961 saw the largest wave of arrests since the creation of the GDR. From August through December, the number of convictions for political "state crimes" quadrupled compared with the "soft line" previously pursued.[5]

The SED clearly felt more secure beginning in mid 1962 and believed that it had managed to stabilize the GDR by sealing the borders and applying "pacification" measures domestically. On 17 April 1962 the Politburo approved a bill concerning "the further development of socialist law," which instructed the courts to use more discretion in meting out punishments and to show more restraint in issuing arrest orders. Within the framework of this "new legal course," some 16,000 prisoners were released beginning in June.[6] Further legal reforms in April 1963 put the rhetoric of the SED party program from the Sixth Party Congress (15–21 January 1963) into practice: "Our state, which serves justice for everyone . . . is the German state grounded in the rule of law."[7] An additional sign that the GDR leadership was relaxing its stance was its 17 December 1963 agreement with the West Berlin senate on cross-border travel. Between 18 December and 5 January 1964, more than 1.3 million West Berliners were once again able to make day trips to visit their relatives in the eastern part of the city (for the first time in over two years).[8] Between 1964 and 1966, four further travel agreements were reached. Beginning in September 1964, all GDR citizens of retirement age could travel to the FRG, initially once yearly. Mandatory daily currency exchange for West Germans visiting the GDR was introduced on 1 December 1964.

With its more secure position, the SED used the Sixth Party Congress in January 1963 to announce that the phase of "Building Up Socialism" was coming to an end and "developed socialism" was expanding as the country transitioned toward communism as an ultimate goal. Targeting the younger generation, the party launched one of the last ideological offensives "planned from above" in the history of the GDR to create "the new socialist man." On 28 September 1963 the draft of a "youth law" was published, and on 4 May 1964 the "Law on the Participation of Youth in the German Democratic Republic in the Struggle for the Comprehensive Construction of Socialism and the All-Around Promotion of Its Initiatives from Leaders in the Economy, the State, Professional Life, Schools, Culture and Sports" took effect. On 7 September 1964, reacting to young people's illegal refusal to participate in military service, the National Security Council initiated a mechanism—unique among the Warsaw Pact countries—that allowed for the creation of unarmed labor units that required neither military ranks nor oaths of allegiance to the flag. The "Unified Socialist Education Act" of 22 February 1965 and the decision of the Council of Ministers on "Boosting the Effectiveness of State Youth Policies" of 15 July 1965 contained further provisions for educating and training all youth to be "socialist personalities."[9]

SED leaders, as well as the majority of their age cohort in the party, had perceived a creeping liberalism in art, literature, film, and television in the GDR since 1963. They believed this product of Western influence on clothing, hairstyles, sexuality, and popular music was corrupting the youth. Delegates to the Eleventh Plenary of the SED Central Committee in December 1965 received a dossier containing numerous reports of juvenile delinquency, "rowdiness," and alcoholism; specific films and books were denounced.[10] The plenary speakers, especially Erich Honecker and Ulbricht, sharply attacked "liberal [capitalist] softening up" among artists and intellectuals, specifically Wolf Biermann, Robert Havemann, and Stefan Heym. Honecker, for example, proclaimed: "Our German Democratic Republic is a clean state. Our state has irrevocable measures for ethics and morality, respectability and good comportment. Our party stands decidedly against the amoral propaganda spread by the imperialists, with their goal of damaging socialism."[11] Moreover, liberalization in the public sphere and in social life posed a challenge to the party's power and served only Western "opponents." In the wake of this meeting, twelve DEFA films (films of the Deutsche Film AG, or German Film Corporation) from 1965 were banned, other projects were broken off, television programs were altered, book manuscripts were left unpublished, and "beat" groups were disbanded. Robert Havemann, who had already been removed from the SED and from his position as a professor at Humboldt University in 1964 after giving some lectures considered too critical, was now excluded from the GDR Academy of Sciences. Despite his previous work for the MfS, he became a dissident.[12]

Socialist society—protected by fortified borders—could not, however, develop without external influences—especially in the more relaxed global context (which the GDR needed because of its lack of international recognition). The SED (and the MfS), in typical fashion, attributed problems in GDR society exclusively to their opponents in the West. After the ZK plenary, repressive measures and surveillance once again increased. On 15 May 1966 Mielke issued a directive "to combat politically and operatively political-ideological deviations and underground activities within youth circles in the GDR." In another instruction issued at the same time, he declared:

> In psychological warfare, the youth in the GDR are a particular target. A coordinated interaction among the state apparatus in Bonn, Western intelligence agencies, and other nuclei of ideological diversion, among West German youth organizations, film clubs and fan clubs, among churches, radio, print media, and television, aims to isolate the GDR youth from the influence of socialist ideology and to force it into passivity, to create an atmosphere of general insecurity and—in certain areas—to create conditions that lead to the formation of youth gangs.[13]

The new criminal code that went into effect on 1 July 1968 expanded the scope of criminal law and listed various "crimes against the GDR" even before crimes against individuals. The party aimed to achieve internal stabilization no longer through "outspoken terror on the part of the justice system," because of its impact on foreign policy, but through covert operations of the MfS.[14] Pragmatically, the party regarded criminal penalties as a last resort when the more usual means of intimidation and the "operational degradation" of targeted persons proved to be ineffective.

The Attractiveness of Socialist Reform Models

At its Sixth Party Congress in January 1963, after the mistakes in the planned economy since 1958, the SED aimed to build "developed socialism" using more "scientific methods." It proclaimed a new economic policy intended to raise productivity and equal the FRG's standard of living by replacing detailed management with broad centralized directives.[15] Ulbricht saw the new structure as a model for the entire socialist camp. But differences with the USSR soon emerged: Soviet leaders found their ally's independent "national" policy suspicious, especially with its missionary zeal. The USSR insisted that the GDR hold to its obligations within the Council for Mutual Economic Assistance. Furthermore, the USSR took advantage of its strong position as a supplier of raw materials to the resource-hungry GDR. The five-year agreement on technological and scientific cooperation between the USSR and the GDR that was signed in Berlin in 3 December 1965 ended the GDR's high-flying hopes that its economic reform plans would serve as a model. Erich Apel—the GDR official who was given much latitude under the economic reform program—committed suicide in his office that very day.[16] In September 1966, however, a special Commercial Coordination department (promoted by the MfS) was established within the trade ministry to secure hard currency through legal and covert means for the state and party leadership. As we shall see, this department was later very relevant to "church business."

Whereas, in the GDR, cultural and economic liberalization suffered a setback at this time, in Czechoslovakia a wide-ranging wave of reform impacted the entire society, including its Communist Party. The reform process accelerated when Alexander Dubcek became first secretary of the party in January 1968. But even before 1968, segments of the Eastern European intelligentsia were increasingly receptive to reform socialism. They criticized "real existing socialism" and used utopian socialist perspectives to challenge it, seeking a "third way" between Western capitalism and Eastern European state socialism. "Convergence theory" became popular; it held that global modernization would present common challenges to social systems across borders. The new US and Allied policy of détente and the Ostpolitik coming from the West German government led to numerous cross-border meetings between politicians, scholars, scientists, and private individuals.

The GDR praised its own policies as a model for all industrialized countries. At the Seventh SED Party Congress in April 1967, Ulbricht put forward the theory that "developed socialism" was an additional, wide-ranging stage between socialism and the now more distant goal of communism. On 31 January 1968 he proposed—within the context of the GDR's sovereignty campaign—to revise parts of the outdated 1949 constitution. But public debates and the referendum of 6 April 1968 on the final text of the constitution were merely cosmetic measures.

In clear contrast to the "constitutional debates" in the GDR, events in Czechoslovakia increasingly slipped beyond the control of the CSSR Politburo and Communist Party. Czechoslovakia's Communist "brother parties" grew ever more alarmed at the open discussions in the CSSR media, the growing pluralism of public opinion, and the new pragmatic contacts with Western countries. The SED saw "social democratic" and "revisionist" tendencies on the rise and conspiratorial "counterrevolutionary forces" at work in the CSSR. After Communist leaders from the USSR, GDR, Poland, Hungary, and Bulgaria failed to persuade Czechoslovakian Communists to take action against the reform—at a 23 March summit in Dresden and at another on 3 August in Bratislava—the five states intervened militarily on 21 August 1968, fulfilling what would come to be known as the Brezhnev Doctrine.[17] Whereas Ulbricht praised the "rescue" of Czechoslovakia, many in the GDR were disappointed and angry that developments they had attached great hopes to were crushed. Reform-oriented intellectual circles in Eastern Europe found their dreams of transforming socialism destroyed by the violent end to the "Prague Spring" and the graveyard-like silence of the "normalization" that followed. At the same time, there were many in Western Europe, as well as among the GDR intelligentsia and some also in the churches, who maintained a belief in a utopian socialism they believed was fundamentally superior to capitalism. The SED leadership, however, found such positions especially dangerous because they threatened the party's monopoly on the interpretation of socialism.

International and German-German Strategies

The GDR's foreign policy and its policy toward West Germany were always dependent upon its relationship with the USSR. The policies of the leading FRG ruling coalition toward the GDR (and those of the opposition), in turn, were constrained by the country's claim to be Germany's sole legitimate political representative and by the Hallstein Doctrine, which held that Bonn would sever (or not initiate) diplomatic ties with any country that recognized the GDR. The GDR's efforts to counter this doctrine and gain international recognition first achieved some success when Ulbricht was received in Egypt in February 1965, but diplomatic recognition remained limited to the Communist bloc. The new Grand Coalition government in West Germany, formed in December 1966, undertook a modified policy toward Eastern Bloc nations. It sought to establish direct contacts with the USSR, and the CSSR promoted itself as a partner in dialogue. The FRG established diplomatic relations with Romania in January 1967, which made Romania the second country (after the USSR) to have embassies in both German states. In February, Warsaw Pact countries decided that no further socialist countries would open diplomatic relations with the FRG until it recognized the GDR; this established the Ulbricht Doctrine, which opposed the Hallstein Doctrine.

The SED now increased its efforts to achieve sovereignty distinct from the FRG through political means and symbolic acts. The words "*gesamtdeutsch*" (Germany in its entirety, all-German) and "*innerdeutsch*" (denoting intra-German affairs across the FRG/GDR border) were dropped from official speech. The SED leadership saw West Germany's Ostpolitik as a sophisticated strategy within an overall plan to undermine the socialist camp with "ideological diversion" and the especially dangerous idea of "social democracy." On 20 February 1967 the GDR Volkskammer passed its own citizenship legislation. Travel to the FRG was supervised to an even greater degree. The pinnacle of the sovereignty campaign was the new constitution, which defined the GDR as a "socialist state of the German nation."

Internally, the GDR state apparatus pushed "ideological vigilance." The MfS equated "ties with the West" with "initiating contact with the enemy" and monitored such contacts with extreme suspicion, recruiting more minors as informers for this purpose.[18] An MfS directive from January 1968 claimed that the West German "enemy" was targeting universities in a centralized strategy of psychological warfare.[19] During times of political risk-taking abroad, the SED leadership fell back on a simplistic concept of the "enemy" and tightened its control and surveillance mechanisms, probably for psychological comfort. Extensive spy networks provided GDR leaders with a great deal of insider information on West German politicians and their strategies, which made them feel justified in their defensive stance toward "ideological diversions." The GDR systematically spied upon West German intellectuals and journalists who met with GDR citizens as they pursued their version of Ostpolitik, in part privately, and in part in the official service of West German politicians.

After the "danger" in the CSSR had been repressed, massive Soviet support brought a first wave of diplomatic recognition to the GDR, largely by Arab countries, in 1969. On 30 May 1969 the FRG modified its Hallstein Doctrine, declaring that it would not automatically break off relations with countries that recognized the GDR. After the left-liberal coalition won the elections in the FRG on 17 December 1969, Ulbricht sent West German President Heinemann an outline of a treaty for "equal relations." On 19 March 1970 the new federal chancellor, Willy Brandt, traveled to Erfurt to meet GDR Minister-President Stoph for the first time, and on 21 May the meetings continued in Kassel. These summits marked the end of the Hallstein and Ulbricht Doctrines and explored the possibilities of relations regulated by treaty. The GDR sought international recognition, and the FRG wanted the SED to make humanitarian improvements and establish stronger German-German relations. However, the SED continued to perceive such relations as a danger. Moreover, the risks of West German Ostpolitik were quite familiar to the USSR, as Honecker's notes from a 18 July 1970 meeting with Brezhnev in Moscow attest. Brezhnev apparently opined that Brandt's aims were the same as those of the rightist Franz-Josef Strauß: a "capitalist system" and "the liquidation of the GDR."[20] The USSR, he said, "would not allow" the GDR to be weakened and "annexed" to the FRG. In Brezhnev's view, the new policy of pursuing treaties should, "by contrast," lead "to a secure separation, a divide between East and West Germany." In August 1970 the West German government signed a mutual non-aggression treaty with the USSR in Moscow, and in December 1970 with Poland, thereby recognizing the then-current borders in Europe as the status quo.

In 1970, Honecker, working in close cooperation with Brezhnev, led the SED Politburo in a concerted effort to force Ulbricht to step down because of his high-handedness and his increasing unreliability. Honecker was named the new first secretary at the Eighth SED Party Congress in June 1971. Loyal to the Soviet Union, he championed the two-German-state principle portraying the GDR as "the socialist German nation."

Kirchenpolitik in the Confined GDR

After 1961 the Office of the State Secretary for Church Affairs put the "differentiation policy" into practice only very slowly in relation to the Catholic Church, concentrating almost exclusively on the Protestant Church. In a 28 June 1963 document for a meeting at the State Secretariat for Church Affairs, the new director of the Catholic Church Working Group, Frank Rupprecht, stated that the next step "for well-planned work" would be "a full political evaluation of the Catholic Church in the GDR."[21] Attached to the document was a questionnaire for all fifteen GDR districts, requesting statistics, political reports, and personal evaluations of leading Catholic officials. Rupprecht used these reports to compose a twenty-one-page "Complex Evaluation of the Catholic Church in the German Democratic Republic."[22] His report noted that the "differentiation policy" had not yet been applied systematically to the Catholic clergy.

Several different attempts to "positively" influence Catholic clergy to support the GDR and its policies had preceded this internal report. The GDR state saw participation in elections as a measurable indicator for evaluating the "progressiveness" of Catholic officials. Obviously, many priests could afford not to vote because the state was not interested in forcing 100 percent participation among this relatively small population segment. The pragmatic approach of other priests—who often made their voting contingent upon some concrete advantage for the local churches or who were worried about their institutions—was not, however, noted in the government analyses, nor were their actual votes (i.e., voting "no").[23]

GDR officials considered their patient "dialogue policy"—whereby the case for socialism and an "affirmative state consciousness" was pitched to both higher and lower-ranking clergy in small groups or individually—to be a more effective means of Kirchenpolitik. On 14 January 1964 the Politburo of the ZK of the SED decided on a "political-tactical" concept with which to approach the Catholic Church. In order to promote differentiation, the decision stated, "more exacting and consequential conversations would be now be possible."[24] The faith in the superiority of the socialist system, which many GDR state and party officials held at least through the mid 1970s, led them to hope that adept political handling and "education" would win religious people over to socialism. These dialogues also presented opportunities for GDR officials to try to chip away at solidarity within the churches and to learn more about their internal workings. They were also well aware that church representatives would attempt to use the dialogues to their advantage.

The dialogues between Catholic ordinaries and GDR state offices, which gradually became an institution, must be distinguished from the GDR state's attempts—both targeted and spontaneous—to engage with middle and lower-level Catholic clergy. Within the BOK, Archbishop Bengsch tried to limit all church-political conversations with state officials to himself or his staff (or at least to have them take part in such conversations). The Catholic ordinaries in the GDR rejected the idea of several bishops meeting together with the state secretary (as was done in Czechoslovakia, Poland, and Hungary) as they did not consider the SED Politburo an opportune partner.[25] Beginning in August 1964, however, State Secretary for Church Affairs Fritz Flint succeeded in meeting regularly with the ordinaries in Görlitz, Magdeburg, Schwerin, and Erfurt—in no small measure because the bishops outside of Berlin wanted these meetings themselves. In Berlin, State Secretary Seigewasser met annually with Bengsch and also regularly with Bishop Spülbeck in Dresden. He had additional unofficial meetings with Rintelen in Magdeburg and Berlin.

The meetings with mid- and lower-level clergy involved officials from the State Secretariat for Church Affairs and district governments, as well as staff from the CDU and the National Front. It was hoped that regular contacts could lead some clergy to make contact with the MfS. The state organs developed a "supervising system" that assigned specific government agents to certain church officials,[26] sending staff from the State Secretariat to visit even the tiniest parishes to manage this. Priests from the CSSR and Hungary who worked with their governments and cooperated with the secret police were invited to the GDR to meet with Catholic clergy and try to persuade them of the virtues of socialism. There were long-term plans for priests from the GDR to travel to Czechoslovakia and Hungary on "vacation exchange" programs.[27] But these did not materialize, except for one visit in August 1964 when two Catholic clergy from Erfurt went to Prague.

To prepare for this "breakthrough," Hans Weise from the State Secretariat had to travel to Prague himself.[28]

For the GDR state, the efforts involved in these measures were disproportionate to the results. The "politics with the mark"—i.e., the special bank accounts district councils used to pay clerical informants who advanced the state "differentiation policy"—were also irrelevant in the case of Catholic clergy in the GDR, with only a few exceptions.[29] The State Secretariat for Church Affairs promised "to win over fifteen Catholic clergy in each district to express support for the GDR" for the twentieth anniversary of the state in 1969. In a 8 September 1969 meeting, Horst Hartwig, head of the agency's Catholic section, claimed to have achieved this goal, "if one considers the Catholic clergy's willingness to engage in dialogue."[30] The state interpreted even a simple willingness to talk with one of its representatives as "support for the GDR."

The church's internal rules for conversations with state officials meant that, despite professions of loyalty in a few individual cases, no Catholic clergy or lay official was prepared to make an official positive declaration regarding the GDR as a state or to express a partisan stand. Yet despite the State Secretariat's initial unified plan, the state differentiation policy gradually drew distinctions among the Catholic dioceses in cities where ordinaries were based. And the state offices also gradually adapted to the personalities of individual ordinaries and their leading staff. In Berlin, the central dialogue between Hans Seigewasser, State Secretary for Church Affairs, and Archbishop (later Cardinal) Bengsch, as chair of the BOK, superseded the pattern of "working with" the diocese. Beginning in 1962, the two usually held an annual summit meeting. Otherwise, the state secretary's representatives and Bernhard Drews (later general vicar), and sometimes also Otto Groß and Theodor Schmitz, advisors to the ordinary, carried out the talks. After Drews died in September 1967, Groß became Bengsch's sole authorized negotiator with the State Secretariat for Church Affairs as well as the Ministry of Foreign and Inner-German Trade (MAI) and MfS.

The State Secretariat analyzed every conversation with Archbishop Bengsch, searching for signs of "progress," and was almost always disappointed with the results. In one conversation of 21 February 1967, described as "difficult and fundamental overall," Bengsch compared the GDR to the Nazi state and characterized the socialist state as "intolerant by its very nature." Thereafter, the Office of the State Secretariat requested a "political profile" of the archbishop,[31] which CDU journalist Hubertus Guske composed on 12 March:

> It seems that he has been wishing for years to coarsely express his true position on the GDR and the Bonn regime . . . He said everything he must have been thinking. The file notes on the content of this conversation represent Bengsch's political profile. His arguments are unmistakably derived from the West German arsenal of lies.[32]

The conversation of 15 July 1968 also had "the features of a fundamental ideological confrontation." Nevertheless, the state believed it had made "progress" because for the first time, Bengsch had agreed to the publication of a news release summarizing the conversation.[33] Following a talk on 13 May 1969, however, State Secretary Seigewasser ascertained that relations to Bengsch and the Catholic Church had "stiffened," and, consequently, he would strengthen regional efforts and limit Cardinal Bengsch's travel to West Berlin.[34]

Increasingly, the talks took on a ritual character and dealt with "factual matters." For matters pertaining to the Catholic Church, the State Secretariat for Church Affairs increasingly lost ground to the MfS, which slowly became the decisive state agency with regard to the Catholic Church in the GDR. Initiatives on the part of the main assistant negotiator, Otto Groß, also led to this development.

The situation in Erfurt was similar to that of Berlin. In talks, Deputy State Secretary Fritz Flint, the Erfurt district council, and Hugo Aufderbeck had hardened their positions. Aufderbeck had come to Erfurt from Magdeburg in July 1962 as an auxiliary bishop with the right of succession, becoming the new ordinary there after Joseph Freusberg's death in 1964. In a report from 7 August 1962, the State Secretariat's office interpreted Aufderbeck's placement as the "destruction" of positive initiatives begun in conversations with Freusberg, Joseph Schönauer in Meiningen, and Joseph Streb in Eichsfeld.[35] With the exception of Streb, a provost in Heiligenstadt who adhered to a kind of autonomous Kirchenpolitik until he retired in 1967,[36] the Catholic Church in Thuringia under Aufderbeck pursued a decidedly anti-Communist course, often making critical remarks in public sermons. In a "complex evaluation" of Aufderbeck in February 1964, the state had already ascribed a hardened viewpoint and a degradation of relations to him.[37] The ZK distributed notes from a sermon he had given at the annual men's pilgrimage to Klüschen Hagis in Eichsfeld in May 1965 to all members of the SED Politburo. The district council in Erfurt was instructed to give Aufderbeck the "necessary warnings" and to make him distance himself from his sermon.[38] The conflict intensified following the women's pilgrimage in Dingelstädt on 18 July 1965; a state "observer" again recorded objectionable statements in Aufderbeck's sermon. But although similar stand-offs in Erfurt ensued in the years to come, the district government did not carry out the threatened sanctions. After a conversation with Aufderbeck on 26 February 1970, a representative of the State Secretariat noted that one "can in no way speak of progress" in the case of the auxiliary bishop of Erfurt.[39]

The state paid less attention to various other centralist, less populous Catholic jurisdictions, even when it ascertained that the officeholders in them were more flexible than church leaders in Berlin or Erfurt. Bernhard Schräder, the auxiliary bishop of Schwerin, negotiated on his own with the district council in Mecklenburg, and sometimes also with a representative of the State Secretariat for Church Affairs. Gerhard Schaffran, bishop of Görlitz, who succeeded Ferdinand Piontek in 1963, acted in a similarly independent fashion. His style was to appear loyal behind closed doors. Even before he became the new bishop of Meißen in 1979, state agents noted that a 1969 conversation with him was "perhaps the best yet . . . with a Catholic bishop."[40]

The regional state organs that had the most notable strategies vis-à-vis the Catholic Church were the district councils of Magdeburg and Dresden. The measures they applied were quite contradictory, not least because of the differing personalities of the local church representatives. In Magdeburg, the state attempted to "differentiate" between specific persons; in Dresden, it followed a strategy of summary repression. The GDR officials in charge of church affairs in Magdeburg, Fritz Steinbach and Fritz Bellstedt, successfully established a personal and almost friendly relationship with the prelate Heinrich Jäger, who, as the de facto representative of Auxiliary Bishop Rintelen, also negotiated with state offices in Halle. No Catholic clergyman in the GDR matched Jäger as an example of the success of the GDR "differentiation policy." Bellstedt noted in a report that "we use our relationship with Jäger to carry out our idea of cooperation with the Catholic leaders in the area." [41] Auxiliary Bishop Rintelen himself held numerous personal talks with the district councils in Magdeburg and Halle, with the deputy of the state secretary for church affairs, and later with State Secretary Seigewasser himself, as well as with the chairman of the CDU district association for Magdeburg, Ulrich Fahl. The first "success" of the state policy of dialogue was that Rintelen no longer prohibited clergy under his authority from speaking with government agencies, as long as they did not take any political positions. Furthermore, Rintelen and Jäger responded to the state's requests to transfer specific clergy who displeased them, although the results of these changes were ambivalent. On 5 December 1966 Rintelen and Jäger had a decidedly political and, in many ways, state-supportive dialogue with the Magdeburg district council and agreed to a joint public statement. The council sent reports of a successful example of "differentiation" to Seigewasser.[42]

The government's handling of church events related to the 1,000-year anniversary of the Diocese of Magdeburg in 1968 was intended to serve as an expression of the "Magdeburg line." In contrast to the greater Dresden region, where the Diocese of Meißen was also celebrating a millennium, the Magdeburg authorities gave the church a fair degree of latitude. On 29 June 1967 Fritz Bellstedt wrote his colleague from the Dresden district council that "our Catholic Church is not burdened by negative forces of the Catholic leadership in West Germany, as is the case with the Protestants."[43] In a 5 February 1968 memo, the Office of the First Secretary of the SED District Leadership in Magdeburg justified the difference in its actions, calling Rintelen "the most progressive bishop in the GDR" and claiming that the 1,000-year anniversary was supposed to produce "a process of differentiation within the church."[44] On 17 July 1968 the government suddenly approved the publication of a Catholic Festschrift—with only minor censorial intrusions—that it had blocked on 19 June.[45] For the GDR as a whole, however, it issued a confidential ruling on 30 May instructing districts to reject requests from West German citizens to visit for church events. Additionally, all requests for printing and "all violations of law by clergy or church institutions" were to be reported to the district councils, and "church requests for additional public transportation" were to be "rejected in an appropriate way, without reference to government directives."[46] Just before the celebrations were to begin in Magdeburg on 7 September 1968, the district council held a final talk with Auxiliary Bishop Rintelen on 3 September, receiving assurances that the event would in no way be political and that all sermons would have only theological content. There was special concern that the church take no position regarding recent events in Czechoslovakia.[47]

More than 20,000 people took part in the Magdeburg commemoration. The four hundred delegates, organized into nine working groups, discussed a wide range of religious and social themes. Religious services for youth overflowed. Over 1,000 people filled Magdeburg's Maxim Gorky Theater for a ceremonial event. Party and state operatives reported extensively on the festivities and had some difficulty making their analyses match up to the premature official predictions of success in "differentiation." An MfS summary of 13 September 1968 listed numerous "dangerous" developments and critical remarks by speakers and participants.[48] In meetings on 11 and 17 September, State Secretary Seigewasser opined that "the millennium celebration in Magdeburg was turned into a Catholic demonstration in a Protestant stronghold—where did these 20,000 participants come from?"[49] The state's flexibility had been "exploited," he said, and "it must be made clear to those comrades who were responsible in Magdeburg that things cannot continue this way." Seigewasser's deputy, Flint, demanded "an end to this willingness for more concessions."

The differentiation policy in Magdeburg thus clearly demonstrated the limits of the state's possibilities. The church interpreted "state accommodation" as the product of its own tactics. The grassroots church community increasingly engaged in a wide spectrum of church-related and socially critical activities (which Rintelen largely tolerated), especially in the Magdeburg and Halle districts. Indeed, contacts with GDR Protestants and with the West became so intense that the state offices had more problems with the Catholic Church in Magdeburg than in any other region in the GDR. State interventions with individuals did little in the end, especially since Auxiliary Bishop Rintelen was removed after he met with Seigewasser on 18 June 1969 and issued a joint statement "in support of the GDR government's peace policies."[50] The Magdeburg district council could not work in the same way with the new bishop, Johannes Braun, because he forced Jäger—who had been useful for the differentiation policy—into the background and removed him as a negotiating partner.

In the Diocese of Meißen, the state based its policies on the view that Bishop Spülbeck represented a perpetual danger. The GDR found no clergy with "positive views" in his entourage who might be used for "differentiation." State "accommodation" was thus correspondingly low. In Dresden, the district council's section for religious affairs under Walter Breitmann and his successor Horst Dohle (directed by the council) pursued an unusually large and systematic "differentiation" policy. Their work with individuals as part of their "handling" strategy led to numerous and gradually more intense contacts with Catholic clergy and lay persons. Some of these contacts later played a large role when the MfS attempted to recruit informers. On 6 April 1967, without any central directive, the Dresden district council composed a one-time thirty-three-page "Evaluation of the Catholic Church (Diocese of Meißen) in the District of Dresden."[51] The report was especially suspicious of Catholic youth work and the church's role among the Sorbs in Bautzen and Kamenz: "The Catholic Church plays itself up as the guardian of the Sorbian national idea, language, and culture."[52] Surveillance of these activities intensified around the celebrations of the 1,000-year anniversary of the Diocese of Meißen in 1968. Horst Hartwig from the State Secretariat had already composed a detailed report on the upcoming celebrations of 5 July 1967, in which he placed them within the political context of the "diversion" of Bonn's Ostpolitik and the tradition of "expansionism" toward Eastern Europe.[53] On the basis of these overheated ideological claims, state entities monitored this Catholic event to a degree unprecedented in the GDR.

When Bishop Spülbeck and some of his staff appeared for a meeting with representatives of the Dresden district council, the state had made great preparations to engage them on "matters of principle": it exhorted the church to schedule celebrations on church property, not to collaborate with the Protestant Church, and not to invite foreign guests; it also prohibited commemorative publications.[54] On 16 January 1968 it presented a "Plan for Political-Ideological Work in Connection with the 1,000-Year Anniversary of the Diocese of Meißen" in the Dresden district council, consisting almost entirely of propagandistic counter-events by state agencies and the National Front.[55] It also planned measures to counter the Meißen celebrations in Bautzen, Leipzig, Zwickau, Karl-Marx-Stadt, and Gera. Informers were deployed, and round-the-clock operations teams were formed. What the state organized for the first time for these millennium celebrations would be a model for future bureaucratic control and attempts to influence the churches. Dohle, the most effective official for church affairs in the entire GDR, made use of this model from 1969 to 1971 in the case of the Meißen synod in Dresden's Hofkirche.

The death of Bishop Spülbeck brought about a change in relations with the district government. Gerhard Schaffran, previously the bishop of Görlitz, was inaugurated as his successor on 17 October 1970. Even before his first official visit to the district council in Dresden on 12 January 1971, the bishop sounded new notes in the church-state dialogue with his vigorous attempts to move the bishop's seat and administration from Bautzen to Dresden. In file notes from 18 November 1970, Dohle wrote:

> The state's previous line was clear: massive disruption of any attempt by the diocese to move . . . That position assumed that there was no interest in transferring a bishop's seat to a socialist metropolis. On the other hand, we must consider that, given the intensity with which the proposed move has been given a renewed push by Bishop Schaffran, it could be accomplished without the approval of the state. If this danger

is too great, then it is worth considering whether the move should be approved and a high political price demanded for it.[56]

Some Catholic officials and members of the CDU constituted a component of the state's differentiation policy. In October 1961, financial support from the National Council of the National Front enabled the publication of the journal *begegnung—Monatsschrift deutscher Katholiken,* which had been planned since July 1960.[57] The first chief editor was Hubertus Guske, a former journalist for the CDU's central organ, *Neue Zeit.* Guske had worked for the MfS since 1959 under the code name "Hubert" and became one of the most important agents in the area of the Catholic Church. Guske tried to use the MfS to influence his career and the journal, as well as to resolve conflicts with church-political officials and the National Council of the National Front to his advantage. Possibilities were limited, however, for a journal with a circulation of only 3,000. Its pretense of independence from state agencies and the CDU was hardly credible, and its journalism was often not serious. The fact that it was read with great curiosity by publication-starved clergy and lay Catholics did not translate into differentiation successes.

The establishment of an international Berlin Conference of Catholics from twelve European countries was something of an entirely different order. It began with 140 participants on 17 and 18 November 1964 "in the capital of the GDR."[58] Conceived of as the Catholic counterpart to the Protestant Christian Peace Conference (founded in Prague in 1958 with the support of all the Communist parties in the Warsaw Pact), its purpose was "to advise progressive Catholics" along the lines of the working group Pax Vobis[59] (founded in Cologne in 1963) and to take advantage of the Vatican's new Ostpolitik. It was, above all, the propagandistic potential that the SED saw in Pope John XXIII's May 1963 encyclical "Pacem in Terris" that prompted it to finance Catholic organizations in the GDR that would serve differentiation purposes.[60] Both the Berlin Conference and the Christian Peace Conference were profiled in the regular church affairs summits held by state offices in Communist countries. Berlin Conference activists selectively quoted papal statements on peace and the personal responsibility of lay Catholics in order to combine political goals with affirmations of loyalty to the church. The oft-repeated public formula was "We [progressive] Catholics in the GDR." Catholic statements were manipulated so that polite refusals appeared to be "salutes," private conversations were played up as "receptions," and simple correspondence was called "an exchange of ideas."[61] A pro forma Vatican answer to a telegram to the pope was called "a high point of our political work." The work of the Berlin Conference was largely discredited in the West after it defended the military intervention in Czechoslovakia in 1968; in the GDR, the organization had no success within the Catholic Church. The Berlin Conference thus shifted its focus from trying to influence the church to campaigning for international recognition for the GDR and support for its foreign policy.

The CDU party leadership was continually concerned with establishing a profile for itself in church affairs, whereas the SED was jealous of its monopoly and suspicious of CDU efforts; however, the CDU's real power was widely overestimated. Nonetheless, when Gerhard Quast, who had worked in Nuschke's office as well as in the State Secretariat for Church Affairs, became head of the CDU section for church affairs, its work gained a degree of professionalism. Quast was involved in the church affairs work of the state and the party. Through his friend Fritz Flint from the party and the State Secretariat, Quast could (at first) look through notes of conversations with church representatives. (Later, he merely received oral reports.) Occasionally, representatives from the Central Committee, the State Secretariat, and the CDU leadership held joint discussions. In general, however, internal affairs in the CDU were completely transparent to the SED because of the numerous MfS informers. Thus, it appears that the CDU's church affairs policies had implicit Communist approval. When they did not, the SED had ample opportunity to intervene via the MfS.

Aside from Frank Ritter, a chaplain from Wurzbach in southeast Thuringia, the CDU did not win over any clergy. The former pastor Karl Fischer became an official non-person after 1965 because of "immoral behavior," and all party and state agencies broke off contact with him at the urging of the MfS.[62] However, some Catholic CDU functionaries did contribute to the differentiation policy by passing on "confidential" notes of personal conversations with clergy to SED state and party offices. CDU Catholics from all parts of the GDR used these reports to demonstrate their ability to engage with Catholic clergy. In Erfurt, Auxiliary Bishop Aufderbeck took up a suggestion from CDU Catholics to discuss the situation of the Catholic Church within the socialist state after Vatican II in a private circle. With Aufderbeck's approval, subsequent conversations took place from 1966 to 1969 involving his chargé Wilhelm Ernst from the Erfurt seminary and two to four Catholic CDU officials from Thuringia. Naturally, their defamatory notes of the meetings were passed on to the CDU leadership, the ZK of the SED, and also the MfS (whenever the CDU officials were also informers). On 20 October 1969 the church affairs department made a presentation to the CDU leadership entitled "Developing a Civic Consciousness among Church Officials in Conjunction with the Twentieth Anniversary of the GDR." It listed 241 Catholic clergy as contacts, including twenty-one described as "mid-level." The report concluded that, "judging by the content of the contacts we have developed, we can assume that the majority are based upon personal connections with Catholic supporters of the CDU. The contacts are not always regular nor directed at the clarification of fundamental political matters."[63]

On the whole, the state's differentiation policy was very inefficient in regard to the Catholic Church, aside from occasionally well-executed moves by the SED or CDU officials mentioned above. Compared with parallel efforts with Protestants, the results were negligible. The developments in Magdeburg were as ambivalent for the state practitioners of Kirchenpolitik as they were for certain church officials. A government evaluation from 6 February 1964 predicted that it would be

> extremely difficult . . . to find points of "differentiation" among the bishops and prelates . . . The Berlin Conference of Ordinaries appears united and closes ranks when dealing with the GDR government; it is resolute not to be "differentiated" in the way the Protestants have been . . . As a rule, Catholic priests are less likely to be swayed by material offers from state agencies.[64]

The State Secretariat for Church Affairs, in a memo from 26 November 1968, ascribed to Catholics greater reservations regarding the Jugendweihe, higher rates of participation in church services and events, and more intense involvement with their religious communities. Moreover, it said that "the Catholic clergy as a whole has shown strong resistance to our attempts at 'differentiation.'"[65] Beginning in 1970, after the changes in bishops in Magdeburg, Schwerin, and Meißen, a representative of the Berlin Conference of Ordinaries took part in all district-level conversations that the State Secretariat for Church Affairs also participated in.

The failure of the state's differentiation policy toward the Catholic Church resulted not only from its schematic methods but ultimately from the larger context of political intransigence in the GDR, which created a climate of capriciousness (as in the events leading to the dismantling of the Universitätskirche in Leipzig in 1968 or the Christuskirche in Rostock in 1971),[66] restriction, and intimidation. Within the rigid, SED and MfS-led hierarchical system, the idea of including Catholics in "building up socialism" was reduced to eliciting servile affirmations. In addition, any "positive" inclusion of Christians in civic and social life remained subordinate to the overall ideological premise of the demise of religion. In February 1968, as part of the training for all district-level church affairs staff in the GDR, Olof Klohr, professor of scientific atheism at the University of Jena, lectured on "The Demise of Religion and the Church."[67] At a similar training session in 1970, Paul Verner, the Politburo member responsible for church affairs, made a speech whose ideological candor was due to the closed doors of the SED:

> Kirchenpolitik is first and foremost work to educate theologians, church officials, and church members to become conscious citizens. This remains the primary way to solve our problems . . . I would like to emphasize that we still consider the prospect of the gradual death of religion to be valid, and that Marxist sociology confirms this . . . The social system in the GDR, socialism, has been correctly programmed. It is in accord with the objective laws of social development.[68]

A few months later, Verner reiterated most of these ideas at an event marking the tenth anniversary of Ulbricht's discussion with Emil Fuchs's "delegation,' but he left out the passages about the educational task of Kirchenpolitik and the death of religion. In this respect, this speech stood in the tradition that Politburo member Hermann Matern also followed in a 1969 speech to CDU officials:

Our imperialist enemies like to accuse the SED of dishonesty toward the churches. They characterize our Kirchenpolitik as a temporary, pragmatic tactic and ascribe to us the intent to liquidate Christianity and the churches. The absurdity of such defamation—whether it is expressed crudely or in more refined ways—is clear. The Marxist German worker's movement can point to a decades-long continuous tradition regarding its position on religion and the church.[69]

This continuity, however, which persisted until the mid 1970s, was based upon precisely this attempt to bring about the "determined" death of religion through socialism.

Activities of the MfS

In 1961 the MfS counted 19,130 employees.[70] With the establishment of the armed Felix Dzierzynski Guards Unit in 1963, this number grew to 30,717 in 1966, and by 1970 the MfS had a staff of 45,580. Its church affairs section in Berlin (renamed HA XX/4 from HA V/4 after an internal restructuring) was headed by Hans Ludwig until October 1969. When he was promoted, Franz Sgraja—a long-time staff member for church affairs—took charge until March 1979. MfS staff levels for church affairs had not changed much since 1957 in the main office or at the district level. In 1968, there were a total of fifty-two MfS employees in all eighteen districts. In Berlin, there were twenty-one, with four fewer officers than in 1957.[71] In January 1968, the MfS issued a new directive concerning informants, differentiating classes of unofficial informers. At the lowest level were IMS (informers charged with securing specific areas or persons), and at higher levels, IMV (informers tasked with directly working with or uncovering persons under suspicion of activity in the service of the enemy) and IMF (for persons with contacts in the West).[72]

In the case of the Catholic Church, in addition to "unofficial" surveillance, the MfS could make use of direct contacts with Prelate Johannes Zinke. This tendency seems to have been arranged with the close cooperation of the ZK and Politburo making parallel decisions. As the MfS considered the offices of the State Secretariat for Church Affairs and the district councils second- or third-rate and handled them with suspicion, it infiltrated them with informers. During Seigewasser's tenure in the State Secretariat for Church Affairs, the MfS did not share important "information" about the Catholic Church with him, but only with Verner in the Politburo and Barth or Bellmann in the ZK or, in special cases, with Ulbricht or Honecker.

When the church designated a church representative to handle contacts with the MfS, it intended to defuse such contacts, but this was only successful at the church leadership level. In general, given the place of the MfS within the regime and its direct connection to the SED leadership, the church hoped this route would give it some influence. For the MfS Catholic Church Unit (HA XX/4,

Referat II), these contacts represented an increase in its role within the state apparatus. It was a classic example of secret diplomacy, where both sides acted within the constraints of their systems and a small circle of initiates. Church officials had to take care to resist certain measures and not to let themselves be used by the state or compromise themselves. Zinke carried on talks with the MfS until his death in November 1968 and wrote reports of these contacts. Remarkably, these contacts led the MfS to designate him not as an informer, but rather as "a representative of Archbishop Bengsch." After the death in September 1967 of General Vicar Drews, who had been the primary contact for the State Secretariat for Church Affairs, Prelate Otto Groß (a close confidant of Bengsch) officially took over this function. One week after Drews's funeral, the MfS officers Hans Ludwig and Helmut Wegener approached Groß to establish further direct channels of negotiation with Bengsch.[73] Because Zinke resided in West Berlin and had health problems, he could only sporadically continue these talks. Therefore, Groß became the cardinal's other representative for these contacts as early as October 1967. Although the talks were identical to those with Zinke, in Groß's case, the MfS registered him as an informer with the code name "Otto."

Groß at least informed Cardinal Bengsch about the subjects of his conversations with the MfS. Many other people in the diocese leadership also knew about the contacts, as did the members of the BOK. Because of both his self-conception as the central authority for the entire Catholic Church in the GDR and the steadily growing need for more intensive talks, Cardinal Bengsch authorized two additional leading church figures to speak with the MfS after they had been approached. Beginning in 1970, Prelate Theodor Hubrich, head of the Caritas Association in East Berlin, relieved Groß by discussing the so-called reunification of families (allowing family members trapped in the GDR to leave) with Wolfgang Vogel, an MfS-connected lawyer. Norbert Kaczmarek, another Caritas official, also functioned as an assistant to the church's main negotiator with the MfS.

Aside from those named above, the Catholic ordinaries wanted no further conversations between church staff and the MfS. The church expected individual Catholic officials to report MfS attempts to establish contact with them to higher-ups so that they could help end them. However, the MfS tried its best to circumvent these church practices. Helmut Wegener, alias "Lorenz," an MfS captain in the Berlin section for Catholic affairs, brought a new level of initiative to registering informers. Many were registered in advance in expectation of cooperation. These usually ended after a few contacts, and sometimes reports detailed conversations that never took place as described. Though often based on things that the registered people had actually said, the "reports" relayed information that had been gained on different occasions and by other means. Wegener's reports as Groß's interlocutor in conjunction with the twentieth anniversary of the GDR, for example, contain several exaggerations of successes.[74] For the GDR's twentieth anniversary, Wegener had promised to deliver nothing less than the installation of papal administrative districts in the East German areas of West German dioceses. But for legal reasons pertaining to existing concordats, the Vatican would only agree to such a measure after the Bonn government recognized Poland's western border and the GDR—which is why this did not happen until June 1972, in the former case, and until July 1973 in the latter.

The flaws and failings of ambitious individual MfS officers did not, however, impede the agency from gathering important information on the Catholic Church, from carrying out differentiation projects, and from sowing confusion and sabotaging certain targets. Relative to other GDR state and party agencies, the MfS was more effective. In individual cases, the MfS was able to establish long-term secret contacts with lower-ranking clergy and thus gain useful information, in part by means of extortion. As a rule, the work of the MfS contradicted the differentiation policy that other government agencies pursued. The MfS explicitly discouraged Stasi informers from making public political (regime-supporting) pronouncements within the CDU, National Front, or Berlin Conference. Informer-priests would be worthless to the MfS if their colleagues distanced themselves because of publicity. This had happened in the case of Karl Fischer (code name "Marduk"), who became isolated within the clergy and thus ever less able to give information to the MfS.[75] Secret MfS contacts with lay Catholics were more common. These lay informers were often recruited among the ranks of the CDU or the Berlin Conference, with notable success. Although church circles regarded these sorts of people with skepticism because of their public political positions, other kinds of informers—like Catholics smuggled into church circles or even those who held honorary or regular positions—were hard to spot. The security services gathered a mosaic of information, which was not really systematically analyzed, as the "operational handling of individuals" did not really take off again until 1969. But by 1971, the MfS began to weave a network of Catholic informers—at least in Berlin, Dresden, Leipzig, Frankfurt an der Oder and in the triangle between Halle, Merseburg, and Leuna—without, however, successfully controlling or directing the Catholic Church.

MfS activities directed at the Catholic Church in the FRG and the Vatican constituted a field unto themselves. The intelligence division Hauptverwaltung Aufklärung was especially involved with these matters.[76] With one exception, Unit IV from the MfS Main Office Section XX/4 had few significant informants devoted to "Western tasks" involving the Catholic Church before 1971. The MfS was able to obtain information via Polish and Hungarian agents in Rome. Regarding his conversation in Rome with the exiled Slovakian Bishop Pavol Hnilica on 4 May 1968, Bishop Schaffran of Görlitz noted, "even in the [Vatican] Secretary of State, not everything is secure. The Holy Father asks repeatedly if certain documents can be delivered there or if they are better kept in his private library. Recently, the main points of a meeting where only six prelates were present were published the next day in a Communist newspaper."[77]

On the other hand, between 1969 and 1973 the Polish secret services received dubious and, in part, fabricated transcripts of conversations between Pope Paul VI and foreign leaders.[78]

Unique among the MfS contacts with Catholics in the GDR were independent attempts by a vicar and a Catholic doctor to engage in a dialogue about worldviews and, by giving information about the church, to promote tolerance and a discussion of commonalities between Marxism and Catholicism. The MfS, however, never treated them as partners in dialogue, according to its files, but as informers.

Aside from direct contacts and informers, the MfS gained information about the churches in several other ways. One was perfecting its penetration of postal, telegraph, and telephone communications. "Measure M" stood for the "operational control of letters," which meant that the MfS copied all mail delivered to and from targeted persons or institutions, with incoming mail first being delivered to the MfS for analysis. "Measure A" or "26A" entailed telephone surveillance of all conversations over a period of months or years. Everything was recorded and transcribed—even phonetic misunderstandings—and preserved in files. "Measure (26)B" was more complicated, involving the installation of listening devices, euphemistically termed "operational technology." The bi-annual reports of the MfS Catholic section from 1966 and 1967 highlighted the need to deploy listening devices—the MfS had failed in attempting to use them against the Catholic Church in 1959, but there were not enough "regular" information sources (informers). There were plans to bug the offices of the Catholic Student Community in Berlin, the Jesuit order in Erfurt, apartments connected with the Focolare movement, Bishop Schaffran's office in Görlitz, and, finally, "all meetings of GDR bishops in Berlin."[79] In early 1967, bugs were to be placed in ordinaries' offices in Berlin, Magdeburg, Erfurt, Bautzen, and Görlitz, as well as in the bishops' weekend homes and in other locations to conduct surveillance on meetings of bishops and leading lay Catholics. But none of these intentions were realized.

The HA XX/4 specialized in "operations employing compromising material," which aimed to "work toward degradation, create problems within the church for leading Catholics, promote the process of differentiation, and create favorable opportunities for [MfS] recruiting."[80] At least six different defamatory letters were sent between 1964 and 1968 under the code name "Saint Michael the Guardian." Clergy and lay Catholics throughout the Diocese of Berlin received hundreds of anonymous letters with detailed accusations of celibacy violations against Catholic clergy in East Berlin. In 1964, these included three Nazi-era cases involving GDR priests, but the self-styled "anti-fascist" MfS soon dropped this tactic to avoid people drawing parallels between their actions and Nazi campaigns against priests. The cases described were a mixture of truth and fiction, and they led in many cases to transfers or defrocking.

Another case of MfS defamation occurred in August and September 1969. The West German magazine *Der Spiegel* reported that Matthias Defregger, later general vicar in Munich, had been an officer on a firing squad in Italy in June 1944 and that Cardinal Döpfner had known this and nonetheless named him auxiliary bishop in 1968. On 30 August 1969 Bengsch received a final "Saint

Michael the Guardian" letter, which listed Catholic clergy in the GDR who had served as military chaplains in the Second World War.[81] The MfS also tried to sow dissent between the cardinal and Catholic students by sending 154 copies of a letter purporting to come from the Catholic Student Community in Halle and Magdeburg in September 1969; the letter was sent to Catholics in the GDR, FRG, and East and West Berlin.[82]

The main targets of MfS surveillance and defamation against the Catholic Church were contacts between GDR Catholics and Catholics in other socialist countries, Catholic educational institutions, religious orders, and the Kolping Association. The MfS especially targeted Catholic student organizations and academic associations. Specific MfS actions depended upon the personnel in HA XX/4 and in the district offices. The institutionalized contacts with Otto Groß, Theodor Hubrich, and Norbert Kaczmarek made the attempt to influence the ordinaries' conference a greater priority beginning in 1969.[83]

Between 1963 and 1969, all the surveillance of office holders in the Catholic Church in the entire GDR (with the exception of the Suhl district) were at first grouped together as a centralized operation called Schleuse (Lock Gate). This unwieldy and unsystematic grouping was opened by the MfS HA V/4 in Berlin in October 1963. Divided between many districts in the GDR, the common denominator was that all parts concerned Catholic clergy who had contacts in other Eastern Bloc countries. The surveillance deployed was sometimes quite considerable, extending from tailing targets in the GDR to joint operations with the secret services of other socialist countries. Astonishingly, the HA XX/4/II wanted to use "appropriate measures" to bring the operation to a conclusion in 1966, when they suddenly perceived a "completely new situation . . . an attack on the GDR and other socialist countries under the cover of the so-called Focolare Movement in the service of the Vatican."[84] The HA XX/4 now occupied itself with gathering intelligence on this Catholic spiritual movement, which had started in Italy. The Schleuse operation had suspected that Bishop Schaffran of Görlitz was coordinating a centralized campaign by the Catholic Church in the GDR, ordered by the Vatican.[85] To gather and analyze information, MfS agents traveled to the USSR, Hungary, Poland, Bulgaria, Czechoslovakia, China, and Vietnam. But they uncovered almost no evidence of a grand conspiracy.[86]

In 1966, the MfS began a campaign against Catholic educational institutions at the Huysburg near Halberstadt, in Neuzelle and Schöneiche, and especially at the seminary in Erfurt. Although its surveillance produced some information (for example, precise notes on the methods West German church offices and individuals used to supply the Erfurt Seminary with religious literature produced in the West), it failed to recruit any informers after 1962.[87] It did succeed in planting an agent in 1961 in the Norbertuswerk, a Magdeburg seminary for older trainees, and another one in 1967 in the Görlitz catechism course for lay Catholics, but these contacts did not yield significant information. In April 1969, a West German publication revealed that Erfurt theology students were receiving doctorates from West German universities. To prevent further cases, the MfS threatened to search the Erfurt seminary and to deny any Catholic professors found responsible in the GDR the right to confer doctoral degrees.

In general, Catholic religious orders in the GDR were under the authority of heads based in Western Europe and were not obliged to report to local bishops. Therefore, some clergy who were members of the various orders in the GDR just permitted themselves to holds talks with Dieter Leutloff, an MfS officer whose code name was "Heinrich." Leutloff initially suspected that the religious orders were the church's "elite troops" steered from the West. The talks must have made it clear even to the MfS that the orders were of no political significance and that there was no "direction" from the West. Nonetheless, Leutloff was able to gather extensive personal and internal church information. The MfS was especially interested in the Jesuits and deployed special measures against them.[88]

MfS actions against the Kolping Association were directed by Edwin Hille from the Berlin district office as of the 1960s. Hille was able to make use of "Schramm," an informer who began working with the MfS in 1953 and continued until the end of the GDR. Hille also built up further contacts with Kolping activists (all lay people) in Berlin and managed a network of informers. Using this information, Hille authored anonymous letters that aimed to tear the Kolping Association apart. But although Hille's work spread numerous rumors and unleashed many suspicions, it had hardly any impact on the work of the Kolping community. As Hille always had to take care not to expose his informers, his "degradation measures" vacillated between fantasy and unconscious satire.

Beginning in the 1950s, the MfS considered the most dangerous element of the Catholic Church to be the Catholic Student Community, especially the academics who emerged from it and were then active in organized academic circles. An MfS report from 29 August 1961 concluded that, based on surveillance since 1958, the students were organized into cells for "passive and active resistance against the GDR."[89] In November 1966, Minister Mielke called Catholic and Protestant student groups "an ideologically destructive concentration" whose activities and contacts with Western students were to be fought.[90] A successful MfS officer, Heinz Nordt, alias "Horn," was tapped to head the work against Catholic students. Operation Schild was launched against the Catholic Student Community in Leipzig, and its pastor's residence—where numerous meetings with West German students took place—was bugged; from 1969 to 1974, this provided the MfS with detailed information. Nordt was able to plant a few students in the group and to recruit marginally among its core members, but he achieved a spectacular success in 1970 when he was able to begin working with the Berlin student pastor Dr. Joachim Berger, whose involvement with the MfS continued to deepen. For six years, Berger furnished the MfS with details on the student community's contacts with the West, its other activities, and meetings of GDR student pastors. Thus, the MfS noticed that the Catholic Student Community was becoming politicized, advocating a "critical engagement" with socialism, which led the MfS to fear its power as an "ideological diversion." Later, the MfS noted the depoliticization of the student organization, largely for reasons internal to the church. The MfS had attempted to force this development with pressure tactics, including the above-mentioned defamatory letters.

In 1962, suspecting "infiltration" and an "undermining" of socialist society in religious discussion circles that professionals took part in—intellectuals educated in the GDR system—the MfS district office in Cottbus began a comprehensive operation, called Mitra, against Catholic doctors' groups in Finsterwalde and Cottbus and against a Catholic attorney in Cottbus.[91] With the help of the administrator of the doctors' dormitory, it also bugged the apartment of a doctor who often traveled to Eastern Europe and the Soviet Union on church business. The doctors were suspected of "espionage under the cover of church organizations and creating political-ideological diversions."[92] After considerable surveillance, Operation Mitra ended in May 1968 with a detailed, 330-page report. Although the operation had been unable to prove that these groups were "directed" from West Berlin, the report concluded that the Vatican had "ordered the Catholic Church in the GDR to now gather all Catholic forces and to form underground groups."[93] Furthermore, it maintained that the Cottbus professionals' group, comprised of clergy and lay Catholics, had "formed an enemy alliance."[94]

In other cases, even the working group Pacem in Terris, set up by the Berlin Ordinaries Conference in 1964, was accused of attempting to "plant" Catholics in key social positions in January 1969.[95] Anton Beer was a Catholic chaplain from Schwerin who participated in an ecumenical group. In 1969, he had accompanied students in Prague placing flowers at the grave of Ján Palach, the Czech student who burned himself to death in protest against the Soviet-led intervention. When he crossed the border, he was interrogated, and subsequently he was watched, along with others.[96] Julius Schoenemann was a physician in Rostock, well-known in the GDR for advocating that Catholics take an active role in society. His apartment was bugged as of 1969, and his career was repeatedly stymied.[97] He fled with his family to West Germany via Hungary in 1972.

The MfS office in Dresden directed special attention to the work of Franz-Peter Sonntag, the Diocese of Meißen's pastor for professionals. Beginning in 1966, he was the target of Operation Black Cloak (*Schwarzkittel*) because he allegedly had the "special mission to influence and recruit the intelligentsia for the Catholic Church."[98] The MfS suspected Sonntag of belonging to the "political-ideological leadership of the Diocese of Meißen" and of "deliberately fostering hostile activity against our state" because of his contacts in Czechoslovakia and his formation of a discussion group in Dresden in November 1967.[99]

In a 10 April 1970 report on Operation Tabernacle, the MfS claimed to have uncovered a "socially dangerous negative group" in Halle: "This group of reactionary clergy and lay Catholics is an ideological bridgehead and a political base for West German imperialism right in the center of the GDR's heavy industry."[100] The MfS saw the Halle Action Group as more "oppositional" than any other Catholic group in the GDR. In their view, Adolf Brockhoff, a former student pastor in Halle and, at the time, a priest in Merseburg, was the group's leader and inspiration. He was accused of "enemy activity" and "creating a political-ideological diversion against social development in the GDR." The MfS began to investigate the Halle Action Group in 1970 on the basis of the GDR criminal law, sections 100 ("conspiring against the state"), 106 ("agitation against the state"), and 107 ("forming an association opposed to the state"). To fight this group, which they saw in ever more hysterical terms, the MfS attacked the person and lifestyle of Pastor Brockhoff with criminal acrimony.[101] Information the MfS gathered with the aid of informants planted in the church led the bishop of Magdeburg to suspend Brockhoff as pastor on 18 June 1971. But the resulting turbulence in the group led only to a temporary disruption of its work. The MfS had calculated that the degradation of an individual would make a group critical of the regime disappear, but this was not the case.

In the 1970s, the security services nonetheless increasingly used such personal "operational measures" against the Catholic Church because they were not associated with the internal political difficulties or unwanted international attention that arrests or formal legal proceedings against a group often provoked. Still, the MfS would turn to these latter measures as a last resort after failing to exercise discipline through the church leadership and when it could anticipate that these leaders would remain passive in the face of state intervention.

The Need for Legitimacy and the Churches

The Berlin Wall did help the GDR to consolidate internally, but the path to economic potency and international recognition was difficult. Prosperity could not be commanded, and the GDR's ambitious goals required raw materials and Western currency. In view of the GDR's need for international recognition and the SED's legitimacy gap inside the GDR, the regime's Kirchenpolitik proceeded along several different (and often conflicting) tracks. Public propaganda for atheism was reduced and mostly carried on in the area of scholarly work on the demise of religion; SED officials spoke mostly internally of their deterministic belief in the disappearance of religion.[102] At the same time, the SED instructed its officials to implicitly stabilize the churches for diplomatic and economic reasons and to allow them to work within the borders of the GDR.

As early as 1964, the SED had abandoned the goal of reaching a public agreement with the Catholic Church. But as late as March 1962, the Office of the State Secretary for Church Affairs had prepared a document entitled "Basis for Regularizing Relations of the Catholic Church in the German Democratic Republic with the Workers' and Peasants' State," which was intended to curtail the influence of the West German church. The document held that, if necessary, such an agreement could be introduced over the objections of the Catholic hierarchy in the GDR "as part of the development of state law." Up until the civil law code was revised in 1965, there was talk that the legal status of the church was "to be reformulated."[103] Documents from the Office of the State Secretary repeated these demands in 1963 and January 1964, but they were absent from a detailed report on 6 February 1964.[104] The idea of a fixed protocol for the Catholic Church was never raised again.

The Catholic Church in the GDR could only maintain its institutions with financial transfers from the church in the West. There were several other sources of funding, such as GDR state grants of 1 million marks per year, their own income,[105] considerable donations from West German business,[106] and a great deal of "illegal" currency dealing by church representatives in West Berlin.[107] But, by and large, the Catholic Church in the GDR was in urgent need of financing by the Fulda (later German) Bishops' Conference and the Bonifatiuswerk der deutschen Katholiken in Paderborn, as well as by the German Caritas Association, with transfers of goods and cash through the Genexweg (that is, the trade office called Geschenkdienst und Kleinexport GmbH). In the Genexweg, donors deposited Western currency, which was exchanged for goods and GDR currency paid to recipients in the GDR. The Catholic Church thus was able to obtain, for example, vehicles, which afforded clergy mobility and greater access to the people (which did not, incidentally, accelerate the state's goal of the "decline" of religion). The SED regime's need for hard currency made them quite partial to such transactions. The Central Committee said as much in a statement on 6 June 1962.[108] In fact, when the West German government considered blocking such Genexweg transfers in early 1965 to reduce the GDR's access to Western currency, Archbishop Bengsch emphatically requested that Bonn keep this trade route open. The Genexweg, he declared, made it possible to keep constant negotiations between the church and the GDR state—which the SED always tried to turn to its political advantage—to a minimum.

Nonetheless, it would soon come to these sorts of constant negotiations. In March 1966, the GDR Council of Ministers remarked in a confidential paper that new agreements should be reached with the "religious communities" to establish "currency parity" and a mechanism to replace the cash transfers through the Genexweg, which were not all that lucrative for the state. Another government decision on 1 April created the Commercial Coordination section within the MAI, whose stated aim was "maximizing the acquisition of capitalist currency." An official was to be named to regulate "commercial relations with the religious communities."[109] On 5 July 1966 Horst Roigk, an MfS special officer and the first head of the new section, invited Prelate Zinke for a discussion and informed him that the Genexweg would no longer be available for Catholic cash transfers. Henceforth, the Catholic Church would have to do as the Protestants were already doing and deliver Western goods or currency to a GDR foreign trade company.[110] The GDR state treasury, in turn, would compensate the church for these goods with East German marks paid into a central account under the name of Archbishop Bengsch or with GDR goods delivered to church institutions. Roigk indicated that the GDR was especially interested in acquiring "coffee, rubber, chemicals, bronze, copper, etc." He also mentioned that he could make considerable building materials available to the church.[111] Zinke noted in his files that he found it advantageous to have in Roigk a "matter-of-fact partner whose materialism was less ideological than concerned with trade and hard currency" because this relationship offset the influence of the State Secretariat for Church Affairs: "we paid in cash rather than in political concessions."[112]

At a 11 and 12 July 1966 meeting, the BOK authorized Bengsch to undertake negotiations to set up the new arrangement. On 5 December 1966 the German Caritas Association asked the West German Trade Ministry to approve the annual delivery of DM 12 million worth of electrolyte copper ingots and electrolyte copper cathodes to the Intrac trading company in East Berlin. In exchange, Archbishop Bengsch would receive 90 percent of the compensation in GDR currency deposited to an East Berlin bank account and 10 percent in East German products.[113] The value of the annual deliveries soon rose to DM 20 million and later to over DM 40 million. Occasionally, there were also special shipments (approved by East and West German customs agencies) of medical and technological office devices. GDR officials referred to the commercial relations with the churches as "church business," whereby they called the arrangement with the Catholic Church "Church Business C" after 1966.[114]

Otto Groß was the church's representative in talks with the main office of the German Caritas Association in Freiburg and its West Berlin branch, the Deutsche Metallgesellschaft in Frankfurt am Main, and the East Berlin Ministry of Foreign Trade, the successor to the Ministry of Foreign and Inner-German Trade. In an October 1967 outline for Cardinal Bengsch's report to the BOK, Groß distinguished between "ideologues" and "economists" in the SED. Underlining the significance of economic arrangements between the church and the GDR state, Groß argued that for the moment, the "economists" had the upper hand, believing that "economic strength will help the GDR determine the political course in the East Bloc." Therefore, he gauged that they were interested in a contented populace and were not out to confront the Catholic Church.[115]

The Catholic Church in the GDR had a position that the SED leadership was not really eager to challenge, despite all its political rhetoric and attempts to enact a differentiation policy. The resources of the West German church provided a lot of cover. Moreover, SED leaders understood that the church's ties to the Vatican could have consequences for the GDR's international relations.[116] Kirchenpolitik was more than an issue of GDR internal affairs; it was also a function of the state's foreign policy and its policies on German questions. The regime's standing in the eyes of other nations was an essential precondition for diplomatic recognition. But "church business" was fundamentally an expression of economic weakness, its economic benefit for the GDR notwithstanding. Moreover, it strengthened the churches in a way that constantly countered the ideologies of the "predetermined decline of religion" and "scientific atheism," not to mention the state's numerous administrative pinprick measures. On the other hand, the SED leadership consoled itself with the belief that the extinction of religion was inevitable and that their financial sustenance by the West was only a provisional phase.

The GDR's need for Western currency did not mean that the churches could have their way with the state in matters of Kirchenpolitik, but it did mean that the Catholic Church could increasingly realize its demands through careful negotiations. For example, since September 1961, Archbishop Bengsch had tried to get a new building erected behind the Cathedral of St. Hedwig in East Berlin and had offered DM 1.1 million from West Germany to accomplish this. Despite the state's general goodwill in this matter, it withheld approval for the building, allegedly because the GDR capital lacked sufficient construction capacity. But in 1967, it quickly granted building permits after establishing Church Business C. The state planning office estimated the construction costs at DM 4 million, and an initial transfer of DM 2 million was made in October 1967. Although construction was scheduled to begin on 1 December 1968, it failed to materialize, so Groß complained to the MfS in February 1969, telling the agency that the rest of the money would not be transferred until construction actually began. MfS section HA XX/4/II then sent two notes, including one to Mielke.[117] Mielke responded with a handwritten note to his direct subordinate, Colonel Heinz Volpert, who, among other things, worked together on special cases with Dr. Alexander Schalck-Golodkowski from the Commercial Coordination section: "Take note of this; I recommend settling the matter." Thus, in 1972, the Catholic Church was finally able to move into a new five-story building in the center of the GDR capital, purchased with Western currency. Another early example of a project similar in scale and financed with copper shipments was the new church and community center in Rostock, which Groß managed to obtain in 1970–1971 after the old buildings had fallen victim to SED city planning.[118]

In addition to being a source of hard currency for the SED, the church also factored into the GDR's diplomatic relations. By 1968, the SED had begun to seek direct contacts with the Vatican to persuade it to change the boundaries of German dioceses to acknowledge the GDR.[119] However, this move limited the SED regime in its Kirchenpolitik at home. Any deterioration of the status quo for the Catholic Church in the GDR would now have a negative effect in the GDR's quest for international recognition rather than constituting a domestic political "win" for the regime. The church could make good use of this reality, thus making itself relevant to GDR foreign policy.

As of the mid 1960s, the GDR regime wanted to avoid confrontations with the Catholic leadership. It was aware of the Catholics' diplomatic value. As BOK chair, Bengsch had formally acknowledged Ulbricht's role as Chairman of the Council of State in numerous communiqués since 1962. This paid dividends when the SED published a draft of a new constitution for the GDR on 31 January 1968. The new draft constitution dropped most sections of the 1949 constitution relating to churches, and section 38.2 now provided that churches and religious communities could regulate their activities in accordance with the constitution and laws of the GDR. On 5 February 1968 Bengsch petitioned Ulbricht on behalf of the BOK, charging that the language of the new draft constitution was a "serious limitation on the fundamental premises of church activity." He requested that freedom of religion and conscience be legally secured.[120] After talks between Bengsch's assistants and government officials, Bengsch followed up on 26 February with a more detailed petition. Fearing that legal moves by the state would threaten the churches, he prepared a paper entitled "Challenges for a Reconstitution of the Profile of the Catholic Church in the GDR in View of the New Realities."[121] Bengsch sought to clarify the legal status of the churches, the status of Catholic Church property, and the relation of churches to "socialist foundations." The state responded: the second draft of the constitution (26 March) and the final version (6 April) ameliorated the language regarding the churches in section 39, and section 20 now granted "freedom of religion and conscience." On 1 April 1968 it was suggested to Otto Groß in a meeting in the Office of the State Secretary that the Catholic Church make a statement thanking Ulbricht for partially responding to its ideas. Groß suggested the wording of such a statement to Bengsch,[122] and it was delivered to Ulbricht on 5 April. One part said,

> We are certain, Mr. Chairman of the Council of State, that the statements you made regarding the draft constitution are to be considered a binding declaration, to the effect that the pastoral and welfare activities of the church in their heretofore recognized form will remain unchanged and that religious freedom 'shall continue to exist as it does and that there are no intentions to alter it.'[123]

Groß was then invited to a meeting—"to receive an explanation"—with State Secretary Seigewasser on 11 April 1968. The state secretary instructed the prelate to inform Cardinal Bengsch that Ulbricht had forwarded his 5 April letter with a note to accord it attention. Fritz Flint, the deputy secretary, assured Groß repeatedly that "nothing" would change and explained that "the State Secretary's message was extremely positive and the letter would be evaluated very positively by the government."[124]

The outcome of the 1968 discussion concerning the GDR constitution was in no way a secure, actionable guarantee that the Catholic Church would survive in the GDR, but it was a legitimation—by the highest echelons of the GDR—of its right to exist and its autonomous status. Regarding his 15 July 1968 conversation with State Secretary Seigewasser, Bengsch noted that Seigewasser emphasized that "the statements from the Chairman of the Council of State permit the activities of the church on their current scale and that 'all remains the same.'"[125] Bengsch did not harbor any illusions about the motives behind this policy: according to an MfS report, at a 13 June 1968 church forum, he said that "if the GDR ever stops needing hard currency, the Catholic Church is through here."[126]

Yet the GDR's appetite for Western currency not only persisted but increased. Moreover, a certain measure of mutual trust (based purely on predictability and familiarity) was developing behind the scenes between the state and the churches; the atheistic pronouncements of the government began to sound more and more like ritualistic invocations of socialist dogma for the sake of continuity. To be sure, the Office of the State Secretary issued a prognostic assessment in January 1970 that proclaimed that state policy in church affairs was "oriented toward limiting the impact of the churches."[127] Horst Hartwig, the section head and author of the statement, foresaw the possibility in the coming years of "limiting the economic power of the church through administrative measures that would be politically defensible." But the GDR's economic needs guaranteed that the exact opposite would be the case: the state expanded its "church business." It required hard currency and raw materials for economic stability, the general standard of living, and also for the lifestyle of Politburo members and the equipment of the security services. For the SED leadership, economic pressures outweighed Kirchenpolitik and the unfulfilled prophecy of the decline of religion in "the developed phase of Socialism."

Political Conflict and the Catholic Church

In his report of 9 January 1962 to the BOK, Bengsch described "a sort of floating political state" that prevailed several months after the wall went up. At the same time, he described what he saw as the church's "prophylactic fear" faced with the uncertainty of the state's intentions.[128] Concerned that the GDR would alter the legal status of the Catholic Church and even force its complete separation from the FRG, the BOK contemplated possible preventive measures. But the state did not advance new legal regulations. In autumn 1963, Archbishop Bengsch declared in a draft memorandum for the (West German) Fulda Bishops' Conference that "the church will only survive in the East if it is supported by the West."[129] The Berlin Wall had "a destructive effect," leading to "a mutual loss of an ability to empathize and understand the other's place." Bengsch expected economic help from the West, as he foresaw that the Catholic Church in the GDR could finance only basic pastoral services from its own resources. Because the regime was fully aware of the need for West German financial transfers, Bengsch believed that "[such transfers] would be a sign of a concrete will to preserve [church] unity." He demanded further that the West German church refrain from "placing additional political burdens [on East German Catholics] through reckless speeches or press articles . . . internal reports on church life . . . excessive political demands (i.e., the question of the Oder/Neisse border) [or] facile condemnations of East German tactics." He wanted West Berlin to retain its function as a quiet "bridgehead" and a "window" to the West for the Catholic Church in the GDR.

For BOK meetings, Bengsch studied GDR policies and atheist propaganda to acquaint himself with the enemy's methods. On 2 April 1964, for example, he treated the ordinaries to an analysis of an article by Otto Klohr in a GDR philosophy journal, in which he saw a "fundamental continuity of the regime's religious strategy," which had the ultimate aim of liquidating the churches.[130] In his November 1965 report, too, he saw "the destruction of religion" as the goal of SED Kirchenpolitik; tolerance of religion was merely "an interim phase governed by political or economic concerns."[131] Such conclusions began to change, however, after Otto Groß's political contacts gave Bengsch qualitatively new insight into the state's policies, increasingly demystifying the supposed strategy of coordinating and planning to eliminate the church. In a report delivered in Rome on 13 October 1967, Bengsch said that "leading officials" assured him that the church need not "fear" the regime's propaganda, because "the arguments made for scientific atheism are finished."[132] In his view, such government statements provided implicit evidence of the state's "respect for the Catholic Church for the sake of its unity," despite their tactical nature.

Bengsch wanted to maintain this "unity" in the sense of politically closed ranks and predictability by setting the entire church on a course of public political abstinence—that is, it was to keep out of all social questions that did not directly concern the existence of the church or central aspects of Catholic belief and morality. Although he saw this posture as an expression of loyalty to the GDR state, he also believed it would serve to expand the church's impact. The policy would also apply in the West German political sphere as hopes for German unity gradually gave way to an acceptance that the GDR was going to last. Ordinaries, clergy, and lay Catholics expressed an awareness of this state of things—and the resulting reorientation of the Catholic Church in the GDR toward other socialist countries in Central Europe—ever more intensely. Bengsch, as the bishop of the whole of Berlin, retained the strongest possible political orientation toward the West. At the same time, he found religious and social trends in Western Europe increasingly distasteful and sought to insulate the Catholic Church in the GDR from them as much as possible.

The GDR regime asked Bengsch, as chairman of the BOK, to publicly support various general and specific political measures and policies at almost every one of his major meetings with Seigewasser. At these usually annual meetings, Bengsch consistently responded that he could not take public political positions because he could not publicly applaud the regime without also offering public criticism, lest he lose all credibility. After one such meeting in April 1963, Bengsch noted that he had managed to preserve his "policy of political abstinence."[133] Bengsch tried to spin this abstinence to the state representatives as a positive response to their repeated requests for loyalty. On 17 June 1964 Flint noted that the archbishop of Berlin claimed to serve the state "when he said nothing about the government's peace campaign, because although he could certainly make a positive statement about it, he says nothing about three other things which he would have to decry, either."[134] When the state initiated a targeted attempt to push Bengsch into making public statements in its support, an exchange of threats ensued, and the government backed off. When the Office of the State Secretary for Church Affairs demanded public statements from the churches on the twentieth anniversary of the end of the Second World War on 8 May 1965, threatening to curtail the archbishop's visits to West Berlin, Bengsch sent Seigewasser a calculated response:

> I think it is undemocratic and unworthy of the government to try to pressure the archbishop into becoming politically engaged in this extortionist manner . . . Under

such circumstances, I cannot guarantee that I will not take a public position on this. I emphasize here that I—and I have proven this throughout my tenure in office—do not seek this kind of public attention but unfortunately can be forced to do it . . . So I request once again that you take my silence and restraint as an expression of loyalty toward the state.[135]

When reminded that Protestant clergy made this sort of political affirmation, Bengsch replied that they also issued critical public statements and that his policy of political abstinence was superior.[136] At the same time, Bengsch repeatedly asserted that the state would not succeed in politicizing the church and making GDR society monolithic in its worldview. On 31 October 1966 Bengsch wrote to Minister-President Stoph that politicized churches "could not make their own unique contribution to the social whole and would not be in the interest of the state."[137] In his view, the Catholic Church was a "fundamentally non-political institution . . . Whenever the church identified itself with the state in the past, it was to the detriment of both institutions." The GDR's ideal of a "unified worldview state" could not last, he claimed, and not just because of the actions of the churches: "the goal of a monolithic worldview is anachronistic in the modern world." Bengsch received no answer to his letter. The state and the party did not enter into discussions about the foundations of GDR society but rather reacted allergically whenever church statements reflected critically—even in the faintest manner—on the GDR worldview.

Bengsch held fast to his line of political abstinence and did his best to prevent any sector of the Catholic Church from making public political declarations, whether supportive or critical of the regime. Seigewasser tried repeatedly to lift the Berlin bishop's restrictions on Catholic contacts with state offices, but Bengsch countered that unregulated political engagement would raise "many negative voices" and that "the state's gain would not be very great."[138] On 2 June 1970 the BOK renewed its stance against taking political positions, which Bengsch had inspired:

1) The mission of the Catholic Church and the Office of Bishop is in principal non-political; 2) if the state denies the existence of a sphere that is above politics, then this excludes the possibility of taking a political position; 3) the freedom to take an unrestricted position in political questions has not been given; 4) political statements that have been made by the church in the past have been misused, without the church having any possibility to object or correct them.[139]

In practice, political abstinence meant that after 1961, the BOK commented publicly on societal matters only in very select situations. One clear position regarded abortion, which the GDR state had permitted. Bengsch criticized this in a sermon on 8 May 1965, and the BOK did likewise in a statement of 1 November 1965.[140] The BOK issued a further statement on 3 January 1972, after the GDR Council of Ministers made another legal decision in December 1971.[141] In a contentious meeting with Seigewasser and leading physicians on

10 January 1972, Bengsch emphasized that this was "a fundamental matter of belief and morality" in which bishops could not act otherwise.[142] In addition, a critical BOK statement regarding the new draft constitution for the GDR was read publicly on 26 February 1968. By contrast, however, the church kept other critical responses to the regime quieter, sharing them only with clergy and not the broader public—letters of protest to the minister-president in 1963 and 1965 regarding family law and youth affairs, and two further letters to Ulbricht about the constitution in February 1968.

Bengsch believed that the BOK should only take public positions when a direct connection to pastoral affairs was at stake. This policy of "political abstinence" was more than the expression of the essential non-political nature of the church and more than a measure to prevent its political instrumentalization. It was also a strategy to avoid political conflict, to preserve the status quo for the churches in the GDR, and to establish a long-term modus vivendi with the state. Thus, bishops weighed these factors as they considered making statements on matters of conscience for Christians. Within the church, they were increasingly questioned as to whether such statements held to the standard of "selective" public pronouncements. Two examples are the continued question of the Jugendweihe and the complex of issues surrounding military service and oaths, which became compulsory in the GDR on 24 January 1962.

The Jugendweihe had evolved from its origin as a materialist catechism into an obligatory civic ritual. It increasingly became a precondition for certain education and career tracks and thus promoted discrimination against Christian citizens. After 1961, the Catholic Church's strong resistance to this ritual led to a vigorous debate within the church. For that reason, the ordinaries softened their position in a pastoral letter to clergy on 4 September 1967:

> Because pressure and fear of being [economically and socially] disadvantaged have been such important factors in the spread of the Jugendweihe, along with a lack of awareness of its fundamentally atheist nature, the bishops have decided—without retreating from their complete rejection of this ritual—to drop their policy of sanctioning youths and their parents and rather to promote appropriate religious activities.[143]

When the official Jugendweihe oath was altered in 1968 to reflect the new GDR constitution, the BOK modified its position even further in a 25 February 1969 position paper, dropping the last sanctions against parents whose children participated in the Jugendweihe. Although they maintained their opposition to Catholics taking part and "offered no new opinions on the church's condemnation of the ritual," they noted that its "true character was becoming harder to recognize in the obscurity of the oath's wording and the propaganda surrounding it and, thus, the participation of parents and youths can often not be viewed as a conscious infraction against the faith."[144]

In the obligatory loyalty oath in the military, initiates had to swear "to defend socialism against all enemies, to offer unconditional obedience to military superiors, to carry out orders decisively," and "to strictly guard military and state secrets."[145] On 6 February 1962 the BOK agreed upon a position on the law for compulsory military service but did not make it public and distributed it to clergy only "for the instruction of the faithful."[146] The ordinaries noted that even during military service, the GDR constitution guaranteed the right to free religious practice, and they defined the military oath as a nonreligious vow because it did not refer to God, adding: "This oath does not force Christians to give up their worldview. This also means that the oath's obligation to preserve the common welfare does not rise to the level of a statement of a worldview." The BOK's position followed the Catholic Church's long-standing, worldwide practice of legitimizing compulsory military service and validating civic duty with the moral doctrine of the "just war." In his "Notes on the Military Service Act" of 9 February 1962, Bengsch tellingly referred to the Fulda Bishops' Conference's definition of an oath as "an act of the most splendid praise of God." He also quoted his predecessor Archbishop von Preysing, who had said in November 1935: "A duty to do something that is in opposition to Catholic belief and morality rooted in God's law cannot be the object of an oath, as it would be a contradiction of divine worship."[147] Bengsch felt that this 1935 commentary was sufficient to dispel any religious reservations. He expressed concern that young Christians would be exposed to "hard atheist influence" during military service and wondered about the "more serious question" of whether they would be able to practice their faith in the military.

Whereas Protestant leaders tried to enter into a controversial and somewhat public dialogue with the GDR state after the introduction of military service—with the result that working for unarmed "construction units" became an option for service beginning in 1964—Catholic bishops did not raise the question of alternative service. In an April 1962 report to the BOK, Bengsch said: "We will not attempt to negotiate with the regime over questions raised by this law, because it has no promise of success."[148] He asserted that critics within the church were motivated "less by religious concerns than an unconscious attachment to Western political ideas." Not least because of his personal experiences in the German military in the Second World War—something he shared with other leading Catholics in the GDR—Bengsch felt that one must remember "that young Christians can withstand this challenge . . . the church does not have the power to avoid our youth being tested."

The BOK's stance led some young clergy and lay Catholics to take critical positions like those of the Protestants. A youth pastor in Magdeburg wrote of his "great disappointment" regarding the BOK's 1962 statement in an internal memo: "it contradicts our reality" and "makes light of a serious matter."[149] After 1965, the Vatican II declarations led many countries to recognize citizens' right to refuse armed service for reasons of conscience and to see alternative national service as legitimate. The GDR option of serving on "construction units" was a far cry from this, however, as these units were integrated into military structures and those serving in them were subject to the same oaths. Protestants thus called increasingly for alternative civil service options. Catholics who worked together locally with Protestants came to similar conclusions.

In April 1966, the Catholic Youth Ministries Office in Magdeburg printed and distributed the 11 November 1965 petition by the Conference of Protestant Church Leaders in the GDR "On the Peace Service of the Church," which the state had attacked. Auxiliary Bishop Rintelen, on a priests' pilgrimage in Magdeburg in May 1966, called this distribution of an official Protestant text by an official Catholic institution a "regrettable, unbelievable, unimaginable fact." He feared that "the conscience of our Catholic young men would be disturbed and conflicted over this." In his view, the Catholic Church should just legitimize refusal of armed service in the GDR: "Gentlemen, where will this lead? What will happen today if every individual could act according to conscience?"[150] Bengsch gave his response in a 10 May 1966 letter to Vicar Willi Verstege in Nienburg, who had told him of the problems a young Catholic "total resister" had experienced, and asked him about the legitimacy of alternative civil service. Bengsch opined that every state had the right to introduce compulsory armed service: "As bishop, I cannot make a general declaration for the Catholic Church that his refusal is a genuine (objectively correct) matter of conscience, when an unarmed military service option is available within the Wehrmacht *[sic]*."[151] On the question of oaths, both for regular soldiers and engineering troops, Bengsch understood those who had reservations about the phrase "unconditional obedience." But he had no support for the case Verstege had brought to his attention and rejected the idea that total refusal to perform military service was "an allowable genuine choice for a Catholic Christian."

The ambivalence of the church's course of abstinence is visible in its handling of public statements on military service. "Political abstinence" was hardly nonpolitical, because the state regarded silence in the face of a demand for a public political statement as a conscious political act—and the SED saw it as arrogant. From the conversations between Bengsch and the Office of the State Secretary for Church Affairs, it is clear that the state viewed Bengsch as an enemy of socialism incorrigibly stuck in "bourgeois human rights" thought categories.[152] The SED believed that under Bengsch's leadership, the Catholics' political reserve merely constituted "cleverer tactics" than the Protestant approach. A 26 November 1968 analysis by the State Secretariat for Church Affairs ascertained that "their tactic aims to exploit legal room for maneuver to the maximum, and not to endanger themselves by entering into conflict and revealing themselves as enemies of socialism."[153] But this church tactic became the more acceptable alternative for the state and the party once a plurality of opinions began to emerge within the Catholic Church in the later 1960s about how to engage in a critical way with GDR society.

Although the Catholic policy of "political abstinence" originally bothered the state—in part because it preserved discipline with the church—GDR officials gradually preferred the policy as they became aware of the ambivalent results their policy of differentiation yielded. Internal documents from the State Secretariat for Church Affairs dated 14 and 25 May 1971 note in reference to the Catholic Church that, "though we try to gain influence, our work must proceed according to the consideration that it is best to let sleeping dogs lie."[154] If one had to reckon with the fact that the Catholic Church would continue to exist in the long term, then "political abstinence" seemed the lesser evil, despite the regime's belief that it appeared to be "a fundamental objection to our state and to socialist society."[155] In addition to protecting the church from political appropriation and division, the policy also expressed a silence that was criticized within the ranks of the church. In 1971, Johannes Braun, the bishop of Magdeburg, claimed "political neutrality" for the church in a conversation with Ulrich Fahl, the director of the local CDU branch. Thereafter, Fahl proclaimed that "the state no longer has any headaches from the Catholics and could not ask for anything more."[156]

What started as a self-protective move now ran the risk of producing paralysis, but it was not always perceived this way within the church. Some clergy, Catholic students, and youths deliberately ignored positions that the BOK, and especially Bengsch, had taken. A whole set of practices began to develop that partially opposed those of the church leadership. As internal theological differences grew visible among the ordinaries, Bengsch could at least use his authority to ensure that Catholic bishops refrained from saying anything as a group that he did not fully endorse or think opportune. Bengsch agitated for what he saw as Catholic solidarity against destructive or heretical tendencies. He directed this line "externally" against state appropriation but increasingly also "internally" against perceived deviations within the church.

Although one must distinguish the policy of public "political abstinence" from the actual views and actions of individual church officials, many clergy and lay Catholics perceived the lack of public protest as a failure of duty on the part of the church. When the spring 1968 reforms in Czechoslovakia offered the Catholic Church there an opportunity to loosen the repressive grip of the Communist government, GDR Politburo member Verner reported to Ulbricht on 31 May 1968 what Otto Groß had reassuringly relayed to state agencies: Cardinal Bengsch was disturbed by the events and "tried repeatedly over the past few weeks to exert a 'moderating influence' upon Czechoslovakian Catholics."[157] But this constituted a deliberate tactic in relation to the state. Bengsch himself had said in a message to the Vatican on 17 May 1968 that "all possibilities that [the Czechoslovakian] liberalization offers should be used immediately."[158] That same month, Bishop Schaffran held talks in Rome on behalf of the BOK. Their purpose was to share detailed information that Catholics in the GDR had gathered about specific people within the Czechoslovakian church with Czechoslovakian clergy to isolate spies. But when the Soviet-led military intervention crushed the Prague Spring on 21 August 1968, the BOK under the leadership of Cardinal Bengsch remained silent—whereas the Protestant Church in the GDR protested. In September 1968, three Catholic and seven Protestant clergymen from Merseburg sent a telegram declaring their distress,[159] but otherwise, the state registered no opposition from the Catholic Church.

On 17 October 1968 the SED Central Committee's Working Group on Church Affairs reported to Verner, after explanations of Vatican tactics, that "[a] cautious, measured posture that avoids pointless political confrontations is also characteristic of . . . the church leadership in the GDR."[160] In February 1969, Prelate Groß even insisted to the MfS that the state take steps to accommodate Catholics in the question of the demolition of the Rostock Christuskirche because, "in contrast to the Protestants, Cardinal Bengsch made no [negative] public statements on military service, the measures of August 13, 1961 [i.e., the Berlin Wall], events in Czechoslovakia, the dismantling of the Leipzig University Church."[161] Groß argued that because fellow Catholics criticized Bengsch for these positions, the state should help him achieve results on the Rostock issue.

A few months later, the very same Groß appealed to Bengsch to make public statements regarding the positive conditions for the Catholic Church in the GDR on the occasion of the twentieth anniversary of the state; he did not mean to undermine the policy of "political abstinence" but merely to manufacture a quotable political gesture. This followed a controversial conversation between Seigewasser and Bengsch on 13 May 1969, whose unsuccessful outcome Groß blamed on Seigewasser's deputy, Flint. Thereafter, Groß was not permitted to accept an invitation to Austria as chief editor of the journal *St. Hedwigsblatt*. Flint wanted to make clear to Groß that "the cardinal must reconsider his position in light of the GDR's twentieth anniversary."[162] After other similar references—including by the MfS—Groß worked before the 3–5 September meeting of the BOK to make sure that the following made it into the minutes:

> We perceive merely more pressure to have Cardinal Bengsch participate in state ceremonies for the twentieth anniversary of the GDR, or at least to make a public statement. However, the cardinal will in no way take part in the state ceremonies. The only thing he will do is to give a sermon on the relation of Christ and the world, to be presented during religious services in Bernau on September 14 on the 100th anniversary of the attack on the Moabit monastery. The sermon will be published in *St. Hedwigsblatt*.[163]

In his Bernau sermon on 14 September, the cardinal then said, among other things:

> We must acknowledge this duty: to love the fellow human beings we are together with, the people here in the GDR. And when, in a few days, the state celebrates its twentieth anniversary, we are prepared to recognize everything that has really served the good of the people, and for the additional reason that Christians have shared in all of this work. And when we look back at twenty years of church life here, we are unable to wipe away the tensions and sometimes heavy burdens, but we are able to say with thanks to God that the church could do its spiritual work and, if we are honest, we can say that it often had more opportunities than it took advantage of . . . And even on things where we cannot reach a consensus, we will struggle for a bearable cohabitation in honesty and liberty.[164]

Prelate Groß delivered the text of the sermon together with guidelines for its interpretation to the MfS, which had already noted in a 15 September 1969 report that Bengsch had "uttered the name 'GDR' for the first time at an official event" and had spoken of "bearable cohabitation."[165] They ventured to remark that religious believers had grown "able to develop a legitimate pride in their collaboration."

The gradual dominance of the categories of political predictability and conflict avoidance in the principle of "political abstinence" was evident in 1971, when the church took no critical position on the much-discussed topic of "the Christian in socialist society." At the 14 June 1971 BOK meeting, Bishop Bernhard Huhn (Görlitz) was tapped to draft a response together with two theology professors from Erfurt, Wilhelm Ernst and Konrad Feiereis.[166] On 20 August Huhn presented the BOK with a draft entitled "The Christian in our Local Socialist Society," summarizing,

> This subject is once again current as the demands mount. The church "must say something about it" because the challenges are increasing, the pressure from the state is not diminishing, and both priests and lay Catholics perceive areas of uncertainty in pastoral practice. [Bishops] have the duty to become informed anew about socialism's self-conception and how Christian citizens can relate to it.[167]

A note from Groß to Bengsch of 3 December 1971, however, put debate about a possible public position on this issue to an end. Groß explicitly stated that no political declaration from one BOK member would be possible with the assent of the others and that the time was "not right."[168] The state would see it as "a sort of declaration of war" and "take extremely harsh ideological countermeasures," perhaps barring Christians from all "government, bureaucratic, and trade" employment; further, the "oath issue would surely be sharpened." Individual Christians would suffer the consequences. On the question of working together in socialist society, Groß responded: "Hasn't this been sufficiently proved over twenty-five years?"

Bengsch made political declarations only in his conversations with State Secretary Seigewasser. For example, on 10 January 1972, after Seigewasser had reproached him for the BOK's position on abortion, Bengsch had openly discussed human rights, expressing his strong disapproval of state pressure in matters of conscience, career disadvantages for Christians, state confiscation of postal parcels, and an education system that produced hypocrites by pressuring people into ideological conformity. Groß quoted the cardinal in his file notes, which he gave to the MfS and finished as follows:

> The State Secretary should think through everything the cardinal said; it is no mere random collection of gripes. He did not go out to solicit complaints; they were brought to him. And it is his responsibility to society and the state to report them. But [Seigewasser] should rest assured that these issues are not subjects for sermons and that by

bringing them up, he in no way intended to disrupt the government and its political aims.[169]

Vatican II and Vatican Policy toward the Communist World

In December 1961, the *Deutsche Zeitschrift für Philosophie* published an article by Alfred Arnold on Pope John XXIII's encyclical "Mater et Magistra" of 15 May 1961. Arnold characterized the pope's words as "a tool in the preparation for ideological war . . . anti-Communism dressed up as religion, with lies, slander, social demagoguery, spiritual terrorism, and a complete lack of perspective."[170] Five months later, the same journal printed a "reader's letter" from Hartmut Rüstau—clearly with the approval of the editors—that heavily criticized Arnold's article. Rüstau wrote that the pope's "anti-Communist language was much milder than in the past" and that the encyclical must be viewed in connection with Khrushchev's praise for the pope's "changed tactics . . . which can clearly be seen as a victory for the socialist camp."[171]

In November 1958, 77-year-old Angelo Giuseppe Roncalli had been chosen to succeed Pius XII as pope; he took the name John XXIII. Although at first he was still surrounded by church figures who were supportive of Italian Christian Democrats and rejected the idea that Catholics could ever vote for socialist or communist parties, the new pope began to distance himself from party politics and advocated working together "with all men of goodwill."[172] Although he believed that Catholics should remain true to the teachings of the church in their social and political engagements, he felt that they should make their own political choices rather than merely fulfill clerical instructions. When the pope warned of the danger of war in 1961, Khrushchev sent him a telegram—on the recommendation of the Italian Communist Party—in November 1961 for his eightieth birthday. To the dismay of many of his colleagues in Rome, the pope sent a thank-you note. As the world turned its attention to the Cuban missile crisis, Pope John XXIII—supposedly at the request of Khrushchev—tried to broker an arrangement with President Kennedy through intermediaries. This episode likely brought the pope and the Soviet leader closer together, and they exchanged Christmas greetings in December 1962. On 7 March 1963 the pope granted an audience to Khrushchev's son-in-law and his wife—the first ever papal audience granted to a prominent Communist.

Pope John XXIII attracted worldwide attention for his 11 April 1963 encyclical "Pacem in Terris," in which he called for international disarmament talks and an end to the arms race. Without neglecting demands for human rights and religious freedom, the pope advocated working together "with all men of goodwill" and saw "positive elements" in historical social reform movements. He condemned the "error," to be sure, but called for dialogue with "those who erred."[173] Primarily aimed at pluralist (Western) societies, the encyclical was timed to coincide with the upcoming Italian elections, but it resonated well within the GDR state and party apparatus, and their propaganda showed their selective appreciation.

In October 1963, two Marxist philosophers published an article on the encyclical entitled "Differentiation in Political Clericalism," which clarified its political objectives. After praising Pope John XXIII, they surmised that "modern Catholicism . . . is not the closed, disciplined, monolithic bloc" that it was often portrayed to be; "differentiation . . . now allows for cooperation in the basic question of war or peace."[174] The East German CDU then published sections of the encyclical in the May issue of the journal *begegnung.* Catholics who were already active in this party now sought to justify their engagement using the pope's words. Immediately after the encyclical appeared, Carl Ordnung, a Protestant CDU official, informed the party leadership that "we can try to win over more circles of lay Catholics and clergy in the GDR for our work."[175] Although his plan was only sporadically realized, he produced a list of names and suggested that every Catholic bishop in the GDR receive a visit from a CDU district leader and a "Catholic friend" to express thanks for "the encouraging and helpful words from the Holy Father." The BOK, by contrast, was moved on 23 May 1963 to release a joint pastoral letter on the encyclical for the entire GDR, which emphasized the passages on human rights and referred people to the complete text of the pope's words in the church newspaper.[176] Such selective interpretation of papal statements would become characteristic of the CDU's differentiation policy and the Berlin Conference, an international peace group active after 1964. The Berlin Conference was also an unintended side effect of the papacy of John XXIII and the Ostpolitik of his successor, Paul VI (Giovanni Battista Montini), elected in June 1963. Without the prospect of "possibilities for differentiation within Catholicism," the Berlin Conference would never have been allowed to form in the GDR.

But John XXIII had a greater historical impact than the selective attention he aroused with his "Pacem in Terris" encyclical when he convened the general council of the Catholic Church, which he announced in January 1959. After a commission made preparations, some 2,400 "council fathers" attended ten "public discussions" in Rome between October 1962 and December 1964. The council issued numerous decrees, statements, and dogmas on a wide range of internal church, ecumenical, and social themes. Due in no small part to the changed perception of the pope's role in world politics, the GDR regime permitted its bishops to travel accompanied to Rome for the council sessions. At the same time, it tried to exert influence so that the council would not be "misused to attack our state, our government, and our peace policies."[177] As a member of the central commission for the preparation of the council, Archbishop Bengsch had already expressed his clear disapproval in Rome of a draft paper on "the spiritual needs of Christians impacted by Communism" on 4 May 1962. These tactics had an impact throughout the council; all attempts by American and other Western participants to condemn Communism in the official council documents were unsuccessful. Bengsch stated further that any one-sided criticism of Communism would hurt Catholics behind the Iron Curtain. For him, "practical materialism" in all political systems was the real problem. Well-intentioned solidarity with the "church of silence" was, in his view, counterproductive for Catholics in socialist countries. He rejected the very term: "The church is in no way silent as a general rule but carries on its spiritual struggle through sermons and teaching . . . It would be a much greater help to this struggle if church representatives in other nations would keep *their* silence about the 'church of silence.'" Bengsch supported the anti-Communist position in the statement but suggested a better tactic: "They can be taught another way that does not so clearly reveal the methods by which the church can overcome its worst enemies."[178]

In December 1965, in part because he feared differentiation attempts by the state, Bengsch also sought to block the passage of a central document at the conclusion of the Vatican Council, entitled "Gaudium et Spes," which assumed pluralist, parliamentary democracy as the norm. Sections of the text addressed pluralism among Christians and the process of arriving at a political judgment:

> It is often the case that [two] people of conscience will come to a different conclusion on the same question. If the two different solutions are then seen by many others— even against the will of the two parties—as clear conclusions based on the message of the Gospels, then it must be made clear that in such cases no one has the right to claim the authority of the church exclusively for himself and his opinions.[179]

Archbishop Bengsch sent a detailed letter in Latin to Pope Paul VI on 22 November 1965, in which he explained his reservations on "Gaudium et Spes."[180] His main issue concerned the authority of the church office; his second concern was the possibility of appropriation by the socialist state's propaganda. Above all, Bengsch rejected "describing almost all questions of today's world," and criticized what he saw as "optimism in the judgment of worldly phenomena"—the praise of "modern culture" and "human progress" while the "defects in our culture" remained unaddressed. Bengsch saw the political abstinence of the Catholic Church in the GDR "undermined by the authority of the council, and the bishops who fulfill their religious and therefore non-political duties in our region will be seen as disobedient by the church and isolated among their peers." Finally, Bengsch stated his opposition to "so-called pluralist society." Catholics, he wrote, "are exposed almost everywhere to the storm of some kind of materialism . . . and almost everything is now a matter of public discussion both within the church and beyond it." Bengsch received no reply to his letter, and only after the adoption of the Vatican Council in December 1965 was he invited to speak with Pope Paul VI. The archbishop of Berlin had first voted against this central document—something he did not deny and that gradually became known within the Catholic Church in the GDR. The existence of his 22 November 1965 letter to the pope was not known, however. In any case, the serious consequences for the church in the GDR in the wake of "Gaudium et Spes" did not derive from the state's easily transparent distortion of it or from CDU policies of differentiation, but rather from a conflict within the church itself over the meaning of the council document.

After the Vatican Council, GDR Kirchenpolitik, coordinated with Polish state agencies, was influenced by an 18 November 1965 letter from Polish bishops to German bishops, and their 5 December reply.[181] Archbishop Bengsch and Bishop Spülbeck had been heavily involved in this, together with the Fulda Bishops' Conference, and the GDR state apparatus came down hard on them for this after their return home. The letters expressed the bishops' wish for reconciliation between the German and Polish peoples and their mutual requests for forgiveness for injustices before and after 1945. Polish bishops were somewhat disappointed by the diplomatic German answer, and the GDR bishops were charged with becoming involved in the foreign policy of socialist countries. The respective state authorities accused the Polish bishops of unpatriotically bending to the Germans, and the East German bishops of acting in an all-German context by signing the letter in common with West German bishops. Aside from the immediate consequences—including serious government "debriefings" of Bengsch in Berlin and Spülbeck in Dresden, both on 16 February 1966—the exchange of letters set the Vatican's policy on the GDR and Poland in motion.

The Polish government concurred with the bishops in their wish to have the Oder-Neisse border recognized in church law by allowing the formerly German regions now under Polish control to become self-contained dioceses. The GDR regime, by contrast, in a policy move that countered their established money-transfer arrangements with the West German churches, sought to dissolve certain church relations with the FRG and to have the Vatican legally establish the contours of the Catholic Church in the GDR. The bishops of Fulda, Osnabrück, Paderborn, and Würzburg were not only now barred from visiting parts of their dioceses on GDR territory, but beginning in September 1966 were also denied day trips to East Berlin, which they had used to maintain direct contacts.

Pope John XXIII had reopened Vatican diplomacy in the Communist world through his contact with Khrushchev and the encyclical "Pacem in Terris." As early as April 1963, figures who would become leaders in Catholic relations with the socialist countries—Cardinal Franz König of Vienna and Archbishop Agostino Casaroli of the Vatican—pursued agreements with the governments of Hungary, Poland, and later Czechoslovakia and Yugoslavia, that would improve the working conditions for the church in those countries. Casaroli's negotiations in Yugoslavia prompted Bengsch to have Spülbeck ask Pope Paul VI in October 1966 to give GDR bishops advance notice of such talks in the future to avoid being manipulated by the East Berlin regime.[182] The pope agreed, but such consultations never materialized.

On 31 October 1966 Bengsch asked the papal nuncio in Bonn to consider adjusting the borders of dioceses to reflect the GDR-Poland border as a preventive measure: "What can today appear as purely a church decision might tomorrow look like a political measure with consequences that are difficult to predict."[183] This kind of statement from Bengsch upset the Bonn government, which considered the question of diocese boundaries in connection with its own Hallstein Doctrine, its non-recognition of the Oder-Neisse border, and the relevance of the Reichskonkordat. Bengsch's awareness that certain realities would have to be confronted sooner or later was ahead of its time. Early on, he saw opportunities, which could not be realized later, to have a hand in shaping the rules of engagement in East Berlin and Warsaw and thereby help the church escape paying a political price. In a 2 March 1967 memo to the Vatican, Bengsch suggested naming administrators for "Western Poland and East Germany," even though the GDR would likely consider it a political success "in its current quest for sovereignty and policy of separation from the FRG."[184] A later arrangement without a direct connection to Western Poland, by contrast, would be an even greater success for the GDR in that such a deal would hardly be possible without prior direct diplomatic coordination with the Vatican. In a 2 May 1969 memo to the Vatican on church-state relations in East Germany, Bengsch suggested that, in the future, the Vatican only appoint acting bishops for the GDR who "receive their jurisdictions directly from the Holy See and not from the diocese bishops resident in the FRG."[185] On 13 May Seigewasser told Groß to inform Bengsch for the first time that "in the future when an auxiliary bishop dies, we will not recognize any successor named by a West German diocese."[186] This issue was discussed at a meeting in West Berlin on 3 July 1969 with Bengsch, the papal nuncio, and the bishops of Fulda, Osnabrück, Paderborn, and Würzburg, who aimed to achieve unity on the direct appointment of "administrators" by the Vatican in the future. The West German ordinaries accepted this formal confirmation of a long inner-church development that had begun when the GDR sealed its border in 1961. Remarkably, the Catholic bishops made this decision while the Grand Coalition of the CDU and the SPD still controlled the parliament in Bonn and the results of the October 1969 Bundestag elections were still unknown.

The elections made Willy Brandt the federal chancellor, head of an SPD/FDP (Free Democratic Party) governing coalition, and the new Ostpolitik that German Social Democrats had prepared well in advance began in earnest. In December 1969, direct talks commenced between the Bonn government and Moscow and Warsaw. By 18–19 November, SPD politicians Herbert Wehner and Georg Leber had held talks in Rome with Archbishop Casaroli, who had been functioning essentially as the Vatican's "foreign minister" since 1967. Their move to have the Vatican recognize Poland's western border (in order to minimize opposition from West German Christian Democrats to their plans for a treaty) failed because Rome first wanted to see such a treaty ratified by the FRG.[187] In March 1970, the Vatican appointed administrative bishops directly for the first time in the GDR: Heinrich Theissing and Johannes Braun became the apostolic administrators for Schwerin and Magdeburg, respectively. On 2 June 1970 the Politburo of the ZK optimistically decided—to "make things clear to the powers in charge of the churches"—that the Reichskonkordat was not binding for the GDR, all Catholic districts in the GDR were to become self-contained dioceses, the BOK was to have the status of a bishops' conference, the papal nuncio in Bonn would have no business in the GDR, and West Berlin Catholic representatives would not take part in the synod of West German dioceses.[188] However, most of these decisions would not be realized. The West German government signed the Moscow treaty in August 1970 and the Warsaw treaty in December, thereby recognizing the Oder-Neisse border.

Only after the West German parliament approved the treaties, which took effect on 3 June 1972, did the Vatican begin to take steps. It established four new dioceses in Western Poland on 28 June 1972, detached the Görlitz district from the formerly German Archdiocese of Breslau, and assigned it an apostolic administrator. By now, the Vatican was long since only able to react to political events. The law of being proactive played out in favor of the GDR, in part because the appeals of the West German Conference of Bishops and Catholic political leaders in the CDU/CSU to the Vatican sought to torpedo SPD/FDP Ostpolitik rather than exact a price from the GDR—which may, indeed, have been prepared to pay one, given the reality of world politics.

Of all the ways the GDR regime, hungry for diplomatic recognition, might have interpreted the Vatican policy toward the Communist world, it still perceived Rome's Ostpolitik for a long time as a gateway to "ideological diversion" for "undermining socialism." A 17 October 1968 analysis by the church affairs section of the ZK on the state of the churches after the Soviet-led military intervention in Czechoslovakia portrayed the Vatican as "oriented toward cautious action that does not cause a spectacle . . . in this way, it achieved everything it could have in Prague (demolishing the Peace Priests' Movement, reinstalling reactionary retired bishops, filling vacant bishops' seats, etc.)."[189] Three years later, a detailed MfS analysis of Vatican Ostpolitik dated 21 July 1971 still saw "a flexible policy" that sought to "sap" the socialist "community of states" using a differentiated approach.[190] The Vatican was allegedly interested in "securing the ownership of property and gaining more liberties for the church." The MfS regarded the Secretariat for Nonbelievers, which had been established in Rome in 1965 under the directorship of Viennese Cardinal Franz König, as only a sham attempt to engage in dialogue with socialism through the study of Marxism and atheism. In reality, the MfS claimed that this organization "aims to use all means—including the activities of the national churches—to 'liberalize' the socialist countries." A further MfS analysis from 26 October 1971 claimed that this Vatican office was "clearly against the socialist worldview and the basis of the socialist state."[191] It appeared to promote dialogue between Christians and Marxists "only to pursue a refined attack against the socialist worldview." In the MfS's view, the Vatican "sought to use current conditions of the worldwide transition from capitalism to socialism in order to work against the underpinnings of socialism."

"Centralism" and Strategies of Kirchenpolitik

It would be a great simplification of complex processes to see concrete BOK policies after August 1961 as the result of the actions of specific leading Catholic figures in the GDR. However, church strategies and patterns of behavior simply cannot be explained without understanding the predominance of Alfred Bengsch's positions, which continued even after his death in December 1979. The manageable size of the Catholic Church in the GDR, and especially the very centralized SED state and its Berlin-based bureaucracy—a hierarchical system of order-giving encompassing the ruling party, the state apparatus, the satellite parties, and the mass organizations—strengthened Bengsch's position. The SED's ideas of the Catholic Church and its functioning were based on its own culture as well as its impression of the church hierarchy from the outside. The GDR regime saw talks and agreements with leading officials as a tried and true means of giving directives it assumed would be passed down a tightly structured hierarchy, and as a way to help "discipline" individuals if necessary. The SED's ideal did not, of course, completely conform to church practice, but many individual Catholic officials used it for their own purposes under the pretext of state pressure.

The term "Berlin centralism" was current in the Catholic Church in the GDR. Catholic ordinaries and clerics often used it critically to describe the role of the bishop of Berlin and his staff, which they perceived as privileged. Bengsch and his people, for their part, saw centralism as a protective function that served to preserve the solidarity of the whole Catholic Church in the GDR. The exercise of power within the church depended upon access to information. Through his contact with the various state offices in Berlin, his access to West Berlin and Rome, and his ability to influence travel abroad for others in the church, Bengsch constantly had the advantage of information over other bishops, ordinaries, and clerics in the GDR. The way he and some of his colleagues then disseminated this information led unavoidably to a kind of "power knowledge." Whether they used it to promote solidarity or a personal agenda in a calculated way depended in large part upon their individual personalities and their political ambitions within the church.

"Centralism" in Berlin was hardly ever questioned before 1965, but broader Catholic debates and generational conflicts after the Second Vatican Council gradually undermined it. In the Catholic Church throughout the West in the later 1960s, new questions arose over the role clerics and lay Catholics ought to play. Some perceived this as a new opportunity, but others found it upsetting and damaging, seeing it as a crisis of authority that needed to be met with even more authority. The GDR population got wind of these tendencies through the Western media, personal contacts, and smuggled literature, so similar developments occurred there as well, especially in the immediate euphoria following Vatican II. The church's "centralism" in Berlin—shaped in its essence by Cardinal Bengsch and especially Prelate Groß—gradually became a decisive factor in its dealings with the GDR state. From the beginning of his negotiating duties in September

1967 to his death in August 1974, Groß established the personalized "modus vivendi" that remained valid until the end of the GDR.

Bengsch was more than the chair of the BOK and its speaker. In personal authority, theological education, and intellectual acumen, he was clearly beyond his fellow bishops. Despite his opposition to "Gaudium et Spes" in 1965, his stature in Rome and in the church worldwide increased due to his diplomatic brilliance in the complex Vatican policy toward the Communist world and his clear loyalty to the pope in the context of some dissenting tendencies within the Western European bishops' conferences—for example, in 1968 over the issue of contraception. Bishop Spülbeck of Meißen was also very important in the BOK; he had personal access to Pope John XXIII and to other foreign bishops, his diocese was not divided between East and West Germany, and he had been considered as a candidate for the seat of bishop of Berlin in 1956–1957 and in 1961. Like Hugo Aufderbeck, the auxiliary bishop of Erfurt, Spülbeck was a serious theological dialogue partner for Bengsch. Despite many differences, Spülbeck and Aufderbeck were loyal to Bengsch as chairman of the BOK, but the same cannot be said of Bengsch in relation to Aufderbeck and especially Spülbeck.

Bengsch's political activities within the Catholic world in the GDR intensified after Groß assumed the role of negotiator with the State Secretariat for Church Affairs and took over Zinke's MfS contacts in 1967. (Zinke, who resided in West Berlin, was in poor health.) Groß was a cleric with an ambition for secret diplomacy. In this key position, and with his close ties to Bengsch, he gradually became the most influential representative of the Catholic Church in the GDR. As such, he was sometimes criticized within the church. In 1969, for example, the Erfurt theology instructor Wilhelm Ernst called him "the most hated man within the [church] hierarchy" who "often claims to speak in the name of the cardinal, whereby many in the church doubt that he sufficiently informs the cardinal or that [Groß] is authorized by the cardinal to make decisions."[192] Although Groß tried to represent Cardinal Bengsch's interests with absolute loyalty in his talks with government agencies, he sometimes used arguments and gave the MfS information that Bengsch would have preferred to keep from state officials.

Groß was never required to account for how he achieved the results that Bengsch wanted. He tried to play state agencies against one another and bet on the MfS as a direct source of information from the Politburo and the ZK. He gave the MfS his notes on conversations between Seigewasser and Bengsch so that the security services could double-check the versions that Seigewasser's office gave them. He added interpretive notes for the MfS on certain subjects in order to spin them in a certain direction. Besides handling affairs for the entire Catholic Church in the GDR, Groß also negotiated for the exchange of American prisoners of war in North Vietnam, brokered Caritas projects in Arab countries, and used the support of the international Caritas organization and the Vatican to spur the inclusion of the GDR in a United Nations world food program. He traveled on business in the West, holding talks, for example, with Herbert Wehner in Bonn in March 1970 on the past and present directions of West German

Ostpolitik and then reporting on it to the MfS. Groß tried to use the MfS for the church's purposes but, therefore, had to play the agency's game when it came to people and groups within the church that it considered oppositional.

In view of the simultaneous balancing act that the church's designated MfS contacts performed, the ambivalence of the policy of "public political abstinence" came to the fore whenever such contacts had political ambitions, wanted influence in the church, and exchanged information in a targeted way for these purposes. Groß tried to use the MfS for "personnel politics," in Cardinal Bengsch's sense, on the issue of appointing bishops in Magdeburg, Schwerin, and Meißen, and a new general vicar in Berlin. The MfS was not able to have very much influence in choosing candidates it felt more comfortable with, and it never made personnel suggestions. But in discussions of personnel matters (which occurred around the time of a changing of the guard), Groß and other sources provided the MfS with a wealth of information.

A process called "Berlin centralism" or "Berlinization" outside of that district was intended to reshape the BOK. This process replaced older departing members with bishops with personal, theological, and political loyalty to Cardinal Bengsch. The motives of the "Berliners" were complex. Besides preserving the "solidarity" of the Catholic ordinaries in the face of the state, notions about theological lines of authority within the church played an essential role. The reorganization of church districts according to a recognition of GDR sovereignty created favorable conditions for the BOK to be reshuffled. When it became evident that the Vatican would follow the suggestions of West German bishops in Paderborn, Osnabrück, Fulda, and Würzburg in installing ordinaries in districts that formally still belonged to them (Magdeburg, Schwerin, Erfurt, and Meiningen), then Cardinal Bengsch's influence grew because of his direct contacts with the papal nuncio in Bonn and with Rome. Bengsch's preventive suggestions about reorganizing Catholic districts in the GDR also contained thoughts about installing coadjutor apostolic administrators with the right of succession in Magdeburg and Schwerin, as well as dissolving the district of Meiningen—without acknowledging the ordinaries resident there: Friedrich Maria Rintelen, Bernhard Schräder, and Joseph Schönauer. Cardinal Bengsch used his influence in the Vatican while Groß used his influence in the state offices to attempt to have these officials gradually removed. The outcome varied across the districts: in Meiningen it failed, in Schwerin it succeeded without public attention, but in Magdeburg it led to major inner-church turbulence and public confrontations.

In general, the church's personnel matters remained internal, hardly garnering notice from the outside except for outwardly obvious changes. The MfS, however, knew quite a bit, in no small part owing to Groß's calculated policy. In November 1969, the Würzburg bishop Josef Stangl asked the episcopal commissioner Joseph Schönauer to step down—routine in church law—to clear the way for the commissioner's office of Meiningen to be dissolved and attached to Erfurt.[193] Schönauer declined, however, and stayed on until 1971 before retiring and settling in Würzburg. In Schwerin, Bengsch and Groß arranged for the bishop's commissioner in Schwerin, Bernhard Schräder, who suffered from health problems, to be replaced by Heinrich Theissing. They did this with the support of the Vatican and the bishop of Osnabrück and without Schräder's knowledge. Theissing was an auxiliary bishop in Berlin with very close ties to Bengsch. Although preparations for this move took over a year, it was only in December 1969 that Schräder was asked to step down and resettle in Osnabrück. The MfS knew long before, however, that an apartment in Osnabrück had been prepared for him.[194] Schräder reacted with a public suit in March 1970. Bengsch was also able to quietly install one of his favorites, Gerhard Schaffran, to replace Bishop Spülbeck in Meißen after he had died in 1970. Schaffran had been the bishop of Görlitz and followed the same theological line as Bengsch. With Schaffran installed, the status of Görlitz simultaneously changed to "the remainder of the Archdiocese of Breslau." In this case, the MfS had very precise information about Bengsch's influence less than two weeks after Spülbeck's death.[195]

Bengsch's attempt to remove the auxiliary bishop of Magdeburg, Rintelen, turned out differently. Rintelen did not obey the rules of secret church diplomacy, which led to an affair with long-term internal church consequences. Bengsch wanted to replace Rintelen because, from the perspective of Berlin, he did not exercise enough discipline over his very pluralistic clergy and because he had too much to do with the local district government and the State Secretariat for Church Affairs. At bottom, the conflict arose because Bengsch wanted Rintelen to acknowledge his political and religious authority, whereas Rintelen viewed Cardinal Lorenz Jäger of Paderborn as his direct superior and felt that his Magdeburg district was autonomous within the GDR. For that reason, Bengsch had considered plans to remove him since 1965. After the state-supported festivities celebrating the millennial anniversary of the Diocese of Magdeburg in September 1968, Bengsch pursued the removal of Rintelen in Rome and Paderborn, arguing that he lacked sufficient authority over his clergy and had too many conflicts with state agencies.

Groß informed these agencies that Rintelen could not be approached with the differentiation policy. By 17 October 1968 the MfS knew that Bengsch was trying to oust Rintelen.[196] On 14 December 1968 Groß and the MfS discussed a successor, Paul Nordhues, an auxiliary bishop in Paderborn; Bengsch and Cardinal Jäger had discussed this choice in Paderborn, and Groß told the MfS that Jäger would restore the necessary order among clerics and lay Catholics in Magdeburg. Nordhues had been the regent of the Magdeburg seminary until 1961, when he legally moved to Paderborn. Although GDR Kirchenpolitik aimed to sever ties with the FRG, the MfS approved Bengsch and Jäger's plan based on Groß's arguments. According to the prelate's notes,

> The state organs, asked how they would view such a plan, stated that they would allow Auxiliary Bishop Nordhus *[sic]* to enter the GDR under the mechanism of the reunification of families, on a list to be submitted by the lawyers Vogel and Stange. Because

of its sensitive German-German nature, the situation must be handled very discreetly. It is essential for them that no internal church difficulties arise.[197]

The Office of the State Secretary for Church Affairs and the Magdeburg district council were not informed about these connections and behaved as before, using the differentiation policy with Rintelen. After Rintelen spoke with Seigewasser in Magdeburg on 18 June 1969, a press communiqué was published. Groß judged it as a disaster: "This communiqué exceeds all of our fears; it is proof that a change in Magdeburg is truly necessary. This press statement opens the door for anyone and everyone to get politically involved with the government. It has broken the unity of the bishops in political matters, and Rintelen has helped the state achieve its goal."[198] After the Vatican finally decided to name a coadjutor apostolic administrator with the right of succession for Magdeburg, Rintelen traveled to Bonn at the invitation of Cardinal Lorenz Jäger, where he met the papal nuncio and was, to his surprise, told that he had to step down.

After his return, however, Rintelen, together with Prelate Heinrich Jäger, informed the SED district leadership in Magdeburg about his pending dismissal and replacement. Gerhard Salzmann, the local SED official, immediately informed the ZK that there had allegedly been "intrigues against Auxiliary Bishop Rintelen, especially after the anniversary celebrations in Magdeburg. Bengsch played an especially sinister role against him at the Vatican. He was accused of making deals with the state."[199] That same day (17 July 1969), Fritz Bellstedt of the Magdeburg district council went with Heinrich Jäger to Rintelen who "had tears in his eyes."[200] State agencies at the central and district levels saw Rintelen's dismissal as a political move against a "progressive" Catholic official, and the MfS, which was involved in a different way, signaled to Groß that a transfer of Auxiliary Bishop Nordhues was no longer possible due to the bad press.[201] Rintelen had not only informed officials in Magdeburg of the decision but also the clergy of the churches that would be impacted. The result was a protest meeting on 19 July 1969 in Halle, as well as a declaration to the Vatican and the cardinals in Berlin and Paderborn against the manner of Rintelen's removal signed by 155 people—about half of all the clergy in Magdeburg.

The protest meeting sparked the formation of the Halle Action Group and started an intensive debate on clergy and lay participation in the choice of bishops, and in the church in general. Rintelen's case touched on a larger feeling within the church of discontent with "Berlin centralism" and a lack of opportunity for participation:

The Paderborn diaspora priests in the "Elbe-Saale department" assumed that "Berlinization" was a fait accompli in church law and secular law, too. Beneath this was a concern about an unjustified centralism directed from Berlin. In recent years, this unfortunately growing mistrust has spontaneously brought together priests of the commissioner's office and lay Catholics—who otherwise hold very different positions—to find common cause and to explain (their feelings).[202]

Rintelen was supportive of the movement to democratize his succession process, but Bengsch and the Vatican ignored it on the basis of existing canon law. Clerics in the commissioner's office of Magdeburg engaged in heated personal battles after an intrigue of Prelate Heinrich Jäger. However, this did not prevent the Vatican from naming Magdeburg Prelate Johannes Braun coadjutor apostolic administrator with the right of succession in March 1970.[203] Long-term, though, there was little of the new direction that Bengsch had hoped for under the new bishop. The new leaders in Magdeburg continued to be sensitive to what they perceived as "Berlinization." They continued to have autonomous connections with local authorities and remained oriented toward Paderborn. By contrast, some of the clergy did not adhere to the new bishop's authority, especially in the Halle area. Otherwise, Bishop Braun refused to engage in his own negotiations with the State Secretary for Church Affairs.

On the whole, "Berlin centralism" had put in charge bishops in Schwerin, Meißen, and Magdeburg who submitted to Bengsch's political discipline more than their predecessors had. The position of the bishop of Berlin among the ordinaries was stronger than it had ever been.

Pluralism within the Church

In an internal report from October 1966, Archbishop Bengsch remarked, as BOK chairman, "the solidarity of the Catholic Church in the GDR has been loosened by a general post-Vatican Council wave."[204] He felt that "many basic principles have been questioned or modified and the preservation of our policy of political abstinence is no longer beyond discussion," but added that "the justifications for this policy" could not "be adequately discussed, let alone published." Bengsch and those who followed his line believed that political and theological pluralism within the Catholic Church was a great danger, given the facts of GDR society, because it would play right into the hands of the Communists and their differentiation strategy. At the same time, the fear that pluralism within the church would lead to a breakdown of unity was also widespread in countries with parliamentary democracies. In the GDR, this kind of argument at first seemed entirely plausible in light of the regime's attempts to selectively co-opt Vatican II, but as in the case of "political abstinence," the terms of the debate soon changed. After initially hoping that pluralism would bolster its policy of differentiation, the state began to see the emergence of different voices within the Catholic Church as unpredictable and even as a threatening "diversion." Bengsch, conversely, increasingly appeared to direct his criticism of pluralism at his own ranks in an attempt to contain trouble and discontent, seeing it as a crisis of authority: "Is it still the case within our church that we serve one another in love? . . . The world must laugh at us when we preach unity and brotherhood; they will say, just look at your own house!"[205]

After Claus Herold, a youth pastor in Magdeburg, wrote a report, read at a West German youth assembly, that was severely critical of the East German bishops in November 1967, a member of the Central Committee of German Catholics in Bonn sent a letter to Bengsch, quoting the report in great detail. The writer noted that the report had allegedly been "composed in secrecy in Magdeburg," and added, "I personally am for strengthening 'Berlin centralism' under the present conditions."[206] In his report, Herold had attacked the "hierarchical centralism from Berlin," remarking that "the block thinking" of the church was "an equally totalitarian answer to the problems of a minority ghettoized behind a wall . . . the state's control—banning books, confiscating periodicals—encourages internal censorship from the church . . . the few religious publications we are allowed contain little more than provincialism (autoeroticism), antiquarianism (a cult of personality), and, at best, apologetics and a few edifying thoughts." Bengsch reacted by writing Herold a pointed letter on 30 December, and Herold, in turn, responded with some self-criticism, requesting a meeting on 5 January 1968. Nonetheless, Bengsch removed Herold as the head of the working group for youth ministries on 15 January 1968 and halted all the work of this organization on account of the "insulting accusations against the bishops" in its annual report.[207] He wrote Herold a polemical letter that same day, declaring that "the limits of freedom and plurality" had been reached.[208] He added: "I understand young people's need for freedom, but it is difficult for me to comprehend how a priest cannot grasp that freedom can easily be confused with caprice." Bengsch's arguments were not grounded in the specific situation of the GDR; they were similar to those Catholic bishops used worldwide in internal church discussion during this era. However, as a rule, Bengsch alluded to pressures from outside, as he did in a BOK report from 2 and 3 December 1968: "Concerning demands from some circles within the church for [freer] discussion and [more] information, we say that, in the specific case of the Catholic Church in the GDR, there are limits."[209]

Information that circulated within the church and in its newspapers was subjected to the censorship of the church as well as the state. Therefore, many Catholic clergy, students, and ordinary people obtained whatever political and religious literature they could from the West through private contacts, as well as West German radio and television, which were available in parts of the GDR. Bengsch held that prolonged public discussions and debates were dangerous for the church, and large segments of the West German Catholic hierarchy in the early 1960s held a similar view. In the September 1963 BOK meeting, Bengsch referred to a speech by Cardinal Döpfner of Munich on the growth of "so-called 'non-conformist' literature," which, Döpfner believed, fomented "discontent with everything institutional in the church" and promoted "the heretical idea of an unhistorical (or charismatic elite) church."[210] Bengsch continued, "Because this literature penetrates our region via the radio, the ordinaries should be more vigilant against this tendency." This model of necessary vigilance against a "false," imported theology would appear again and again in the years to come in Bengsch's and other GDR ordinaries' positions. In February 1969, Bengsch described this Western influence as a "disease":

> We can observe a disrespect of church authority among many young clergy. Council decisions are now seen as a basis for discussion rather than a teaching that must be obeyed. This lack of insight into the essence of church teachings is the basis for the proliferation of individual theological views, which can be frequently observed today. The theological views of many young clergy have come from Western sources, been taken out of their context, simplified, and insufficiently thought through. Thus, untenable theological concepts have arisen, and when these have been corrected by bishops—as is their duty—it has been misunderstood as authoritarianism. This crisis of authority, transplanted from West to East, is, at the present moment, a disease afflicting the church, which cannot be cured by good theological and inner-church information.[211]

Western media, in part, spread this "disease." After a discussion that was, as usual, controversial, Bengsch suggested to the State Secretary for Church Affairs on 1 March 1971 that they should join forces against the damaging influence of Western television:

> The state should finally recognize in this case that we can indeed work together to educate our youth and that the church must be granted more latitude. Through religious instruction in school and by meeting the spiritual needs of our people, we can help clear away many things that might later also be harmful for the state. The state does not want our youth taught to be alcoholics, either, which can happen from many television programs from West Germany.[212]

In an internal speech draft, Groß said on 23 June 1971 that it was "certainly understandable that we do not want just any sort of social-political model pushed on us as imports from abroad, no matter where it comes from."[213]

These sorts of "imports," however, were of great interest to young Catholics, including clergy and students. In student congregations, young Catholics also began to work closely with Protestants. In April 1968, for example, the first joint student pastor conference in the GDR took place. In the post–Vatican II euphoria, Catholics in many countries wanted to "create facts" by changing practices, in the hope that the church would later endorse them. These attempts at pluralism impacted the Catholic Church in the GDR as well, and in some cases led to sharp—often irreconcilable—personal differences. Bengsch tried to resolve these conflicts not with dialogue but by tactically applying his authority, especially in personnel matters. Bengsch felt that it was his mission to save church unity, and many supported him in this, including the Vatican, West German bishops, many Berlin-based clergy, and many Catholic clergy of the older generation.

Other bishops in the GDR reacted in various ways to the movement for pluralism. Rintelen, the rather passive auxiliary bishop of Magdeburg, generally supported the clergy under him and thus provoked Bengsch to instigate his removal. Starting in 1965, Bishop Spülbeck of Meißen began preparations for a diocese synod to implement the decision of the Second Vatican Council; he had serious conflicts with Bengsch and Vatican officials after the synod opened in June 1969. Auxiliary Bishop Aufderbeck of Erfurt tried to integrate different tendencies within the church to avoid polarization. In April 1968, together with Bishop Schaffran of Görlitz, he organized the first Erfurt Dialogue Circle, which invited Catholic clergy and professionals from across the GDR to discuss heterogeneous ideas about the future of the churches under "real existing socialism." Within this group, expressions of uncertainty regarding the proper understanding of "spiritual office" and authoritarian efforts with charismatic pretensions revealed the church's shortcomings in managing internal conflict, a circumstance that was very unusual in GDR society. The Erfurt Dialogue Circle recommended that a group of ten to twenty clergy and lay Catholics from across the GDR be formed to advise the BOK on the situation of the church in the GDR; this came before the Vatican Council's call for advisory councils to be established at the central and regional levels.[214] When these were discussed at a meeting on 15 February 1969, members of the Erfurt group tried to persuade Bengsch to include "members of opposition factions" as well. He rejected this because these groups called for bishops to recognize the GDR, endangered state tolerance of inner-church publications by mailing their own literature, and supposedly "promoted isolation because it favored their protest stance." This sort of pluralism, said Bengsch, "was not part of the church as a whole," and the attacks on the BOK threatened church unity and played into the hands of the state's differentiation agenda. Moreover, Bengsch defended himself against the accusation that the church restricted information:

> Some of the church's discussions with government offices cannot be carried out in the public eye. Many of the possibilities for activity that the church enjoys are based upon spoken personal agreements with state offices, which require discretion. Thus, the cardinal and the [Berlin] Conference of Ordinaries are often confronted with the problem of not being able to explain things fully to the church community. This gives rise to the impression of an authoritarian style of leadership . . . The trust of the faithful in the leadership of the church is the foundation for the work of the Conference of Ordinaries.[215]

In July 1963, after Pope John XXIII's encyclical "Pacem in Terris," Auxiliary Bishop Aufderbeck of Erfurt helped found the Pacem in Terris Working Group with the BOK that sought, through the study of Marxism and the practical work of the church's social teachings, to analyze their socialist environment, to counter the state's ideological appropriation of concepts like "peace" and "justice," and to develop ideas for pastoral work. Theo Mechtenberg, a student pastor from Magdeburg, became its leader. Inspired by the decisions of the Second Vatican Council, especially the document "Gaudium et Spes," the group sent Bengsch a document on 14 December 1966 calling for "a dialogic relation of the church to the world in the form of critical engagement with socialism."[216] They admitted that the model of "Gaudium et Spes" could not be directly applied to the GDR but also held that the dialogic model could not be dismissed outright.

That same year, the group suggested that the church start a "pastoral-socio-logical institute" in order to involve lay Catholics in an analysis of the work environment of the GDR. Soon it was encouraging Catholics to take on jobs with a higher level of social involvement without joining the SED. Yet because Bengsch rejected the political and theological premises of the group, and because the BOK reserved a preeminent place for itself regarding the lives of Catholics, specific international contacts were soon blocked, and the group's members were cut off from information. Church leaders sought to integrate the group tightly into hierarchical church structures and ultimately render it ineffective. When Mechtenberg left the group in the fall of 1971, it almost completely lost its relevance within the church. In other words, church leaders who supported Bengsch managed to achieve their aim.

A more amorphous form of pluralism up until the 1970s was the "noncon-formity" of individual clergy—who often worked in much smaller circles. As in West Germany, bishops in the GDR used the term "nonconformity" in a clearly negative way to characterize what they saw as irresponsible dissent within Catholicism,[217] although the definition of this term and its application to specific individuals were naturally vague. In general, it referred to Catholic clergy who had demonstrated disobedience to church authorities without actually commit-ting an offense for which they could be removed from office according to canon law. In essence, the bishops wanted to distinguish between those clergy who were loyal and those who were not. In the GDR, they labeled a few individual priests in various dioceses nonconformist, but mostly reserved the designation for the Halle Action Group. Cardinal Jäger from Paderborn sent a letter from Rome to Auxiliary Bishop Rintelen on 28 November 1969, declaring his views on the public protests by clergy in Magdeburg: "The revolts by clergy are increasing! Even the Halle letters are known [here] and are attracting attention because of their tone. What a shame for the good clergy there!"[218] A position paper Bishop Schaffran sent to all BOK members on 26 February 1970 proves that this was not an isolated case in the GDR. Schaffran argued, "The issue of priests' groups con-cerns us all, regardless of where these groups are based; their sphere of operations crosses diocese boundaries."[219] Schaffran distinguished between the positive work of these groups and the "dangers" they entailed, which he understood as every-thing from "a collection point for discontent" to the formation of "a so-called underground church." Therefore, he wanted the BOK to "not only take admin-istrative steps to contain" such groups, but also to "begin positive initiatives."

One of the "groups" Schaffran referred to was comprised of the authors of a letter addressing "our celibacy crisis," which clergymen from Leipzig (Clemens Rosner and Theo Gunkel) and Gera (Bernhard Sahler) distributed in January 1970. Sent to all clergy in the Diocese of Meißen, it reached 340 people, who were asked to give their opinion on the possibility of allowing non-celibates to serve as priests. The letter attracted a great deal of attention among clergy and a strongly negative reaction from bishops in the GDR, not only because it coincided with a statement by the Netherlands Bishops' Conference that was critical of celibacy but also because the West German "Priests' Solidarity Group" in Frankfurt am Main published it.

Another group that garnered criticism was the Protestant-Catholic Letters Circle. Karl Herbst, a Catholic priest in Rötha and secretary of the Diocese of Meißen's ecumenical commission, and Günter Loske, a Protestant minister from Petersburg near Halle, had run the circle since 1958. They made theological texts and commentaries on ecumenical issues available to interested members of both churches in the GDR. However, in 1968, Herbst distributed comments critical of the papal encyclical "Humanae Vitae" and published texts from Western theologians such as Hans Küng, after which the BOK expressed its disapproval in its 23–24 February session:

> A careful review of the recent publications of the "Protestant-Catholic Letters Circle" finds that Karl Herbst's reflections are one-sided, confused, theologically incorrect, and capable of being misunderstood. They thus damage ecumenical efforts. We therefore note that this "Protestant-Catholic Letters Circle," which resulted from a private initiative, does not have the approval of the ordinaries.[220]

On 20 July 1970 Heinrich Bulang, chapter vicar of the Diocese of Meißen, instructed Herbst to stop all work with the Letters Circle on the argument that "it is better to be silent than to unintentionally misinform, even if in good faith."[221] In accordance with Catholic canon law, Herbst lost his "author's permit" and was also prohibited from participating "privately." Furthermore, Bulang told Catholic clergy who had supported the Letters Circle that they needed to conscientiously reconsider "receiving and reading these publications in their current form."[222]

In another major development, student congregations discussed the possibilities and limits of Christian engagement within socialist society.[223] They also debated the "democratic" restructuring of the church—for example, the free election of pastors—which led to conflicts with the BOK and prompted the MfS to call for stricter control of the churches. The West German student movement of 1968 had very much enlivened the Catholic Student Community (Katholische Studentengemeinde, KSG) in the GDR. Thereafter, the bishops in Berlin intervened several times in this community, removing a student pastor, considering blocking the free election of speakers, refusing to recognize elected student spokespeople, installing new pastors, and, after a Fasching event in February 1970, considering dissolving the KSG. An MfS report from 15 September 1969 gives a sense of the state of relations between the students and the bishops: it describes a "birthday present" Bengsch had received—a tank draped in crosses and church banners with the inscription "for the annihilation of the KSG." Moreover, the BOK had informed the MfS that Bengsch would no longer personally open packages because he feared stink bombs or even explosives.[224]

In 1971, the Berlin KSG announced that the theme of its Fasching celebration would be "Post–Vatican Council Pig Breeding: Alfred [Bengsch]—we are on our way!" As in no other Catholic institution in the GDR, an independent political and religious engagement developed in the student milieu up through about 1971. Centers of Catholic student activity included Berlin, Halle, Jena, Leipzig, and Magdeburg.

The so-called Korrespondenz (Correspondence Group), formed by ten young professionals and students in Halle in 1966, was a byproduct of the KSG, influenced by Adolf Brockhoff, a cleric in Halle. Its members reprinted and distributed 100–200 copies of theological articles from Western journals, adding their own commentaries as well as their names and addresses. In addition to current events, they discussed subjects such as the role of Christians in the GDR and Christian-Marxist dialogue, and they criticized forms of communication within the church. Dr. Winfried Schülke, for example, wrote in a first letter during Easter 1966,

> We think about our church in the GDR, appearing to the outside world as a unity, but preserving this unity only through activities and initiatives directed by the church's pastoral offices. It has not yet discovered the opportunity for pluralism, which means lay Catholics taking responsibility for their activities. Think how many possibilities there are for a genuine democratization of interactions between bishops, priests, and lay Catholics, how many chances for Christian deeds that have not yet been imagined in church offices.[225]

The group hoped that "public opinion" could be shaped by distributing this literature—but it failed in this aim because some rejected the ideas presented, and even those in favor were suspicious of the group. Many concluded that if they were tolerated by the state, they must be supported by the MfS.

The Halle Action Group was formed after the July 1969 clergy protest in the Holy Cross Congregation in Halle and the controversial "campaigning" surrounding the choice of a successor to Bishop Rintelen. The congregation prompted Claus Herold to write a seven-page text, "Hot Summer in Magdeburg," which was distributed in sixty numbered copies. The loose circle emerging from this spark soon drew attention to itself with assemblies and informational circulars. Catholics from all over the GDR responded, going well beyond the region of Halle and Magdeburg. After a gathering on 27 September 1969, several priests and lay Catholics officially formed the group "on the basis of various initiatives"; the first draft of its "declaration" mentions goals such as "solidarity," "open discussion and information," "action to democratize the church," and "assuming a critical social function."[226] "Democracy will be practiced within the group," they promised, "to establish a model." In a programmatic statement from 4 April 1970, the group called for the "democratization" and "humanization" of the church:

> We want to work for an interpretation of faith appropriate to the times and to pro-
> mote, within the church, consciousness, the strengthening of will, the freedom to
> express one's opinion, the unhindered flow of information, the transparency of admin-
> istrative processes, participation in decisions by church leaders, and a review process
> for these decisions. We strive to make the discontent and the activism of many indi-
> viduals more effective through the formation of a larger group.

The Halle Action Group began to organize regular "full assemblies" that sometimes attracted more than 100 people. It sent informational letters to clergy in
Magdeburg, ordinaries, and interested persons with excerpts from Western articles and commentaries. In the years that followed, the circulation of its literature
ranged from 350 to 600. The group's hopes for a broader impact in other church
jurisdictions did not succeed, however, even though it did have some members
from other dioceses. The Halle Action Group endured a serious crisis between
1971 and 1973, when the credibility of Adolf Brockhoff was challenged; the
group was polarized when he was suspended as a priest for violating celibacy. In
the long term, there was a shift in focus away from church reform issues toward
larger social questions; thereafter, the group lost relevance within the church.

The state's perception of pluralist developments within the Catholic Church
ranged from rather general analyses of the Office of the State Secretary for
Church Affairs (which often lacked insight) to the narrow, schematic view of
the MfS, which had a great deal of information on the movements. After a few
initial misperceptions, state officials soon came to the conclusion that this phe-
nomenon was not appropriate for their differentiation policy: people critical of
hierarchical practices within the church could not be politically instrumentalized
because they were also critical of socialist society. Therefore, they believed that
the church pluralist movement needed to be watched and possibly suppressed.
At the same time, they saw the church's preoccupation with internal conflict as a
welcome distraction from potential conflict with the state. GDR officials felt that
"structural reform" and "modernization" in the church were dangerous, because
they would make the church more attractive to youth and the intelligentsia, aim-
ing "at the heart of our society."[227] The Halle district council issued an analysis on
19 November 1969, claiming that the Catholic Church, with its young "activist
clerical forces," was seeking to modernize and, in contrast to the Protestants,
demonstrated "a higher degree of religious organization and participation in
events" in Halle.[228] In a 10 April 1970 report, the MfS expressed its fear that
the Halle Action Group was attempting "to adapt the Catholic Church to our
current stage of social development and remove obstacles to this by throwing all
conservative and intransigent elements in the church overboard."[229] Even when
government officials overestimated the popularity of the church reform movement in their reports, their fear of a "modernized" church that appealed to the
masses revealed that theological "conservatism" and "political abstinence" were
much more predictable for the GDR state, and therefore preferable, even though

this meant that they had to accept the Catholic Church's continuing existence over a longer term.

The Debate Over "Engagement" with Socialist Society

On 10 November 1965 the Halle branch of the MfS reported confidential "tips on the plans, intentions, and working methods of religious groups" to Horst Sindermann, first secretary of the Halle district SED:

> We have learned from intellectuals with Catholic ties that the Catholic intelligentsia will now take a more active part in our society, allegedly to assist capable people to assume positions of responsibility. The previous passive attitude of the intelligentsia is held to be responsible for the placement of incompetent people in numerous state positions.[230]

It was no coincidence that this news emerged at this time. After the Berlin Wall was erected and the reality of two German states sank in, and in the wake of Vatican II and its challenge to engage in "dialogue with the world," a tendency to show conditional support for the GDR and to participate in socialist society in specific ways (without renouncing church membership or joining the SED) gained strength among professionals and students in the Catholic Church.

One way to "cooperate" with GDR society, which most East German Catholics found quite unattractive, was through the state-sponsored pro-regime activities of the CDU, the National Front, and the Berlin Conference of Catholic Christians of European Nations. Aside from an episode involving Hubertus Guske and the Erfurt Priests' Seminar, only Adolf Brockhoff briefly tried to engage in a dialogue with the CDU, and with Otto Hartmut Fuchs of the Berlin Conference in particular, which quickly proved futile.[231] The Berlin Conference, financed by the GDR state, sought to maintain a profile of loyalty to the pope and therefore wanted nothing to do with the church's internal critics. After 1968, representatives of West German "critical Catholicism" were no longer invited. Guske and Fuchs noted, in their report to the ZK after a conversation at the Vatican on 17 July 1970, that Catholic officials praised their rejection of church "rebels."[232]

In its session in Magdeburg on 11–12 July 1966, the BOK took up the issue of "engagement in the public and state sphere." First, the ordinaries decided that "the misunderstood term 'engagement' should be avoided" and replaced with the Vatican Council's concept of "'the presence of the Christian in the world' and 'the Christian's service to the world.'"[233] They felt that it was possible for qualified Catholics to pursue careers that could "lead to conflicts of conscience, given the political situation" in the GDR, and that such individuals needed to "maintain contact with their pastors and also be ready to accept a change in career or position as part of the bargain." The BOK further stated that, under Archbishop

Bengsch, the leaders of the working groups for youth, student, and professionals' pastors would be authorized "to discuss this question with appropriate lay Catholics and to evaluate the options."

In an October 1966 report—in a section with the heading "Church Unity and Solidarity in the 'GDR'"—Bengsch noted that growing numbers of Catholics were calling for engagement in social and political life. This was not surprising, he thought, because "professional advancement and government permission for travel, importing, or construction demand a certain level of collaboration as a price."[234] Bengsch saw this attitude as a "lack of caution" vis-à-vis the Communists because "any chipping away" at Catholic unity would only provoke greater pressure from the state. He felt that discussions of "engagement" were understandable five years after the erection of the Berlin Wall, but he largely put the responsibility on developments in the West: Bonn's unsteady policy on German-German questions, the Western powers' refusal to risk a change in the status quo, reports about the church's supposed failures in the Nazi era, and widespread criticism of the close ties between German Catholicism and CDU politics.

Diametrically opposed opinions prevailed in Catholic student congregations and among youth, student, and professional pastors. Wolfgang Trilling, a priest in Leipzig, sent a paper by the Student Pastors Working Group entitled "Questions of World Service in the Contemporary World and Our Situation" to the BOK chairmen on 5 December 1967. This paper referred to the Vatican II document "Gaudium et Spes," which Bengsch had rejected, and stressed that what was now important was "the church of the pilgrimage rather than the triumphant church, not secrecy but openness, not stiffness but movement, not monologue but dialogue."[235] Furthermore, the working group argued that

> [opportunities] for service out of a sense of Christian responsibility must always be sought. If this is countered with the objection that any cooperation helps to build socialism, then a distinction between what one is actually doing and its ideological interpretation can be a basis for our contribution to the just construction of this world. Possibilities for intervention can only be determined, however, from a very clear Christian conscience. No one can be free of the danger that, in an ideological state, the Christian is "the dumb one" and can have a negative experience.

These very different positions within the church were radicalized in the years to come. Whereas young clergy and lay Catholics called for social engagement regardless of its potential ideological use or even basically affirmed socialism while criticizing it, Bengsch saw the end of a unified church position as a victory for the state and a threat to the church's work. And independent of this internal Catholic debate, the GDR state was suspicious of Catholics' desire for dialogue and social engagement: it feared that they sought to undermine socialist society and incite unrest.

Alongside these demands for "engagement" (also referred to as "Christian world service" in accordance with the theological concept), many students, professionals, and some clergy began, after 1966, to join their colleagues in West Germany in calling for "dialogue" with the "world," and in particular with Marxism. Statements, such as the following from Winfried Schülke on Easter 1966 in the *Korrespondenz*, set the tone:

> If we believe that the mission for engagement in public life and state administration in our world is also a Christian mission, then the recognition of the state authority of the GDR is the only starting point from which cooperation is possible and in which criticism and corrective suggestions are not automatically suspicious.[236]

For Bengsch, this amounted to "dialogue intoxication" and was completely unacceptable. A statement he co-authored in 1966, entitled "From Priests in Both Sections of the Diocese of Berlin," apodictically declared that

> In an ideological state, there is no possibility for public dialogue . . . The profound illusion that one can learn the rules of the game in an atheistic state though the scholarly study of atheism is probably one of the biggest reasons for the well-intentioned but naïve enthusiasm for "dialogue" by Christians in Western countries. There can be no dialogue between the wolf and the lamb. There is nothing up for discussion between the hunter and his prey.[237]

The St. Paul Society was one group that promoted scholarly dialogues between theologians, philosophers, and Marxists from Western and Eastern Europe beginning in 1964. In April 1967, the group met for the first time in Mariánske Lázne, Czechoslovakia, to discuss "creativity and freedom in a humane society," but no representatives from the GDR took part. Erfurt theology professors Wilhelm Ernst and Wolfgang Trilling had been invited to represent the GDR, but the BOK strongly discouraged them from participating. They acquiesced yet voiced their frustration, in a letter to the BOK dated 27 April 1967, that an important opportunity had been missed out of fear that it might have been politically exploited: "Participation would be justified merely by the chance to meet Marxists and theologians from neighboring countries, regardless of the subject discussed, the course of the meeting, or its implications for the regime's religious policies."[238] They questioned "whether we as a church in the GDR, in the long run, are subjecting ourselves to, or remaining within, the kind of isolation that the GDR itself experiences among Eastern countries" and claimed that there were "clear signs that in our field a genuine dialogue with Marxist theory is possible and, indeed, is expected from the other side."

Winfried Schülke and some friends did, however, participate unofficially in the conference. In a letter of 30 May 1967, Schülke reported this to Bengsch and lamented "the church's own responsibility for an isolation that was not always forced, its fearful clinging to a privileged status once it had been won, and the resulting inertia regarding new situations such as this conference and its opportunity for dialogue with Marxism."[239] Trilling further emphasized the isolation of the church in a programmatic lecture in Leipzig on 12 October 1967 that found great resonance among clergy and lay Catholics. In his lecture, "The Path of the Catholic Church in the GDR," Trilling called for a break with "ghetto thinking" and the "comfort of the Catholic nest" in order to pursue a Christian-motivated dialogue to realize the church's mission in the world.[240] Lay Catholics, he said, must be brought on board "to share decisions and responsibility"; it was not a question of "comfortable conformity or collaboration" but of "our service in the world, to humanity."

The hopes for a genuine Christian dialogue with Marxism were broken when Warsaw Pact troops intervened to suppress the Prague Spring in August 1968. Skeptics within the church felt that these events confirmed their views. Yet well before that, state organs had been suspicious of such dialogue and had taken steps to undermine it. As early as 18 January 1968, the Office of the First Secretary of the SED District Leadership in Dresden had referred to the St. Paul Society as "an organ of political and ideological diversion."[241] Christian-Marxist dialogue, it claimed, "primarily serves to weaken our ideology" and "to organize opposition to socialist development." The Dresden MfS branch conducted operative surveillance on the Dresden priest Franz-Peter Sonntag (Operation Black Frock), who had initiated a dialogue group among professors at the Technical University of Dresden in November 1967 (Operation Dialogue), as well as on the group itself.[242] On 26 November 1968 the State Secretary for Church Affairs wrote a Prague Spring memo, referring to the meeting of the St. Paul Society in Marián-ske Lázne as "a variant of the clerical dialogue concept in agreement with Bonn's so-called new Ostpolitik and the Vatican's bureau for non-believers" and related it to "the counterrevolutionary tendency" that had grown in Czechoslovakia until August 1968.[243] It called a Vatican document on "Dialogue with Non-Believers" an effort to strengthen "its offensive against Marxism" that sought "to create the basis for a legal opposition" in the socialist countries.

Because of these SED fears, Catholic Church attempts to initiate dialogue and critically engage with socialist society were considered suspect from the beginning and regularly criminalized under statutes controlling "group formation." After 1969 the MfS increasingly confronted Prelate Groß—himself an opponent of these tendencies within the church—with this government line and asked him to have Bengsch intervene.[244] Yet despite socialism's obvious unwillingness to conduct a dialogue—which the liquidation of the experiment in Czechoslovakia laid bare—Catholic supporters of dialogue and change within the church did not disappear.

Rather, the polemic sharpened and more radical ideas were voiced, for example, in Adolf Brockhoff's lecture series "The Theology of Revolution." On 3 December 1968 he addressed about a hundred people in Merseburg, expressing the need for a "turnaround" changing the "dictatorship of the proletariat" in the GDR to a "democracy" on the path to "revolution."[245] He made a similar speech on 5 January 1969 at a Catholic student event in Halle, where the discussion turned to "the possibility of employing guerilla methods to optimize socialist society."[246] Brockhoff's provocative ideas launched lively debates and demonstrated that Catholic professionals would have long-term influence in the GDR.

Joachim Garstecki was another activist Catholic in charge of youth ministries in the Diocese of Magdeburg. Within the framework of the millennium celebration in the diocese, at a meeting of the "youth" working group on 8 September 1968, he characterized the task of the church's work with youth as a contrast to developments in the GDR, which he even described as "creeping fascism."[247] The more undemocratic the state became, he argued, the more democratic the church's work with youth had to be. The "lack of socialist order" had to be exposed and the youth educated in how to compromise as well as how to protest both within the church and society.

In February 1969, a Catholic student working group posted a document called "Thoughts on Christian Peace Service in the GDR" in the Berlin office of the KSG and sent it to clergy in the Diocese of Berlin. The group maintained that only those "who wish to participate in building socialism" could perform peace service.[248] Moreover, "neither unconditional loyalty nor political affront qualify as peace service. We must identify with our reality; we are citizens of the GDR." On the other hand, the document described alternative military service as a "construction soldier" *(Bausoldat)* as "a clearer path for the fulfillment of peace service," and expressed solidarity with those who refused to participate in any and all forms of military service *(Totalverweigerer)*. For the MfS, these ideas constituted "a surreptitious attack on the social evolution of the GDR."

On 16–17 May 1970, 350 to 380 Catholic students from across the GDR (according to MfS estimates) took part in a pilgrimage to Rosenthal bei Kamenz, which also served as a convention. In eight working groups, they sought to develop "concrete ideas for the complete transformation of the working methods of the Catholic Church in the GDR."[249] They dealt with themes such as "the social engagement of students" and "appropriate student contributions to establishing the framework of scholarly inquiry," and concluded that

> the church must be present today where the affairs of the world are decided, to hinder negative developments and to promote positive ones. [We must] adapt our [arguments and manner of speech] to match those with whom we must work, otherwise they will allege that our ideas are in opposition to the basic tenets of socialism . . . The notion of "socialist democracy" will help us in our quest to offer reasonable criticism and to make a contribution . . . We need to rid ourselves of the reluctance to work under this flag, because only in this way can our ambitions be realized. We should thus make constructive use of the FDJ.

The MfS feared that the Catholic students would succeed in pushing through this kind of "diversion" at the upcoming church synod and made various attempts to silence the students, including asking the bishops to dissolve student organizations.

State officials saw the push for dialogue and engagement coming from both Catholics and Protestants as damaging, viewing it as "ideological diversion" even as they believed it could make the churches more modern and thus more attractive. A 1969 report by the Office of the State Secretary for Church Affairs declared it

> false to claim that church officeholders who are theologically progressive or who promote modern methods in the church are also progressives in society . . . In every case, modern theology and an adaptation of church forms to keep up with social developments in socialism must be judged as negative and politically reactionary.[250]

In a 19 June 1970 evaluation of its Operation Tabernacle against the Halle Action Group, the MfS held that its members believed that "a Catholic Church dominated by conservative bishops serves the interests of the state. Such a church would become obsolete much faster than a modern one whose work is 'oriented toward society.'"[251]

Especially after 1969, the state's fears, expectations, and threats, on the one hand, and Cardinal Bengsch and Prelate Groß on the other, began to have a reciprocal impact. Bengsch and Groß, for their part, considered voices for engagement and dialogue from within the Catholic community suspect, as they sensed that they were being steered by the MfS, and damaging, because they fractured church solidarity and went their own theological way. Meanwhile, once the MfS, having conducted surveillance and criminalized these tendencies within the church, began to demand that Groß (and thus Bengsch) confront and discipline those involved, anger at internal church critics began to grow among the Berlin ordinaries, because these groups now seemed responsible for threatening smooth church-state relations at the highest level.

At first, leading conservative church officials were not sure which role the state was actually playing. Was it interested in stability and predictable church-state relations, or in destabilizing the church by promoting criticism of the conservative hierarchy? Yet it soon became clear that the state was banking on predictable officials rather than unpredictable activists. In a 23 January 1969 conversation with the MfS, Groß made clear that he rejected the movements within the church that the MfS had criticized. At the same time, he signaled that Bengsch would not dissolve the Berlin Catholic Student Community: if he did, it would then continue to work underground and might be used by the state against the Catholic Church.[252] A certain convergence of interests soon emerged between the GDR Communists in power and the staunch anti-Communist Berlin ordinaries. The practice of discreet negotiations between central state agencies and church leaders was threatened by the demands for more information from within the church, and Bengsch and Groß were disturbed by agitation in their own ranks. In a 3 December 1969 conversation in the Office of the State Secretary for Church Affairs, for instance, Groß was quoted as saying that Bengsch could no longer keep developments within the church in Magdeburg under control and that political engagement by Brockhoff—who was influential there—had very strong support; equally concerned government officials noted in their report that "this matches our assessment, as well."[253]

Because of the conflicts and personal attacks within the Catholic Church, which escalated after the summer of 1969, Bengsch issued an unusually direct response to his colleagues in Berlin one week after he had participated in a very tense meeting with Seigewasser on 9 April 1970. Although Bengsch himself never commented upon the sharp differences within the church in his meetings with state officials, Groß—according to a 22 April 1970 MfS report—interpreted Bengsch's change in attitude following the meeting with Seigewasser as follows:

> There are already many groups of clergy that call themselves "progressive" and demand changes in the structure of the church, the free election of bishops, and such like. At the same time, these clergy oppose the state. Apparently, the state has only noticed up to now that these clergy are engaged in church-internal oppositional politics . . . [These clergy] are of the opinion that the GDR state finds a conservative Catholic Church to be in its own best interests . . . and believe that, by contrast, a more modern church would be more energetic and, in contrast to the conservatives, would take a stand on societal issues. Such a church would be much less comfortable for the regime. [Groß], Bengsch, and most other leading figures within the Catholic Church in the GDR count as "conservatives" to them. Consequently, Bengsch has refrained from taking a position on various internal church issues because he did not want to provide even more fuel for the opinions of this group of clergy. Sometimes, he is of the opinion that the state only takes vigorous action in areas where it encounters no resistance.[254]

To be sure, the MfS did not need Groß to tell them that critics of Bengsch within the Catholic Church were also against the state. But Groß's expression of sympathy for state action against people who, in a formal sense, were authorized by the BOK had a special meaning. After the Catholic leadership had initially suspected that the MfS was steering the oppositional groups to foster division within the church, these groups, in turn, began to make public accusations against Bengsch and Groß—for example, that they worked for the MfS or at least cooperated indirectly with the state. In September 1971, a young theology professor from Münster who had contact with the Catholic opposition groups wrote in a West German journal that "well-informed circles within the church are convinced that there is a subtle collaboration—without any concrete agreement—between the [GDR] State Secretary [for Church Affairs] and the [GDR] ordinaries to restrict the freedom of movement for theological dissenters."[255]

The state did not need any nudge from the Catholic Church to be "cautious" about religious movements. It saw Christian-inspired engagement in socialist society as a "diversion" that needed to be combated. In 1969, the Office of the State Secretary stated clearly that

> The promulgation of bourgeois and imperialist ideologies under the rubric of "critical" cooperation has grown. The superficial innocuousness of this idea cannot hide

its intention: a lookout point for the church within socialist society in an attempt to become a partner of equal status, and to then steer social development in another direction.[256]

In a 4 December 1970 speech in Magdeburg, Politburo member Paul Verner spoke of attempts by the Catholic Church

> to occupy crucial positions within our state apparatus with the goal of obstructing development in general and conducting a so-called "dialogue" with us as Marxists. Under these conditions, our encounter with the Catholic Church is much more difficult than in years past. It is disguising itself and making many progressive statements whose deeper reasons are not always immediately apparent.[257]

The state's insecurities corresponded to Cardinal Bengsch's fears, which were motivated by other concerns. In a 14–15 June 1971 report to the BOK, Bengsch lamented the loss of unity among the Catholic clergy:

> Small groups exist that use the term "engagement" and believe that they see a genuine alternative to capitalism in socialism. Uncertainty reigns among the believers as well. The reasons for this may lie in a general uncertainty that impacts other areas of life, or in the fact that there is a series of changes within the church, or in the expectation that church authority would give in to the norm of what is factual.[258]

The Synod of the Diocese of Meißen in Dresden

Of even greater importance than the heterogeneous movements for pluralism that emerged after the Second Vatican Council was the Synod of the Diocese of Meißen in Dresden, held between 1969 and 1971. For the first time anywhere in the world, and in a small "diaspora" diocese, this synod wrote texts on and established guidelines for the current definition of church tasks and structural reform to implement Vatican II, garnering attention beyond the Catholic Church in the GDR.

Bishop Otto Spülbeck played a key role in organizing this meeting. As early as 9 January 1963, Spülbeck, who enjoyed a personal connection with Pope John XXIII and applauded his theological openness, had expressed his enthusiasm over Vatican II in a report to the BOK: "[It encourages us] to present ourselves charismatically and to be daring, not to be so concerned with the past, not to take too much of a defensive stance or to succumb to instinctive reactions that are full of anxiety and caution."[259] Even before the Second Vatican Council was concluded, Spülbeck sent a letter, dated 6 September 1965, to all clergy in the Diocese of Meißen announcing a special synod for 1967. Another pastoral letter from Spülbeck of 30 January 1966 then announced the synod to all Catholic communities. By October 1966, more than 1,000 individual applications had been received from across the diocese. As a result, the synod could not take place in the originally proposed time frame but opened on 13 June 1969 in Dresden's Hofkirche. In April 1968, members of the organizing commission had developed a general theme—"God's People in the Diocese of Meißen"—which they presented to the synod for consideration and finalization on 5 May 1969. The synod consisted of 149 delegates (including sixty lay Catholics); some had been elected by priests and the laity while others had been appointed by the bishop. Decisions required a two-thirds majority and, according to canon law, counted only as recommendations until they were made effective by a bishop's decree. The synod met three times—on 13–15 June 1969, 9–12 October 1969, and 12–14 June 1970—before the death of Bishop Spülbeck on 21 June 1970, when it was suspended. It was then concluded in two more sessions under his successor, Bishop Gerhard Schaffran, on 24–26 September and 22–24 October 1971.

The GDR state held a fairly negative view of Vatican II. A 1965 MfS report described some of its conclusions as philosophically simplistic and stagnant thought rooted in natural law that needed to be revised, along with overly optimistic triumphalism, clericalism, and a lack of collegiality within the church. Consequently, the state was also wary of the synod. It responded at the central and especially the local level by trying to intercept as much official and unofficial information relating to the synod as possible. At the same time, it sought to influence the content of decision-making through certain delegates. Although the regime succeeded in obtaining a wealth of information, its actual influence upon the synod was insignificant. On 18 April 1969, to prepare the government response, the deputy minister of the interior of the Dresden council informed State Secretary Seigewasser that "differentiation work [was] taking place with Catholic clergy and with some progressive members of the synod, but, admittedly, the prospects for differentiation are small."[260]

In advance of the synod's first session, the state had already taken steps to shape it according to its own narrow interests. The Dresden district council invited Heinrich Bulang, deacon of the Cathedral in Bautzen, to a meeting on 27 May 1969, telling him that no foreign guests would be permitted to attend and that the synod should take care not to reach any decisions directed against the GDR constitution or the "building up of socialism."[261] Above all, Bulang was told that the general description of the synod should be amended to specify that the Catholics in attendance would be citizens "in the GDR." As president of the synod, Bulang made this request to the synod and declared it to be the state's wish, but the motion was rejected 85 to 45. After another meeting, the description was amended the next day at the suggestion of the bishop: where it read "a socialist social order," the phrase "like we have here in the GDR" was added. Other than this one small reference, the Office of the State Secretary for Church Affairs noted, the GDR was never named.[262]

The state's other efforts consisted in decreeing a system of "handlers" for individual members of the synod in Dresden, Leipzig, and Karl-Marx-Stadt. On 20 June 1969 the deputy minister of the interior in the Dresden district sent identical letters to district, city, and neighborhood officials notifying them of the Catholic synod participants who resided there. Each was to be assigned a "handler" who would initiate "targeted political work" with them. The work was to be accomplished with finesse: "The handlers should take care that the subject's identity as a synod participant be elicited from the subject himself . . . Because this job entails a precise application of Kirchenpolitik, the handlers should be carefully picked."[263] However, most jurisdictions within the Dresden district supplied useless reports, if any. Those that the Church Affairs Unit evaluated as "very good" were detailed reports on the offices and, in some cases, the private lives of the synod members.[264]

The theme of the synod—"God's People in the Diocese of Meißen"—worried the state in both its draft and final forms, as it sensed the danger of a "modernized" and "popular" Catholic Church. In an 18 April 1969 letter to Seigewasser, the deputy minister of the interior for the Dresden district expressed his fear that the synod "would take on a certain leadership function and prepare the way for further synods in the GDR . . . creating a church with mass appeal within socialist society . . . which could make more effective use of our own social structures to spread its ideology."[265] In a 30 June 1969 paper, Horst Hartwig, an analyst for the Office of the State Secretary for Church Affairs, noted an "indifference to the system" in the synod as well as "ideological activation" within the church.[266] He found that "the church wants to set itself up as 'the champion of human rights and freedom for citizens'" and to "increase the availability of clerical publications." On 9 January 1970 the Office of the State Secretary for Church Affairs concluded that the Meißen synod was part of a church strategy of "long-term penetration" of socialist society.[267]

The "God's People in the Diocese of Meißen" platform was reworked after some discussion in the June 1969 session. Then it was adopted by a vote of 127 to 17 as the first decree of the synod in the second session in October and given the title "Aims and Duties for Renewal in the Diocese of Meißen Following the Second Vatican Council"; it took effect on 26 March 1970 on Bishop Spülbeck's decree. In a summary of the progress of the synod of 14 July 1970, Horst Dohle said that the decrees would only increase the state's fear of a more attractive church, especially with the prospect of a joint synod encompassing all GDR Catholic districts in the coming years: "It shows that under Spülbeck's leadership, the Diocese of Meißen has become one of the most liberal in the GDR and has thus unleashed activities in the direction of a Catholic Church with mass appeal, and this cannot be in the best interests of the state."[268]

The synod's first decree was indeed "indifferent to the system" and contained only a few passages relevant to Kirchenpolitik:

> [Section 3] We live in a socialist social order that is characterized by atheism. Materialism, both in the philosophical and practical sense, determines our environment. In this situation, we must affirm our historical time and place. We strive to recognize the will of God in it . . . [Section 8] The mission of the church is not tied to any politi-

cal, economic, or social system. Even in a socialist social order, like we have here in the GDR, the church must proclaim its message and perform its service in such a way that it will be trustworthy . . . We show consideration for every human being who may think differently, we respect every honest conviction, and every choice of conscience. We are ready to work together in the spirit of Christ's love with all people of goodwill.[269]

In the sections on "Brotherhood and Responsibility," "Freedom and Authority," and "Orders in the Church," there were many passages that, although not motivated by Kirchenpolitik, provoked energetic resistance from representatives of a more conservative theology.

Berlin ordinaries sent Peter Riedel to observe the first session of the synod in June 1969. He wrote a mostly negative and critical report, which he gave to Bengsch and also to leading clergy in Meißen, expressing reservations that were especially theological and partly political.[270] Looking at the structures of the synod, anticipating that the synod sought the church to take political positions, and perceiving that it attempted to publicize internal Catholic discussions, Riedel saw the synod as "an endangerment of secret negotiations between the church and the state" and "a threat to unified Catholic action in questions of Kirchenpolitik." Moreover, he feared that it might cause the state to "demand political declarations" and intervene "in internal church affairs." He said: "It is unrealistic to want to establish democratic structures—which are legitimate in and of themselves—to this degree in a totalitarian, ideological state." The report prompted Spülbeck to refute all its points in an 8 October 1969 letter to Bengsch, declaring: "What you say about dangers and consequences for Kirchenpolitik is incomprehensible to me. My stance here is surely clear . . . In my opinion, it is unjustified to suggest that the synod lacks sensitivity to Kirchenpolitik." The state's analysis of the situation matched Spülbeck's opinion. If it had perceived the things that Riedel had feared, it surely would have noted them. In the final analysis, the state observers noted, the internal church discussion at the Meißen synod remained "indifferent to the system," a debate over theological views that only implicitly had political relevance.

In January 1970, the West German journal *Herder-Korrespondenz* contained an article praising the Meißen synod, noting that "the advisory function of the councils was expanded into 'a partnership with equal responsibility.'"[271] Cardinal Bengsch did not want the line taken by the Meißen synod to be perceived in any way as determinative for the anticipated synod for the whole GDR, so he turned to the Vatican. During his visit to Rome on 4–12 May 1970—which Prelate Groß discussed with the MfS on 16 May—he spoke with Cardinal Franjo Seper, the prefect of the Congregation for the Doctrine of the Faith. Both men criticized the Meißen synod and agreed that a statement expressing disapproval of Bishop Spülbeck be discussed at the upcoming BOK session in June. In fact, on 8 May 1970 the papal nuncio in Bonn sent a letter to Bishop Spülbeck expressing the fear of "the Holy Congregation of Bishops" that the Meißen synod had overstepped its bounds; he also referred to the above-quoted sentence published in *Herder-Korrespondenz* four months previously, which had "particularly fomented" concern about the role of the officials.[272] Two days after the third session of the synod had concluded on 14 June 1970, Bishop Spülbeck prepared a detailed paper in defense of its decrees in anticipation of the upcoming BOK meeting on 23–24 June, where the Meißen synod was to be critically discussed. He concluded with the words: "Naturally, all have the freedom not to accept the theological direction of our synod. Diverse opinions are possible here. We believed, however, that we had to choose this path so that our industrial diocese in diaspora be made aware of the service which is now required."[273]

The work of the synod did pause shortly thereafter—due to Bishop Spülbeck's untimely death. On 21 June 1970, on his way back from a pilgrimage, Spülbeck died suddenly of a heart attack at the age of sixty-six. After he was buried in Bautzen eight days later, the BOK met in a special session, where Bengsch remarked that the Meißen synod's view of the church was "one-sided."[274] He continued: "A pastoral practice was prejudged, which puts a great strain on work of the church in the GDR . . . Legal and canon law questions that weigh heavily upon the work of the church in the GDR are prejudged in general . . . Therefore, the work of the commissions and the secretariat of the Meißen synod should be laid to rest." With Spülbeck's position vacant, the synod's work halted until a new bishop was elected by the Bautzen Cathedral Chapter. Bulang, the chapter vicar, wrote to Pastor Karl Herbst on 2 July 1970 that Spülbeck's death had been caused by the pressure he was under:

> I cannot hide from you that these critical theologians from all areas—we have them in our diocese, too—have caused the most serious concern in the highest offices of the church . . . I cannot conceal from you, moreover, that our dear Bishop Otto had to die because thoughtless advisors brought him to the point where he—along with a part of his work—had to collapse.[275]

On 18 July 1970 Bengsch wrote to the nuncio to suggest Bishop Gerhard Schaffran of Görlitz—whose theological views matched Bengsch's—as Spülbeck's successor. Bengsch argued that the "split between conservative and progressive representatives" that had emerged at the last session of the synod was so severe "that no one from either of the 'parties' has a good chance as a successor."[276] His arguments were effective: Schaffran was selected and inaugurated in September 1970. In two concluding sessions held without prejudicial character, Schaffran successfully transferred the Meißen synod into the general synod of the Catholic Church in the GDR and thus ignored the decrees of 1970.[277] In a letter to the papal nuncio on 22 December 1970, Bengsch disclosed that the new bishop had encountered "a general wish to continue the synod."[278] Bengsch reported further that Schaffran and other experts had requested external evaluations on the decrees, which Wolfgang Trilling—"whom Bishop Schaffran held to be the theological inspiration for the [Meißen] synod's decrees"—had ordered. In addition, Bengsch lamented that the publication of the first decree of the synod in *Herder-Korrespondenz* had made its content known to "virtually the whole Catholic Church in Germany . . . together with the information that influential GDR offices want to extract the practical implications from this decree."[279]

Notes

1. See Otto Wenzel, *Kriegsbereit, Der Nationale Verteidigungsrat der DDR 1960 bis 1989* (Cologne, 1995).
2. Falco Werkentin, *Politische Strafjustiz in der Ära Ulbricht* (Berlin, 1995), 264ff.
3. See Inge Bennewitz and Rainer Potratz, *Zwangsaussiedlungen an der innerdeutschen Grenze: Analysen und Dokumente* (Berlin, 1994).
4. Jochen Staadt, *Die geheime Westpolitik der SED 1960–1970: Von der gesamtdeutschen Orientierung zur sozialistischen Nation* (Berlin, 1993), 54–61.
5. Werkentin, *Politische Strafjustiz,* 286.
6. Ibid., 273.
7. Ibid, 276.
8. Staadt, *Die geheime Westpolitik der SED,* 82–88. Interestingly, Archbishop Bengsch, assured of the Vatican's strict confidence, had already sent a personal note to Ulbricht on 28 November 1963, asking for restrictions on personal travel between East and West Berlin to be relaxed. Ulbricht's response is unknown, but Bengsch thanked him in a 21 December 1963 letter for allowing travel by Christmas (ROO, H I).
9. See Armin Mitter and Stefan Wolle, *Untergang auf Raten: Unbekannte Kapitel der DDR-Geschichte* (Munich, 1993), 384.
10. Cf. Günter Agde, ed., *Kahlschlag: Das 11. Plenum des ZK der SED 1965* (Berlin, 1991), 290–330.
11. SAPMO-BArch, DY 30, IV 2/1/191.
12. See Robert Havemann, *Dialektik ohne Dogma* (Reinbeck, 1964); and Silvia Müller and Bernd Florath, eds., *Die Entlassung: Robert Havemann und die Akademie der Wissenschaften der DDR 1965/66* (Berlin, 1996).
13. Mitter and Wolle, *Untergang auf Raten,* 386.
14. Werkentin, *Politische Strafjustiz,* 298.
15. Jörg Roesler, *Zwischen Plan und Markt: Die Wirtschaftsreform in der DDR zwischen 1963 und 1970* (Berlin, 1990).
16. See Peter Przybylski, *Tatort Politbüro: Honecker, Mittag und Schalck-Golodkowski* (Berlin, 1992), 2:150–61.
17. On East Germany's military role, see Rüdiger Wenzke, *Die NVA und der Prager Frühling 1968* (Berlin, 1995).
18. See Jörn Mothes et al., eds., *Beschädigte Seelen: DDR-Jugend und Staatssicherheit* (Bremen and Rostock, 1996).
19. Mitter and Wolle, *Untergang auf Raten,* 406.
20. Peter Przybylski, *Tatort Politbüro: Die Akte Honecker* (Berlin, 1991), 287.
21. BAP, DO-4, 2628.
22. BAP, DO-4, 1296.
23. See the ZK analyses from 1963–1971 in SAPMO-BArch, DY 30, IV A 2/14/4 and BAP, DO-4, 498.
24. SAPMO-BArch, DY 30, J IV 2/2/917, Anlage 6, Punkt 4.

25. See State Secretary Seigewasser's 14 September 1963 letter to Paul Verner, BAP, DO-4, 382.
26. BAP, DO-4, 2752.
27. Ibid.
28. Note of 18 June 1964 entitled "Organization of a five-day visit by Streb and Ruppel to Prague," BAP, DO-4, 2752.
29. Except for isolated gifts of material goods and import licenses, only Karl Fischer, the former pastor of Neustrelitz, and Josef Streb, a provost in Heiligenstadt, received benefits (Fischer monthly from 1955 to 1964 and Streb annually from 1967 to 1974). See Peter Beier, *Die "Sonderkonten Kirchenfragen": Sachleistungen und Geldzuwendungen an Pfarrer und kirchliche Mitarbeiter als Mittel der DDR-Kirchenpolitik, 1955-1989/90* (Göttingen, 1997).
30. BAP, DO-4, 382.
31. See the file notes by Horst Hartwig, BAP, DO-4, 115, and the complementary remarks by church official Otto Groß of 12 February 1967, ROO, A III 31.
32. BAP, DO-4, 115; BStU, ZA, AP 12052/92, p. 120. The text was obviously also sent to the MfS, for whom Guske worked from 1959 to 1989 as an informant with the code names "Hubert" and later "Georg."
33. See the state's notes on 23 July 1968 by Fritz Flint (BAP, DO-4, 2638) as well as the file notes by the CDU Department of Church Affairs (Gerhard Quast) from 19 July (ACDP VII-013-3062). On the church side, there are notes by Bengsch himself (ROO, A III 30) and Otto Groß (ROO, A VIII 6).
34. Nothing of the kind took place. See the state's notes by Horst Hartwig (BAP, DO-4, 355) and the CDU notes from 3 June 1969 (ACDP VII-013-2164). Church notes from 13 May are by Otto Groß (ROO, A III 29).
35. BAP, DO-4, 350.
36. See the file of informer "Stern," BStU, ZA, AIM 2758/68. Tellingly, Streb was the only Catholic clergyman in the GDR who was the subject of a publication from a non-church press: Franz Gerth, *Joseph Streb* (Christ in der Welt, 44), (East Berlin, 1978).
37. SAPMO-BArch, DY 30, IV A 2/14/7.
38. SAPMO-BArch, DY 30, IV A 2/14/2. Cf. Aufderbeck's pointed sermon ("We shall decisively resist imported godlessness") of 27 May 1965 in Josef Pilvousek (ed.), *Kirchliches Leben im totalitären Staat: Seelsorge in der SBZ/DDR 1945-1976* (Hildesheim, 1994), 277f.
39. BAP, DO-4, 355.
40. Minutes of the State Secretariat for Church Affairs on 22 and 28 April 1969, BAP, DO-4, 382.
41. Report by Bellstedt, 12 February 1963, LV S-A der PDS, LPA-Magdeburg, IV A 2/14/718, p. 3.
42. Reports of 8 and 20 December 1966, LV, S-A der PDS, LPA-Magdeburg, IV A, 2/14/720.
43. LV S-A der PDS, LPA-Magdeburg, IV A 2/14/721.
44. Report by Gerhard Salzmann, LV S-A der PDS, LPA-Magdeburg, IV A 2/14/979.
45. See Franz Schrader, "Erfahrungen mit der Herausgabe einer wissenschaftlichen Festschrift zum 1000jährigen Jubiläum der Gründung des Erzbistums Magdeburg," *Wichmann-Jahrbuch des Diözesangeschichtsvereins Berlin* 32/33 (1992–1993): 147–55.
46. LV S-A der PDS, LPA-Magdeburg, IV B 2/14/979.
47. District council file note of 5 September 1968, ibid.
48. BStU, ZA, ZAIG, Z 1574.
49. Minutes dated 11 October 1968, BAP, DO-4, 400.
50. See the evaluation by the Magdeburg district council of 9 October 1969, BAP, DO-4, 325.
51. HStA Dresden, Bt/RdB, 47605.
52. SAPMO-BArch, NRNF, Abt. Christliche Kreise, 3174.
53. BAP, DO-4, 2727.
54. Notes by the Dresden district council, 23 January 1968, HStA Dresden, Bt/RdB, 26603. See also the church notes from 11 January, ROO, A VIII 3.

55. HStA Dresden, Bt/RdB, 26603.

56. BAP, DO-4, 843.

57. Conformity to the changing political climate was reflected in the journal's subtitle, "A Journal of Progressive Catholics" (added in January 1968), and beginning in 1979, "Journal for Catholics in Church and Society." See Renate Hackel, *Katholische Publizistik in der DDR 1945–1984* (Mainz, 1987).

58. See Bernd Schäfer, "'Um "anzukommen" muß man sich "ankömmlich" artikulieren': Zur 'Berliner Konferenz' (BK) zwischen 1964 und 1993," in Michael Richter/Martin Rißmann, eds., *Die Ost-CDU: Beiträge zu ihrer Entstehung und Entwicklung* (Weimar, Cologne, Vienna, 1995), 111–25.

59. See Guske's detailed report to the MfS on "Pax Vobis" (17 September 1963), as well as a 17 October 1963 report on a visit to the GDR by its chairman from Bonn, Karl Wilhelm Gerst, BStU, ZA, A 835/85, pp. 139–49.

60. SAPMO-BArch, DY 30, J IV 2/2/917.

61. For typical examples, see notes to Archbishop/Cardinal Bengsch by several Berlin Conference activists, such as Otto Hartmut Fuchs, Hubertus Guske, Alfons Malik, Max Reutter, Karl Grobbel, and Gerhard Desczyk, ACDP VII-013-3006.

62. BStU, ZA, AIM 205/66, Bd. II, p. 188 (File for Informer "Marduk").

63. ACDP VII-013-2153.

64. SAPMO-BArch, DY 30, IV A 2/14/7.

65. BAP, DO-4, 822, p.3.

66. Georg Diederich, *Aus den Augen, aus dem Sinn: Die Zerstörung der Rostocker Christuskirche 1971* (Bremen and Rostock, 1997).

67. BAP, DO-4, 1144.

68. SAPMO-BArch, NY 281/81 (30 October 1970).

69. Quoted in *begegnung* 9, no. 11 (1969): 4.

70. Jens Gieseke, "Die hauptamtlichen Mitarbeiter des Ministeriums für Staatssicherheit," in Henke et al., eds., *Anatomie der Staatssicherheit: Geschichte, Struktur und Methoden*, Vol. 4 (Berlin, 1995), 1: 1–107.

71. Clemens Vollnhals, "Die kirchenpolitische Abteilung des Ministeriums für Staatssicherheit," in Clemens Vollnhals, ed., *Die Kirchenpolitik von SED und Staatssicherheit: Eine Zwischenbilanz* (Berlin, 1997), 90.

72. For a discussion of these categories in relation to the Catholic Church, see Bernd Schäfer, "'Inoffizielle Mitarbeiter' und 'Mitarbeit': Zur Differenzierung von Kategorien des Ministeriums für Staatssicherheit im Bereich der katholischen Kirche," *Kirchliche Zeitgeschichte* 6 (1993): 447–66, especially 450 and 452.

73. BStU, ZA, AIM 2716/75, Part 1, pp. 85–89.

74. See Gerhard Besier and Stephan Wolf, eds., *"Pfarrer, Christen und Katholiken": Das Ministerium für Staatssicherheit der ehemaligen DDR und die Kirchen* (Neukirchen/Vluyn, 1992), 276.

75. BStU, Ast Frankfurt/Oder, AIM 205/66.

76. The MfS planted a secretary, "Edith Dötsch," in the main Catholic Church offices in Bonn in 1969. On 3 November 1975 she fled to the GDR together with her husband Walter (active in the planning staff of the CDU/CSU parliamentary group) and an agent named "Dieter Hänsche" who had worked in the Catholic News Agency (KNA) since 1970. See the article in *Die Welt,* 7 November 1975. Like other socialist countries, the GDR had agents in Rome. The Benedictine Eugen Brammertz (who died in 1987) from the San Anselmo abbey had been an MfS agent in Rome since 1975. Alfons Waschbüsch, too, worked for the MfS; he worked in Rome and Wiesbaden for the Catholic News Agency (KNA) and knew Brammertz from his time in the St. Matthias cloister. Brammertz recruited Waschbüsch for the MfS and paid him for documents from the German section of the Vatican Secretary of State. The documents originated from Erwin Josef Ender, an unsuspecting German prelate in this section.

77. DAB V/5-7-1.

78. BStU, ZA, HA XX/4, 127.
79. Arbeitsplan der HA XX/4/II für das II. Halbjahr 1966, BStU, ZA, HA XX/4, 1060, pp. 438–49.
80. Arbeitsplan dated 1 January 1967, BStU, ZA, HA XX/4, 1060, p. 301.
81. BStU, ZA, HA XX/4, 2472, pp. 1–5.
82. BStU, ZA, HA XX/4, 1061.
83. See the HA XX/4/II Arbeitsplan from 15 January 1970. BStU, ZA, HA/XX/4, 1528, pp. 27–32.
84. BStU, ZA, HA XX/4, 1060, p. 438.
85. See the 18 January 1965 report in BStU, Ast Cottbus, AOP 967/68, vol. IV, p. 225.
86. See the 3 March 1966 report on Schaffran in BStU, Ast Dresden, XX/4, 283, p. 8.
87. BStU, ZA, HA, XX/4, 2440, p. 421.
88. BStU, ZA, XIII 711/63 and XV 1581/71 "Schober."
89. BStU, ZA, HA XX/4, 2509, pp. 1–22.
90. Quoted in Besier and Wolf, *"Pfarrer, Christen und Katholiken,"* 260.
91. BStU, Ast Frankfurt/Oder, AOP 967/68, especially VI 979/62. Forty-seven persons were investigated.
92. Report of the MfS district office in Cottbus of 10 February 1964. The author is grateful to Prof. Dr. Josef Horntrich (Cottbus) for sharing files the MfS had on him.
93. BStU, Ast Frankfurt/Oder, AOP 967/68, Bd. IV, p. 303.
94. Ibid., p. 329.
95. BStU, ZA, AIM 2716/75, Pt. II, vol. 1, pp. 27ff.
96. BStU, Ast Schwerin, AOV 10/1974 esp. II 600/70. The author is grateful to Anton Beer for allowing him to view the files kept on him.
97. BStU, Ast Rostock, AOPK I 997/73. The author is grateful to Dr. Schoenemann for allowing him to view files kept on him.
98. BStU, ZA, AP 4835/92 and BStU, Ast Dresden, XII 308/66 esp. AOP 1035/75, vol. 1, p. 7.
99. See the report of 11 April 1969, BStU, Ast Dresden, XII 308/66 esp. AOP 1035/75, vol. 1, pp. 43–53. The dialogue group was the target of a separate MfS operation. See BStU, Ast Dresden, XII 805/68, esp. AOP 1438/74.
100. BStU, Ast Halle, AOV 2145/72, esp. VIII 1635/70, vol. 1, pp. 15 and 17. The author is grateful to the late Deacon Helmut Langos (Merseburg) for access to files on him related to Operation Tabernacle.
101. The author is grateful to the late Adolf Brockhoff for access to MfS files on him.
102. See Olof Klohr, "Probleme des wissenschaftlichen Atheismus und der atheistischen Propaganda," *Deutsche Zeitschrift für Philosophie* 12 (1964): 133–50. Klohr held the position— unique in the GDR—of professor of scientific atheism at the University of Jena from 1962 to 1968.
103. BAP, DO-4, 650, p. 12.
104. BAP, DO-4, 498; BAP DO-4, 468; and BAP DO-4, 1296.
105. In 1967, for example, the Diocese of Berlin took in 15.8 million marks. See the letter from Cardinal Bengsch to Herbert Wehner of 17 June 1968 (ROO, J II). The total included 12 million marks in voluntary tithes and 3.8 million in collections.
106. The clothing retailer C & A (Brenninkmeyer) is one notable example. See Archbishop Bengsch's letters of thanks between December 1961 and July 1966 for three donations totaling about 1 million marks, DAB, V/5-20-1-1.
107. It is astounding that the MfS hardly ever uncovered (or wanted to uncover) transfers of goods and currency by Catholic clergy, which were illegal according to GDR law. See BStU, ZA, AIM 6973/73, Pt. 1. Theodor Schmitz, the former general vicar in the eastern portion of the Diocese of Berlin, by his own admission, exchanged about DM 800,000 every year between 1970 and 1982 at the black market rate of 1 to 2.5. See Theodor Schmitz, "Kirchenfinanzen in der SBZ/DDR, 1945–1989" (unpublished manuscript, 1996).

108. SAPMO-BArch, DY 30, J IV 2/3/813.
109. Deutscher Bundestag, 1. Untersuchungsausschuß, Drucksache 12/3462 vom 14.10.1992.
110. Armin Boyens, "'Den Gegner irgendwo festhalten': 'Transfergeschäfte' der Evangelischen Kirche in Deutschland mit der DDR-Regierung, 1957–1990," *Kirchliche Zeitgeschichte* 6 (1993): 379–90.
111. File notes on the 5 July 1966 conversation by Zinke. ROO, A II 3.
112. Ibid., undated file note.
113. Deutscher Bundestag, Beschlußempfehlung und Bericht des 1. Untersuchungsausschusses vom 27.5.1994 und 3 Anlagenbände, Drucksache 12/7600, p. 2706. See also Hellmut Puschmann, "Zur Brückenfunktion des Deutschen Caritasverbandes," in Ulrich von Hehl and Hans Günter Hockerts, eds., *Der Katholizismus-gesamtdeutsche Klammer in den Jahrzehnten der Teilung? Erinnerungen und Berichte* (Paderborn, 1996), 127–38.
114. "Church business A" referred to the supply of raw materials by the Lutheran Church in West Germany, in operation since 1957. "Church business B" designated the ransom (in the form of shipments of raw materials) paid by the Lutheran Social Services agency in Stuttgart for the release of prisoners. See Armin Volze, "Kirchliche Transferleistungen in die DDR," *Deutschland Archiv* 24 (1991): 59–66.
115. ROO, J II.
116. See Bernd Schäfer, "Verselbstständigungohne Zugewinn: DDR, katholische Kirche und Vatikan von 1965–1972," *Stimme der Zeit* 213 (1995): 321–32.
117. BStU, ZA, AIM 2716/74, pt. 2, vol. 1, pp. 69ff.
118. See Diederich, *Aus den Augen, aus dem Sinn.*
119. See Schäfer, "Verselbstständigungohne Zugewinn," 327.
120. See Lange et al., eds., *Katholische Kirche – Sozialistischer Staat DDR: Dokumente und öffentliche Äusserungen 1945-1990* (Leipzig, 2nd edition 1993), 227–30.
121. DAB, V/5-8-2. The section on legal questions is dated 1 March 1968.
122. Ibid.
123. ROO, A VIII 6.
124. Notes by Otto Groß, 11 April 1968. DAB, V/5-8-2.
125. Bengsch's report of 15 July 1968 is attached to the minutes of the BOK meeting of 2 September 1968. ROO, A III 30.
126. BStU, ZA, AP 11284/92, p. 3.
127. BAP, DO-4, 225.
128. ROO, A III 15.
129. ROO, H VII.
130. ROO, A IV 3.
131. DAB, V/5-7-1.
132. Ibid.
133. Notes to Bengsch's minutes of the meeting, 8 April 1963, ACPD I-028-031/1.
134. "Notes on the June 16, 1964, meeting with Archbishop Bengsch," BAP, DO-4, 2752, p. 8.
135. Letter of 13 April 1965. DAB, V/5-7-2.
136. See Seigewasser's 10 October 1966 report on a conversation with Bengsch. BAP, DO-4, 355.
137. DAB, V/5-7-2.
138. File notes by Otto Groß on a 13 May conversation between Seigewasser and Bengsch, 14 May 1969, BStU, ZA, AIM 2716/75, Part II, vol. 1, p. 98.
139. ROO, A II 27.
140. See *Herder-Korrespondenz* 20 (1966): 12ff.
141. See Lange et al., *Katholische Kirche – Sozialistischer Staat DDR,* 209 and 247.
142. File notes by Otto Groß of 10 January 1972, BstU, ZA, AP, 12446/92, p.192.
143. Lange et al., *Katholische Kirche – Sozialistischer Staat DDR,* 225.
144. Ibid., 237.

145. The complete text, unchanged since 1962, is found in Ministerium für Nationale Verteidigung, ed., *Wehrdienstgesetz und angrenzende Bestimmungen* (East Berlin, 4th edition 1984), 32.
146. ROO, A I 18.
147. Ibid.
148. ROO, A III 15.
149. Claus Herold, "Katholische Jugendseelsorge," in Bernd Börger and Michael Kröselberg, eds., *Die Kraft wuchs im Verborgenen: Katholische Jugend zwischen Elbe und Oder 1945–1990* (Düsseldorf, 1993), 284.
150. Cited in ibid., 286.
151. ROO, A I 18.
152. BAP, DO-4, 822.
153. Ibid.
154. BAP, DO-4, 382.
155. LV S-A der PDS, LPA-Magdeburg, IV B 2/14/980.
156. Report by Fahl, 22 March 1971. LV S-A der PDS, LPA-Halle, IV D 2/14/472.
157. SAPMO-BArch, NY 182/1098.
158. DAB, V/5-7-1.
159. See the report on an 30 August 1968 visit by the Office of the State Secretary to the Leipzig region, BAP-DO-4, 365. The ten clergymen were called in individually for "debriefings" with the district council. The author is grateful to the late Adolf Brockhoff of Hünstetten-Wallrabenstein, a priest in Merseburg in 1968, for access to private files.
160. SAPMO-BArch, DY 30, IV A 2/14/5.
161. Notes by HA XX/4, "Geplanter Abriß der katholischen Christus-Kirche in Rostock," 24 February 1969, BStU, ZA, AP 12446/92, p. 90.
162. File notes of 22 July 1969 by the CDU section for church affairs on a 21 July conversation with Flint, ACDP VII-013-2164.
163. ROO, AIII 29.
164. Cited in Lange et al., *Katholische Kirche – Sozialistischer Staat DDR*, 241.
165. BStU, ZA, AP 12446/92, p. 61.
166. ROO, A IV 5.
167. ROO, A II 27.
168. Ibid.
169. BStU, ZA, AP 12446/92, pp. 191–99.
170. Alfred Arnold, "Mater et Magistra: Werkzeug der ideologischen Kriegsvorbereitung," *Deutsche Zeitschrift für Philosophie* 9 (1961): 1446–60, here 1460.
171. Hartmut Rüstau, "Bemerkungen zur Enzyklika 'Mater et Magistra,'" *Deutsche Zeitschrift für Philosophie* 10 (1962): 653–56.
172. Cf. Elisa A. Carrillo, "The Italian Catholic Church and Communism 1943–1963," *The Catholic Historical Review* 77 (1991): 644–57.
173. See the original Latin text in Heinrich Denzinger and Adolf Schönmetzer, eds., *Enchiridion Symbolorum Definitionum et Declarationum de Rebus Fidei et Morum* (Freiburg, 35th edition 1973), 801–19.
174. Dieter Bergner and Gernot Preuß, "Differenzierung im politschen Klerikalismus: Zur Enzyklika 'Pacem in Terris'," *Zeitschrift für deutsche Philosophie* 11 (1963): 1189–1202.
175. ACDP VII-013-3003.
176. Lange et al., *Katholische Kirche – Sozialistischer Staat DDR*, 200ff.
177. See the SED Politburo notes of 11 September 1962. SAPMO-BArch, DY 30, J IV 2/2/847, attachment 3.
178. See Hansjakob Stehle, *Geheimdiplomatie im Vatikan: Die Päpste und die Kommunisten* (Zurich, 1993), 391.
179. Karl Rahner and Herbert Vorgrimler, eds., *Kleines Konzilskompendium: Sämtliche Texte des Zweiten Vatikanums* (Freiburg i. Br., 1984), 492.

180. See Schmitz, "Eurer Heiligkeit demütigster und gehorsamster Diener": Warum Kardinal Bengsch die Pastoralkonstitution des Zweiten Vatikanischen Konzils ablehnte" in *Deutsche Tagespost*, 22 April 1995, 13. The original Latin text is found in ROO, A V 20.
181. For more details, see Schäfer, "Verselbstständigung ohne Zugewinn," and Theo Mechtenberg, "Briefwechsel polnischer und deutscher Bischöfe 1965: Die Reaktion der Machthaber in der DDR," *Deutschland Archiv* 28 (1995): 1146–52.
182. DAB, V/5-7-1.
183. Ibid.
184. Ibid.
185. DAB, V/5-7-1.
186. 13 May 1969, file notes by Otto Groß, also delivered to the MfS. BStU, ZA, AIM 2716/75, Part II, vol. I, p. 100.
187. BStU, ZA, AIM 2716/75, Part II, vol. I, pp. 247–50. Chancellor Willy Brandt was also unsuccessful in a follow-up attempt with the Vatican in July 1970. See BStU, ZA, HA XX/4, 127, pp. 227–30.
188. SAPMO-BArch, DY 30, J IV 2/2/1287 (attachment 8).
189. SAPMO-BA-rch, DY 30, IV A 2/14/5.
190. BStU, ZA, ZAIG, Z 1947.
191. "Strategie und Taktik des Vatikans und seines Sekretariates für die Nichtglaubenden gegenüber den sozialistischen Ländern," BStU, ZA, HA XX/4, 463, pp. 48–54.
192. Notes by the CDU mayor of Weimar, Franz Kirchner, on a conversation with Ernst. SAPMO-BArch, DY 30, IV A 2/14/11.
193. See the MfS report of 20 November 1969 in BStU, ZA, ZAIG, Z 1764, p. 3.
194. Ibid., p. 1.
195. BStU, ZA, AIM 2716/75, Part II, vol. II, pp. 76–80.
196. Report of 10 October 1968, BStU, ZA, AIM 2716/75, Part II, vol. I, p. 7.
197. "Betr. Nachfolge des Weihbischofs Dr. Rintelen in Magdeburg," ROO, J II.
198. Letter of 23 June 1969 to an unnamed West German prelate, ROO, J II.
199. SAPMO-BArch, DY 30, IV A 2/14/11.
200. Magdeburg Council notes from 28 July 1969. BAP, DO-4, 844.
201. File notes by Groß, 31 July 1969, ROO, J II.
202. "'Heißer Sommer' in Magdeburg," undated report from late August 1969 by Claus Herold, a priest in Halle. BAP, DO-4, 464.
203. The MfS wanted to know as early as 20 November 1969 if the Vatican saw Braun as a successor to Rintelen. BStU, ZA, ZAIG, Z 1752, p. 2.
204. DAB, V/5-7-1.
205. Sermon by Bengsch in Bernau, 14 September 1969, quoted in Lange et al., *Katholische Kirche – Sozialistischer Staat DDR*, 242.
206. ROO, A II 22. Letter of Herbert Prauß to Cardinal Bengsch, 20 December 1967.
207. Letter of Bengsch to Prelate Bernhard Huhn, Görlitz, of 15 January 1968. ROO, A II 22. Bengsch asked Huhn to assume responsibility for youth ministries in the GDR.
208. The author is grateful to Father Claus Herold, Halle, for a copy of the letter. See also his article, Claus Herold, "'Zwischen Elbe und Oder': Rückblicke auf die zweite Hälfte des 'anderen Weges,'" in Bernd Börger and Michael Kröselberg, eds., *Die Kraft wuchs im Verborgenen: Katholische Jugend zwischen Elbe und Oder 1945–1990* (Düsseldorf, 1993), 132–36.
209. ROO, A III 30.
210. ROO, A III 15. Protocol IV.
211. Minutes by Schoenemann of 17 February 1969, on a conversation of Bengsch with representatives of the Erfurt Dialogue Circle, ROO, A II 9.
212. File report by Otto Groß, BstU, ZA, AP 12066/92, p. 73; ROO, A VIII 6.
213. ROO, J II.
214. Minutes of 23 October 1968, with a list of participants. ROO, A II 9.

215. ROO, A II 9.

216. ROO, A III 31.

217. The term first gained currency in West Germany in a pastoral letter from the Fulda Bishops' Conference in 1963, criticizing the position of the Catholic writers Heinrich Böll and Carl Amery on Rolf Huchhuth's play *The Deputy.*

218. Jäger used the regular mail for this personal letter, making it possible for the MfS to open and copy it. BStU, ZA, AIM, 145/88, Part I, p. 17.

219. ROO, A II 27. An earlier draft of the letter, sent to Prelate Paul Dissemond as secretary of the BOK on 17 February 1970, was much more pointed. Schaffran called for the bishops to be punished, remarking that their "bishop's staff" was useful for more than mere "decoration." ROO, A V 24.

220. ROO, A IV 4.

221. Karl Herbst, *Jenseits aller Ansprüche* (Munich, 1972), 198f.

222. Ibid, 203f.

223. Peter-Paul Straube, *Katholische Studentengemeinde in der DDR als Ort eines ausseruniversitären Studium generale* (Leipzig, 1996), 99–133.

224. BStU, ZA, AP 12446/92, pp. 69–73.

225. DAB V/5-9-3.

226. I am grateful to Father Claus Herold (Halle) for access to materials on the Halle Action Group in his private possession, from which this and the following quotations are taken.

227. This is from a February 1968 report entitled "New Forms and Methods Employed by the Churches for Political-Religious Influence, Especially of Youth," BAP, DO-4, 1144.

228. LV S-A der PDS, LPA-Halle, IV B 2/14/826.

229. BStU, Ast Halle, AOV 2145/72, vol. 1, p. 13.

230. LV S-A der DPS, LPA-Halle, IV A 2/14/1297.

231. See notes by Horst Hartwig from the Office of the State Secretary for Church Affairs on a conversation with Fuchs on 13 October 1966, when both still believed that Brockhoff could be "molded into a progressive clergyman," BAP, DO-4, 2752.

232. SAPMO, BArch, DY 30, IV A 2/14/37.

233. ROO, A IV 1.

234. DAB V/5-7-1.

235. ROO, A II 19.

236. DAB V/5-9-3.

237. DAB V/5-7-1.

238. DAB V/5-9.

239. DAB V/5-9-3.

240. Klemens Richter, ed., *Wolfgang Trilling. "Trauer gemäß Gott": Leiden in und an der Kirche in der DDR* (Altenberge, 1994), 17–31. The text could not be printed in the GDR because of government censorship as well as rejection from within the church in Berlin. The text was first published in 1993.

241. HStA Dresden, Bt/RdB, 26603.

242. BStU, Ast Dresden, XII 805/68, especially AOP 1438/74.

243. BAP, DO-4, 822.

244. See the 23 January 1969 "meeting report" by MfS Captain Helmut Wegener, BStU, ZA, AIM 2716/75, Part. II, vol. 1, pp. 26–39. In this conversation with Groß, the MfS was concerned with the Pacem in Terris Working Group, the Magdeburg student priest Theo Mechtenberg, the Berlin Catholic Student Congregation, the former Berlin student chaplain Eberhard Kirsch, the St. Paul Society, Adolf Brockhoff, a priest in Merseburg, and the former Magdeburg youth chaplain Claus Herold.

245. The author is grateful to the late Adolf Brockhoff for sharing with him the MfS transcripts of his lecture.

246. Straube, *Katholische Studentengemeinde*, 321–26.

247. BStU, ZA, ZAIG, Z 1574, p.5.
248. The full text of the document as well as MfS reports about it are found in Straube, *Katholische Studentengemeinde,* 331–36. For the original, BStU, ZA, AIM 2716/75, Part II, vol. 1, pp. 44–53.
249. As quoted in MfS reports from 20 August 1970. BStU, ZA, XX/4, 534, pp. 30–42.
250. BAP, DO-4, 1323.
251. The author is grateful to the late Adolf Brockhoff for access to his personal MfS files.
252. BStU, ZA, AIM 2716/75, Part II, vol. 1, p. 36.
253. SAPMO-BArch, DY 30, IV A 2/14/11.
254. BStU, ZA, AIM 2716/75, Part II, vol. II, pp. 36ff.
255. Quoted in Klemens Richter, "Aufbruch oder Resignation? Zur Situation der katholischen Kirche in der DDR," *Deutschland Archiv* 4 (1971): 972–976, 973.
256. BAP, DO-4, 1323.
257. LV S-A der PDS, LPA Magdeburg, IV B 2/14/980.
258. ROO, A IV 5.
259. Report attached to the minutes of the 8–9 January 1963 BOK meeting, p. 12 (ROO, A III 15).
260. HStA Dresden, Bt/RdB, 29715.
261. Horst Dohle, "Information und erste Einschätzung über die erste Arbeitstagung der Diözesansynode des Bistums Meißen vom 13.-15.6.1969 in Dresden," in HStA Dresden, Bt/RdB, 29715.
262. Analysis by section chief Horst Hartwig, "Zur ersten Sitzung der Meißner Synode," 30 June 1969, BAP, DO-4, 826.
263. HStA Dresden, Bt/RdB, 29715.
264. Ibid.
265. Ibid.
266. BAP, DO-4, 826.
267. BAP, DO-4, 255.
268. HStA Dresden, Bt/RdB, 29715.
269. After Spülbeck's death in June 1970, the text was never published in the GDR. It first appeared in print in December 1970 in the FRG in *Herder-Korrespondenz* 24 (1970): 576–81.
270. For this and the following quotes, see Spülbeck's letters and Riedel's report in ROO, D III 2.
271. *Herder-Korrespondenz* 24 (1970): 5.
272. Referenced in a 26 November 1970 letter from the papal nuncio, Konrad Bafile, to Cardinal Bengsch, DAB, V/5-6-3.
273. ROO, D III 2.
274. ROO, A IV 4.
275. Herbst, *Jenseits aller Ansprüche,* 196.
276. ROO, J II.
277. On 9 November 1970 the papal nuncio Konrad Bafile asked Schaffran for his personal estimation of the synod. Schaffran, now bishop of Meißen, responded on 12 December that he hoped "to respond to the many doubtlessly well-intended forces and, at the same time, to put a stop to the few dangerous forces. In the consciousness of most priests and lay Catholics, the synod held in the diocese was a great act of the church, and I have a dilemma: to take in these well-intended forces and simultaneously to keep out dangerous tendencies that cannot be reconciled with church teachings. Furthermore, Decrees I and II have only been adopted as an experiment for three years. I hope that these can be superseded by the decrees of the upcoming general synod and therefore lose their relevance." OAB, File 116.02/00, vol. 1.
278. DAB, V/5-6-3.
279. Bishop Schaffran sought the expert opinion of the following theology professors: Georg May (Mainz, on canon law); Leo Scheffczyk (Munich, on dogma); and Rudolf Schnackenburg (Würzburg, on exegesis). Wolfgang Trilling solicited opinions, via Hans Werners, a pastor in

Münster, from the systematic theologians Karl Rahner (Münster), Josef Ratzinger (Regensburg), and Walter Kasper (Tübingen). May sharply rejected the synod's decrees, as did Scheffczyk, but all other experts gave them positive evaluations and held them to be consistent with "church teaching."

Chapter 5

1972–1989

The GDR as a Sovereign State under International Law

External Stabilization and Internal Erosion

Under Chancellor Willy Brandt, the Bonn government's Ostpolitik pursued the long-term aim of gradually overcoming the European political status quo, i.e., the division of Germany, through the initial recognition of that status quo in international law. In contrast, the Soviet Union, the GDR, and other Warsaw Pact states hoped that the international recognition of two German states would stabilize the status quo. They always felt that overly close German-German relations presented a danger, but they believed that they could check this by increasing internal security measures and spreading propaganda in support of separation.

After the FRG had signed treaties on the East with the Soviet Union and Poland in August and December 1970, direct talks began between Michael Kohl, a GDR diplomat, and Egon Bahr, the West German state secretary in the federal chancellor's office. On 3 September 1971 the four victors in the Second World War signed the Quadripartite Berlin Agreement. West Berlin was not recognized as a constitutive part of the FRG, but its special ties to West Germany were confirmed, as was its diplomatic representation by Bonn. The Transit Agreement, signed on 17 December 1971, was the first inner-German agreement between Bonn and East Berlin, establishing rules for travel between West Berlin and the rest of West Germany. On 20 December, the West Berlin city government and the GDR regime reached a further agreement regarding visits to East Berlin from West Berlin.

A Basic Treaty between the FRG and the GDR, which was to be concluded as soon as the FRG ratified treaties with the USSR and Poland, was to regulate general relations between the two German states, based upon mutual diplomatic recognition. One temporary hitch in this process occurred when the conservative opposition tried to topple the SPD/FDP government in Bonn with a vote of no confidence on 27 April 1972, as the coalition found itself under increased pressure with a shrinking parliamentary majority. But Willy Brandt's government remained in power and, after tough discussions, secured the passage of the treaties on 17 May 1972; they took effect on 3 June 1972 together with the Quadripartite Agreement. Negotiations over a Basic Treaty between the FRG and the GDR began immediately thereafter and led to a signed agreement on 21 December 1972, after the SPD/FPD government had won a stable majority in new elections in November. The FRG recognized the GDR as a state but did not recognize its citizenship. The Basic Treaty was ratified by West Germany's parliament on 11 May 1973 and took effect on 21 June.

In the following years, there were intensive official and unofficial diplomatic and political contacts between East and West Germany, as well as further agreements on trade and transit. Between 1972 and 1978, the GDR was recognized by 123 more nations. On 18 September 1973 both German states were simultaneously admitted to the United Nations. On 2 May 1974 the "permanent representatives" of the two German states opened their offices in Bonn and East Berlin, respectively. In order to avoid "all-German" overtones, the GDR altered its constitution on 7 October 1974, expunging all references to "the German nation." The phrase "socialist state of the German nation" from the 1968 constitution was replaced with "socialist state of workers and peasants." On the same day, a twenty-five-year friendship treaty with the USSR was demonstratively signed. The recognition of the European status quo in international law was completed with the signing of the Conference for Security and Cooperation in Europe in Helsinki on 1 August 1975 by almost all European states, as well as the US and Canada. Although the USSR, which had called for such a joint European security conference since the 1960s, thus accomplished the recognition of the full sovereignty and equality of all of the Warsaw Pact countries—in particular, the GDR—it had to accept the human rights clauses in the Helsinki agreement as part of the bargain.

With the signing of the Helsinki accords in 1975, Erich Honecker emerged for the first time as a statesman on the international stage. In 1976 he obtained the agreement of the heads of the GDR Council of State to formally secure all final decision-making power in the GDR in his hands, and thus became a political figure that the Soviet Union could not do without, despite some reservations and intrigues on their part.[1] When tensions between the Communist world and the West increased sharply around 1979–1980 with the Soviet intervention in Afghanistan, the Western boycott of the Moscow Olympics, and the rise of the Solidarnošč movement in Poland, Honecker temporarily emphasized his distance from the FRG. On 9 October 1980 the minimum amount of money that

Western visitors to the GDR were required to exchange was raised drastically. In a 13 October speech in Gera, Honecker enumerated four demands for the FRG that would remain persistent issues in relations between the two Germanys in the years to follow: recognition of GDR citizenship; dismantling the Central Registry of [West German] State Judicial Administrations in Salzgitter with its database of GDR human rights violations; upgrading the permanent missions of the two countries to embassies; and adjusting the border along the Elbe River to the river's middle. At the same time, he approved Chancellor Helmut Schmidt's visit to the GDR, which after considerable preparation in 1980 was postponed because of the international situation and finally took place on 11–13 December 1981.

Both Helmut Schmidt's government and the one that followed, the conservative CDU/CSU/FDP coalition under Helmut Kohl, which came to power in September 1982, were interested in preserving talks and "channels" to the regime in East Berlin.[2] The same was true in the GDR, as Honecker sought to play up his so-called peace initiative before and just after the West German Bundestag reached a decision on 22 November 1983 on the stationing of mid-range nuclear missiles. Even after this important turn, Honecker continued special relations with Bonn until the Soviet leadership exercised its authority and blocked his planned trip to the FRG in August 1984. During the crisis in Soviet leadership—Brezhnev's illness and death in November 1982, followed by the brief tenure of his successors (Andropov died in February 1984 and Chernenko in March 1985)—Honecker was able to play an unprecedented role in German and international relations as the GDR head of state. This role would not have been possible without cross-party support in West Germany for a "coalition of reason" and a "community of responsibility" between the two Germanys. Indeed, in many ways there was an increase in official and unofficial contacts between East and West German emissaries after the CDU regained power in 1982. The new West German government sought its own successes in inter-German relations, and the business community wanted to expand trade. In the opposition, the SPD—the "inventor" of Ostpolitik—saw itself reduced to a minor role and tried to compensate with a "parallel foreign policy" toward the GDR and the USSR, which was not coordinated with the Bonn government.

A first dramatic success for West German secret diplomacy with the GDR was the "billions-credit" negotiated in July 1983 by Alexander Schalck-Golodowski through Josef März, a meat wholesaler and former CSU party treasurer, and Franz-Josef Strauß, the chairman of the CSU. This deal, which was of eminent importance for the GDR's ability to obtain credit from and make payment to the international market, was achieved without the state's committing to measurable political concessions. In 1984, a further credit of DM 950 million was extended. With Gorbachev's rise to power in the USSR and the decrease in international tensions, relations between the two German states deepened. West German politicians discussed a wide range of themes both officially and privately with their East German counterparts: travel, trade relations, cases of arrest or application to leave the GDR, city partnerships, and exchanges between experts. Often these contacts had a convenient domestic political side for the West German politicians involved.

Attempts to Thwart "Publically Effective" Dissent

After Honecker had replaced Ulbricht as the general secretary of the SED Central Committee in May 1971, the party's ideological drive gradually began to slow down, despite the continuity of ideological sloganeering and the party's monopoly in ideological education. The SED's Ninth Party Congress in May 1976 was the last time that reference was made to ideological mobilization "to create socialist man" in "a socialist human community" and to future visions of "a gradual transition to Communism."[3] Official party historiography retroactively described the period from 1961 to 1971 as "the path to a developed socialist society" and cast the period under Honecker as "the further unfolding of developed socialist society." With the proclamation of the "irrevocable victory of socialism on German soil in secure alliance with the Soviet Union," the party saw the GDR as "an indivisible part of the socialist community of states," especially given its broad international recognition after December 1972. The basic issues had been decided and society's structures established; the SED's task was to preserve its power.

Under Honecker, the party tried to win over the population with the "unity of economic and social policy." It promised to raise the standard of living by supplying high-quality consumer goods and constructing modern apartments for a society rooted in security and order, which was to produce a feeling of "comfort" and "sense of home" in the GDR. The SED's promises and later proclamations of success in its own propaganda, however, were far from the everyday reality in the GDR. The gap between West German consumer society and the GDR grew and grew, even though the GDR did experience some improvement in the perpetually inadequate supply for domestic needs. The so-called Intershops, opened in 1974 to ordinary GDR citizens, sold West German consumer goods for hard currency. The SED thought that these shops would release some of the pressure of the pent-up demand, but they were also a continuous visible admission of its own economic weakness. As West German currency became a de facto second currency for GDR citizens, the state needed more and more hard currency to finance its social and economic policies as well as to maintain its own public appearance and—not least—to equip its military and security agencies.

Unlike any other socialist country, the GDR was able to obtain a considerable amount of hard currency using a variety of means: agreements with the FRG on traffic with West Berlin, overdraft credits (so-called swing credits), the mandatory minimum currency exchange for visitors from the West, the Intershops, the "gift service" of "Genex" (valuable goods ordered for GDR citizens by Western sponsors through GDR firms operating in Denmark and Switzerland),

and various other enterprises of "commercial coordination" run by Alexander Schalck-Golodowski (such as trade in art and antiques, the arms trade, foreign firms, and "church business"). Nonetheless, the GDR racked up increasing debt to Western countries due to the credit practices endorsed by Honecker together with Schalck-Golodowski and Günter Mittag (the minister of the economy in the ZK). By the end of the 1970s, GDR debt amounted to DM 30 billion and by 1989 had grown so large that the country was bordering on insolvency.[4]

Dissent had increased in the wake of the 1975 Helsinki accords, which the GDR had signed—along with its passages on human rights and basic freedoms. It was also strengthened after the GDR accredited West German journalists as a result of the Basic Treaty with the FRG. Sensational events became points of crystallization for the reciprocal impact of oppositional acts in the GDR and West German media coverage of them, sharp reactions from the SED and the security services, and first attempts to form oppositional groups in the GDR. These events included the self-immolation of Oskar Brüsewitz, a Protestant minister, on 18 August 1976,[5] and the Politburo's decision to revoke the GDR citizenship of folk singer Wolf Biermann while he was on tour in West Germany. Robert Havemann became a leading dissident figure when he was placed under house arrest in 1976 (he died in 1982). Other dissident initiatives such as that of Rudolf Bahro, or the so-called SED Opposition Manifesto, made an impact in the GDR via their publicity in the West.

Although SED doctrine regarding internal security remained unchanged, and the personnel and technological equipment of the MfS continued to expand, the increase in dissident activity forced the state to make strategic choices. It wanted to repress the opposition, but such a course had to be weighed against the impact it could have upon the GDR's international reputation. The regime strove to prevent oppositional activities by "obstructing" them via MfS surveillance and the psychological "degradation" of targeted persons. Yet although the regime aimed to stop the "public effectiveness" of the opposition by any means, it had little success. The SED saw public expressions of dissent as dangerous, therefore justifying a tough MfS response, up to and including arrest. From 1982, however, oppositional groups could not be so easily dispatched but became permanent fixtures, most of them under the umbrella of the Protestant Church.

One particular form of "dissent"—filing a legal application to leave the GDR as a result of the Helsinki accords—was viewed in very different ways among those in the opposition, the churches, and in the general population. Permission to leave was granted to 20,000 GDR citizens between 1972 and 1977, and the number of applications to leave rose sharply thereafter: 8,400 in 1977; 21,500 in 1980; 50,600 in 1984; and 78,600 in 1986. The figures for 1984 and 1986 were especially high after a follow-up conference to the Helsinki accords held in Madrid in 1983 resulted in a legal basis for "family reunification" in the GDR. The repressive and capricious treatment of applicants by the SED leadership and the MfS led to ever greater problems. When some of them occupied embassies in East Berlin and Prague in 1984, this issue became public and a serious international concern for the regime, especially in connection with the thirty-fifth anniversary of the state in October 1984. Problems only increased in the years thereafter, as the SED preferred to personally attack and repress individuals who wished to leave rather than address the root causes of these individuals' desire to emigrate.

The GDR and the Vatican

After the FRG ratified treaties with the USSR and Poland in June 1972, the GDR began to plan a diplomatic initiative to take up direct negotiations with the Vatican. The GDR's wish for the church to adjust diocese boundaries to accommodate political borders set in motion a series of developments that were interrupted by the death of Pope Paul VI in August 1978 and then took a new direction under Pope John Paul II. In this period, secret agents of various Communist governments in Bonn and Rome kept the GDR remarkably well informed about the direction of developments within the Vatican. By contrast, the GDR had only rudimentary information about discussions within the BOK and the (West) German Bishops' Conference.

The Vatican line—represented above all by Archbishop Agostino Casaroli as secretary of the Council for the Public Affairs of the Church, which had the support of Pope Paul VI and Cardinal–Secretary of State Jean Villot irrespective of power struggles in Rome—demanded diplomatic autonomy in relation to the local Catholic churches and advised German bishops from both East and West to consider the general situation of the church in Eastern Europe. On the one hand, this stance contextualized the openness in canon law regarding the "German Question"; on the other, it sought to make maximum use of the extremely favorable status quo for the Catholic Church in the GDR compared with other Communist countries. It was on behalf of Catholics in other Communist countries that the Vatican sought to establish a constructive diplomatic relationship with East Berlin.

The Vatican's representatives, who began negotiating directly with SED politicians and GDR diplomats in 1973, justified their policy as far-sighted and shaped by "higher insights."[6] They acknowledged East German Catholics' reservations about making Catholic districts within the GDR independent and energetically opposed West Germany's persistent reservations. The chairmen of the BOK and German Bishops' Conference—Cardinal Bengsch and Cardinal Döpfner—conferred closely on this and took identical positions on not realigning church jurisdictions with current political borders, notwithstanding their differences over the question of the status of West Berlin in canon law. They were treated very differently by Vatican diplomats, however, as Bengsch's absolute theological loyalty to Rome protected him, whereas Döpfner was regarded as being critical. Some East German bishops—Johannes Braun (Magdeburg), Gerhard Schaffran (Dresden), and Heinrich Theissing (Schwerin)—did not completely agree with Bengsch on this question from 1973 to 1979, and were sympathetic to the idea of promoting GDR dioceses under canon law.

To the dismay of the West German episcopate, the pope and leading figures in the Vatican supported the Ostpolitik of the SPD-led government in Bonn in principle, as they hoped it would enable them to make progress in the legal situation of the churches in Poland and the GDR. In the view of the German Bishops' Conference and the Bonn Central Committee of German Catholics, however, the Vatican's Ostpolitik, first and foremost, had negative consequences for the political fortunes of the CDU/CSU. In its mostly unsuccessful attempts to influence Rome, the German Bishops' Conference frequently pointed to upcoming elections in West Germany and possible "loyalty conflicts" that "German Catholics" (as CDU/CSU voters) might experience because of Rome's policy toward the GDR. For example, when the new West German government under Helmut Schmidt temporarily took a harder line toward the Communist world in 1974, Cardinal Döpfner wrote to the pope on 24 November: "It would be disastrous if the impression arose that the West German government rejects Communism more strongly than the Catholic Church . . . many in Germany are unsettled [by the Vatican's Ostpolitik] . . . the authority of the Holy See is threatened in a way that could all too easily spread to disciplinary and religious questions as well."[7]

The GDR took its first diplomatic steps toward the Vatican by passing a Politburo memorandum on 18 July 1972 entitled "Measures to Regulate Catholic Diocese Borders to Correspond to State Borders as the Necessary Consequence of the Ratification of the FRG/USSR Treaty."[8] The memo was passed from the GDR embassy in Belgrade to Mario Cagna, the papal nuncio there. On 24 August 1972 GDR Prime Minister Willi Stoph held talks with Cardinal Bengsch, explaining the GDR's diplomatic initiative and requesting his support. On 26 August Bengsch sent a report on the conversation to the nuncio in Bonn, expressing his approval that the GDR regime viewed the Vatican as a dialogue partner. It was "a better starting point than the Protestants had," he said, adding that the BOK "would be an incomparably less favorable" partner.[9] Further, Bengsch said that the GDR would not dispute his administrative responsibility for West Berlin and would even "permit frequent visits as a concession." The first direct contacts between Vatican representatives and the GDR then followed in Belgrade on 9 October 1972.

Bengsch dispatched Otto Groß to Munich on 24 September 1972 to speak with Cardinal Döpfner and to discuss the meaning of the Bengsch-Stoph meeting. The Döpfner-Groß talk was in part controversial because of the disputed status of West Berlin in church administration, but the special relations of the churches in each of the German states were to be preserved, as was the system of financial transfers from West to East.[10] On 14 September Groß had composed a position statement for Bengsch, which the BOK was to approve in its session the next day and send on to the Vatican.[11] The BOK then passed it with slight modifications, taking the position that church talks with the GDR should insist upon the free selection of bishops, free access to Rome, the support of church institutions by the Vatican, official acceptance of the church's current areas of activity in the GDR, and the protection of church property. As a concession to GDR wishes, the BOK proposed that the church establish distinct Catholic districts within the GDR, whereby "a final settlement will only be reached when these become independent dioceses."[12]

It was soon clear, however, that the Vatican sought to negotiate based upon its own interests, not those of the Catholic Church in the GDR. On 24 January 1973 SED Politburo member Werner Lamberz called on Archbishop Casaroli in Rome without consulting with GDR Catholic leaders before or after the meeting. According to Lamberz's notes on the visit, Casaroli cautioned him about "the psychological aftereffects of the 1933 Concordat" in West Germany and, at the same time, signaled that

> He, Casaroli, wanted to think aloud. In the four districts in question where Catholics lived, apostolic administrators could be named as a first step . . . The second step would follow this one. The essential thing about the first step is that its direction is clear . . . Church-state relations in the GDR are positive, indeed more than positive. The Vatican wishes to preserve this and even to improve it. Casaroli expressly asked whether the GDR regime had the intention of maintaining this state of affairs in the future. Comrade Lamberz replied that the GDR regime did not have the intention of changing its relations with the Catholic Church in the GDR.[13]

To the horror of the Catholic Church in the GDR, the Vatican actually wanted to begin serious diplomatic relations with East Berlin and have a papal nuncio in residence in "the capital of the GDR." Had this taken place, it would have constituted a higher level of state recognition and would have subverted the previous "arm's length" posture the Catholic Church had exhibited toward the regime. Moreover, it would have broken Cardinal Bengsch and the BOK's local church monopoly on negotiations with state officials. It would have made it possible for the state to try to employ the nuncio as a watchdog for local Catholic activities. Cardinal Bengsch dispatched Otto Groß to make his profound objection to this turn of events known to GDR officials,[14] and he tried to intervene in Rome.

The GDR was also very interested in diplomatic relations with the Vatican but eventually had to keep its distance because the Soviet Union prohibited such ties to avoid allowing differentiation within the Communist bloc. Practically speaking, Warsaw Pact countries could only achieve diplomatic relations with the Vatican if the Soviet Union approved them first. Thus, the issue of a papal nuncio in East Berlin never got beyond the hypothetical stage, but the Vatican and the SED Central Committee never gave up their hopes in this regard.

After the ratification of the Basic Treaty between the two Germanys on 18 May 1973, Pope Paul VI declared the bishops of Erfurt, Magdeburg, and Schwerin to be "permanent" administrators. They were to report directly to the Vatican, so the formal jurisdiction of the West German dioceses there was suspended. For the GDR, these steps were only a minimal accommodation when measured against the ambitions of their summer 1972 memorandum. The GDR now pursued negotiations with the Vatican, expressing its wish for the diocese and state boundaries to become fully aligned ("normalization") by means of further legal steps. The Vatican sought guarantees for the relatively favorable status quo of the Catholic Church in the GDR and hoped for improvement. Contacts occurred not only through the GDR embassy in Rome, but also on the sidelines of the Conference on Security and Cooperation in Europe, where a conversation between Archbishop Casaroli and GDR Foreign Minister Winzer took place, and at the European Security Conference in Geneva.

On 25 June 1974 the SED Politburo decided upon a new, detailed "Directive for the Continuation of Talks between the GDR and the Vatican."[15] These instructions for negotiations set the alignment of the diocesan borders as the clear goal. Only on the condition of Vatican reciprocity was the party willing to offer an agreement that would guarantee the current level of activity enjoyed by the Catholic Church in the GDR for the future. At the same time, the party did not want to prod the Vatican toward the hoped-for decision by threatening to make the situation worse. On 10 July 1974 the GDR ambassador in Rome, former Minister of Culture Klaus Gysi, visited Casaroli with his government's invitation to continue bilateral negotiations in Berlin at the level of the foreign minister. In response, all BOK members signed a letter to Casaroli on 5 September 1974, requesting that, given the Vatican's resolve to take up the GDR offer, the Vatican representative consult with GDR bishops before visiting the country and remain in close contact with them.[16] On 17 April 1975 Politburo member Werner Lamberz presented a confidential note to Casaroli asking him to speed up his visit. After receiving this, Casaroli said he was not only prepared to come for direct talks but also to attend some state functions and spend two days as a guest in a GDR government hotel. When Casaroli eventually visited the GDR on 9–14 June 1975, he was certainly influenced by information he had received in Rome from the BOK, as well as from West German religious and political figures, on the situation of Catholics in the GDR. During his visit, he met twice with Foreign Minister Oskar Fischer and once with State Secretary for Church Affairs Hans Seigewasser. For the GDR regime, the concrete results of the visit were paltry.

The Vatican, however, continued to feel diplomatic pressure to move in regard to the GDR—especially after the CSCE Helsinki meeting—and did not want to jeopardize the status quo by being inflexible. To defend its diplomacy with East Berlin to Cardinal Bengsch, the Vatican pointed to pressure from the GDR regime. However, the bishops in the GDR and their deputies could not observe this pressure; in fact, the regime's internal plans did not anticipate a scenario limiting Catholic activities. The principal motive of Vatican Ostpolitik was still to secure progress for the entire Roman Catholic Church in Eastern Europe by establishing better relations with the GDR because of its unique church-state relationship.

In 1976, the MfS found out that the Vatican had decided to create a regional conference of bishops in the GDR before establishing independent dioceses. Cardinal–Secretary of State Jean Villot confirmed this in a letter to Cardinal Bengsch on 10 April 1976. The GDR bishops were asked which canon law measures should thus be introduced. The GDR regime saw these measures as an anticipatory action by the Vatican to secure a more favorable negotiating position in the question of establishing independent dioceses.[17] Despite massive intervention by the German Bishops' Conference and the Central Committee of German Catholics, the Vatican held to its decision and made only the small concession of delaying the announcement until after the West German elections on 3 October 1976. On 26 October the Vatican published a declaration announcing that the independent Berlin Bishops' Conference (Berliner Bischofskonferenz, BBK) had been established in accordance with a 25 September decree.

On 28 October, the GDR Office of the State Secretary for Church Affairs described what had been accomplished as "contradictory" but "a step in the right direction" and "the furthest-reaching measure yet in relation to the recognition of the situation of the GDR in international law."[18] In a decision on further relations with the Vatican of 9 November 1976, the SED Politburo expressed its satisfaction with this "positive step" but noted that "the basic question of redrawing diocese borders to match the GDR border" had not yet been resolved. Therefore, it concluded that it should show the Vatican its willingness to "set up a papal nuncio for the capital of the GDR and name a GDR ambassador to the Vatican" on the condition that the border issue be resolved. At the same time, referring to the situation of Cuba, Yugoslavia, and Poland, the Politburo made clear that this would in no way create a precedent for other socialist countries. To show its willingness to cooperate with the Vatican, the Politburo decided that the state should treat the Catholic Church in the GDR more generously, for example, by providing financial support for charitable activities and for subsidizing priests' salaries, considering certain construction requests, and allowing GDR bishops more contacts abroad.[19]

Not until the autumn of 1977, when GDR bishops made their quinquennial visit ad limina to Rome, were they informed that the church intended to establish GDR dioceses because there were no guarantees for the status quo. Although the German Bishops' Conference and Cardinal Bengsch opposed further steps toward making GDR districts into independent dioceses (though not all East German bishops and BOK members held this view), the Vatican nonetheless asked the BBK in March 1978 to vote on the issue. The varied reactions of East German bishops to this request led, in the end, to a BBK resolution that administrative districts should be established if the Holy See felt that a change was unavoidable.[20] On 5 June 1978 the papal nuncio in Bonn was informed that "[t]he Berlin Conference of Bishops finds the status quo of the Catholic Church in the GDR to be by far the best in the Communist world, above all, concerning the freedom of pastoral activity. The status quo cannot, of course, be guaranteed for the future, but nor can it be secured by altering the borders of the dioceses."[21]

Thereafter, the Vatican prepared the decree to establish new administrative districts and informed the governments in Bonn and East Berlin.

Pope Paul VI died on 6 August 1978, and as it turned out, the decree was never signed. On 22 August GDR Ambassador Gysi sent a telegram from Rome to East Berlin describing two conversations with Casaroli immediately before and after the pope's death. "The basic features of Ostpolitik" would remain secure, he reported, "but its emphasis and tone" might be altered at any time. Moreover, Casaroli did not appear to expect to remain in office.[22] First, however, Gysi was recalled from Rome on account of undiplomatic private affairs. In the end, Casaroli was promoted to cardinal–secretary of state after Jean Villot's death in 1979. As early as 25 October 1978 the MfS concluded in a report that "power relations" within the Vatican were shifting to the detriment of GDR interests.[23] GDR Foreign Minister Fischer was able to hold a meeting with the new pope, John Paul II, on 28 October (it had been scheduled long in advance), but they did not aim to make any concrete agreements. To be sure, the establishment of administrative districts remained on the Vatican agenda until 1979 but then faded into the background. The GDR had no diplomatic means for pressuring the Vatican to make church boundaries square with political borders. To worsen conditions for the Catholic Church in the GDR would have been politically counterproductive both internally and externally. Vatican claims of GDR pressure lost credibility when the SED actually improved the church's situation in the following years, even though it had, in the end, been snubbed on the issue of diocese borders.

The GDR state apparatus continually analyzed the new Polish pope and his policy toward the Communist countries. After an initial phase of uncertainty, its characterizations became more and more negative, especially in regard to developments within Poland. On 12 April 1979 the MfS put together a first detailed analysis of "Essential Questions of Vatican Policy after the Election of Wojtyla as Pope."[24] It was based on sources from Rome as well as from Polish security services, which described John Paul II as an extreme anti-Communist. The MfS concluded that "political decisions regarding GDR dioceses are not expected in the immediate future" and that the new pope "does bring much goodwill to 'German questions'. . . He is an anti-Communist, but first and foremost a Pole."

In the following years, the GDR regime saw the new pope's course as especially dangerous, especially in the "counterrevolutionary" Solidarnošč phase in Poland from August 1980 to December 1981. It believed that the pope, in alliance with the West, was both openly and secretly mobilizing the power of the Catholic Church to overthrow socialism in Poland. In contrast, the MfS did not accuse the pope of a negative influence upon the Catholic Church in the GDR. Responding to questions that the Polish security services posed to their colleagues in other Communist countries about papal influence, the MfS said on 14 August 1981 that, as concerned the Catholic Church in the GDR, it was not the Vatican but West German Catholics who negatively influenced the East German Catholic Church, which, for its part, usually tried to avoid controversy.[25]

In Rome, Casaroli's former key role in Vatican policy toward the Communist world was sharply curtailed in favor of the many direct contacts that Pope John Paul II enjoyed with important church officials in socialist countries. At the same time, the GDR leadership softened its judgment of the pope after he showed more and more diplomatic skill in his many visits abroad, which made it attractive for SED General Secretary Honecker, who needed to promote his international reputation, to meet with him. Increasingly, the GDR differentiated between the "Polish pope" and the Vatican head of state.

In these years, Honecker styled himself as an international "politician for peace." When he was able to arrange an audience with John Paul II on 24 April 1985 during his state visit to Italy, he had the international impact of a meeting with the pope and the spectacle of a full state visit in "Berlin, the capital of the GDR," in mind. But the BBK chairman, Cardinal Joachim Meisner, who was known for his good contacts in Rome, annoyed the GDR state organs responsible for church affairs in this matter and was perceived by them as a hindrance. As the Vatican had not consulted Meisner on the Honecker visit, he tried to block the papal audience, or at least to involve himself in it, noting that he, as BBK chairman, had until now avoided a meeting with Honecker.[26] However, the BBK was merely able to supply the pope with information on the problems of GDR Catholics and, after Honecker's papal audience—where he delivered unauthorized greetings to the pope on behalf of "Catholics in the GDR"—to plead for greater government tolerance for GDR Catholics. Honecker's official present certainly made an impression at the Vatican: in contrast to West German President Richard von Weizsäcker, who gave the pope a golden watch, Honecker presented a Meißen porcelain Madonna by Kändler.

The GDR-wide convention of Catholics in Dresden in July 1987 seemed an occasion for the pope and Cardinal Meisner to plan for a "counter visit" that would sidestep the capital city. However, after complex internal state moves and church intrigues,[27] this idea did not come to fruition. In the end, the pope's GDR visit was amicably agreed upon for 1991, with both sides beginning preparations in 1988. The SED Politburo approved a papal visit "in principle" as early as 12 August 1986.[28] In the tightly controlled GDR public discourse, the issue of the pope became "a matter for the personal attention of the SED General Secretary *[Chefsache]*." As Klaus Gysi, now state secretary for church affairs, put it on 22 December 1986 in an internal memo advising church affairs officials in the GDR district offices: "In conversations [with GDR Catholics], we must refer more forcefully to the pope as our chief witness. We must differentiate, and under no circumstances may we argue against the pope."[29]

The State's Need for Currency and the Churches

Under Honecker, an increasingly pragmatic SED leadership ascribed an ever more important function in internal and foreign affairs to the churches, which had no alternative but to adjust to the continued existence of the GDR. SED members largely believed in the historically determined demise of religion under socialism, but the policies of the leadership showed a different emphasis. As the GDR's foreign debt grew, so too did the state's need for hard currency. As a result, Kirchenpolitik became more important in light of the so-called church business, which was placed under the control of Politburo members Honecker, Günter Mittag, and Erich Mielke in 1972.

The financial transfers from West Germany under the provisions of Church Business C totaled approximately DM 630 million between 1966 and 1989, whereby the GDR state then gave the Catholic Church 360 million in GDR marks and DM 270 million for previously approved new construction as well as medical and technical equipment. Because of the artificially fixed rate of currency exchange and various deals with the copper supplied from the West, the GDR could earn about DM 15 million per year from the Catholic Church through the Commercial Coordination and Church Business C programs. These and other hard currency funds flowed into MfS bank accounts 0528 and 0559, as well as into the general secretary's account number 0628, set up in 1974, which Honecker controlled personally. The funds partly went to equip the state security services and were also used to make up for GDR goods shortages and to provide financial assistance to allied Communist countries.[30] In light of all the opportunities to profit from the church, the MfS church affairs division HA XX/4, which was not involved in church business, wanted to find another way to benefit. It thus took advantage of a situation in 1982 when Roland Steinke, head of the Berlin Caritas organization, was found to be involved in extensive black market currency dealings. By threatening prosecution and simultaneously offering to drop charges if direct "restitution" payments were made to the unit's director, Lieutenant Joachim Wiegand, it was able to "earn" DM 250,000 in cash, which Prelate Gerhard Lange from the BBK delivered after an internal church agreement was reached.[31]

The Catholic Church was also involved, via Prelate Zinke in the early 1960s, in Church Business B: the ransom of political prisoners. Later, it was also involved on occasion when lists were compiled of those willing to emigrate within the context of "reunification of families." Wolfgang Vogel, a GDR lawyer, played more than a mediating role in this, even though he claimed in his memoirs that the churches invented the practice of ransoming prisoners, emigrants, and those who occupied embassies. (The GDR differentiated the monies for these cases by referring to ransom for prisoners as "restitution for damages" and for the rest as "compensation for the costs of their education at state expense").[32]

Manfred Seidel and Manfred Wünsche were two of the state's key players in the currency transfers and other business with the Catholic Church. Seidel had replaced Horst Roigk, who had transferred to the MfS division HA XVIII in 1966. He had an impressive career there, ultimately moving to the Ministry of Foreign Trade. Within the MfS, church business was monitored by the Deputy Minister's Working Group for the Commercial Coordination Division (Arbeitsgruppe Bereich Kommerzielle Koordinierung beim Stellvertreter des Ministers, AG BKK). Until 1989, Seidel functioned as Alexander Schalck-Golodowski's deputy for "commercial coordination"; his duties included direct negotiations with Catholic representatives, including Otto Groß (until 1974) and later leaders of the Central Office of the German Caritas Association, the East Berlin Caritas directors Roland Steinke and, after 1982, Hellmut Puschmann. Wünsche, from Berlin-Karlshorst, a lawyer brought on by Seidel, was a glitzy figure who took on jobs for the Catholic Church in the GDR and in the FRG via his friendship with Groß. In addition, Wünsche acted as a "confidential lawyer" for the MfS as well as for Working Group S in the foreign intelligence Hauptverwaltung A (HVA); nonetheless, it was not always clear to the security services that he worked for them.[33] Wünsche had direct contacts with the head of the German Caritas Association in West Berlin as well as with representatives from the East Berlin ordinaries.

In the context of the larger flow of money to the GDR from West Germany, church-related financial transfers—so necessary for the basic existence of the GDR churches—played a proportionally small role in the financial stabilization of the GDR. Between 1970 and 1989, the Bonn government gave the GDR a total of DM 14.1 billion. Within the same period of time, an additional DM 5 billion passed from West to East Germany through private hands in the form of presents and money spent during visits. By contrast, the Protestant Church received about DM 2.5 billion from the West German churches between 1957 and 1989 and the Catholic Church netted DM 530 million between 1966 and 1989.[34]

The GDR's need for hard currency was so great that, beginning in the early 1970s, the churches were pressured to participate in hard currency–financed construction and renovation projects for religious buildings and housing. Naturally, both Protestant and Catholic representatives tried to take maximum advantage of these opportunities.[35] The GDR Intrac firm was to pay the costs, and state enterprises would then carry out the construction work. On 1 November 1972 the GDR Council of Ministers authorized Seidel to conclude deals up to DM 44 million annually for the Protestant Church and up to DM 15 million for the Catholic Church. Seidel was "to secure that the opportunities arising from these relations should be exploited for their high economic value."[36] The Council of Ministers expected "intakes," i.e., profits, of about DM 40 million annually. While the Protestants concluded the first "hard currency special construction program" with Seidel in 1973, the Catholic Church invested less than DM 10 million annually in Western-financed construction projects from 1972 to 1974. Between 1975 and 1982, the annual average was DM 15 million. Increased construction wishes then pushed the total over DM 20 million.[37] On 18 June 1976 Paul Dissemond and Gerhard Lange were asked to come as representatives of the ordinaries to the Office of the State Secretary for Church Affairs to discuss replacing the system of hard currency financing for individual Catholic construction projects with a broader basic construction agreement with the Catholic Church, something that was then sealed in a previously planned meeting between Seige-wasser and Bengsch on 11 August.

The Catholic Church was especially interested in building churches, community centers, and preschools in newly constructed neighborhoods. GDR city and district bureaucrats were very cool to these construction proposals for ideological and practical reasons: they feared a religious presence in the new, modern GDR developments and worried about the limited construction capacity; they thus regularly rejected individual proposals. In such cases, however, central state offices intervened with decisions based upon political tactics and economic considerations that—with the exception of preschools and some individual churches in certain areas—largely matched the wishes of the Catholic Church. Faced with resistance from within the SED and some discontent among the non-churchgoing population, Honecker increasingly made these decisions personally.[38]

Chairman of the State Planning Commission Gerhard Schürer described the formal path for approval of hard currency–financed church construction projects to State Secretary for Church Affairs Klaus Gysi in February 1981:

> These capital expenditures should be summarized for a five-year-plan time frame and presented by the State Secretary for Church Affairs—after approval by the Chairman of the State Planning Commission, the Minister of Building, the responsible SED district leaders and the district councils, as well as by the SED Central Committee Church Affairs Working Group—to the Politburo of the SED Central Committee for final approval.[39]

In practice, however, Honecker sent coded notes to all SED district-level first secretaries and decreed that such proposals would be approved, in principle. An example of this comes from this note of 2 May 1985: "Construction proposals from churches and religious communities in the GDR for the years 1986–1990 are, as a principle, approved. Payment for these construction proposals is exclusively through convertible currency within the framework of the GDR export program."[40]

The churches—in particular the Catholic Church and the Mormons—continually proposed new construction projects throughout the 1980s and demanded high-quality work from the state as they were paying in hard currency. Yet GDR construction capacity was taxed as these church projects competed with others; materials became scarce and the number of incomplete projects rose. Because the state needed the hard currency profits, it was in a weaker position vis-à-vis the churches over construction matters. In 1987, the "Valutabau" working group was set up within the Ministry of Building, yet it was unable to alleviate the discomfort GDR officials felt in this situation. On 28 September 1987 Schalck-Golodowski wrote a worried letter to Mittag, expecting church leaders to "complain directly" to Honecker because of the "considerable backlog" of unfinished church projects.[41] Indeed, Honecker decided personally on these matters, in direct consultation with Schalck-Golodowski and Mittag. Honecker answered critics from within his own ranks on 10 August 1988, when he sent a two-page information sheet entitled "Information on Procedures for Approving Construction Projects for Churches and Religious Groups Permitted in the GDR" to all Politburo members and candidates.[42] Although the document left the actual procedure for decision-making unmentioned, it did calculate that the GDR profited from the "special construction program" to the tune of DM 50 million annually.

"Commercial coordination" was a clever way to conceal the GDR's hard currency needs. Capitalist methods were to be employed to receive funds from "the capitalists" in order to win the struggle between the two systems. The East German churches' financial dependence on the West offered the SED the opportunity both to profit and, at the same time, to make the churches more loyal to the GDR. For their part, the churches saw pragmatic possibilities within the state's chosen course—a chance to secure their existence and to expand their activities with the help of their better-off brethren in the FRG. The various church businesses had advantages for both sides that could not be overlooked. They also created mutual dependencies, although the churches had no alternative because of the state's policies. Each side was implicitly influenced by the other. For the GDR churches, church business guaranteed their existence as long as the GDR needed sources of hard currency. As a consequence, expectations and perceptions changed on both sides. The SED leadership accepted that the churches were not headed for extinction, and that such a thing actually was not desirable as their existence had financial and political positives for the GDR state. The churches, in turn, knew that the state was not about to liquidate them in the foreseeable future, but would rather use them for its own purposes and integrate them.

Consequently, political tactics shifted to align with the new reality. For example, throughout the 1970s SED Politburo member Paul Verner still preached the gospel of the historically determined decline of the churches in his speeches on the basics of Kirchenpolitik to state and party church affairs officials from the entire GDR. By 1980, however, he used the same forum to proclaim the new ideology: "The line followed by our party is correct: the churches should be more strongly at home within socialist society, and we should aim to make it possible for their power and ability to influence—both internally and externally—to be more effective for the GDR."[43] Academics who researched "scientific atheism" at the Marine Engineering School in Rostock-Warnemünde had oriented themselves to the new line as early as 1979. In November 1978, Olof Klohr and Wolfgang Kaul still presented papers with titles like "Causes and Trends of the Extinction of Religion in the GDR."[44] By 1979, though, the theme had become "On the Tendencies of the Regression of Religious Life Expressions in the GDR."[45] They no longer predicted that the churches would disappear, but only that they would "become smaller" and be reduced to "an active core."

State "Differentiation" Policy in Relation to the Catholic Church

In the early 1970s, the GDR state bureaucracy had a pyramid structure. Church affairs divisions were no exception: SED party organs directed them, and the MfS carried out directives and watched over them. When important matters were in question, they became "matters for the personal discretion of the highest instance" *(Chefsache)*—the general secretary of the SED Central Committee. Ulbricht and his successor Honecker were alike in this regard, although Honecker had a greater interest in church affairs because, with the international recognition of the GDR in 1972, they had greater political significance at home and abroad. Paul Verner was responsible for church affairs within the SED Politburo beginning in 1957, but this was only one of several areas he was in charge of. When (genuine) health concerns compelled Verner to step down from his offices in 1984, church matters were turned over to Werner Jarowinsky, who had just become a full Politburo member; however, his main duty was to head the ZK's Secretariat for Trade and Supply. Verner and Jarowinsky were the direct supervisors of the four-person Church Affairs Working Group in the ZK. The group was headed until March 1977 by Willi Barth (born in 1899), then by Rudi Bellmann (born in 1919) and, beginning in January 1989, by Peter Kraußer (born in 1941). In addition, there were individual officials within the party apparatus (within the district-level SED first secretaries' offices) who were involved in religious affairs. At the *Kreis* level, the SED did not devote personnel to church issues.

The greatest numbers of GDR officials working on church policy were found in the Office of the State Secretary for Church Affairs and at the church affairs units within the district councils; individual staff members also worked in some city and county councils. The MfS, however, saw itself—in the service of the SED leadership—as the decisive state branch in church affairs questions through its HA XX/4. The MfS tried to influence events and decisions by using its informers within the church affairs policy bureaucracy, who were sometimes planted rather than recruited. As "partners in political-operative cooperation," these persons could be found in all of these divisions working simultaneously for both state organs. In contrast to his predecessor as state secretary for church affairs, the late Hans Seigewasser, Klaus Gysi—in office beginning in May 1979—sought direct contact with the MfS and was therefore more closely tied to the distribution of MfS information on behalf of the SED leadership. But that did not keep MfS HA XX/4 from using all means at its disposal to spy on Gysi, obtaining information on his schedule and correspondence from informers.

Where the Catholic Church was concerned, only the CDU officials Fritz Flint (1960–1977) and Hermann Kalb (1977–1989) actually functioned as empowered deputy representatives of the state secretary for church affairs. In every other instance, because of the "specific political composition" of the leadership, it was the main department leader from the SED who was the actual representative.[46] From 1957 to 1982, this was Hans Weise; then Peter Heinrich through 1989, when he was simultaneously an MfS special duty officer. The section for Catholic affairs was headed by Horst Hartwig from 1965 to 1972. Horst Pätzke was then in charge through 1982, when he was abruptly removed. Dr. Klaus Kurth added this job to his many other duties from 1983 through August 1985, when Hartwig then relieved him and headed the section again, remaining until the end of the GDR.

Olof Klohr, who held a chair in "scientific atheism" at the University of Jena, was transferred to a college in Warnemünde in 1969 when the chair was eliminated. He built up the research group there through 1972. Its mission was "to prepare programs of study and teaching materials for colleges and universities for required special courses in scientific atheism and to train instructors."[47] Beginning in 1979, the research group produced diagnostic studies and a handbook for the SED Central Committee, with detailed statistics on all religious communities in the GDR for use by central and regional offices of the SED, MfS, and other state offices concerned with church affairs. After 1981, within the Institute for Marxist-Leninist Philosophy at the Academy of Social Science in Berlin, there was also a working group for "Worldview Issues Concerning Cooperation between Communists and Religious Believers." It conducted scholarly research on behalf of the state and the party and aimed to coordinate "atheism research" in Warnemünde and elsewhere. In December 1980, Wolfgang Kliem, who would later direct this group, proposed a GDR research program specifically on Catholicism, but it was never realized.

The GDR church affairs apparatus tried to approach the Catholic Church with a "differentiation" strategy aimed at dividing its members one last time in the 1970s, when Hans Seigewasser was still state secretary for church affairs. In contrast to the state efforts of the 1960s, the intensity of the campaign gradually diminished because its methods—individual talks with bishops and other clergy that would then be paired with political praise—remained unsuccessful. Moreover, after the GDR was recognized under international law by Western countries, the political pressure for churches to make supportive public statements, so common in the GDR's early years, had let up. The churches still received routine requests and reminders, but the state seemed to be aware they would lack resonance even before they were sent.

Nevertheless, at a 24–25 January 1972 conference of district-level church affairs officials from across the GDR, State Secretary Seigewasser still took a militant tone in his presentation on the Catholic Church: "The Catholic Church in the GDR still has not retreated from its position of 'destructive silence' on fundamental political questions. This is nothing more than concealed political aggression. It corresponds to the basic posture of the Catholic Church if aggressive and provocative actions are now seen."[48] The state made considerable efforts to overcome this posture—such as a countrywide signature campaign for a "public letter" from "progressive Catholics" in May 1972 in advance of the pastoral synod—but they had little effect. A 17 August 1976 analysis by the Catholic section of the Office of the State Secretary held that the regime could "neither accept nor tolerate the motives for alleged political neutrality and abstention that Cardinal Bengsch and the other bishops preach."[49] In the end, however, the state interpreted Catholic political abstention—which it could not change—as the lesser evil compared with the prospect of an openly critical church. In the 1980s, Catholic political reticence was seen as an accommodation, and even as a *Geschäftsgrundlage*—a foundation upon which business could be conducted.[50]

The routine work of the Office of the State Secretary concerning the Catholic Church consisted of preparing and following up on Seigewasser and Flint's annual talks with Bengsch (and occasionally, other bishops), evaluating reports from district-level governments, and providing guidance to them on situations involving the Catholic Church. Other work included "political conversations" held with Catholic clergy, which were intended to convince them of "the advantages of socialism," as well as attempts to mobilize "progressive" lay Catholics. However, these tasks were mired in the same kind of stereotypes that characterized the Office of the State Secretary's regular reports on the situation of the Catholic Church in the GDR. In one typical example from 22 June 1978, it was said that the bishops' basic stance was "to escalate the opposing worldviews of religion and Marxism-Leninism into an irresolvable, ongoing conflict of conscience" so fundamental that it "commands a 'true Christian,' on account of the ideological implications of GDR politics, to stand at a critical distance from socialist development."[51]

GDR government offices hoped for more opportunity for "differentiation" after the death of Cardinal Bengsch in 1979. Bengsch had enjoyed clear dominance as the BBK chairman and could use his authority to mask any differences of opinion. When Gysi was tapped by the Politburo to be the new state secretary for church affairs on 7 November 1979, he and his staff took an active role in this endeavor. The differentiation efforts of central and regional GDR government offices had generally been no different in the 1970s than they had been previously. No differentiation was possible within the Diocese of Berlin due the loyalty Bengsch commanded from clergy. The state thus concentrated its efforts on Magdeburg (where the state had had some success at differentiation, although the problems this created outweighed its value) and Meißen, where Bishop Schaffran accommodated the state's wishes more readily than his predecessor Otto Spülbeck had. In the Diocese of Schwerin, talks with the new bishop, Heinrich Theissing, led neither to conflict nor to accommodation, to say nothing of the recruiting of "loyal Catholic officials."[52] The same result was evident in Bishop Bernhard Huhn's district in Görlitz, although he carried on general discussions with state offices on worldviews concerning human rights and "the Christian view of humanity."[53]

GDR officials repeatedly characterized Bishop Hugo Aufderbeck from Erfurt-Meiningen as "militant," especially during pastoral synods. For example, on 14 March 1975 the Office of the State Secretary referred to him as "a fanatical enemy of atheism" set on a "course of confrontation": "He is the spiritual leader of a line of thought which feels that the church will be more effective in demonstrating its vitality under socialist conditions if it is argumentative and militant in issues of worldview rather than critically distant and politically abstinent."[54] Even though state officials later softened their judgment of Aufderbeck, they took note of his clear sermons and their "negative influence" in the majority-Catholic region of Eichsfeld.[55] Even after Aufderbeck's death on 17 January 1981, sermons in Eichsfeld were a point of contention between the regime and the Catholic Church. Gerhard Müller, the SED first secretary in Erfurt and an exponent of "communist principles," attempted to get SED members and their spouses to officially renounce their membership in the Catholic Church and to staff positions with open cadres. This almost led the pulpit to call for a boycott of local elections in 1984 and did lead Müller to retreat after Hermann Kalb, the deputy of the state secretary for church affairs, intervened.

In the districts of Erfurt, Suhl, and Gera in Thuringia, state attempts at differentiation—including through the MfS—were also unsuccessful. Bishop Braun, in office in Magdeburg since 1970, faced a crisis of authority among segments of his clergy after the internal turbulence of the previous years. On the state side, he faced the expectations that had developed based upon the state's relations with his predecessor, Rintelen, and Prelate Jäger. On the whole, the district council found differentiation efforts and "political-ideological work" to be difficult in the Magdeburg Catholic Diocese.[56] Admittedly, the state was able to recruit some individual clergy to participate passively in National Front events, unlike in other Catholic districts, but not in the Berlin Conference. The state could certainly negotiate with General Vicar Theodor Hubrich, but he was also busy with very important contacts in Poland and organizing pastoral care for Polish guest workers in the GDR under the auspices of the BBK.

Repeatedly dissatisfied with Catholic activities in Magdeburg, the state intervened at the central and regional levels. On 17 June 1973, for example, a youth pilgrimage to Petersberg (near Halle) led to "provocative actions" that made waves in the ZK and the SED. An April 1975 report by the Halle district council noted that there was close cooperation between Protestants and Catholics in Magdeburg, intensive Catholic work with youth, and "not one positive statement" from a Catholic official on the occasion of the twenty-fifth anniversary of the GDR on 7 October 1974.[57] In July 1977, a group called the Protestant-Catholic Correspondence Working Group—initiated on the Catholic side by Dieter Tautz, a vicar from Osterburg—sent a petition with sixty-one signatures from clergy of both faiths to the Magdeburg bishops Werner Krusche and Johannes Braun; it anticipated many of the demands that would reappear in the "peace movement" of the early 1980s.[58] And lastly, the Halle Action Group—ignored by the bishop of Magdeburg—continued to meet regularly. After focusing on church reform up until 1971, the group had lost resonance within the Catholic Church due to personal rivalries and a focus on ideas of "democratic socialism." But the group again entered the debate within the church after the 1975 Helsinki accords ushered in more discussion of human rights, and especially after the emergence of the 1980s peace movement. The Halle Action Group also reemerged on the authorities' radar screens in the early 1980s but was not seen as a potential target for differentiation efforts.

The state's positive response to the Diocese of Magdeburg's numerous build-ing requests stabilized the situation, at least at the level of the church leadership. Indeed, the issuance of construction permits often functioned like a sedative. On the other hand, millions flowed into Magdeburg from the mother Diocese of Paderborn, thus deepening the clergy's ties to West Germany.[59] In the state's view, the Catholic Church's building projects in the Magdeburg area were dis-proportional. Yet in general, internal church developments in Magdeburg were independent of the designs of the state. Because of serious personal differences in the leadership of the diocese, Bishop Braun removed Hubrich from his position as general vicar in 1985, without the state having been involved through its dif-ferentiation policy. Hubrich then directed the Caritas operations in Magdeburg until he was named bishop of Schwerin in December 1987. After the internal Catholic conflicts that followed Hubrich's removal—also without state involve-ment—a papal delegate was sent to Magdeburg in a very unusual move to review the situation among the clergy there. By the autumn of 1989, the state perceived the majority of clergy in Magdeburg and Halle as out of control.

In the Diocese of Meißen, Bishop Schaffran brought up the issue of construct-ing a new bishop's residence in Dresden (moving the seat of the diocese there from Bautzen) in every conversation he had with government officials in Dres-den after 1970.[60] He tried to accelerate official agreement by generating church circumstances favorable to such a move in small increments by relocating church buildings or changing their function. Horst Dohle, head of the church affairs unit for the Dresden council, and his successor after 1975, Gerhard Lewerenz, both demonstrated an ability to support requests they felt were legitimate, building personal relations with church officials and scoring "political successes." Schaffran could flatter the state representatives with rhetoric without making measurable commitments. He thus held to the "political abstinence" line and tried to use all means available to advance the new construction. The SED district leadership and the Dresden district council had already approved the building in Dresden of a structure worth DM 3.5–4 million in hard currency on 6 November 1975: "Construction is approved because the GDR urgently needs hard currency. The one condition is that it not be erected in Dresden's city center."[61] The bishop was informed of this only later, after government officials had reached agreement on which plot of land was to be the site. After negotiations between the bishop, the state secretary for church affairs, and the district council, a Vatican resolution on 25 March 1980 officially moved the bishop's seat from Bautzen to Dresden and renamed the diocese "for all time" as "Dresden-Meißen." State and party officials celebrated what appeared to be a generous move on their part.

The regime was unable to bank any differentiation successes from these events, however. A 20 July 1978 analysis by the Dresden district council on "long-term influence upon the Catholic leadership of the Diocese of Meißen" described the posture of the Catholic officials there as "more low-profile, individual, and guarded than the Protestants . . . [seeking to] maximize their position [by avoiding conflict with the state]."[62] Except in the case of Sorbs in Kamenz and Bautzen, GDR officials failed in their attempts to hold conversations with Catholic clergy outside of the rules the church had established for such talks.

Only in the 1980s did the state advance in its efforts to dialogue with individual Catholic clergy in Dresden. In 1981, Bishop Schaffran authorized his long-time negotiator with the Dresden district council, Günther Hanisch, to also hold talks with the MfS, after Hanisch informed Schaffran that he had been approached. Schaffran similarly authorized Prelate Othmar Faber to hold talks in 1984. That same year, the diocese's new general vicar, Hermann Joseph Weisbender, told the Dresden district council he wished to have direct contact with the local SED leadership under First Secretary Hans Modrow, who was handling church affairs in a much more active way than other district-level party organizations in the GDR. Thus, in Dresden an unusually close contact with the SED party apparatus developed.

Meanwhile, the CDU played practically no role in policy toward the Catholic Church anymore, despite individual contacts and attempts to influence the pastoral synod in 1972–1975 and the 1987 Catholic convention in Dresden. In 1974, the CDU had to accept the demotion—due to the intervention of the jealous state secretary for church affairs—of its own church affairs' division head Gerhard Quast, whom the SED found too active. His successor, Wulf Trende, was no longer kept in the loop of information concerning Kirchenpolitik by the ZK and the state secretary. After the CDU had completed its role in establishing the Alliance of Protestant Churches in the GDR (Bund der Evangelischen Kirchen in der DDR, BEK) in January 1969, it lost its relevance as a mediator in church affairs. It was not invited to help plan and execute a summit meeting between Honecker and the BEK in 1978.

With the CDU's decline, Catholics' desire to try to achieve influence through this party—which had always been minimal—sank even further. There were still sporadic contacts between CDU members and officials, as well as individual Catholic bishops and other clergy, but these did not amount to serious attempts at differentiation. Those Catholic CDU members who were also MfS informers (a common occurrence) were usually just making denunciations rather than supplying useful intelligence. Exceptional situations existed in Eichsfeld, where the CDU had a disproportionate significance for both the Catholic Church and the SED, and among Catholic Sorbs in Kamenz and Bautzen. But these exceptions did not diminish Trende's retrospective judgment of the situation on 10 November 1989: "Of all the churches in the GDR, Roman Catholics had the worst relations with the CDU—not to say they had none at all."[63]

The Berlin Conference of Catholic Christians from European States, an SED-financed and CDU-supported organization renamed the Berlin Conference of European Catholics in 1978, was also only marginally important for Catholic clergy in the GDR.[64] Its methods were too transparent and opportunistic, as the long-time Berlin Conference chairman, Otto Hartmut Fuchs, acknowledged in an internal memo from 1978: "The more authentically Christian, that is to say Catholic, the Berlin Conference can formulate its agenda, the more attention, understanding and approval it will find among its target groups for its political peace work. In order to 'attract,' one must express oneself in an 'attractive' way."[65] The Berlin Conference was useful to the MfS because a large number of Catholics from the GDR who participated could be recruited as informers and because foreigners who came to its events were seen as potential assets. Moreover, allied Communist countries had an interest in the propaganda value of the organization.

Berlin Conference officials were partially successful in establishing contacts with leading GDR Catholic officials through Eastern European participants in its meetings. This was the case in Dresden in 1980 and 1988, and in Erfurt in 1985, but not so in Neubrandenburg in 1983. Their "success," however, also fit in well with Catholic officials' wish to learn more about the Berlin Conference and its methods, as well as to be able to speak with Catholics from other Eastern European countries about their situation. For many Eastern European Catholics, this was their only opportunity for such a meeting. Therefore, the Vatican unofficially encouraged Catholics from, say, the Baltic countries to participate. Within the GDR itself, Berlin Conference activity merely resulted in empty political exercises and expensive political tourism. In May 1989, the BBK was able to block Berlin Conference participation in a workshop of the European Ecumenical Gathering in Basel. The SED had to accept it when the church shunned the Berlin Conference in this way. Their funds had already been slashed in 1988. In an interview with the journal *begegnung* on 16 August 1988, the newly named State Secretary for Church Affairs Kurt Löffler called for "the urgently needed establishment of national work in the GDR, as it exists in other countries"—although the Berlin Conference had been in existence for twenty-four years.[66] During discussion in November 1989 over whether the Berlin Conference should continue to be funded, Trende, the CDU section chief, argued that it should be dissolved. The chairman of the National Front, Werner Kirchhoff, wrote Minister-President Hans Modrow on 6 December 1989 that financing the group was no longer justified. Looking back on his experiences, he remarked:

The Berlin Conference has not succeeded in establishing the sort of contacts with Catholic clergy in the GDR that produce results. Nor has it been able to recruit priests to participate in its events or even to realize planned unofficial meetings. Attempts by the Berlin Conference to gain recognition from officials of the Catholic Church have been brushed aside or rejected outright, even after the departure of Cardinal Meisner.[67]

Activities of the MfS

From 1971 on, the MfS increased its staff continually, counting 90,577 full-time employees in its main office in 1986. After a small decrease in 1987–1988 and then another increase, it had reached 91,015 by 31 October 1989.[68] But in contrast to other departments, the number of staff devoted to church affairs in section XX/4 remained constant for a long time. There were 21 in 1972 and 24 in 1982, but this figure increased to 32 in 1983 with the establishment of an unofficial church-based peace movement and the growth of opposition networks. It was slated to grow to 44 in 1988.[69] In 1979, Joachim Wiegand (alias "Wagner") replaced Franz Sgraja as head of HA XX/4; he came from Unit IV (work connected with the West) and had been its deputy director since 1975. After the sudden death of Helmut Wegener in December 1974, Unit II (devoted to Catholic Church affairs) was run by his deputy, Major Hans Baethge (aliases "Ebert" and "Heine"). Its staff numbered six in 1988. Although the ministry's internal classification of its "unofficial informers" changed in 1979, the first step for registration as an "unofficial informer" remained the category IMS.

Catholic leaders maintained ongoing contacts with MfS officers from HA V/4 and HA XX/4, generally with a unit chief *(Referatsleiter)* but sometimes also with a section chief *(Abteilungsleiter),* and had internal authorization and a duty to report back. Beginning in 1958, Prelate Johannes Zinke handled these regular contacts, which then passed to Otto Groß in 1967 and became increasingly important for church-state relations on both sides. After Groß died in August 1974, the MfS approached his close confidant and BOK secretary, Prelate Paul Dissemond. Because of his position in the BOK, Dissemond was a natural successor, so Cardinal Bengsch authorized him to handle the MfS contacts. He was registered by the MfS as an "unofficial informer," first with the designation IMV and, beginning in 1979, as IMB with the code name "Peter."[70] When he gave up his job as BBK general secretary in May 1987, the church then authorized Josef Michelfeit to take over the MfS contacts; he was Dissemond's successor and a confidant of Cardinal Meisner. The MfS had signaled—in vain—that it wanted Prelate Gerhard Lange as its contact person; since 1974, he had succeeded Groß in handling contacts with the Office of the State Secretary for Church Affairs. Thus, the MfS failed in its aim to have one single Catholic contact person for all state offices, as had been the case with Groß from 1967 to 1974. Cardinal Bengsch had already deliberately divided responsibilities between Lange and Dissemond after Groß died.

These meetings with central offices—which provided a forum for the regular exchange of information and for making agreements—became very significant within the state's Kirchenpolitik. For the Catholic Church, the contacts revealed the far-reaching power of the MfS (for example, in vetting travel abroad) and the true power structure of the regime. Within the church, the status of the contact people rose considerably. Everything was "discussed in advance" or even "clarified" at these personal meetings: all travel by Catholic officials to or from the GDR; all major Catholic events—pilgrimages, conferences—whether abroad or in the GDR; any Catholic concerns or complaints about events within the GDR; and government concerns or objections regarding Catholic activities. For the MfS, the personal meetings helped it fulfill its aim of preventing any conflicts before they spilled over and became public. But they also came with the expectation that the MfS agents would continually be able to exercise influence upon their Catholic counterparts and gradually "win them over," thus neutralizing the social impact of the church.

In two Catholic dioceses, the institutionalized contacts also developed for dealing with regional and local issues. The MfS Catholic affairs unit in Berlin (HA XX/4) took care to prevent its central authority from being diminished but did not really use these contact meetings to further a differentiation agenda. Within the church, these central and regional meetings were less than transparent to outsiders, and it is even unclear to what extent they were transparent within the MfS itself. In Magdeburg, the new general vicar and auxiliary bishop, Hubrich (whom HA XX/4 had already approached in 1970 when he was the Caritas director in Berlin) was visited by MfS officers in Berlin and also by Major Armin Dobberphul from the MfS regional office in Magdeburg beginning in 1972. Hubrich—reporting back to Bishop Johannes Braun—carried on these talks until he left to become the bishop of Schwerin in December 1987. He had further talks with the MfS there until July 1989, even meeting his contacts once in an MfS-owned guesthouse near Berlin. After Hubrich stepped aside as general vicar of Magdeburg in 1985, MfS officers held meetings with his successor, Manfred Kania. Additionally, Bishop Braun authorized Provost Hans-Peter Gospos from Halle to maintain contact with the MfS after he reported being approached in 1981. The choice of Gospos was clearly an attempt to influence and control the Halle Action Group since Gospos's critical views of this group were well known. He held some rather secret "handshake agreement" talks with the MfS and was given the code name "Gustav."

Another regional channel for government contact with the MfS was opened in the Diocese of Dresden-Meißen, when Bishop Schaffran authorized Provost Hanisch to meet regularly with the MfS after its Dresden office approached him in May 1981. This connection continued after Hanisch was transferred to Leipzig in 1984, when the bishop authorized Prelate Faber to carry on the Dresden meetings with the MfS. Both Hanisch and Faber made oral and written reports to the bishop and, beginning in 1984, exchanged almost all of their own notes on MfS meetings with each other.

For the MfS, these institutionalized contacts were only conditionally suited to steering church decisions, because—despite occasional secret exchanges with Catholic representatives—a significant number of high-ranking Catholic officials knew about them. Thus, when MfS contacts took positions too close to the regime's, or if they made the impression of "doing the state's bidding," they aroused suspicion. Because the MfS was unsuccessful in recruiting leading Catholics as confidential informers, the ministry's work was limited to using operations to control individual bishops and to apply the differentiation policy. Attempts to infiltrate informers into ordinaries' offices failed in 1980 in Dresden, in 1986 in Erfurt, and in 1989 in Schwerin. Only in 1986 was the Dresden MfS office able to plant informer "Erika" as a secretary in the building department of the bishop's office and, later, in the Caritas office. The MfS acquired a wealth of information through this informer but could hardly act on any of it lest she be discovered.

By contrast, the MfS managed to obtain important information from the BBK, probably by using listening devices in government buildings near their meeting rooms in the late 1980s. The regular MfS "information reports," which summarized BOK/BBK meetings until the late 1980s, contained only selective, general information that it could have gathered in talks with Catholic representatives. But beginning around 1985, the MfS managed to partially transcribe the BBK meetings, probably by using improved technology to listen in on a room, then sort out the voices, reconstruct the dialogue, and make a report with explanatory commentary from the state's point of view. Thus, it usually took weeks before the Politburo and ZK received an MfS report about a meeting. The reports always ended with the warning "For personal reference only due to the high risk of endangering the source!" Beginning in 1985, the MfS made similar reports on meetings between representatives of the BBK, the German Bishops' Conference (DBK), and the West German Central Committee of German Catholics, which were held in the same room as the BBK sessions. Before these meetings could even take place, Dissemond or Michelfeit had to first clear the agenda with the MfS, as well as clear border crossings for West German participants.[71]

Another significant source of information for the MfS was from church leaders' phone calls and trips to the West. The MfS systematically tapped phone conversations within West Berlin or between West Berlin and the rest of West Germany. If the information gleaned from these conversations was relevant to Kirchenpolitik, the MfS passed it on to HA XX/4. The bishop of Berlin and his entourage frequently made what they believed were unmonitored phone calls while on visits to West Berlin (which, of course, were state-authorized). When they traveled, the MfS broke into their suitcases and photographed documents in them, not only at East German airports but also at (West) Berlin-Tegel.[72]

After 1972, the MfS only succeeded in adding one more long-term secret collaborator to its recruits among the Catholic clergy. The minimum criterion for the MfS to count someone as a "recruit" was an initial conversation, as long as the target kept it secret and there was a prospect that "information" might be gathered. In this manner, MfS officers from various regional offices found several "debriefable" sources—clergy who met with MfS representatives in their parsonages—for various stretches of time. Similarly useful to the MfS were a handful of members of monastic orders, although in the 1970s these orders were not as high on the MfS agenda as in previous years. Again, Sorbian clergy were an exception; the MfS had long considered them to be especially "negative." In the end, however, the tension between them and the Dresden ordinaries and Bishop Schaffran could be used effectively for differentiation. After the dean of Kamenz made himself available to the MfS in 1974, the security services were able to recruit five priests in the Sorbian district as sources over the next twelve years without the knowledge of Catholic leaders in Dresden.[73] In 1987, the CDU's church affairs division quoted one Sorbian clergyman from Storcha, who himself was never an MfS contact, as saying, "Sometimes the Communists do more for us than the bishops."[74]

For HA XX/4 and the MfS district offices, lay Catholics who could be recruited or even planted within the church were more useful sources than the clergymen they were able to "debrief." A network of informers within the Catholic milieu was already in existence at the beginning of the 1970s. This network varied in intensity across regions but maintained its stability over the long term. For example, in Berlin in 1970, HA XX/4 was able to recruit a former Catholic priest from Görlitz who had become a secretary to Bishop Schaffran; he cooperated with the MfS right up until 1989—and not only on Catholic matters.[75] In 1976, a further MfS contact person, Egbert Brock, a former priest who was then editing the journal *begegnung*, joined the ranks of two professional informers within the Berlin Conference, Hubertus Guske (code name "Hubert/Georg") and Georg Wipler (code name "Bruno").[76] In Dresden, CDU members were prominent as informers, like those with the code names "Küster" and "Werner Albrecht."[77] In Erfurt, by contrast, the MfS "Catholic front," handled by Officer Frank Gensmann, was rather thin, apart from long-time informers like "Siegfried."[78] One significant informer in the Heiligenstadt district was "Alois Saul," recruited by Officer Erwin Stolze in 1977.[79]

In Halle, the MfS had access to the Halle Action Group through informers "Budgereit," "Dr. Herzog," "Helmut," and "Siegfried Weiß," although the latter two also informed other members of the circle of their MfS contacts.[80] A more serious case of inside informers began in 1983, when "Rechner," as well as the priests "Joppe," "Gustav," and "Gregor Finzenz," provided the MfS with significant help in its fight against the group.[81] One of the few meaningful informers in the sparse MfS "Catholic front" in the northern districts was recruited in Waren in 1982, when he was still a minor.[82] He later informed on the Catholic student organization in Rostock as well as on Protestant peace groups.

There were many regions, however, such as Erfurt and Magdeburg, where the MfS could not find informers for its Catholic network. Qualitatively, the MfS got the most information and thus exercised the greatest influence in the Halle and Dresden districts, as well in individual cities including Bautzen, Berlin, Leipzig, Eisenhüttenstadt, Frankfurt/Oder and Karl-Marx-Stadt. The destruction of many HA XX/4 files in Berlin (as well as in regional offices in Berlin, Magdeburg and Suhl) in late 1989 makes judgment difficult, however.

The number of "operational checks of individuals" and "operational measures" against individual lay Catholics and priests surpassed the number of MfS informer operations after the ministry concluded its centralized "Schleuse" operation in 1969 and followed it with several individual operations. These usually ran for a few years, aside from the surveillance of the Halle Action Group[83] and the Mecklenburg pastor Anton Beer[84]—which continued almost without interruption beginning in 1970—and impacted hundreds of people across the entire GDR.

The MfS organized large-scale surveillance and intelligence-gathering around major Catholic events. An internal MfS document from 30 November 1975 noted that, following the final assembly of the pastoral synod that met in Dresden between 1973 and 1975, "original copies of all materials and decisions from the synod were now available, having been obtained by five informers from HA XX/4 together with other informers, especially from the Dresden office, and cooperation from departments VIII, VI, M, and the technical (photography) division of the Dresden office."[85] A number of state security and police personnel watched every dedication ceremony, every bishop's funeral, and every new bishop's inauguration, far exceeding the usual security arrangements. The measures drafted by Erich Mielke for "political-operative measures" during Cardinal Bengsch's funeral in 1979 were exceptionally extensive, even by this standard: 1,034 MfS agents and 395 police were to be deployed, and six "detention points" were set up in case of mass arrests.[86] The MfS recorded almost every detail of Pope John Paul II's visit to Poland in June 1979.[87] The surveillance of Warsaw Cardinal Józef Glemp's visit to Berlin on 22–24 October 1984 was so exacting that the MfS officer concluded his final remarks on the Polish visitor's exit across the border with the exclamation: "It ends well, so all is well. Thank God!"[88]

Examples of extensive MfS surveillance abound: in July 1986, Cardinal Meisner wrote the following words to all clergy in the Diocese of Berlin: "On August 13, 1961, a wall was built through the middle of Berlin."[89] To acknowledge this event, he established that all Catholic services on the weekend of 9–10 August should include a reading of special prayers. Because of this "hostile act" and "intervention in state affairs," the director of HA XX/4, Major-General Paul Kienberg, ordered that all Catholic services in the districts of East Berlin, Potsdam, Neubrandenburg, Rostock and Frankfurt/Oder be monitored on those days. Similarly, measures taken during the Catholic youth congress in Berlin in May 1985 (operation code name "Kreuz") were also large-scale, as were those for the Catholic convention in Dresden in July 1987, where the mail and phone calls of 1,500 delegates, youth, and their local hosts were monitored.[90] For the 1988 and 1989 meetings of the Ecumenical Convocation for Peace, Justice, and the Conservation of Creation in Dresden and Magdeburg, the HA XX/4 intervened with even greater intensity on the church front but was increasingly frustrated by its minimal influence.

The MfS repeatedly made plans to influence Catholic seminaries and other training facilities by infiltrating them and recruiting instructors, but these remained unrealized. A 1977 report ascertained that "the Catholic Church interprets the constitutional principle of the separation of church and state as granting absolute freedom in the training of new clergy . . . They make every state attempt at influence or control impossible . . . The students are effectively shielded."[91] Only one instructor was ever recruited—Joachim Berger, a former Berlin student pastor who taught homiletics at Neuzelle beginning in 1976; he furnished the MfS with information on theology students and other instructors under the IM code name "Johannes." In Erfurt, the MfS got only second-hand information about the seminary from other Catholic informers and from one seminary student with the code name "Ernesto," who was regularly debriefed by MfS officers between 1984 and 1989 when he traveled to his home in the Karl-Marx-Stadt region.[92] The MfS saw itself as unable to influence the "bourgeois ideology" of the seminaries. The MfS regional director for the Erfurt district admitted in his report on the first quarter of 1988 that "the situation in the Erfurt-Meiningen bishop's office and in the seminary" was not under the ministry's control because of an "insufficient 'unofficial base' [i.e., informers]."[93]

After 1972, the "handling" of the Kolping Association essentially consisted of the intrigues of the MfS officer Edwin Hille from Berlin. In addition to the informers "Schramm," "Mahlsdorf" and "Drescher"—all active until 1989— Hille was able to recruit Schramm's wife ("Irmchen") in 1974 as well as "Franz Schmidt" and "Hermann Marquart" in the mid 1980s.[94] Because of the central position of "Schramm" and "Irmchen" within the Kolping Association, the MfS was able to monitor it across the GDR, taking additional operational and informer measures in some cities.

MfS "handling" of the Catholic Student Community (KSG) diminished after the mid 1970s,[95] as the up-and-coming generation of Catholic students did not pursue the agenda of social and church reform (which the state had viewed with alarm) as vigorously as that of the past decade. The HA XX/4/II annual plan of 10 January 1973 prominently declared that "the uncovering, dismantling, and defeat of enemy footholds and activities—especially among students" was to be a priority, in particular the surveillance of contacts with Poland, meetings between former members of the Berlin KSG (Operation Luke), connections with the West Berlin–based Berlin Education Center (Operation Zentrum), and the partnerships "directed [from abroad]" between the KSG and West German Catholic university groups.[96] The HA XX/4 used informers and bugs between 1971 and 1974 to monitor about thirty former KSG members in Berlin whom it perceived as "so-called Catholic young professionals . . . engaged in anti-state agitation and . . . the formation of an anti-government group . . . under the guise of an internal church opposition movement," allegedly organized by the former seminary student and deacon Helmut Lück.[97]

Until 1976, when the Berlin student pastor Joachim Berger was transferred to the seminary in Neuzelle to be an instructor, the MfS received excellent information on all GDR-wide student pastor conferences, student pilgrimages, and contacts between the KSG and West Germany. Then the information flow broke off abruptly and remained frozen through 1989, because the MfS could not recruit another Catholic student pastor as a secret informer. As a rule, the MfS did not have any problems infiltrating the KSG—a rather open organization—with at least one student informer, so it did receive a minimal level of information. As an example, a Catholic student from the KSG Zwickau was arrested and convicted of "agitation against the state" based on information a student informer supplied during the MfS's Operation Sacrament in 1985.[98]

The MfS also kept an eye on *Hauskreise,* informal religious discussion groups that met in private homes, and Catholic professional groups in the 1970s and 1980s. In a 1975 memo, the security services stated their concern that "circles among the intelligentsia would spread bourgeois ideologies upon a religious platform, attempt to block socialist development, or to foster or bolster anti-socialist attitudes."[99] These circles—Catholic and Protestant—were said to be "ever more conspiratorial, targeting new recruits." The MfS tried to keep tabs on the organized lectures and leisure programs of these groups, but as with the surveillance of the KSG, this abated as inner-church relations underwent "depoliticization."

In general, the MfS was not going to tolerate any "anti-state" activities. Yet it was willing to accept that sections of the intelligentsia were influenced by "bourgeois ideology" as long as this had no impact on the general public. The MfS did not want open repression to lead to internal disturbances and damage the GDR's carefully crafted foreign-relations image.

The Poland Seminars that Günter Särchen from the Magdeburg bishop's office had organized for decades were only partially monitored from 1980 to 1983.[100] The peace circle in Leipzig led by Hans-Friedrich Fischer—unique in the Catholic Church in the GDR—was only superficially observed in the 1980s because suitable informers were lacking.[101] However, on the rare occasions when Catholic groups had an impact on the "general population," the MfS perceived them as crossing the Rubicon of "anti-socialist activity" and forming a "political underground"—and it reacted accordingly. This happened in January 1987 when Vicar Gerhard Packenius of Weißenfels organized an ecumenical environmental group; the MfS managed to get Packenius transferred through the actions of informers within the church.[102] The MfS also had its disappointments: in the case of the Potsdam-based Arche group, which met in the basement of a Catholic nursery school, the MfS was unable to get the church to expel or even to control it.[103] This also occurred in the case of a peace group in Dresden-Johannstadt that was concerned with human rights and, after 1986, very responsive to the "new thinking" coming from the Soviet Union under Gorbachev.[104]

Because of constant state pressure, however, there was no church solidarity with such activities or with the individual Catholics who organized them. Sending the signal that this kind of action was beyond the scope of the church's responsibility, the church "privatized" the risk of dissent. Individuals now faced greater potential danger from state agencies. As a rule, church offices in the GDR would not take responsibility for dissident activities or material distributed with the heading "for internal church use only" unless they personally agreed with their content. When government agencies tried to use massive pressure to force the Catholic Church to make a choice between taking responsibility or officially distancing itself on a given issue—for example, when matters concerning the Halle Action Group came to a head in 1984–1985—the church was pushed to the breaking point.[105]

The Halle Action Group had a measurable public impact, posing a challenge to MfS officers in Berlin and Halle. The group organized biannual assemblies and distributed 600 copies of its literature across the GDR, prompting occasional reports in the West German media about its positions. The MfS officers in Halle led the way in operations against the group; within the MfS, Halle was seen as having the most success with the Catholic Church. To the surprise of the MfS, the Halle Action Group remained active (despite internal differences) after the ministry had concluded Operation Tabernacle in 1972, so the Halle MfS office began new measures (Operation Academica) against the circle's leading member on 17 July 1975. The Halle Action Group was now identified with "anti-social-ist thought" and "open demands to change certain social relations in the GDR," working through the Catholic Church. The MfS pursued a long-range agenda against the Halle Action Group: "anti-state tendencies" were to be suppressed and "negative" persons were to be "destroyed." It did not attempt to dissolve the whole group until 1984 but worked instead—unsuccessfully—to intimidate and discredit leading members. It was more valuable for the MfS to have the group continue so that informers could gather information on it than to force it to go underground and possibly gain more sympathy in the GDR and in the West. Although the MfS operational plan called for the group's prosecution for various crimes, HA XX/4 and the Halle office concluded that "from the perspective of Kirchenpolitik" and "because of the political situation," no punitive legal mea-sures would be taken.

This changed, however, beginning in 1982, as the peace movement grew within the Protestant Church and at its fringes. The Halle Action Group took up this cause, and its members also participated in other peace groups. From 1982 until 1985, the MfS tried to exploit the evidence it had against the Halle Action Group in an indirect way so that Catholic leaders would take disciplinary action against clergy in the group. The MfS and other state agencies sought to accom-plish this by arranging personal "conversations" with Catholic officials in Halle (Provost Gospos), Magdeburg (Bishop Braun and Auxiliary Bishop Hubrich), and Berlin (Prelate Dissemond and Prelate Lange). Threatening consequences for "church-state relations," as well as the cancellation of certain negotiated or silently tolerated areas of church activity, they tried to pressure the church to deny the Halle Action Group use of its buildings and to have bishops forbid clergy to be members of the group. The MfS also held so-called *Zersetzungsgespräche* (talks aimed at neutralizing persons) with circle members, threatening them with crimi-nal prosecution and telling them that leading Catholic officials did not consider them a church group but a private affair.

Catholic leaders had mixed reactions: Auxiliary Bishop Hubrich recommended that the security services ignore the Halle Action Group, but the Berlin prelates and Gospos signaled that they would remain passive if the state pursued criminal charges against the group. On 15 November 1985 leaders of the Halle Action Group appealed to all BBK members to recognize them as an official group according to canon law (a *consociatio*), in view of the threats from the government. BBK leaders referred them to their local ordinary, Johannes Braun, for this kind of request. In a note to Cardinal Meisner on 19 November 1985, the BBK's man for talks with the Office of the State Secretary for Church Affairs, Prelate Lange, stressed that "responsibility for the Halle Action Group's comportment toward the state must be borne by the Halle Action Group."[106] He recommended that the group not be recognized as a church-authorized assembly. Lange likewise rejected the idea of the head of the BBK speaking with government officials on behalf of the Halle group, because "it might give [the circle] a kind of 'fool's freedom' to say just anything." He cautioned that strict limits be set on church intervention if indeed the state took legal action against the circle. Lange said that the basic question remained "whether it is possible and indeed responsible for the Catholic Church in the GDR and its bishops to tolerate a permissive organization under the protection of the church, at least if nothing that affronts faith or morals happens in this group." Bishop Braun of Magdeburg was not prepared to protect the Halle Action Group from the threat of state action, either. His general vicar, Theodor Hubrich (who had just been relieved of his duties effective 1 January 1986) wrote Claus Herold, a priest in Halle, about the bishop's intransigent position on 27 November 1985: "Unfortunately, I must inform you that any kind of intervention is impossible for the moment, which you can certainly understand. In fact, without a single exception, all of us here warned him about the consequences."[107]

However, the state's widely expected move against the Halle Action Group in the wake of its not being recognized by the Catholic Church did not take place, thus sparing the church a spectacular test of its ability to hold together. At the end of its extensive operation, the MfS realized that the remaining force would have to act in order to dissolve the group. Yet ultimately it chose not to do so, despite Catholic leaders' indication that they had partial understanding for such a move, in order to avoid conflict. The MfS feared that such an action might stir popular sympathy for the group and create a "martyr effect" through the Western media. After dramatically ramping up operations in 1984–1985, the Halle office of the MfS concluded Operation Pulpit on 22 August 1986 and ended Operation Academica on 9 October. The Halle Action Group was now classified on paper as a nonpolitical, religious-educational institution, and the MfS claimed it had successfully fulfilled its aims. The Halle Action Group itself, intimidated, held back for a few months and then tried to vary the way it distributed its literature but remained unchecked and politically active through the autumn of 1989.

This example shows how the very precise ideas of GDR government agencies on the suppression of opposition from church quarters often clashed with the reality of the GDR's internal and international political situation. In fact, the government usually deluded itself with wishful thinking in this regard. A case in point is the following statement by Horst Dohle, personal aide to the state secretary for church affairs and one of the most influential Kirchenpolitik strategists in the GDR, who praised East Germany's allegedly model policy toward the churches in a speech to Polish party functionaries in Warsaw on 18 November 1986:

> Having churches take responsibility for themselves has proved effective . . . We are thus interested in a strong high- and mid-level church leadership that also has the disciplinary authority to guarantee secure positions toward the state. This is especially important in regard to some marginal groups within our churches who, though small in number, try with the help of Western media to use an anti-socialist platform to satisfy their neurotic need to be noticed. The solution for us is not to expel these groups from their church as soon as possible, thereby pushing them underground, but to discipline and control them within the church.[108]

The Pastoral Synod and Church Attitudes toward the Internationally Recognized GDR

As the first meetings of the synod in the Diocese of Meißen were underway in Dresden in June 1969, the decision to hold a synod of all Catholic dioceses in the GDR later had already been made. The (West) German Bishops' Conference had decided at its spring assembly in Bad Honnef in February 1969 to convene a synod for all West German Catholic districts including West Berlin, which prompted Cardinal Bengsch and the BOK to respond. The BOK could safely assume that the GDR regime would not let East German Catholics participate in a synod called by the German Bishops' Conference, nor would it countenance the Catholic Church in the GDR adopting the decisions made there. Thus, the BOK knew it had to convene its own synod in the GDR, although this could be interpreted politically as a step toward the recognition of two German states. Cardinal Bengsch came to this conclusion unwillingly, finding it abhorrent given his own theological convictions. But a synod had some advantages: it would make internal church discussion in the GDR about Western religious models possible and give Bengsch a high-profile opportunity to counter tendencies he disapproved of coming out of the Meißen synod.

After a preparatory commission was formed in the spring of 1970, the BOK, on 8–9 January 1971 in Heiligenstadt, finally decided to hold the synod. As first steps, it created a "central working group" and a "central office" in Dresden; a joint pastoral letter from all BOK members on 28 February 1971 announced a "pastoral synod for all dioceses in the GDR."[109] In July 1971 the "central working group" formed two commissions and seven subject groups corresponding to the themes to be discussed: proclaiming the faith and fulfilling the faith, prayer and ritual life, marriage and the family, deaconry and congregation, evangelism and social action, religious orders and services, and ecumenical issues. Out of some 12,000 entries, the seven subject groups prepared preliminary papers that were discussed in congregations and at "pastoral congresses" in individual dioceses in

1972. On 15 March 1972 the statutes—which the Vatican approved only after five drafts—were published. These maintained that decisions taken by the synod would not be legally binding. Discretion over the implementation of synod recommendations rested with the BOK and individual bishops, the real "lawgivers" within the church. By the time the first full assembly convened in Dresden's Hofkirche in the spring of 1973, 121 synod members had been chosen by various boards and 21 further persons had been appointed by the bishops. Pope Paul VI named Cardinal Bengsch president of the synod in 1971. In all, 9 bishops, 71 priests, and 71 lay Catholics participated.[110]

The Vatican had made clear in a 26 September 1971 letter to the bishops that approval of the synod was conditional upon its being "free from all outside influences."[111] At the outset, GDR government agencies were not prepared to accommodate this and tried to politicize the synod and apply pressure. On 27 January 1972 State Secretary Seigewasser, in an internal memo to staff, characterized the pastoral synod as the project of the West German Catholic Church in the service of the Vatican: "It must not be allowed to proceed as its initiators and organizers (the upper clergy) want it to. Cardinal Bengsch will certainly intervene with disciplinary measures for clergy to counter our intentions, and others will eventually do so as well. This should not cause us to lose courage, and we must keep trying."[112] The state's interventions, however, ultimately led to a depoliticized synod, which accorded well with the vision Cardinal Bengsch and a few other bishops had for it, namely, that it should be an internal church-pastoral event. As the synod proceeded, the state adapted its analyses to what was actually happening, and, in the end, interpreted it as being in the state's own interest.

Still, the planners had to cope with state-backed opposition during the preparation phase. On 3 May 1972 eleven Catholics from the Berlin Conference and the National Front's Christian Circles Working Group (including nine CDU members) signed an "Open Letter from Catholics in the German Democratic Republic" prepared by the ZK and then published after consultation with the signers.[113] The signatories wanted the synod to proceed but to adopt a certain political concept in the form of a statement in favor of the socialist order in the GDR. These "progressive Catholics" declared that "the majority of Catholics of our country are convinced of the longevity of the socialist societal order in the GDR and of the future triumph of socialism in the entire world."[114] It continued: "Only through a positive relationship to this society, our society, can the Catholic Church in the GDR be true to its mission, which emanates from the gospels, to serve mankind. We ask our bishops and priests to work together for a Catholic Church in the GDR oriented toward the future and toward social justice." The signers wanted the church to take "a position in support of the state that is clearer than any previous one . . . that is already accepted by a majority of Catholics in the GDR." "As a church in a [recognized] sovereign state, the Catholic Church in the GDR has a claim to national independence within the framework of the church worldwide."

Between 15 May and 20 July 1972, only 3,665 Catholics in the entire GDR signed on to this statement, despite massive threats. No Catholic clergy supported it. On 3 August 1972 several of the original signatories delivered the petition to the Berlin ordinaries and to the "central office" in Dresden as preparations for the synod were underway. The National Front's National Council drew the following twisted conclusion about its efforts on 23 August: "If the Catholic Church threatens not to hold the synod if there is outside influence, then we can be sure that no one besides the Catholic Church will stop the synod."[115]

The state-financed helpers like the National Front were deceiving themselves, however. In the intervening time, continued contacts between the GDR and the Vatican had awakened the SED's interest in the synod as a showcase for the GDR's tolerance, especially as it anticipated concluding a basic treaty with the FRG, as well as the international recognition such a move would bring. The SED wanted to avoid furnishing the Catholic Church with the pretext of state pressure for canceling the synod. The only ZK Politburo decision regarding the synod, from 23 January 1973, called for the state and party apparatus to work to achieve the redrawing of diocese boundaries to correspond to national borders, with the explicit instruction that "no direct reference to the pastoral synod" should be made.[116] Moreover, officials were to work to ensure that bishops at the synod would neither attack the GDR nor take measures against it. Foreign guests of the synod and an offical observer from the Vatican were to be admitted on an individual basis. For its part, the Vatican, in view of the upcoming GDR-Vatican talks, expected the BOK to limit the synod to internal church subjects and not create any political problems. The BOK understood "outside influence" and "the freedom of the synod" in a double sense: it would reject state attempts to interfere by means of the CDU and the National Front, as well as resist demands from within the church that it take socially critical positions. In a conversation with the Schwerin district council, Bishop Heinrich Theissing drew a parallel between these two things and distanced himself from both, citing the Vatican: "Anything that is not directly part of the synod will be considered external. Any attempt to influence it—even on the part of church forces—would be an outside influence."[117]

As the "central working group" received contributions from the Catholic base suggesting subjects for the synod, government offices also learned of these texts. Draft Paper Five, "Evangelism and Social Action," had especially excited them, as it included a long list of "provocative" suggestions. It called for Catholics in the GDR to collaborate "in the realization of the human cause . . . [and] the earthly mission of Christians . . . within a specific society," for the church to "fulfill its concrete mission within each and every state structure" without affirming "the ideological basis for the GDR state and every measure that results from it," for "clarification from the official church on its relationship to the state," for joint action "with Christian brothers of all confessions," for the church to campaign for justice and peace, for acceptance of conscientious objections to armed military service, for the creation of an alternative civil service, for contributions to "the humanization of work," for a modified emphasis on the Jugendweihe, for "dialogue with non-believers and those distant from the church," and for "missionary paths for pastors." [118] The MfS saw all this as a "hostile conception" of how to change social relations in the GDR. The paper was, in fact, a collection of positions for "critical engagement" and "dialogue" that had formed in Catholic academic circles in the wake of Vatican II in the 1960s. The MfS had registered these positions, monitoring them with operations, and had repeatedly mentioned them reproachfully in talks with Otto Groß.

The state had serious objections to the content of this and other preparatory documents for the synod, which they brought to attention of Bishop Schaffran in a meeting in the Dresden district council office on 12 June 1972. Schaffran suggested that his deputy, Hermann Joseph Weisbender, should meet with Dohle so that the state could point out the objectionable passages. According to the state's notes, Schaffran said that many of the papers merely provided a pressure "valve" that allowed some people in the church to let off steam: "We—the bishops—determine what remains at the end of the day; we are the ones who take out the red pen. That is secured by our statutes. We are dealing here with suggestions to keep us busy for the next fifty years, and most will be off the table by the fall of 1972." [119]

In the end, the BOK used the state-organized "Open Letter" in its 12–13 September 1972 session in an effort to scale back the themes for discussion, which it had planned to do anyway. The ordinaries called for "an oral communication to priests and to the pastoral assemblies of all dioceses" that would clarify that

> A free and open treatment of all the questions raised in the "Open Letter" is not possible . . . as long as such conditions exist, Paper Five cannot be dealt with at the pastoral synod. The [BOK] has a duty to examine whether the freedom of the synod and of the individual participants is there to the extent that the pope's approval of the synod explicitly stipulates . . . The [BOK] expresses the hope that the synod can take place as a purely internal church process to set pastoral goals. [120]

The other preparatory suggestion papers were relativized at the pastoral congresses in the dioceses because the majority of the participants followed the pastoral line, as did the delegates who were chosen at the congresses. Those advocating reform within the church, and that the church take on a more socially critical role, were visible but clearly in the minority. And the CDU "progressive Catholics," so eager to please the state, were not at all a presence. Hans-Joachim Zobel, a lay Catholic elected as one of the vice presidents of the synod in March 1973, informed Dohle that "the cardinal is having a panic attack about the synod. He fears it may produce difficulties for our relation to the state and difficulties for the bishops, the church, and the unity of the Catholic Church in the GDR." [121]

Before the first full assembly of the synod opened in Dresden's Hofkirche on 22 March 1973, the Dresden district council (which, together with the state agencies in Berlin, was responsible for monitoring the event) held three talks with Bishop Schaffran to inform him of the government's expectations. The government representatives appealed to their allegedly mutual interest in avoiding conflict, suggesting that the synod avoid "provocative" statements and decisions. Schaffran argued that the bishops could make clever use of the meeting agenda to ensure that long discussions about the preparatory position papers would not occur, and that the (non-controversial) subject of "faith today" would dominate. In one of the conversations, the bishop said: "The decisive question is how much bandwidth, how much plurality, to allow for different opinions, and where one steps in with authoritarian power to prevent too much room for diverse opinions."[122]

Government agencies tried to collect information on all of the synod participants in order to aid their search for intelligence, as the synod meetings were not public. The Leipzig and Halle districts gathered detailed information in their areas in February 1973.[123] In Magdeburg, synod participants were summoned to "conversations," and their "workplace performance" was scrutinized.[124] In Dresden, Dohle had secret contacts with Zobel, who nearly caused a scandal when he took part in a World Peace Conference in Moscow, delivering an official greeting there on 12 September 1973. GDR media reported on this and identified him as a "vice president of the synod." Alongside criticism of his participation by West German Catholics, some opponents of Cardinal Bengsch's course praised Zobel's actions. Bengsch, in turn, had strongly criticized Zobel because his visit to Moscow had opened the synod to outside influence and endangered its independence. After speaking with Bengsch, Zobel publicly explained his actions to the pastoral synod on 19 October 1973: his visit to Moscow had been a private affair and did not impact the synod, an internal church matter. Cardinal Bengsch then declared his confidence in Zobel and pronounced that the synod's further activities would enjoy freedom. He thanked all of the delegates, especially those who did not come from regular church positions, for their work, although, he added, "we know that various visits and conversations have taken place between individual members of the synod and offices that do not belong to the synod, to the church, or to the state."[125]

Not all synod members revealed these contacts, however. At least one synod member had secret meetings with the MfS and gave them material. Two lay Catholics from the Dresden main office also gave information to the MfS. Two former priests prepared theological analyses of the synod for the security services. By the second full assembly of the synod (19–21 October 1973) at the latest, the MfS had complete minutes of the synod's discussions. However, because the full assemblies of the synod were not public, the state could not make any public use of the information it gained, and it took no public stance on the synod. In an evaluation dated 3 April 1973, the Office of the State Secretary for Church Affairs justified this position as based in the "fact" that the state respected "the synod as an internal affair of the church" and that "the international community will consider this a measure of an even-keeled relation between the churches and the state in the GDR."[126] The real fact—that the state conspired to obtain internal church information—was supposed to be kept secret for the sake of the GDR's international image.

The synod met for six plenary sessions: 22–26 March and 19–21 October 1973; and 21–24 March and 7–10 November 1974; and 10–13 April and 7 and 9 November 1975. A seventh, final session took place on 29–30 November 1975. In the end, after working intensively in the plenary sessions and on expert commissions, participants produced a total of nine drafts with the necessary majority on the topics "Faith Today," "Ministering in the Parish," "Aspects of Missionary Service in the Parish," "Services and the Orders of Life in the Parish," "Foci of Christian Life in Matrimony and the Family," "Christ in the Professions," and "Service of the Church for Conciliation and Peace." The pastoral synod was a formative pastoral and ecclesiastical event whose meaning lay primarily in the certainty of its implementation. In spite of all the different views within the church, it contributed to a more conscious sense of fellowship among Catholics in the GDR, even though the work of the synods hardly continued, and the failed reception of many of the decrees within the church led to disappointments in the years to come.

On the other hand, state and party organs observing the synod—who secretly sought influence—geared their observations toward the "Analysis of Power Relations" with the pragmatic intention of favoring the line within church political structures, in each instance, that seemed to be the least detrimental. Controversial debates on the priorities of the synod arose at the first plenary in March 1973; Bishop Aufderbeck overcame a conflict among almost a third of the synods and the line of the other bishops with his suggestions for compromise. The state apparatus established that this made Aufderbeck a representative of "a more militant line," which he pursued, apparently, by rallying "negative groupings" around himself. Hence, the ZK inferred that its mission was to expand "the circle of powers around Cardinal Bengsch in order to strengthen their position vis-à-vis the more militant powers."[127] Indeed, there would be no confrontation with Aufderbeck or the synod, not even in conversations with Catholic officials or synods. As early as the second plenary on 29 October 1973, the ZK ruled that Bengsch had "established his position' and "commanded the scene."[128] After the third plenary, on the other hand, it marked the appearance of a "faction" of twenty to twenty-five synod participants seemingly determined to cause a "confrontation" with the state. Bengsch was supposedly "not willing" to lead "the open confrontation": "The champions of a course of confrontation are at the same time champions of a modernist theology, for pluralism within the church and the promotion of a so-called lay-apostolate, attacking certain taboos." The differences of opinion within the church were overall of a "simply tactical nature, but not at all based on principle." Both of the last plenary meetings and the final session in 1975 confirmed the estimation of the government posts that the "negative powers" in the synod could not assert themselves because of their minority status, and because of the established hierarchy in the synodal statute. Bengsch was allegedly intent on "counteracting the public attacks on the socialist state as well as positive votes for the socialist state and social orders by emphasizing the exclusively inner-ecclesiastical, pastoral character of the synod, [and] maintaining the hierarchical principle of the Catholic structure and the privileges of the bishops."[129] After the final session of the pastoral synod, agents of HA XX/4 in the MfS called upon their ecclesiastical interlocutors in the Berlin Diocese's Ordinariate on 30 November 1975 to make sure Cardinal Bengsch held the line of "not allowing any post-synodal institutions" to be established. His ambitions were to "get the church order back under tight control after the conclusion of the pastoral synod and to proceed in a strategically clever manner against oppositional efforts within the church."[130]

Although the assemblies and the decisions of the pastoral synod caused no great headaches for the SED, other events that took place in this same period revealed that the Catholic Church did indeed constitute a very real security risk for the SED. The social program of the youth pilgrimage of the Episcopal Commissariat of Magdeburg to Petersberg near Halle on 17 June 1973, using the slogan "Mask 73—Act, Don't Be Acted Upon," presented politically critical cartoons and parodies, displayed posters, and presented songs by Wolf Biermann. To the state organs, these were shocking "debaucheries" and "open, but also furtive, subtly declamatory attacks against the socialist social order."[131] The actions made waves at the regional and district levels and then up to the ZK and HA XX/4, which made their way back to Magdeburg, where Prelate Gross expressed the church's displeasure to Bishop Braun and Vicar General Hubrich.[132] Hubrich conducted the service at the youth pilgrimage, presumably without knowing about the social program. The regional church leadership finally distanced itself from the social program of the pilgrimage, as well as from the responsible youth pastors, in conversations with government posts in Magdeburg and Halle, also announcing that a transfer of one of the clergyman that had taken place before the event was a disciplinary consequence. Additionally, the state granted the church permission to take more exacting ecclesiastical control over the preparations of pilgrimages. Fritz Flint, in a conversation with Prelate Gross at the State Secretariat for Church Affairs on 1 August 1973, threatened that, "in the event of a repeat offense, the entire affair would have to be tried at the central state level." Gross seemed to concur. With respect to the church situation in the district of Halle, Flint interpreted Gross's explanations as implying "that we could very well cooperate much more closely in combating . . . such developments, consulting with each other more often in order to prevent endangering [our] amicable relations, even expanding this cooperation."[133]

But there was no inkling of such an amicable relationship when Cardinal Bengsch or the BOK broke taboos themselves. In the summer of 1973, the state proposed a new "youth law" that would replace the clauses of May 1964, publicizing it in the GDR press. On 21 September 1973 the bishops took a position on this via a detailed letter from Cardinal Bengsch to Premier Stoph. It was not read in the churches, however, and when the state did not respond, it was presented to the clergy on 18 October 1973 for informational purposes.[134] More than anything else, Bengsch criticized the propagated cultivation of the "social-ist character" in the proposed youth law, which was "unacceptable in the view of Christian belief" because it was "formulated by Marxist-Leninist ideology." "Society," he continued in the letter, must not be allowed to bestow "personal dignity . . . on young people." The state's claim to contribute to the develop-ment of character, he argued, was "an exercise of power in a realm of human life to which state force is not entitled." In closing, he, and with him the bishops, invoked "innumerable personal and confidential contacts with children, youths, and parents," and for this reason claimed to be speaking "in the interest not only of young Christians, but also young people, and, finally, society":

> In all earnestness, we must call attention to the issue that the ideological totalitari-anism of the state and all of its organs, especially within the entire educational sys-tem, according to our understanding, does not represent progress, but rather regress, because it imposes coercion on the human being, which in the long term will only cause major harm to the individual and society.

The government completely ignored the bishops' "request for benevolent and objective scrutiny" of this petition. The law for the "Participation of Youth in the Design of the Developed Socialist Society" went into effect, unchanged, on 28 January 1974. By December 1973 the state had already assimilated students in grades 4 through 7 into the Thälmann Scouts, whose uniforms incorporated a new, red neckerchief, creating a second ideological level of the Scouts orga-nization. In the summer of 1974, an international pedagogy conference of the socialist states advocated that "socialist character" be developed by means of state education in all public corners. On 17 November 1974 the BOK responded, decreeing that a pastoral letter on Christian education, which Bishop Aufderbeck and the Erfurt theology professors had been preparing for a year, be read at all Catholic services in the GDR.[135]

By mid November 1974, the MfS had apparently gotten hold of this letter, which it then provided to Verner and Barth in the ZK as an introductory "brief." The MfS interpreted it as "a consciously false portrayal of the standing of devel-oped socialist society in the GDR and a furtive attack." Further, the MfS alleged that the letter "falsified and arbitrarily construed" the constitution of the GDR from 1968 and the UN Declaration on Human Rights from 1948. Moreover,

> In the context of the criticism of the socialist educational policy, the leading role of the party and working class, with their Marxist-Leninist worldview, is repudiated, and a politically pluralist society is recommended as worthwhile. With that, the pastoral word not only argues against the ostensible limitations of the freedoms of religion and conscience in the GDR but also "promotes" combating the Marxist-Leninist worldview for the benefit of religion on the basis of a "bourgeois understanding of freedom."[136]

With its critical Catholic testimonies on societal development in the GDR, unheard since a similar bishops' statement in 1960, this pastoral letter seemed like a "battle cry" to the state.[137] In it, the bishops expressed their need to protest publicly: "We must speak out in order to protect the adolescent generation from harm. We must intervene for their freedoms of religion and conscience and for their right to education." The state's "educational monopoly," they argued, limited "the choice of school type, educational path, and career," and also defined "a biased idea of man." This monopoly was not acceptable and contradicted the UN Declaration on Human Rights because parents had the "first right" and the church "a special right" to educate. The normative worldview of dialectical materialism "often distorts and skews" religion and Christianity, such that it misrepresented religion "with the media of propaganda and also pressure of conscience." In contrast, Christian education focused on conveying the idea that a human being is more than "the fruit of his labor" and that "development of conscience" comprised "the core of education."

In contrast, the bishops maintained in the letter that the GDR state

> placed ethics and morals at the mercy of the party and the state. Whatever is legally sanctioned or permitted is considered ethically good. According to this line of thought, individual conscience has no other function than complete incorporation into development. We ask: Can a society really be the benchmark of all things? Are the state and the party permitted to have ethics and morality at their mercy? Is something good simply because it is legally sanctioned or permitted?

Finally, the letter addressed the "limits" of the cooperation of young Christians in society and called upon church members to provide testimony of their faith and loyalty to the church, even if it should carry professional disadvantages.

After the ZK became aware of this text, State Secretary Seigewasser summoned the advisor from the Berlin Ordinariate on 13 November 1974 to his administrative office. This was Gerhard Lange, whom Cardinal Bengsch had appointed the new delegate of the BOK in "negotiation duties" on 10 October 1974 after his predecessor Prelate Groß had died.[138] The state secretary formally objected to the public reading of the pastoral letter by pretending that it "put intense pressure on' the relations of the Catholic Church with the state and was an "intervention into exclusively state affairs."

One day later, by order of the cardinal, Lange conveyed to the state secretary's office that the BOK had been informally advised of the state's objection at the funeral of Auxiliary Bishop Karl Ebert in Meiningen, which had occurred that day.[139] The bishops stood by their decision and approved a declaration that Lange was to present to the state secretary for church affairs one day after the letter was publicly read on 18 November. It explained that discrimination against Christians in the state educational system had been repeatedly aired as a grievance in recent years. Because the state had not reacted to these grievances and had approved the youth law, including its provisions to develop the youth's "socialist character," the bishops saw it as their duty "to direct a pastoral letter to believers about the development of the Christian character." This was not "politically" motivated, but rather a "stance on worldview." It was not about intervening in "an exclusively governmental task" but about protecting Christian parents' right to rear their children as they saw fit.[140] When Lange read this to State Secretary Seigewasser and Delegate Flint on 19 November, the West German press was already spreading news of the pastoral letter. Highly irritated, the state representatives angrily replied: "No church in the socialist states, neither in the USSR nor in Hungary, not even the Wyszynski Church in Poland, would have dared to do what the Catholic Church in the GDR has done . . . We reserve the right to determine appropriate procedures as to how, what, and when something becomes public; but an irregular situation has occurred which cannot be ignored."[141] At the end of the state comment on the conversation, Seigewasser noted that Bengsch needed to be summoned "to a discussion of principles." His opportunities to visit West Berlin would also have to be scrutinized, as would the international travels of bishops and clergy.[142]

At the same time, however, the government posts began strategizing in respect to the ongoing negotiations with the Vatican about the hoped-for independent dioceses reflecting the borders of the GDR. Visible measures against the pastoral letter would have been counterproductive for this, so the ZK sought other solutions. Politburo member Verner decided that only Seigewasser should speak to Bengsch: "The entire discussion should avoid threatening the Catholic Church with sanctions. It should make clear that a worsening of relations between the state and the church would only disadvantage the church in the end." This restraint was a "political decision," and "confrontations" would not be allowed to obtrude.[143] The discussion between Seigewasser and Bengsch proceeded accordingly on 6 December 1974: both sides again described their differing positions without attaining convergence.[144] Bengsch rebutted Seigewasser's accusation of an ecclesiastical attack on the state by claiming that the state had launched an attack through its educational policy so that the bishops could not remain silent any longer. The state secretary declared the discussion on educational affairs in the GDR "taboo," to which Bengsch responded that "human rights come before socialism." Seigewasser's rhetorical posturing notwithstanding—he claimed, for example, that the church could have more "strictness" if it so "desired," but that the state "itself" had "no cause" to become more strict—the conversation concluded with common resolve to maintain the mutually beneficial "modus vivendi" between the state and the Catholic Church.

Bengsch's daring on behalf of all Catholic bishops in November 1974 was unprecedented. The state's reaction and its lack of compromise regarding issues of education and upbringing ultimately contributed to finding balance in the "modus vivendi," and to it playing an even more dominating role in church-state relations. The Catholic Church in the GDR did not want this modus to be anchored in writing; rather, it wanted to avoid making a binding agreement with the state, preferring a legally dubious abeyance. In this way, a kind of customary law developed by means of ecclesiastical work opportunities and the negotiated contacts with Rome and the West. The church found itself at the short end of the stick but could rely on the GDR's need for an international reputation and foreign currency. Since the mid 1970s, the state's church negotiators had gradually expanded their positions—which the state described as a generous concession—expecting up-front predictability and resolution of the church-political problems in return. Theoretically, the state organs, although they sometimes could not reach consensus among themselves, could always limit the opportunities of the church and take away what they had once given. However, political decision-makers almost always found that the public furor accompanying such measures was too high a price to pay. They did not go beyond aggressive posturing behind closed doors, the actual character of which became clear for both sides only after the fact. At the time, however, the state's threats were real and church leaders' uncertainties were no figments of the imagination.

In this context, the church's Berlin negotiation delegates on behalf of the BOK and the BBK to the MfS and the state secretary for church affairs became important fixtures. Whereas clergy and church employees adhered to strict directives regarding discussions with government posts at the regional, district, city, and community levels, the central contacts were not subject to this rule and proceeded according to their own principles, formally responsible only to the chairman of the BOK/BBK.[145] Groß enjoyed a unique position as the sole political contact for seven years and essentially laid the foundation for the future "modus vivendi." But after he died in August 1974, his church-political functions were divided among Prelate Dissemond, as delegate to the MfS discussions, and Lange, as the negotiation partner of the Administrative Office of the State Secretary for Church Affairs.

Dissemond was active in this capacity until at least May 1987; Lange carried out his role until December 1989. There was no rivalry between them in terms of internal church issues, but there was personal rivalry with respect to their leading functions in the church, which the state organs certainly noticed. Lange strongly wished to be additionally recognized at the MfS level after Dissemond's departure, but Cardinal Meisner did not allow it. The time frame and intensity of these prelates inevitably led to opposing "knowledge of domination" *(Herrschaftswissen),* and with that, gradually to partial convergences of interests among the negotiators on both sides. Predictability and avoidance of conflict advanced to become the highest maxims of these institutionalized channels: representatives on all sides considered themselves the agents of order and regulated their own camps to prevent and smooth out "problems." Once accomplished "collectively," the convergences were consolidated. The state's new skillful deputy state secretary for church affairs, Hermann Kalb, significantly contributed to this pattern.[146] In a conversation at the Administrative Office of the State Secretary on 28 November 1977, Lange made a remark, here quoted by a state representative, that timelessly sums up these relations: "I count among the successes of my predecessor and myself that the we kept the number of possible controversies as small as possible. If nothing happens, then I am already delighted."[147]

To preserve this climate, extensive favors and gifts were often exchanged, and minutes were frequently contrived at the official level. The personalized atmosphere became better and better until the end of the 1980s, influenced on the church side by its underestimation of the state's calculating policy, which could paralyze the church in some instances. Dissemond and Lange's explanations on the occasion of the 2 March 1987 inaugural visit of the new Secretary General of the BBK Josef Michelfeit to the Administrative Office of the State Secretary for Church Affairs were symptomatic of the church's view of the level of these "relations":

> Using the area of travel affairs as an example, [Dissemond] made clear that the church's amicable adjustment requires a certain restraint, or sometimes, an understanding, for state interests. By strictly adhering to the predetermined viewpoints for evaluating church leaders' travel requests, the state has almost never deemed it necessary to decline a travel application. Prelate Lange sought to characterize the essence of the state-church relationship as it developed over the years by explaining that it was not about a kind of diplomacy that tried to pull the wool over the eyes of the partner, but rather about an open explanation of bilateral interests and the search for realistic, navigable avenues for solving problems.[148]

The benchmark of "predictability" brought with it the tendency for the church to not publicly ennoble church protest but rather to direct it toward the state, almost compulsorily, as an exhibit with accompanying dilution. Public directness of the sort that occurred when the pastoral letter on Christian education appeared in November 1974, when the church could "remain silent no longer," did not recur during the incumbency of Cardinal Bengsch, who passed away in December 1979. Only in the annual closed-door policy discussions with State Secretary Seigewasser did the bishop of Berlin express his unmasked and resolute political criticism; publicly, he manifested his self-understanding of the political abstinence of an exclusively pastorally oriented church.

Bengsch and his employees harshly rejected Erfurt Bishop Aufderbeck's suggestion for a new pastoral letter on questions of socialist education. Bengsch's and Aufderbeck's different positions on the necessity of public discourse had already become clear a year before when obligatory military defense lessons were introduced at the GDR polytechnical secondary schools on 1 September 1978.[149] After the state had made this intention public, the Alliance of Protestant Churches in the GDR petitioned for its withdrawal. The alliance then had a discussion with State Secretary Seigewasser on 1 June 1978, the tenor of which proved unsatisfactory. Consequently, it had the petition read in all Protestant parishes on 25 June. The Catholics, because of the activities of the Protestants and requests from Catholic student unions, deliberated on this topic and finally approved a petition of protest that Cardinal Bengsch was to hand over to State Secretary Seigewasser at their usual discussion on 12 June 1978.[150] Bengsch used this opportunity, in turn, to reiterate his positions on educational issues from the previous years, but did not find it auspicious to repeat them publicly.[151] The text of the BBK's petition was finally forwarded to the Catholic clergy in the GDR on 28 June 1978, "not as a pulpit sermon" but rather "for the instruction of the parents and students," after the Protestant protest had been read three days before.[152]

Aufderbeck thoroughly expressed his disapproval of the state's intention on 23 July 1978 in the presence of a West German television crew at the women's pilgrimage in Dingelstädt in Eichsfeld:

> Military defense instruction is connected to teaching hate, to awakening idea of friend or foe. Military defense instruction is connected to mistrusting peoples. Military defense instruction stands in contradiction to the usual propaganda of peace and fellowship among peoples . . . We should first keep our eyes open and be strong, not just parrot what others say, so that things are not done that are said to be "voluntary," such as the boys' military training camp in the 9th grade.[153]

Such differences of opinion within the BBK as to whether and when bishops ought to make public declarations in the name of the church on societal developments also determined Bengsch's final year in office, during which he acted against Aufderbeck with direct acerbity. With Bengsch's death on 13 December 1979 the church lost its dominating personality, which allowed its smoldering differences within to become stronger over the next decade. The outwardly adjured continuity of the "course of Cardinal Bengsch" ceased to be reality. With that, new constellations and convergences in church-state relations emerged.

Catholic Identity and Heimat

When Erich Honecker received a delegation of the Communist Party of France under the leadership of its Secretary General Georges Marchais for a meeting on 25 April 1980, he wanted to impress his guests with numbers that showed "successful economic and social policies" of the GDR. He alleged that these policies had led to "great changes in the development of the consciousness of the people," and that even the Protestant Church no longer posed "notable difficulties" after the summit talk with Bishop Albrecht Schönherr on 6 March 1978. Nor did the Catholic Church, he proclaimed, elaborating: "In a situation of intensified confrontations with class, since there are attempts to create a fifth column in the GDR, the church stands behind its state, even though we have a separation of church and state. That has an influence on development in the FRG as well."[154]

This snapshot of Honecker's world of thought contains the SED's expectations regarding religious communities under the requirements of state socialism. The churches had been pushed to "not cause any difficulties" and, on this basis, were being trained to affirm the GDR without being attached to all-German contexts, which kept them from being a "fifth column" of the Federal Republic of Germany—an element of uncertainty –in the eyes of the SED. This security policy perspective, and the appraisal of the role of the church deduced from it, contained a rational core that consisted in the internal acceptance of general societal frameworks as the prerequisite for church functioning, even for the Catholic Church in the GDR. As a result, the constancy of the socialist bloc in Eastern Europe and the GDR, after the development of a "Catholic identity in the diaspora" even before 1961, had led to a consciousness of *Heimat,* or "being at home," that was not merely local or individual. It was neither the German Democratic Republic nor even its socialist self-definition that was affirmed, but rather, ever more often, "this land," or "our land."

The international recognition of the GDR, which confirmed the political status quo in Europe, had ratified the forced drifting apart of the Catholic Church in both German states. Even though the personal, inner-German church contacts and the material Western transfers in the 1970s and 1980s were often more intensive than in the first decade after the erection of the Wall,[155] the partial, legal self-development of the Catholic Church in the GDR was an authentic outward expression of its internal independence. The Catholic Church as "World Church" under the direction of its holy leader in Rome did not define itself in national contexts. For the leadership of the "Local Church" in the GDR, this supranationality was a decisive point of reference for abstracting itself from inner-German status questions in a way that rose above legalisms and political systems. Günter Gaus, the first permanent representative of the Federal Republic in East Berlin between 1974 and 1981, properly defined Bengsch's worldview as "first and foremost of a relationship of three states to each other, and defined by each other: the Catholic Church in the GDR as one state, the GDR as the second, and the Vatican as the third."[156]

Catholics in the GDR distanced themselves from the politics of the SED with the question of what it means to be Christian, discussing how this fact was to influence day-to-day life in the society of the GDR or how it might change that society. In this respect, the synod of the Diocese of Meißen between 1969 and 1971, and the pastoral synod of the local Catholic jurisdictions between 1972 and 1975, were self-evident signs that Catholics were developing an identity under the restrictions of the GDR, in spite of all of the differences that existed within the church. This identity was understood in theological terms as a "challenge" and "mission" sent by God, even though disagreement about the resulting consequences abounded.[157] Most of the bishops and many of the clerics felt affirmed—not least by the developments in West Germany after the Second Vatican Council and its aftereffects even in East German Catholicism, as well as by the all-too-clear presence of "practical materialism" in the West—that one could live more authentically and in a more Catholic manner under the societal regulations of the GDR and their protection from "destructive" modernity and plurality. When this "materialism" began to develop from a low but rising level of consumption even in the GDR, the church perceived this as nearly a crisis in convergence that spanned the whole system of both German states.[158] In his first interview in the Federal Republic after his transfer from Berlin to Cologne on 14 April 1989, Cardinal Meisner compared Catholics in both parts of Berlin, leaving no doubt about what he saw as the "healthier" environment for the Catholic faith:

> I have always perceived the clear differences, also in the strength of the faith in the church, but I have told myself realistically that the Christians in the Eastern sector of my former Diocese of Berlin are no better than those in the Western sector. They just have less opportunity to sin. That is, under the societal situations in the Federal Republic, the Christians in the GDR would probably present us with the same image.[159]

Still, GDR Catholics seldom described the "GDR" as their "home." Instead, they used politically distancing terms like "here," "where we live," "this land," and, increasingly, "our land." During Cardinal Bengsch's tenure, such phrases would hardly have been uttered out loud for church-political reasons; such ideas were largely repressed for the sake of a "placeless" theology, except for some discussion at the synods. This stance kept the church from conveying an image of resignation about the political situation. In the 1980s, that would change. Catholics, especially those in the generation socialized in the GDR, began to publicly pose questions—for example, about the church's place in society and its responsibility for contributing to changes in society.

In the following years, the church's course of abstaining from political discourse eroded gradually in an interplay of bishops' statements and critical queries and expectations from the church base. This happened despite retarding and not always causally related events. Differing approaches between 1982 and 1987 had the following basic principles—which were more or less explicit—in common: the Catholic Church wanted to become more public and, with its specific understanding of faith, cautiously called for Catholics to penetrate society and play a critical role in its makeup. When the first GDR-wide meeting of Catholics from all jurisdictions took place in Dresden in July 1987, at least 100,000 people participated. In this "socialist metropolis," a euphoric feeling of church fellowship dominated. Some 3,000 delegates openly and critically discussed a wide array of church and social topics, though usually at prescribed events. Never before had a self-confident Catholic identity been visible in this way.[160] Cardinal Meisner and Bishop Joachim Wanke spoke about "our country" as a matter of course on the final day, and the following statement by the cardinal met with enormous, spontaneous applause:

> The Christians in our country would like to contribute their gifts and abilities to our society without having to follow a different star than that of Bethlehem. Many idle energies and quiet reserves would become active if the abilities and professional competencies of the individual citizen were the most pivotal for professional service![161]

The audience understood the metaphor of the Star of Bethlehem to be the antithesis of the Red Star. In a clear sign of tolerance, GDR television broadcast this statement and the reaction it evoked in its evening abstract on 7 July 1987. In his closing remarks, Erfurt's Bishop Wanke, after expressing his gratitude to the hosts in Dresden, euphorically called out: "If there is anything characteristic of our country, then it is the joyful readiness of the people to celebrate any time, anywhere, to organize a small (or large) party, to participate in it, to be invited to it. The GDR has become a real party society!"[162]

The state did not know how to make use of this obviously developing consciousness of *Heimat* within the Catholic Church. Only the SED district leadership under Hans Modrow, who had been advised by Horst Dohle, believed it valuable to make an unusual decision to grant the Catholic Church a "political domicile" in the district as a potential partner. This was a result of their local experiences with the meeting of Catholics and the contacts with Bishop Gerhard Schaffran and his Vicar General Hermann Joseph Weisbender on 11 September 1987.[163] However, this was soon to become obsolete vis-à-vis the leadership of the Diocese of Dresden-Meißen that had newly assumed power in January 1988. Generally speaking, in the 1980s perpetual uncertainty and anxiety entered the politics of the SED with the emergence of an independent peace movement and oppositional groupings within and on the margins of the Protestant Church. This led to uncertainty in the state's Kirchenpolitik, too, so that the Catholic Church was expected to continue its silent course of political abstinence just as it had under Cardinal Bengsch. But instead, the Catholic "frontline" caused problems for the state's Kirchenpolitiker (church politicians), which, although essentially smaller than those generated by the Protestant Church, still made state officials wonder whether the Catholic Church was following these Protestant tendencies. An "informational document" from the Working Group for Church Affairs at the ZK on 28 October 1985 established—and from this perspective it was certainly true—that relations with the Catholic Church had changed:

> For some time now, attempts in the Catholic leadership—particularly represented by Cardinal Meisner—have been growing more apparent that aim to demonstratively establish and expand personal positions with offensive measures . . . With this attempt . . . the danger becomes greater that [Meisner] is departing from basic principles that have been meaningful since the time of Cardinal Bengsch. He is clearly drifting from the protected and customary foundations of reasonable, concerted, bilaterally maintained relations to the state.[164]

In the context of further conflicts with Cardinal Meisner in the fall of 1986, the state Kirchenpolitiker also refrained from writing a detailed interpretation of a pastoral letter of 8 September 1986 that had been addressed to priests and the ministry, entitled "The Catholic Church in the Socialist State," because the critical and reserved tones toward the socialist state outweighed the affirmative ones.[165] The CDU's Main Department for Church Questions, however, provided a more precise interpretation: the text visibly demonstrated that the "hibernating stance that could be observed in GDR Catholicism up to this point" had been overcome.[166] Bishop Wanke of Erfurt, alongside the auxiliary bishop of Schwerin, Norbert Werbs, was one of the main authors of this pastoral letter. The former hinted retrospectively in October 1987 that it had been

> intended more to encourage Christian testimony in society and the public than to serve as a warning of the dangers of such testimony. The letter of the bishops takes the declaration of the last council that the church is not bound to any particular political system seriously (cf. "Gaudium et Spes" 42, also 76). Christians can fulfill God's will under any political conditions. Moreover, the state and its ideology do not so totally occupy all areas of life that no room for Christian testimony and discipleship remains. The question is only how that can happen without the church and the individual Christian being forced to sail under alien flags.

Moreover, Wanke added, Catholics knew they were connected with Christians of other confessions "in light of the challenges of societal disbelief": "Certainly being Christian, being Catholic in the GDR means constantly 'walking a tight-rope' . . . The paths leading off to the right or the left, toward assimilation or expatriation, are very tempting."[167]

On the issue of "emigrating," and thus on the questions of remaining in the GDR or applying to leave, bishops and other Catholics in the 1980s held a variety of views—always affected and suffering from the situation in the country despite generally encouraging people to stay.[168] Catholic parishes, and especially church social organizations, were greatly affected by applications for exit permits. On the other hand, church organizations commonly protected applicants by taking care of them if they were dismissed by state institutions or companies due to their application. In a wave of emigration such as in the first half of 1984, the announcements from the Catholic sphere vacillated between exhortations to Catholics to remain in the *Heimat* and concealed anger at the government, whose politics were responsible for the applications. Cardinal Meisner, preaching at a consecration ceremony for abbesses in Alexanderdorf, declared that "God put us in this place [and] for that reason we will not leave this country," and, before a group of pilgrims from the GDR in Rome on the occasion of the Holy Year in April 1984, said that the Catholics "in Saxony, in Brandenburg, in Lusatia, in Thuringia [should] build huts . . ."

The state registered such statements with gratification, and the West German media interpreted them as a subliminal affirmation of the GDR. Yet Meisner reacted by composing a letter on his own initiative to Premier Stoph, which he presented to government posts on 25 April 1984. After highlighting the development of a religiously founded concept of *Heimat,* he identified hardships caused by state politics and reiterated the desire for more generous travel regulations: "We wish very much that the state-introduced causal research will bring about measures that will render many reasons for wanting to emigrate superfluous."[169]

On 19 May 1984 at the Catholic Academy in West Berlin, he publicly stated that 80 percent of applications for exit permits were "submitted based simply on the ideology of real-existing socialism." Agency journalists who were present noted these and other remarks, and the media of West Berlin made them public. This sparked immediate and hot controversies with the state organs of the GDR and its "church-policy advisors" of the Berlin Ordinariate.[170] Up until his transfer to Cologne in February 1989, Meisner challenged the government of the GDR to do something to simplify travel. After hopeful would-be emigrants occupied the Erfurt Cathedral in June 1988, Meisner personally intervened, contacting his church-policy delegates to arrange for those affected to be successively expatriated to the West after they had left the church building with the requisite permission. Further occupations of the Cathedral of Saint Hedwig in Berlin in the same year, and again in the Erfurt Cathedral in July 1989, progressed in a similar fashion, although the state and the church took care to keep these procedures out of the public eye so as to prevent a vacuum effect. In their desperation, some who wished to leave the country used any opportunity to get out as quickly as possible. In exceptional cases, the church discreetly intervened with state organs or negotiated with lawyer Wolfgang Vogel about the list he compiled on "Bringing Families Together," especially when those hoping to leave offered the church real estate and were to receive settlement capital in West German marks from the German Caritas Association as payment. Aside from sympathy for individual decisions, the church hierarchy still implied in Catholic parishes that a Christian was to remain in solidarity with his or her *Heimat,* regardless of any discontent with its political and societal system. But that also raised pressure to effect changes in the GDR, and members of the church increasingly asked the BBK to use its Kirchenpolitik and audience with the state to this end. The exclusively theological justification for remaining in the *Heimat* no longer sufficed to deal with this pressure.

The Church in Public and Differences in Kirchenpolitik

After Joachim Meisner, who had been an auxiliary bishop in Erfurt for the previous five years, was inaugurated as the bishop of Berlin in 1980, the BBK held a special session on 17 May 1980 to elect a new chairperson to succeed the late Cardinal Bengsch. This election proved to be very complicated. Among other reasons, the bishop of Berlin and the BBK chair had been one and the same person up to this point, but Meisner was widely held to be too inexperienced in Kirchenpolitik to take on the latter role. It took two rounds of voting for the bishop of Dresden, Gerhard Schaffran, to receive the majority. The Berlin members of the BBK and their chair comprised most of the opposition, not only because they thus lost importance in affairs of Kirchenpolitik but also because the "bridging function to the World Church due to the responsibility for West Berlin" was thus lost. In a letter to Schaffran of 28 June 1980, the auxiliary bishop of Berlin,

Johannes Kleineidam, noted that the personal union between 1950 and 1979 had "certainly always had [its] essential meaning for the greater freedom of our conference and the church in our country." Yet, he continued, Schaffran's election could "have a signaling effect for certain people" with respect to a "stronger integration of the church into the state-social structure."[171]

Kleineidam's remarks bore the influence of his criticism of Schaffran's decision to make an inaugural visit to Honecker in the latter's capacity as chair of the State Council of the GDR. But in light of overriding Ostpolitik deliberations, Schaffran did receive approval and encouragement from the Vatican for such an approach, which would have been unthinkable under Cardinal Bengsch.[172] The Administrative Office of the State Secretary for Church Affairs then prepared for the visit with Prelates Lange and Dissemond, who were also to participate in the meeting with Honecker. The BBK urged Schaffran to use critical words at this meeting in order to prevent the state from misappropriating what he might say, which had happened to the head of the Protestant Church when he met with Honecker on 6 March 1978.[173] The originally scheduled date of 10 October 1980 was pushed back to 15 January 1981, probably due to the political situation in Poland. The church withdrew the intended public reading of a prepared speech with critical passages by Schaffran when the state announced that confrontations would result. Instead, the church signaled that Schaffran would deliver these positions on issues of ideological worldviews and problems of public education orally.[174]

The state was pleasantly surprised by Schaffran's election as chair of the BBK because it regarded him as the Catholic bishop "who in recent years was and is the one who most clearly strives for an amicable arrangement with the state organs." In this respect, the state fostered hopes that Schaffran's incumbency would lead to "a more far-reaching and faster cultivation of the positive elements of church-state relations in the GDR."[175] The 45-minute conversation between Honecker and Schaffran on 15 January 1981 largely consisted in polite and ceremonial banter and scored a symbolic win for the GDR overall. Church records indicate that they chatted about the separation of church and state, the issue of bishopric boundaries, and world peace.[176] Notable in the atmosphere was Honecker's offhand remark that the GDR had become "smarter" in handling the church over the course of time. Otherwise, the secretary general pointed out that he had "always gotten along" with Catholics from his home in the Saarland: "The Catholic church tower loomed behind the garden of his father's house and he could not imagine it being gone."[177] In no way did Honecker and Schaffran address objective questions; they made no agreements. Yet due to Honecker's skill at talking about nothing, Schaffran did not broach the subject of the discrimination of Catholic youth in the educational system, as the BBK had expected, which other bishops later criticized him for.[178]

The media of the GDR conveyed an impression that a harmonious, amicable agreement had been reached at the highest level between the state and the Catholic Church. Yet a long pastoral letter prepared for the Lenten fast on the issue of the Jugendweihe and Christian education, scheduled for 8 March 1981, quickly undermined this idea. The letter was intended to prevent a possible "spirit of January 15, 1981" analogous to the Protestant one of "March 6, 1978."[179] Bishop Aufderbeck of Erfurt, who had already diverged from Cardinal Bengsch's line in 1978, when he publicly criticized the introduction of military defense instruction in the GDR, had already composed a pastoral letter entitled "The Christian Idea of Man" on behalf of the BBK in the fall of 1979, together with professors of theology from Erfurt. On 12 October 1979 Cardinal Bengsch had rejected it in an almost cynical letter to Aufderbeck: "To whom do we make our claim that no one for the sake of his conscience may suffer discrimination through defamation or societal underevaluation? To the state? At most, [the state] could guarantee legal equality, not social equality. No state can do that, and no state does it."[180] After Bengsch's death in December 1979, Bishop Heinrich Theissing of Schwerin already urged, on 30 January 1980, that the BBK put forth an operative word on the Jugendweihe, which was long past due.[181] Afterward, all the bishops sought to preserve the impression that they were not diverging from Bengsch's recently practiced course, yet the mere fact of a pastoral letter that included social criticism already marked a clear departure. After various drafts, the Lenten pastoral letter finally found its final form in February 1981 and had just become known to the MfS. In response, the state put a mechanism in place intended to strictly prohibit the public reading of the pastoral letter during Catholic Church services in the GDR just weeks after the Honecker-Schaffran summit talk and before the upcoming Tenth Party Congress of the SED.

On 26 February 1981 the MfS sent a brief to Honecker and Politburo member Verner, enclosing the pastoral letter.[182] Above all, passages in the section entitled "Do We Christians Still Have a Chance in our Country?" prompted the state security arm to suggest that State Secretary Gysi prevent the public reading in a discussion with Bishop Schaffran. The most incriminating passages in the letter were as follows:

> Parents are not allowed to dismiss their first right to rearing, and no one is permitted to take it away from them. Even the state, in its educational goals, must respect the will of the parents. This teaching of the church is also consonant with the United Nations Charter, the General Declaration of Human Rights, and the Final Act of Helsinki. All of these declarations are legally enforceable in the GDR . . . Even more profoundly, the hurtful issue of the Jugendweihe restricts the right to freedom of religion of thousands of Catholic parents and children. Again and again it is decreed: Participation in the Jugendweihe is voluntary. But if Catholic parents and children take advantage of this voluntariness, they are usually under such moral pressure from the school, the companies in which the parents work, or social institutions that there can be no voluntariness. But at the same time, Christians who want to live with God cannot express a celebratory affirmative to the unquestioned atheist aims of the Jugendweihe. This cannot be expected of Christians! It is an injustice to force them by means of moral pressure. It does not matter who applies this pressure; that person is violating the free-

doms of religion and conscience to which every citizen of the GDR, whether atheist or Christian, has a constitutional right.[183]

On 28 February 1981 State Secretary Gysi spoke with Bishop Schaffran in his apartment in Dresden-Pillnitz for eight hours, describing the pastoral letter as an "open act of confrontation." In his "brief" of 2 March on this discussion, Gysi summarized his arguments to Schaffran as follows:

> What does this letter aim to achieve? The Western press would do its part for the interpretation and circulation of this issue. Do you want that? The Polish situation is smoldering in the background. What our Catholic pastors would make out of this letter here at home cannot be predicted . . . In the present situation, such a pastoral letter could only be seen as a withdrawal, or at least a disavowal of the spirit and atmosphere of the meeting with the Chair of the State Council. In other words, the letter is clearly directed against this meeting and also endangers what was attained under Cardinal Bengsch. The church leaders must be clear on all of these aspects.[184]

However, the state's threats did not have the desired effect. On 6 March 1981, two days before the proposed public reading of the pastoral letter, Hermann Kalb, delegate to the state secretary, called on Bishop Schaffran in Dresden and then presented the chair of the BBK with a verbal note (Kalb was not prepared for surrender):

> Dear Bishop Schaffran! Be herewith advised that the public reading of that pastoral letter of which you informed me at our last meeting in Pillnitz is forbidden by the state. The public reading of such a pastoral letter with unfounded attacks against our state would not contribute to a further development of amicable relations between the state and the Catholic Church, but rather could only damage them. Respectfully, Klaus Gysi.[185]

Yet neither this verbal note nor the detailed conversations between Kalb and Schaffran that followed[186] stopped the public reading on 8 March 1981 in all Catholic churches of the GDR. The services were especially closely monitored by the HA XX/4 and the regional authorities of the MfS.[187] During the scheduled session of the BBK on 9–10 March 1981, the bishops hotly debated the state's approach and a possible church reaction to Gysi's note.[188] The result was ultimately a stalemate between the state and the church. The Catholic bishops decided against reacting to the note and informing the church public in order to avoid dreaded state sanctions. The state was not interested in publicizing the ineffectiveness of the note and its consequent loss of face. Had it implemented sanctions against the church, the Western media would have diffused and commented upon the state's futile interventions before the Tenth Party Congress of the SED. The Working Group for Church Affairs at the ZK "directed" the "responsible Comrades for Church Affairs" in the administrative regions not to react at all to the pastoral letter of the BBK, remarking that "the possibility, and also the strength and power, to effectively intervene" were available, yet the state had determined that it was currently "not in our interest to [do so] before the Tenth Party Congress and the elections. Such a confrontation would be welcomed by the West and it would avidly exacerbate it."[189]

After these aggressive state attempts to influence the church's public statements, the MfS and other state organs had a stronger impression of the church's departure from the predictable practices it had exercised under the authority of Cardinal Bengsch. They perceived more and more actual and supposed evidence that they had to pay special attention to the Catholic leadership, as well as react unofficially with secret arrangements and threats.

In November 1982, the layman Günter Särchen, director of the Working Post for Pastoral Support at the Episcopal Commissariat of Magdeburg, published a 100-page circular entitled "Reconciliation—The Mission of the Church" intended "for internal church use" at the higher level.[190] When a copy leaked to the MfS, the church leadership tried to pass off responsibility. Särchen, who for decades had interacted with contacts in the Polish church and regularly conducted "Poland Seminars" behind the church walls of the GDR,[191] had put together German translations of Polish texts on the relationship between church and state and the role of Solidarnošč, which had all previously been published in the Polish press. He aimed to work against the unilateral news coverage in the GDR media. This act was "a political novelty" for the MfS because, for the first time, an official ecclesiastical "anti-socialist heritage of thought [was being] promoted within the Catholic Church in the GDR."[192] The MfS intervened to bring the issue under negotiation at the BBK session on 7 December 1982, where it was to be established that the circular was an arbitrary act of Särchen, and that he and his supervisor, Bishop Johannes Braun, should be advised not to let the incident repeat itself. As a result, antipathies within the church developed: Bishop Braun, whom the state threatened with consequences, put Särchen under his own watchful eye, and the Berlin Ordinariate encouraged government posts to let the bishop "run aground."[193]

Three months before this, Schaffran's power in the BBK had been transferred to Bishop Joachim Meisner, even though Schaffran's term lasted until the summer of 1986 by the statutes of the Roman Canon Law. This transfer also resulted from the state's counterproductive attempts to exert influence. Among other things, this political change of personnel cleared the way for the pastoral letter of the BBK on World Peace Day, which was read openly on 2 January 1983 in all Catholic churches of the GDR. Between October 1981 and December 1982, considerable suggestions, expectations, and drafts of this letter were deliberated within the church.[194] Most of all, the peace movement, which had captivated the Catholic youth, and the issue of a "social peace service" in the GDR convinced the BBK that it must say something about this set of problems. As early as 15 December 1981, it had agreed upon a text for a pastoral letter of peace. After martial law was declared in Poland on 13 December 1981 the BBK revised the text again, ultimately approving it on 4 January 1982 after final consultation with

Bishops Meisner, Theissing, and Schaffran. In this case, unique in the history of the GDR, state organs had an opportunity to directly influence a Catholic pastoral letter: the experiences of March 1981 had led church negotiators to inform the MfS relatively early about the intended pastoral letter, including its content, editorial revisions, and constellations within the BBK.[195] As a result, the MfS knew that Bishop Schaffran had taken part in the final decision, which gave it opportunities for influence. To the dismay of Bishops Theissing and Meisner, Schaffran vetoed the public reading on 4 January 1982, rendering the entire text irrelevant in light of the BBK's traditional principle of unanimity. For Theissing, this unprecedented event was the "darkest hour in the history" of the BBK because it broke the bishops' "unity" for the first time, triggering an end to Schaffran's incumbency as chair. At the BBK session in April 1982, he managed to prevent his colleagues from voting him out of office only by definitively promising to step down at the end of September 1982.[196]

State organs viewed the issue of a critical Catholic pastoral letter on peace with consternation: they believed that such a letter would associate the Catholic Church with certain "negative" developments in the Protestant churches. While the state and party apparatus gladly noted throughout 1982 that the Catholic bishops remained silent, this BBK "silence" spurred accusations within the church, as well as initiatives below the leadership level.[197] Bishop Wanke of Erfurt wrote a new draft that became the basis of a text approved by all bishops in December 1982. The MfS received it only two days before the public reading, without church commentary. As expected, the security organs determined "that the 'pastoral letter' contains several political statements, which—even if formulated with more restraint—are consonant with certain opinions formulated by the Protestant Church in the GDR on the so-called independent peace project."[198] After the public reading on 2 January 1983, a commentary appeared in all East German newspapers on 7 January criticizing the BBK's pastoral letter within the context of a polemic against the West German media. That these media "received, at this time, the blessing of certain dignitaries in the GDR who are steered by Rome does not make the matter any better but impels reflection not only among the mass media of the GDR but also in some dignitaries who are GDR citizens."[199] This commentary marked the first time since 24 December 1965, when an article on the exchange of letters among Polish and German bishops appeared in the official SED paper *Neues Deutschland,* that the SED had reacted publicly to a statement of the Catholic Church in the GDR. Again, it used "GDR citizenship" to implicitly question Catholic bishops' "right to reside" in the GDR if they made political statements allegedly coordinated with "foreign" institutions.

The SED viewed this pastoral letter as an attack, and above all it connected the letter to the change in the chairmanship of the BBK, where "without a doubt a situation of unpredictability in state-church relations [had] emerged."[200] State Secretary Gysi, on the directive of the ZK of the SED, summoned the new chair Meisner to a discussion by on 20 January 1983—purposely scheduled before

Meisner's trip to Rome to receive his cardinalate. The purpose of this "discussion" was to ask Meisner concretely "whether, in light of facts gathered by the MfS, he sought to change the church's course toward the GDR government, which would inevitably have consequences for the relationship between the Catholic Church and the socialist state."[201] A day before the meeting, Prelate Lange called the State Secretariat as the delegate of the BBK and told them, among other things, that he had spoken with Meisner for ninety minutes, but that Meisner's ability to be judicial was limited. The state's note-taker quoted Lange as saying that, in his "humble personal opinion, it would be advisable if it were made clear to the bishop that a change of course would endanger everything."[202]

At the meeting, Gysi threatened Meisner with consequences for the unity of the Diocese of Berlin and his travels in the West, reproaching him with a long "list of sins" about statements and actions. He asked him, among other things: "Does the Catholic Church intend to break from the principles of church-state relations maintained by Cardinal Bengsch and intervene in issues of state politics in the future? . . . Is the Catholic Church not arrogating powers to itself with its criticism of the state's efforts to secure peace that contradict the principle of the separation of church and state, as well as the church's previous understanding of itself?" In this context, the pastoral letter of peace was described as "conscious political aggression."[203] The SED hoped this intimidating discussion would clarify the situation to the bishop of Berlin, who was soon to become cardinal, and bring him back onto the "predictable" course of Cardinal Bengsch.

Meisner's escorts at this discussion, the advisors in Kirchenpolitik, Prelates Lange and Dissemond, also fostered this hope. Even though these two were personal rivals, competing with one another to expand their individual influence in church-political matters, they concurred in their negative judgment of Meisner. Their key positions in church politics and their liaisons with the state apparatus made them extraordinarily well informed about many church activities. They could exploit this information within the GDR system, passing it on or withholding it as necessary to exercise major influence in the church over personnel issues, travel applications, and theological or publicity events.

The state organs (and Meisner's advisors) would have ample opportunity to find "unpredictable behaviors" in the bishop of Berlin and supposed threats to the status quo of the Catholic Church in the GDR, as well as to introduce "learning" processes through its communicative channels. In a brief of 2 February 1983 on Meisner's reactions to his discussion with Gysi, the MfS had already determined by conferring with Meisner's close associates that he viewed the status quo as a given rather than as an accommodation of the state, and made uninformed decisions that could be attributed to his need for recognition. Further discussions with the state secretary would be required to educate the future cardinal in Kirchenpolitik.[204] On 7 November 1983, in a discussion with Hermann Kalb, Lange requested that the "information exchange" between him and the Administrative Office of the State Secretary, as well as the corresponding Berlin centralism, be increased. This was "important for his advisory function to the cardinal" and would "support the cardinal's efforts to discipline the local bishops." This would require the office to exert influence "on important church-state activities at the central level," including activities that local councils occasionally decided "on their own authority."[205]

Prelates Lange and Dissemond represented continuity in personnel from the era of Bengsch to that of Meisner. They repeatedly distanced themselves from some of Meisner's undiplomatic activities and statements, disavowing him in their talks with government posts. One such undiplomatic statement occurred in a lecture on 19 May 1984 at the Catholic Academy in West Berlin. Meisner had remarked that 80 percent of travel applications in the GDR were "lodged simply because of the ideology of actual existing socialism," which "was so gray that the human being suffocates from it and searches for ways to dodge it." Lange and Dissemond organized a campaign to assuage the GDR government that was almost farcical. Lange wrote a submissive declaration dated 25 May 1984, approved by Meisner and passed on by the delegate in the Administrative Office of the State Secretary, in which the cardinal distanced himself from what seemed to be misquotations in the Western media.[206] Prelate Dissemond had told the MfS at the same time that the original lecture did indeed contain these quotes and therefore could not be handed over, and Lange had explained to the Administrative Office that certain parts in the tape recording were unusable, so that Meisner had later inserted corresponding parts from memory. In addition, Dissemond told the MfS that he and Lange hoped that the GDR government would make it clear to Meisner that such conduct could have serious consequences on the relationship between the state and the Catholic Church. Further, they promised to influence Cardinal Meisner, "who often made autocratic decisions, took on unrealistic and extreme positions, and doubted certain instructions and established practical experiences of his close associates as no longer applicable."[207]

Every departure from the usual practices under Bengsch was criticized by the state organs and viewed by Lange and Dissemond as dangerous for the status quo of the church. The state sought to find a common realpolitik between Prelate Lange and the Administrative Office of the State Secretary (mainly Hermann Kalb), as well as between Prelate Dissemond and the MfS (Hans Baethge, Joachim Wiegand), to counterbalance the cardinal's "unpredictability," as well as that of other bishops and unruly parts of the Catholic laity. The state partners of the church negotiators encouraged them to perceive themselves as guarantors of predictability over and over again. Secretly distancing themselves from Meisner, Lange and Dissemond retreated from their diplomatic status as church delegates, partially positioning themselves between the fronts.

However, from May 1987 on the MfS had to accept Meisner's confidant, Josef Michelfeit, the new secretary general of the BBK, as Dissemond's successor, because Meisner rejected the state's desire to retain Lange as the sole negotiator. At the same time, upon Dissemond's official resignation Lange's importance grew, as he became the sole "guarantor of predictability." Lange and Dissemond had engaged in something that state and party functionaries characterized as a "channel" and the MfS had already automatically called "cooperation." When "settlements" and "limiting damage" were not enough, these advisors of the BBK had often encouraged their state interlocutors to explain the situation to Meisner or other bishops.

In the view of state Kirchenpolitiker, Meisner had abandoned the "business fundamentals," namely the line of "political abstinence" practiced by Cardinal Bengsch. Since the early 1970s, the state had come to regard this "political abstinence"—which had become a symbol of church resistance to state demands for public affirmation—as the lesser evil and, in light of the developments in the Protestant churches, the preferred role for churches in the GDR. On 15 December 1980 State Secretary Gysi had told Prelate Dissemond that the church's abstaining from making political statements would be viewed as its loyalty to the state,[208] and guidelines of the Administrative Office of the State Secretary from 4 November 1982 even commended the strategy:

> As long as the Catholic Church leadership wants to pursue its own interests with its former fundamental line of "political abstinence," this will not conflict, at least not considerably, with the interests of the state. This line was never disruptive and is even less so at present and for the foreseeable future. On the contrary, a church that decrees itself "politically abstinent" offers advantages to an extent, even though one must reckon with oppositional detractions, such as the previous and present, ideologically motivated, dismissive attitude by the episcopate in the GDR toward our educational policy.[209]

When Cardinal Meisner fell under the critical purview of the state and political organs, the director of the Working Group for Church Affairs at the ZK, Rudi Bellmann, wrote a nostalgic comment "On the 'Business Fundamentals' of the Relations of the Leadership of the Catholic Church in the GDR to the State under Cardinal Bengsch." He did not judge the political abstinence of the Catholic Church unreservedly as positive but described it as a "sustainable platform for a constitutional and transparent relationship." Bellmann did regret that Bengsch had avoided every public opportunity to support the state and its politics, yet he recognized that it had the positive effect of generally putting an end to "attempts at intervention in state matters, as well as demonstrative, provocative activities that incited the public." Bengsch's principles, Bellmann wrote, consisted in "'not marketing' questions and problems that concerned his relations with the state and society of the GDR, but quietly carrying out existing oppositional positions." In this way, church-state relations were carved out in a "predictable and objective" way.[210]

Bellmann's remarks, however, were hardly more than mere nostalgia. In 1984, the BBK had announced a GDR-wide Catholic Assembly for 1987 without consulting state organs or providing them with advance information. This constituted further evidence that the church had acquired a new consciousness and abandoned these "business fundamentals."[211] According to state reports, Meisner wanted to "demonstratively enlarge and expand" church positions, tried "to ignore the state order," and persisted in a "distancing . . . that occasionally turns into an affront."[212] Further, he "constantly" distanced himself "in a demonstrative way" that had an entirely different quality from the actions of his predecessors. He had lost his "sense of reality and any sense of proportion for the politically doable"—and did not behave as another unnamed "high-ranking Catholic Church representative" had, whom Gysi quoted as having said: "Support the state, and it will support you."[213]

Aside from ritualized but ultimately empty threats to limit the church's sphere of activity, however, the state and party organs could exert influence only through personal channels. The state could not carry out its threats because doing so would endanger its reputation in the West. Consequently, it could not call upon the "business fundamentals," and it made no serious attempt to impose sanctions on any sector. What the state organs described as "accommodation" and "advance support" for the church (for example, in recognizing the formal cross-border unity of the Diocese of Berlin, allowing travel and import opportunities, a valuta program for nonstandard buildings) could only be called off at a high cost to foreign policy, which the GDR leadership very much shied away from in the 1980s.

Cardinal Meisner behaved in a similarly dismissive fashion regarding an inaugural visit with Honecker as the chair of the State Council after being elected chair of the BBK. For a long time, he tied the possibility of such a visit to the condition that a GDR functionary provide a publishable, quotable interview on the voluntariness of the Jugendweihe. Although the Administrative Office of the State Secretary informed him that such an interview could be done, the SED leadership could never actually decide to take such a step, so the inaugural visit never took place. Additionally, Cardinal Meisner attempted in 1986 to invite the pope to visit the Dresden Catholic Assembly, at which the cardinal would also have met the general secretary of the SED for the first time. The SED leadership viewed such an implausible request—which failed to consider the imposition on Honecker, who would have to travel outside the GDR capital to visit the pope deep on his own territory—as unacceptable and provocative. Not until 1987 did things smooth out a bit, when both the state and church leadership explored the prospect of the pope visiting the GDR some time between 1989 and 1991.

With the celebrations of the 750th anniversary of the city of Berlin in 1987, Meisner was eventually poised to meet Honecker. The cardinal had to address the issue of whether to participate in the official festivities in both parts of the city—on 23 April in West Berlin and on 23 October in East Berlin. In a 19 January 1987 memo, Prelate Lange had expressly advocated that Meisner participate in both events because doing so would "improve the climate" and, since it was possible he would encounter Honecker, fulfill a precondition for the papal visit.[214] While Meisner refused to meet with the chair of the State Council before the act of state in East Berlin without an interview on the Jugendweihe,[215] Prelate Lange argued, on 15 February 1987, that they should stage a symbolic encounter during the event in the Palace of the Republic on 23 October 1987.[216] In making his case in a memo to Cardinal Meisner, Lange maintained that although the GDR was still an ideological state that dispensed with "legitimacy in the sense of being supported by a majority of its people," it still seemed "to enjoy a similar de facto recognition . . . domestically as well as in the rest of the world." He continued: "At least the existence of the state as such is no longer debated; but with that it has become a factor for which—more willy than nilly—allowance is made." Lange held that a meeting between Honecker and Meisner would be highly interesting. Yet the event's presentation to the public would be decisive, and Meisner and the church would have the upper hand in this "through our direct access to the most important Western media people, who would certainly not ignore our interpretation."

The meeting itself was arranged to seem coincidental: on 23 October 1987 State Secretary Gysi led Cardinal Meisner into a restaurant upon entering the Palace of the Republic, where the ZK working group leader Bellmann appeared to inquire whether Honecker might greet the cardinal personally. Finally the chair of the State Council turned up and conversed with Meisner for about five minutes.[217] In Meisner's account of it, the encounter "was not necessarily intentional, but certainly foreseeable." Honecker expressed his satisfaction with the unity of the Diocese of Berlin, praised the pope, and spoke "with admiration" of the Catholic Assembly in Dresden because "he knew that there were over 100,000 participants." After the break in the ballroom, Honecker introduced Meisner to West German Minister-President Oskar Lafontaine of the Saarland and Mayors Klaus von Dohnanyi of Hamburg and Klaus Wedemeier of Bremen, who were in attendance, describing him as "our cardinal." Meisner thus believed he had gotten around a formal inaugural visit and had minimized "political 'abuse.'" When West German CDO politicians criticized this meeting, he remarked that "[i]t cannot just be the church's responsibility to use its resources to affect and attain in politics what (Western) politics even seems incapable of."[218]

However, this symbolic encounter between Meisner and Honecker—held shortly after Honecker's visit to the Federal Republic in 1987—was only one of many episodes in the tense relationship between the state organs and the Catholic Church. SED Kirchenpolitiker continued to view many of the BBK's actions under Cardinal Meisner as departures from the "business fundamentals"—for example, its decisions to announce major public events without consulting the state, to strengthen international connections by inviting theologians and bishops from West and East to events in the GDR, and to thematize the position of the Catholics and their constructive and critical treatment of society through pastoral letters.

An important step toward overcoming the "political abstinence" of the Catholic Church was the Catholic Assembly in 1987 in Dresden. Despite many church disputes over its preparation and some significant confrontations with the government posts behind the scenes, the mere fact of the meeting itself primed a stronger Catholic self-confidence. The collective experience involved up to

100,000 participants meeting in Dresden between 10 and 12 July 1987 to discuss church and societal topics via 3,000 delegates in closed sessions.[219] In a letter to Cardinal Meisner of 15 July 1987, Jens Reich, a molecular biologist in Berlin, conveyed his personal euphoria over Dresden, which was largely representative:

> I must thank you for your address at the celebratory mass on the large meadow in Dresden. It gave courage and direction to the twofold life in the diaspora and addressed the problems and boundaries of our cooperation with the political system, the willingness to cooperate in state and society (with limits of conscience: 'without having to follow another star . . .'), but also the unpaid bonds of guilt: the absent inner peace, paternalism, curfew, discrimination in education, etc. Special thanks, as well, for naming these in a manner free of excitement . . . The church congress was a grand celebration and a grand event![220]

After the Catholic Assembly, the state organs regarded its outcome as positive on the surface. They had feared "high-profile, negative activities," as well as echoes in the Western media about the "church from down below" that still resounded in the wake of the church congress of the regional Protestant Church of Berlin-Brandenburg in East Berlin three weeks before. The Catholic Church had ultimately forced the Catholic Assembly on the state organs by making and publicly declaring an autonomous decision without briefing them first. Although they had earnestly considered prohibiting the assembly, they abandoned such a course out of concern for foreign policy consequences. All they could do was focus on mitigating the damage so that the event would be justified from the outside as a generous demonstration of tolerance.

At the same time, some state agents held isolated hopes that the assembly would create "new opportunities for 'gently pulling' the officeholders to socialist society," as Andreas Graff, department chair of the Dresden SED district leadership, put it, because of the cooperative, local experiences they had had in its preparation. Yet these proved to be a fallacy.[221] The leadership of the Diocese of Dresden-Meißen, under Bishop Schaffran and Vicar-General Hermann Joseph Weisbender, had direct discussions with the SED leadership in Dresden during their last years in office up to the resignation of the sick bishop after his seventy-fifth birthday on 4 July 1987.[222] This departure from the BBK line of avoiding such contacts with SED party organs occurred in 1986 and 1987, when Bishop Schaffran twice met with the first secretary of the SED district leadership, Hans Modrow,[223] and Weisbender met with associated party organs. Both the state and the church had repeatedly aired the idea of maintaining direct contacts with this relatively open district secretary until agreements were reached during the visit by the chair of the Soviet Advisory Council for Religious Affairs, Konstantin Chartchev, at a multilateral meeting of Warsaw Pact state secretaries for church affairs in Dresden in June 1985.

But under the new diocesan leadership of Dresden-Meißen as of 1988, this line of discussion came to a halt through the conscious passivity of the church.

The direct contacts of the years 1986 and 1987 did not—in form or content—constitute a particular course of Kirchenpolitik toward the state that the church public could have perceived. Rather, they were acts of two ambitious Catholic clerics of the older generation at the head of the diocese, who counted Hans Modrow and his colleagues among the rare species of "reasonable Communists," and who believed they could attain a stable, and even cooperative, modus vivendi between the party and the church in the Dresden region as a sort of a personal legacy, and to this end ignore traditional church regulations regarding such discussions. They were not very conscious of the state's "differentiation" intentions. For this reason, the BBK and its advisors in Berlin watched Schaffran and Weisbender with at least as much skepticism as the Politburo of the SED observed the Dresden district leadership, which it suspected of "perestroika" under Modrow, a known Gorbachev sympathizer.

In contrast to such personal maneuvers, during this time an earnest philosophical dialogue began between Christians and Marxists after a scientific symposium on "Society and Ethical Values" had taken place in Budapest on 8–10 October 1986. A joint symposium of the Roman Papal Council on Nonbelievers and the Hungarian Academy of Sciences, it constituted the largest and most meaningful dialogical meeting between Catholic and Marxist scholars up to that point.[224] Aside from the atheism researchers Olof Klohr of Rostock-Warnemünde and Wolfgang Kliem of Berlin, Professor of Philosophy Konrad Feiereis from Erfurt also participated. It was the first time that a Catholic theologian from the GDR had engaged in such discussions. His contribution, "Cohabitation and Cooperation of Christians and Marxists in Society," gave a detailed interpretation of historical and current Marxist-Leninist tendencies toward atheism and looked ahead to prospects for a dialogue in mutual tolerance.[225] This was an innovative approach, especially since the Paulus Society in the mid and late 1960s, by order of the bishops, had had to get by without Catholic participants from the GDR in its efforts to promote dialogue.

After the 1986 gathering, Feiereis gave numerous lectures in the GDR on such dialogue and also led discussions with Marxists, some of whom argued astonishingly openly. Feiereis himself grew more critical as the state became increasingly intransigent in 1988. This did not remain hidden from the MfS, which monitored the dialogue and its protagonists with suspicion. State organs at least wanted to hinder an all-too-public discussion by preventing Feiereis from publishing his contributions in the GDR.[226] The Marxist theoreticians, however, whom the state tolerated, could publish their ideas, which were usually abstracted from the concrete situation in the GDR. Starting in 1988, talk of "Marxist religious studies" emerged.[227] The "Theory and History of Religion and Atheism" now was to be taught for the first time in the course of the SED's year-long apprenticeship program, and in 1989, the GDR Ministry of Higher and Technical Education established a five-year plan for the postgraduate study of this subject.[228] Overall, however, these peripheral activities remained irrelevant to the relationship between the church and the state, the more so as the state course toward the churches once again grew more severe, ultimately culminating in open conflicts.

A significant event around which these conflicts ignited was the Ecumenical Convocation for Peace, Justice and the Conservation of Creation (Ecumenical Convocation), whose first plenary assembly took place in Dresden in February 1988. At the end of 1987, the BBK had decided—after lengthy internal debates—to send twenty-five Catholic delegates to participate in it. The initiative for an ecumenical convocation of all Christian churches in the GDR came from the municipal ecumenical convocation in Dresden on 13 February 1986. It referred to the ideas of the World Council of Churches, the pope, and above all the West German physicist Carl Friedrich von Weizsäcker. Protestant regional bishops, especially Johannes Hempel of Dresden, approached the Catholic Church expecting it to participate. The church was "challenged like never before from the side of the ecumenical bodies of the GDR on the topic of 'peace.'"[229] In a discussion between Cardinal Meisner and the regional Protestant bishop of Thuringia, Werner Leich, who was chair of the Alliance of Protestant Churches in the GDR (BEK), Meisner expressed the Catholic Church's fears of instrumentalization as well as its reservations about political tendencies in the Protestant churches. Still, Meisner and Leich agreed to establish a collective working group to clarify church-state issues.[230] In a greeting before the synod of the BEK on 19 September 1986, Bishop Wanke emphasized that it was important for the churches

> to reach greater unity not only in the area of teaching but also in the area of action . . . In light of the great problems of humankind, Christianity is challenged to speak with one voice. The graveness of the problems, the endeavor for happiness and the success of human life and cohabitation, for freedom, justice and peace, for the maintenance of our environment and the earth for future generations—all of this commandingly calls us to take collective action as Christians and as well-meaning people in general . . . Therefore, I, as a Catholic bishop, would welcome it if we succeeded at uniting the voices of Christians in this country in an impressive testimony of peace in freedom and justice and truth. At the end of such a long road or process, a clear and unambiguous church testimony must certainly stand with which no other extrinsic interests can interfere.

To these remarks—unusual for the Catholic Church—Wanke added that Cardinal Meisner had signaled to Leich that the Catholic Church was "fundamentally open" to the ecumenical convocation.[231]

The BBK was still uncertain, however. On 2 December 1986 it decided that, in order to keep all options open, the Catholic Church should participate in the preparations for the Ecumenical Convocation in an observing capacity.[232] When the Association of Christian Churches in the GDR, to which the Catholic Church also belonged only as an observer, officially invited the church to the Ecumenical Convocation, a decision finally had to be made. Again and again, Catholic parishes, especially Dresden, and individual priests and laypersons pressured the BBK to participate fully.[233] A discussion group in the parish of St. Paulus in Dresden-Plauen asked the BBK in a letter of May 1987 "whether we should watch how others toil at extinguishing the burning house?"[234] The expectations from below and the Protestant churches' decision put the Catholic bishops under pressure to act. Between the end of October and the beginning of December 1987, the BBK held several advisory meetings, and ultimately, on 15 November, it made the preliminary decision to allow the church's working group Iustitia et Pax, which it had established in 1983, to participate as Catholic delegates, provided certain conditions were met.[235] The delegation would consist of twenty-five people including expert advisors, and would be led by Monsignor Dieter Grande. A unanimous decision at the BBK session on 2 December 1987 made this formal, although the idea of delegating the working group *en bloc* ran into criticism within the church, as other Catholics had been excluded. Additionally, the BBK stipulated that there be a Catholic representative in the Ecumenical Convocation's presidium, a special Catholic spokesperson, and the option of a Catholic exit "if the freedom of the delegates no longer appears to be secured because of influence by powers outside of the participating churches and church communities."[236] With this decision, the already crumbling fundamentals of the Catholic Church's political abstinence in the GDR were ultimately washed away. From 1988 onward, the mechanisms of state-church channels of communication and of their monopolies in state-church relations at the central level began, step by step, to falter as well.

Perestroika

Developments in the USSR and Consequences for the SED

At a time when three secretaries general of the Communist Party of the Soviet Union (CPSU) in a row had been ill, leaving a vacuum at the top of the party, Erich Honecker was bestowed with a particular role within the socialist camp. Nothing was more untimely for this role than the Twenty-Seventh Party Congress of the CPSU in February 1986, when the new secretary general, Mikhail S. Gorbachev, presented a sensational program in his report of 25 February. This program encompassed the "acceleration of social-economic development," the "democratization of society," and "socialist self-government," as well as a new "foreign policy strategy" for ending the arms race.[237] The party congress gave rise to an alternating international and national dynamic, such that Gorbachev took on a global role associated with many hopes without necessarily being aware of the actual processes unleashed in his mission to institute "perestroika." The expectations of the West and of the reform powers in the CPSU, as well as developments in Hungary and Poland, propelled the secretary general forward much faster than he had expected.

These developments generated anger and fear in the SED leadership under Erich Honecker, which sought to seal itself off from them. The Politburo and the ZK grew increasingly worried that the new leadership of the CPSU, with its policies toward the West, could undermine the stability of the GDR and, in the long term, put its very existence up for negotiation. Starting in the fall of 1986 at the latest, Honecker distanced himself from the course of perestroika and from Gorbachev personally, to whom he unambiguously expressed the fears that the GDR leadership had regarding the new course from Moscow on 3 October 1986: "It is important for us to fight on one, and not on two, fronts."[238] Honecker's and other SED functionaries' aversion to perestroika as a threat to the stability of the GDR transformed into a blatant haughtiness vis-à-vis the "backward" Soviet Union. They monitored "perestroika" tendencies within the SED, for instance in the district leadership of Dresden under Modrow, with suspicion, caustically attacking them within the party. In an interview with the West German magazine *Stern* in April 1987, Kurt Hager, the member of the SED Politburo responsible for culture and science, had already tried to set the SED's public course toward Soviet developments. He compared perestroika in the USSR with changing wallpaper, asking rhetorically "whether one must repaper his apartment" just because his neighbor has done so.[239]

To the SED, the USSR henceforth showed itself to be a state that put the GDR in danger of destabilization, while West Germany—in its government, the SPD, and business—seemed almost full of useful stabilizers by comparison. In 1987 Honecker realized his lifelong dream of making an official state visit to the Federal Republic in order to emphasize German two-state status and the international sovereignty of the GDR. The Soviet Union was suspicious of such a visit, intended to counter that of Federal Chancellor Helmut Schmidt to the GDR in December 1981, and managed to prevent one until 1986, when Honecker finally prevailed using his sovereignty.

In the run-up to the visit, Honecker did not want anything to happen that might have led to a cancellation. For this reason, the SED in 1987 portrayed itself to the outside world for quite some time as unusually tolerant, while the MfS had to monitor and operate all the more intensively behind the scenes, especially in church matters. It did not halt activities at the church congress of the Regional Protestant Church of Berlin-Brandenburg in June 1987, but it intervened severely against the same types of activities just months later. In this context, local state organs generously supported the organization of the Catholic Assembly in Dresden in July 1987. Moreover, *Neues Deutschland* and GDR television covered the event with unusual breadth.

On 28 August 1987 *Neues Deutschland* published "The Fight of the Ideologies and Collective Security," a dialogue paper developed by a joint commission of the SED and the SPD; three days later, SPD politicians discussed it on live television in the GDR.[240] In September 1987, thousands of people were allowed to protest in the official, GDR-wide Olof Palme Peace March and the Pilgrimage Route between the Zion Church and Gethsemane Church. Pacifist and oppositional groups were able to display their posters uncensored and unhindered. Honecker visited Bonn, Essen, Saarbrücken, and Munich on 7–11 September 1987. In the end, the GDR leadership viewed the mere fact of the visit as an important success; furthermore, it had not had to make political concessions in the agreement that Honecker signed while in West Germany.[241]

Yet the SED leadership had to pay a price for refusing to accept perestroika, as well as for allowing a hint of tolerance before and during Honecker's FRG visit: an oppositional movement began to spread. Primarily housed in Protestant Church facilities, it was able to draw attention to itself with fliers and self-printed newspapers. Anxious to clamp down on these activities, the MfS finally had its day on 24 November 1987, when the SED leadership allowed it to deal with opposition housed in the "Umweltbibliothek" of the Protestant Zion Parish in Berlin by storming it, closing it, and making arrests. Several weeks before, the state organs had passively looked on as right-wing extremist skinheads attacked and violently ransacked a punk concert in the Zion Church. The Anti-Nazi League, founded by those who had been attacked, prompted the MfS to its repressive action, which immediately triggered solemn vigils, peace prayers, and demands for the release of those arrested.

After several prisoners had been released and new arrests had been made, the situation escalated when planned demonstrations by oppositional groups on the margins of the official memorial march for Karl Liebknecht and Rosa Luxemburg led the state to "take in" around 120 people. Several of them were either deported to the West or received a fixed-term travel visa after imprisonment and long negotiations between the state and the Protestant Church. By February 1988, the MfS backpedaled again internally and stated that its "main line" for combating these tendencies should be "political." On 23 March 1988, HA XX/4 claimed in statements made in preparing for an advisory meeting with the Polish state security organs that the measures it took after 17 January 1988 had been "forced" on it.[242] The number of exit travel applications now rose dramatically; applicants got organized and used orchestrated campaigns to generate publicity.[243] By the end of 1987, around 112,000 applications had been submitted, whereas there had been only about 78,000 at the end of 1986. Among the 112,000 applicants were 52,800 skilled workers and 11,500 individuals with tertiary or technical qualifications, and 87 percent were under forty years of age.[244]

Meanwhile, the state parties in Poland and, above all, Hungary had begun reform processes. It was an obvious consequence of perestroika in the Soviet Union that the USSR no longer wanted to interfere with the internal matters of its alliance partners; with that, Moscow's Brezhnev Doctrine of limited sovereignty of socialist European states became obsolete. By June 1989 Hungary was already far removed from the other socialist countries. People like Honecker regarded it as having arrived in the "bourgeois camp" with no hope of a reversal. In the same month in Poland, Solidarnošč won the elections held in agreement with the government hands down, whereupon power in Warsaw was divided. Honecker and the party organs in the GDR tried to seal themselves off from these developments. On 3 March 1988, when Honecker met with Leich in his capacity as chair of the Conference of Church Leaders of the Alliance of Protestant Churches in the GDR, Honecker made clear that the GDR solved "its problems differently than other socialist countries . . . Some thought [that] with perestroika in the Soviet Union, general freedom has broken out, but that is not the case. Hopes that they linked to perestroika and glasnost lost any foundation with regard to the GDR."[245] Henceforth, Honecker propagated a socialism "in the colors of the GDR"—for example, at the conference of the ZK of the SED on 1 December 1988.[246] At the same time, the Twelfth Party Congress of the SED was to be moved up by a year to 15–19 May 1990, in order to come before the next party congress of the CPSU and to minimize the effects of the worsening health of Honecker, who was again running for secretary general. On the occasion of a conference of the Thomas Müntzer Committee on 18 January 1989, Honecker announced that "the wall . . . will still exist in 50 and even 100 years if the reasons for it have not yet disappeared."[247]

The Ecumenical Convocation for Peace, Justice, and the Conservation of Creation and the Failure of Kirchenpolitik Mechanisms

The mechanisms of influence and differentiation that had been in play between the church and state for decades—the targeted talks with church representatives that vacillated between threats and accommodations—began to falter at the end of 1987. Developments would soon spin out of the control of both churches' long-standing negotiators with the MfS and the Administrative Office of the State Secretary for Church Affairs. Opposition could increasingly be found in Protestant circles, and unfolding events now often contradicted church leaders' positions. Catholic defenders of the status quo in the church-state relationship had to witness how not only the delegates of the Ecumenical Convocation but also growing numbers of Catholics oriented themselves toward the developments in the Protestant churches or took an active part in them. The state's threats and exhortations often meant little because church partners were hardly in a position to enforce the state's expectations to guarantee a conflict-free church-state relationship, and at least some of them were no longer willing to even try. If, on the other hand, the state itself took repressive measures to underscore its threats, it only exacerbated the situation, and the GDR leadership descended further into a defensive posture.

The state's perception that positions in the Catholic Church were "converging" with those of the Protestant churches became a constant issue. The MfS became aware through its agent "Erika" in the Caritas Association of the Diocese of Dresden-Meißen that the working group Iustitia et Pax had compiled a "procedural manual" for the Ecumenical Convocation.[248] The director of HA XX/4, Colonel Joachim Wiegand, stated in his letter to the MfS district administration in Dresden on 10 December 1987 that "the suggestions of the paper essentially coincide with analogous demands of Protestant circles," and so "the working group 'Iustitia et Pax' is becoming an operative focus."

After the arrests and expatriations that occurred in the context of the Lux-emburg-Liebknecht demonstration of 17 January 1988, activities both at the base and in the leadership of the Protestant churches gave rise to inquiries in the Catholic Church about whether a church statement was needed. For this reason, on 1 February 1988 Cardinal Meisner directed a letter to the priests and ministries in the eastern part of the Diocese of Berlin expressing concern for the people who "want to leave their Heimat" and those "in danger of being forced out of their *Heimat*."[249] He criticized the language used in the GDR press and schools, having expected "forms of statements and expressions" that would enable Catholic Christians to "exhibit social responsibility." Finally, Meisner wished Protestant leaders "longed-for success" in their efforts to mediate. But this let-ter achieved notoriety on account of passages that were highlighted by Prelate Lange to the Administrative Office of the State Secretary, as well as in the East Berlin church newspaper *St. Hedwigsblatt,* and therefore also in the West Ger-man press: Meisner had stated that the "intercessional worship services" in the Protestant churches served "mainly informational purposes and political goals." For this reason, such a service could not be described as a "worship service" but, as it "no longer first and foremost serves to honor God, then, in our Catholic thinking, it is a questionable undertaking. In the end, it must have a damaging effect on the service of the church."[250] These statements notwithstanding, the ZK believed Meisner's letter displayed a "'process of opening up' toward convergence with positions of the Protestant churches with complete disregard for Catholic fundamentals."[251]

At the latest, this "process of opening up" began to find expression at the first plenary assembly of the Ecumenical Convocation on 12–15 February 1988 in Dresden. There, frank discussions took place among the delegates in the working groups and in the plenary. To be sure, the churches still had reservations about dealing with one another and the oppositional groups that had assembled in a separate "meeting center" in Dresden. Yet gradually, in the working groups and advisory meetings that convened between the two plenary sessions, a dynamic unfolded that permitted the delegates to cooperate more and more, regardless of their Christian denomination. On the Catholic side, though, Prelate Lange led the battle for his policy of "predictability" and "political abstinence" with the Administrative Office of the State Secretary for Church Affairs in what was for him an "inconsolable" situation. When he suggested that pulling the Catholic Church out of the Ecumenical Convocation could be an option, the GDR state hoped that it would be able to torpedo the assembly unofficially by getting indi-vidual churches to resign.[252]

In the absence of other intermediaries between the people and the state, the Protestant churches had taken on the role of the people's advocate regarding problems within East German society in the Western and GDR public. This occurred at the latest on 17 January 1988, when Protestant representatives took public positions and made attempts to mediate. A significant expression of these problems was the summit talk between Honecker and Leich on 3 March 1988. During its session on 8 March 1988, the Politburo spent a good deal of time on this controversial conversation. It determined that State Secretary Gysi should "work out suggestions for curbing the church leadership's presumption that it can exercise state functions."[253]

It was no coincidence that on 10 March 1988, Prelate Lange handed over a "verbal note" by Cardinal Meisner from the date of the lecture, "only in his capacity as bishop of Berlin," to the Office of the State Secretary.[254] Meisner remarked that the events in Berlin since November 1987 had also "caused dismay and unrest [in the] Catholic Church parishes": "The resulting circumstance confuses Catholic Christians who know that their duty in the church is to advocate for the common welfare in the various areas of life and work." For this reason, Meisner asked for "legal rules" for approving visitor trips and admission to secondary and tertiary schools, for applications for travel permits, and for a civil service alternative to military conscription. The presentation of such a verbal note was without precedent in the Catholic Church. The ZK explained this "foray" as the Catholic Church's attempt not to seem "idle" in light of Protestant activities. Peter Heinrich, director of the head office in the Administrative Office of the State Secretary, was to speak to Lange and downplay the verbal note "as an internally and confidentially communicated statement of opinion."[255] In the first discussion between Heinrich and Lange on 11 March 1988, Lange told Heinrich that the Catholic Church had felt "at home in this state, in this society" since the 1987 Catholic Assembly in Dresden, and that this event finally acknowledged the current state of affairs, overcoming the idea that history would "turn out differently." Henceforth, Lange continued, the Catholic Church wanted to consciously "commit itself to tasks" in the GDR, which was why the verbal note was a "very constructive paper" expressing the "Catholic Church's supportive care of the state and society." The church did not want "to leave the field to the Protestant Church," especially as the latter proceeded with its actions in a much "too undifferentiated" manner. At the same time, Lange assured Heinrich that this verbal note was confidential and would not be published, and that Meisner expected an answer from the state secretary for church affairs. The government posts, though, did not appreciate this "offer," and at the end of April they told the Catholic Church that Honecker had already provided all the relevant answers in his conversation with Leich on 3 March 1988.[256]

A few days later, the verbal note had already lost all relevance because Prelate Lange felt he had to use all means at his disposal to "dispel" a "conflict" in the church-state relationship and reestablish "predictability": Cardinal Meisner had given a sermon in the "Maria Frieden" church in Mariendorf in West Berlin on 5 May 1988, referring to Berlin's "desecration" by the "Wall," in which he also had rejected "class hatred and race hatred." The Catholic news agency in West Berlin had registered these lines for the West German press. Just as foreseeable as Hermann Kalb's aggressive reaction were Lange's frustration (he referred to Meisner's behavior as a "relapse") and his attempts at appeasement.

In Lange's explanation of Meisner's sermon, which he had handed over to Kalb on 30 May 1988, he remarked: "It would be good if the doubts raised by this regarding Catholic reliability could be dispelled, because, if nothing else, [this reliability] passed the test at the Catholic Assembly in Dresden; for if the papal visit is really to come to pass, then it is indispensable that we work together with reliability and trust."[257] In fact, a papal visit was already in the works for 1991. The Politburo of the SED had agreed to it "in principle" in its session on 23 August 1988,[258] which the new state secretary for church affairs, Kurt Löffler, told Cardinal Meisner on 30 August 1988. The Vatican was interested in a "pastoral visit" but did not want to accept any preconditions.[259] An open question was whether West Berlin should be included in the itinerary: while the church insisted upon this, the state organs wanted to avoid it at all costs. Although the basic framework of the visit had been set out on both sides by the end of 1988, no concrete negotiations on the papal visit would take place in 1989.[260]

Aside from Meisner's repeated demand for a quotable public statement on the voluntary nature of the Jugendweihe, the central diplomatic relations of the Catholic Church continued to be conducted behind closed doors without addressing smoldering societal conflicts. Tensions between the SED and the Protestant churches, on the other hand, became greater and greater. In advisory sessions of the Working Group for Church Affairs, all churches were referred to as the "spear tips" of the Western "adversary" in their own country. They were said to have assumed a "political mandate" and a "representative role" vis-à-vis the state because they supposedly called for the "necessity of decisive and substantial changes to society."[261] As for the Catholic Church, the organs of the SED and the state were now exclusively interested in its political abstinence so as not to have to confront both churches at the same time. In the summer of 1988, the ZK declared that the "opening" of the Catholic Church, "as in the Protestant Church, is not worth pursuing." The Catholic Church was not to promote a "process of opening," but rather, keep everything "as it is."[262] But the second plenary meeting of the Ecumenical Convocation in Magdeburg on 8–11 October 1988 continued the process of Catholic convergence with positions of the Protestant Church. Lange and the MfS had hoped that the Catholic bishops would end their participation in the proceedings due to the working group texts of the Ecumenical Convocation in Magdeburg, in order not to endorse the course of the Protestant churches, but these hopes were unfounded. On 25 November 1988 Lange asked for permission to speak for the Catholic Church, even requesting official help from Kalb, who immediately forwarded it to the MfS contact person Peter Heinrich at the Administrative Office:

> Dear Peter! The Catholic Church leadership would be thankful for clues as to whether, and if so in what areas, cooperation is developing with the Protestants on the church's basis whose goals have negative roots. The Catholic Church intends—because of the

previous results of the Ecumenical Convocation—to work against such tendencies in order to keep its local churches out of "misappropriations."[263]

By 26 October 1988 the MfS had "actively registered" all but 34 of the 175 delegates, advisors, and international guests of the Ecumenical Convocation in its files with entries filled with personal details.[264] According to an "analytical overview" of 27 December 1988, 150 people had already been registered, 48 of whom had been directly "processed" in Operative Personenkontrolle (OPK) or Operative Control of Individuals and Operativer Vorgang (OV), or Operative Measures against Individuals.[265] The direct influence of the MfS on the Ecumenical Convocation was small, however, because very few informers were present among the delegates. In the Catholic delegation, comprised of thirty-one people after subsequent nominations, there was not a single one.[266] The constant discussions of the MfS and other government posts with leaders from the church and individual delegates could no longer influence the trajectory of things, which had taken on a dynamic of its own.

The Department of International Relations in the Administrative Office of the State Secretary implied on 19 January 1989 that the Ecumenical Convocation arrogated a "political mandate" to itself. The working texts were said to "defame" the social relations in the GDR: "As a whole, they are politically negative checklists of demands on the socialist state, which constitute the concrete enactment of the churches' assumed role as representatives." The Catholic Church, though "more distanced," still contributed to " this line."[267] The Protestant Church Department of the Administrative Office formulated it even more clearly on 23 January 1989, with an appreciation for historical developments: "It is new for the attitude of the Catholic Church and the small free churches and religious communities in the conciliatory process that they obviously aid attacks against the GDR. With that, for the first time since the Reformation, a consensus has been reached, though not a theological but a political one."[268] The state's Kirchenpolitiker anxiously awaited the concluding plenary assembly of the Ecumenical Convocation in April 1989.

After Kurt Löffler took over as the state secretary in July 1988, he drafted a "conception to offensively assert the policies of the party and the government in the sphere of churches and religious communities,"[269] but he could only realize it on paper. Because the Politburo's intransigence and lack of will to reform remained constant and escalated to the perception of a state of siege on eastern and western fronts, the state organs of Kirchenpolitik had to barricade themselves in the fortress and try to steer the outposts. In an advisory meeting on 16 January 1989 in the ZK of the SED, Werner Jarowinsky ordered the Administrative Office of the State Secretary for Church Affairs to maintain a "constant on-call status" to "develop . . . a bearing that derives from an ostensible style of representation."[270] As of January 1989 the Administrative Office also had at its disposal a computer and an Operative and Status Center (Operativ- und Lagezentrum, officially abbreviated OLZ), which functioned as the "administrative center" for the "coordination of operative-political actions with the uniform implementation of state policies in church affairs."[271]

A brief of the SED district leadership of Dresden from 22 March 1989 characterized the "politicization and the misuse of the churches" as "far advanced." According to the brief, the Protestant Church had withdrawn from discussions with the state and presented an "organized" front of ignorance about developments—such as the "typical example of its representative role"—especially with respect to the Ecumenical Convocation.[272] A substantial number of state representatives and MfS officers traveled to the third and final plenary assembly of the Ecumenical Convocation on 26–30 April 1989 in Dresden. Löffler wanted to speak to both Protestant and Catholic bishops and threaten them with grave consequences if the Ecumenical Convocation papers at issue were approved. On the Protestant side, he was able to get hold of Regional Bishop Johannes Hempel, who afterward, on 30 April 1989 before the forum of the Ecumenical Convocation delegates, summarized his talk with Löffler and rebuffed the state's attempts to apply pressure, further stimulating the delegates to approve the compiled texts.[273] The state quickly organized an appearance by the former bishop Gerhard Schaffran, who was very ill, so that he might influence individual Catholic delegates in Dresden-Strehlen, but this had little effect.[274]

The twelve texts resulting from the Ecumenical Convocation were politically quite explosive and made blatant demands for social change—especially the third paper entitled "More Justice in the GDR." As expected, the texts could not be published with a state printing permit. Instead, they were reproduced and distributed in church institutions across the country. In a first attempt to take stock of the situation on 30 April 1989, HA XX/4 concluded that the situation had grown dire:

> With the antagonistic and aggressive powers' assertion of themselves, the achievement of consensus among the base powers, as well as among the churches and church leading forces, the documentation of the achieved breadth of the first ever inter-denominational convocation in this sort of ecumenism in the GDR over the period of more than one year, a new level and a new quality of church procedure was attained.[275]

At the presentation of the concluding documents to the church delegates on 30 April 1989 in Dresden's Kreuzkirche, Bishop Huhn emphasized that the Ecumenical Convocation had shown "that Christians in our country would like to give answers from the depths of their Christian faith and out of reliance on their Christian hope to questions and problems which are not to be ignored. 'Open the windows!' Yes! No return to the ghetto, but also no selling out of what is genuinely Christian."[276] On the same day, Monsignor Grande remarked, as the Catholic delegate in the steering committee of the Ecumenical Convocation at the concluding press conference, that "a new, general thrust has developed that will bring about a change of self-perception and give rise to alertness and hope."[277]

The results of the Ecumenical Convocation, which were successively approved by the leadership of the churches and found their way into church parishes and groups, accelerated the death throes of the state's Kirchenpolitik. Kirchenpolitiker still attacked individuals, holding "talks" to educate and intimidate church leaders and delegates, but this tactic was counterproductive. The absolute intransigence of the SED leadership regarding reforms and changes in society, as the Ecumenical Convocation had called for, could only produce "failures of Kirchenpolitik" and further fuel the discontented mood. Especially in the paper "More Justice in the GDR," state and party organs saw "a platform for those who want escalation and are looking for confrontation." They arrived at this appraisal at an advisory meeting on 23 May 1989 in Leipzig, at which Peter Krausser from the Working Group for Church Affairs at the ZK met with church affairs employees of the SED district leaderships. They also determined that the churches essentially held "the uniform notion . . . that changes in the GDR must be brought about like in the Soviet Union." The Ecumenical Convocation had revealed "how superficial our approaches are": instead of retaining state control, they had put the churches in the driver's seat.[278]

The state's Kirchenpolitik had long been completely intertwined with the general development in the GDR as the reform pressure from below, communicating with the reform bottleneck from above, allowed the number of exit permit applications to climb. Moreover, as of July 1989, GDR citizens eager to leave their country occupied the embassies in Hungary, and then also in Poland and the CSSR. More and more East Germans fled to Austria and then the Federal Republic through the western Hungarian border, which had hardly been secured since May 1989. The Politburo's blatant sympathy for the brutal suppression of the Chinese democratic movement in Beijing at the beginning of June 1989, the SED's demonstrative backing of the Romanian ruler Nicolae Ceausescu, and a pithy speech by People's Education Minister Margot Honecker, which was printed and distributed on a mass scale, roused additional oppositional forces to try to overcome the stagnating regime in a political manner. Parts of the oppositional movement began to unhinge themselves from the churches and form an independent political grouping, the New Forum, which, by petitioning to be allowed to register as a political organization, challenged the monopoly of the SED and the bloc parties in a hitherto unheard-of fashion.

The state's attempts to use the methods of the 1950s to deal with the churches, like founding the League of Freethinkers (VdF), which took an unmistakably anti-church line of attack, were anachronistic and, tellingly, had not originated with the Kirchenpolitiker of the state and party apparatus.[279] The VdF had been initiated by a Politburo resolution of 6 December 1988 and was essentially run and supported by the MfS.[280] The constitutive assembly to found the VdF took place on 7 June 1989 in Berlin. From the standpoint of church-state affairs, this decision, viewed in the churches as a threat and a call to arms, was counterproductive. Cunningly, the churches suggested that the VdF organize the Jugendweihe on a voluntary basis instead of the state schools.

In February 1989 there was a change in the leadership of the Catholic BBK after Cardinal Meisner had been confirmed as the archbishop of Cologne and "released from citizenship in the GDR" following a long tug of war among the Vatican, the Cologne diocesan chapter, and the state governments of North-Rhine Westphalia and Rhineland-Palatinate. Meisner's deputy, Bishop Wanke of Erfurt, administered the office of the chair of the BBK while it was vacant. Many names circulated in the Western press and within the church as to Cardinal Meisner's replacement in Berlin, and GDR government posts were well acquainted with them, wanting to accept only a "GDR citizen" as the new bishop. Surprisingly, on 24 June 1989 Georg Sterzinsky, who had been the vicar general of Erfurt up until that point, was confirmed by the Vatican after his election by the Berlin chapter and ordained as bishop in Berlin on 9 September 1989.

The unrest and tension in the population ultimately reached the BBK as well. During his summer vacation in July 1989, Bishop Huhn led discussions with Catholic clergy and, picking up on their arguments, penned "several noncommittal thoughts" that he presented to the secretary of the BBK and thereby the other bishops.[281] He asked rhetorically whether "our church (bishops? pastors?)" would not have to "take a position more strongly and audibly (!) on problems of the people in our country." Was the "certain abstinence still justifiable," was the justification of "not endangering our pastoral care" still valid "even today"? He maintained that, although the church evaluated societal processes in terms of ethical standards, this happened "too slowly, too infrequently, too secretively." The desire for greater church involvement, however, should "not be seen as an ecumenical competition." Still, the Protestant Church knew better how "to quickly take a position on current hardships," while the Catholic Church was suspected of "a ghetto mindset" because its efforts were so seldom published. Huhn concluded that the bishops would have to react more quickly and more concretely to "give testimony to the truth, promote trust in the church" and support the "process of 'renewal.'" In the current situation, the government had to be the "recipient of church position statements": "If no one else is there, the church has the duty to point out injustice." The government should be petitioned to engage in discussions on the resolutions of the Ecumenical Convocation not only with bishops but also experts. Professional groups of laypersons should be formed, and all of this should be made known to the Catholic parishes. Modes would have to be found that would "make the BBK able to take positions more quickly than now."

With these thoughts, Bishop Huhn had broached both the structural and content-related issues of Catholic Church diplomacy. In the church, processes of a non-simultaneous development had been going on for a long time, which became clear when more and more laypersons and clerics began to take action autonomously and on their own authority without waiting for those rare occasions when the Bishops' Conference made a public announcement. Because the BBK's "representative role" vis-à-vis the state was hardly perceivable in the Catholic Church, this role was called for and taken on ever more strongly from below. The Catholic bishops were no longer challenged only by GDR policy, but also from within the ranks of their own church. The BBK's principle of achieving "consensus" for all public political statements proved to be immobilizing in this situation more clearly than ever. Therefore, Bishop Huhn's thoughts from July 1989 had no immediate consequences for the bearing of the BBK.

The Catholic Church in the Dissolving GDR

The ever-growing stream of GDR citizens presenting themselves at FRG embassies in Eastern European states to force their emigration to West Germany, or fleeing to the FRG over the Hungarian-Austrian border, had a severe impact on Catholic parishes and charitable church organizations in the GDR as well. The wave of emigration, which reached a climax when the western Hungarian border was definitively opened on 11 September 1989, prompted many groups and people, including the churches, to make increasingly explicit demands for pluralism and open dialogue in the GDR. For instance, the working group Education for Peace, led by Catholic Eva Storrer of Güstrow, who previously was a member of the steering committee of the Ecumenical Convocation, made the following demand in writing to the bishops of Mecklenburg, Christoph Stier and Theodor Hubrich: "Give clear signs of encouragement by using open words in the parishes and the church press, but also to delegates of the state and the parties."[282] The Catholic members of the Ecumenical Society for Peace in Dresden-Johannstadt turned to the members of the BBK on 11 September 1989, expecting them "to make it consistently clear to the officials in the party and the government" that "open dialogue in authorized discussion sessions" was necessary.[283] The Catholic bishops, though, initially acted publicly only by calling for people to remain in the GDR. In a note from the minutes of the BBK session of 4–5 September 1989, which was published in church newspapers, they proclaimed that due to the wave of emigration, they would "raise the issues of problems and their causes in discussions with the government posts," but they neither named these problems nor demanded public dialogue.[284] The government posts, though, were still not even ready to engage in such diplomatic discussions with the churches.

The episcopal ordination of Georg Sterzinsky on 9 September 1989 in Saint Hedwig's Cathedral in Berlin was closely watched in the East and the West. It was "in form and words timeless and universal, a 'pure worship service.'"[285] One day after the opening of the western Hungarian border, on 12 September, Bishop Wanke conducted an extensive interview with the press office of the BBK that was made public on 24 September and 1 October 1989, respectively, in the Catholic Church newspapers in the GDR. Yet on 14 September Lange had already given it to Löffler in advance as previously agreed with the state secretary. Löffler then forwarded it to Jarowinsky in the SED Politburo on 18 September 1989, without broaching the church's proposition to hold discussions and on the assumption that Bishop Sterzinsky "would have used his influence to present the critical tones in a more balanced way."[286] Wanke had put forth the chief assertions of the interview more emphatically on 17 September 1989 during his sermon on the occasion of the fall pilgrimage before tens of thousands at the Erfurt

Cathedral square.[287] For one thing, he reflected on the pros and cons of emigration, rhetorically naming and establishing problems in society: "Even if many people leave, we Christians still have good, faith-based reasons to stay here." The bishop reiterated complaints on the ideologization of the educational system and the discrimination against Catholic Christians and called for discussions with "the responsible parties" to acquaint state representatives with the causes of the emigration movement: "Administrative directives do not help much when more openness and honesty in society are needed, and distrust and spoon-feeding must be overcome. If we must continually ask for these things to be overcome, then we will still have to live with the weaknesses of some people and structures. No one knows exactly for how long."

Such patience had long since run out elsewhere: After the closure of the Czech-Hungarian border, the wave of emigration shifted to the FRG embassy in Prague. In the GDR itself, the number of emigration applications increased in leaps and bounds. At the same time, political opposition groups (like the New Forum, Democratic Uprising, and Democracy Now) were forming, collecting signatures, and publicly challenging the SED's monopoly of power. In this situation, the Fifth Synod of the Federation of Protestant Churches, which had convened in Eisenach on 15–19 September 1989, responded with several resolutions:

> We need:
> - a general awareness of the problem that reforms are urgently needed in our country;
> - open and public engagement with our societal problems;
> - everyone to cooperate responsibly in our society;
> - responsible, pluralistic media policies;
> - democratic diversity of parties;
> - freedom of travel for all citizens;
> - economic reforms;
> - responsible handling of societal and personal property;
> - opportunity for peaceful demonstrations;
> - an election procedure that makes it possible to choose among agendas and persons.[288]

Löffler summed up the state's view of these resolutions on 27 September 1989 in an internal advisory meeting: they constituted "a counter-revolutionary agenda"; the Federal Synod had attained "a new level of cooperation with the opponent"; the Protestant Church offered itself as "an alternative to the question of power"; it rejected the "authority of the state"; it called for "open resistance," instigated "blatant and open interference in state affairs," and suspended the state "legal system (by demanding elections and the right to demonstrate)"; and it wanted to "eliminate the fundamentals of socialism" and sought "open confrontation."[289]

In this situation, it was in the domain of the Episcopal Commissarat of Magdeburg that the Catholic leadership broke its habit of lagging behind in public statements. Pressured by leading clerics of his administration, and consciously deviating from the other members of the BBK, on 20 September Bishop Johannes Braun signed the most sensational pastoral letter—which his leading clerics had drafted—that the Catholic Church had ever presented in the GDR. It was read publicly in all worship services throughout the districts of Magdeburg and Halle four days later.[290] The letter addressed causes of the wave of emigration in all clarity and demanded that the exact number of emigrations and applications for exit permits be published. It also attacked the SED with a harshness Catholic leaders had never before displayed: "A group or a party that claims to always be right is not capable of dialogue, not capable of introducing reforms. For where no mistakes are made, there can be no correction." Braun called upon all listeners to engage in activities to restructure society:

> I ask you to consider intervening: Share with me your fears, your hopes, your wishes, your needs, your suggestions! I encourage you to talk in all the groups of your parish about things that have gotten under our skin in order to develop ideas and submit proposals. Whether or not our opinion is desired, we feel compelled by God to raise our voice, to bear our concerns together so that the rudder will change course before it is too late. I do not want to be misunderstood: We cannot copy the Federal Republic of Germany. We cannot follow the path of those in the Soviet Union, Hungary, or Poland. We must find a path that suits us and is supported by a broad spectrum of the population. We must eliminate misunderstandings in order to create a democratic society where as many people as possible can feel at ease.

The letter was very well received in the Catholic Church well beyond Magdeburg and was even circulated among Protestants. The Bishop of Magdeburg received over 1,000 letters with position statements and suggestions signed by around 15,000 people.[291] This missive from Magdeburg forever suspended the Catholic Church's political principle of "consensus" and the "political abstinence" of the BBK.

At the central church level, the representation of the BBK at festivities devoted to the fortieth anniversary of the GDR on 6 and 7 October 1989 in the Palace of the Republic in Berlin was being debated. Then the events in Dresden began, nearly overnight, to eject a further Catholic district from the hitherto existing political strategy of public restraint. In order to celebrate the fortieth anniversary without "negative" headlines in the international public, the SED Politburo had suspended visa-free travel to the CSSR on 3 October. The next day, GDR citizens were deported to the West from the German federal embassy in Prague in trains that traversed the territory of the GDR. This led to violent confrontations at Dresden's main train station and across the city between latecomers who had been denied entry to the CSSR and the Dresden district security forces.[292] In this context, fifty-two people occupied the Catholic Hofkirche in Dresden's center that same day, managing, thus, to force their exit to West Germany.[293]

In the following days, more protests and smaller demonstrations occurred in the city center of Dresden. The largest protest march, on the evening of 8 October 1989, stood poised to be violently dispersed, as cathedral Vicar Frank Richter and Chaplain Andreas Leuschner from Dresden-Pieschen, who had both participated in the demonstration with the Catholic parish youth, took up negotiations with the security forces, finally ushering in a peaceful solution. First of all, a spontaneous "Group of 20" formed with the involvement of clergy. The SED, through its representative Wolfgang Berghofer, the chief mayor of Dresden, received this group—as a first-ever oppositional "dialogue partner" in the GDR—on the morning of 9 October 1989. That evening, open council meetings with tens of thousands of people were held in the four largest churches in Dresden's city center, among them the Catholic Hofkirche, as sanctioned by Bishop Reinelt. These meetings provided information on the discussion process that had been introduced.

Also that evening, unauthorized demonstrations taking place in Leipzig were the largest (70,000 participants) in the history of the GDR. As in the preceding weeks, these grew out of the peace prayers in the Protestant churches, but on this night such prayers had also been held in the Catholic Propsteikirche for the first time. Although a large contingent of state security forces had gathered and preparations for the dispersal of the demonstrations had been completed, the evening remained peaceful. This was due to breaks in the SED chain of command between Berlin and Leipzig, which, though they cannot be reconstructed in their entirety, marked the beginning of the state's gradual shift away from the massive use of violence that had already gotten under way. Security forces had engaged in several violent acts in Berlin, Leipzig, Dresden, and other cities around 7 and 8 October 1989 and made many temporary arrests—some in a brutal manner.

On 8 and 9 October 1989, the Regular Council of the BBK (Bishops Wanke and Huhn) met for a special advisory meeting with Sterzinsky in Berlin. Reinelt from Dresden was also briefly present. According to an MfS brief from 8 October 1989, the bishops wanted to get involved in the current situation because they had

> been pressured to do so by numerous requests and demands from Catholic priests and laypersons to become active . . . Since a number of clergy are meanwhile engaged in political actions, for example, in initiatives for foundation associations (among them 'New Forum,' parties), these bishops are of the opinion that it is now time to determine how to proceed, and what the bishops and the BBK should do.[294]

The bishops decided to give the government another tepid "verbal note" presenting the Catholic Church's perspective "on the most recent domestic events."[295] They "encouraged" the government "to consistently continue pursuing" the path of improving travel opportunities. In the present situation, "neither the exodus nor the exclusion" of GDR citizens was the "right path." In the "shared responsibility of the church for the common good," it was up to the church "to contribute to the development of relations in society and the state that correspond to the rights and dignity of the human being and social responsibilities." They denounced violence as a means of solving problems but did not explicitly call the state's monopoly on violence into question. Rather, they merely emphasized that this should not cause the state "to forego peaceful political solutions." Moreover, the bishops emphasized the basic rights in the GDR constitution and the necessity of "comprehensive discussions among the responsible state parties and all groups of peoples": "The bishops are strengthening their preparedness to participate in such discussions, either personally or through delegates, within the framework of the responsibilities of their church office."

Lange presented this note to Kalb on 9 October 1989 with the optimistic interpretation that the BBK was, at last, once again speaking "with one voice." The BBK had to issue a statement, Lange believed, because "significant portions of the Catholic youth and the groups organizing under their roofs were drifting over to the Protestant churches." Lange further noted that Protestant Regional Bishop Leich had tried to convince Wanke to make a collective declaration, yet this was prevented when Sterzinsky objected.[296] Within the church, the verbal note and its nature were not made known. Instead, all priests and church social networks in the GDR received a letter by Wanke of 9 October 1989 that implicitly reiterated passages from the note, like the church's offer to engage in discussions with the state. This letter was intended to serve recipients as a basis of information for the branches of their parishes.[297]

Although the BBK had only signaled within the church that it had asked the state to engage in discussions, the interplay of the emigration wave and the nationwide spread of political initiatives and evening street demonstrations actually brought such discussions into the realm of possibility. These events subjected the SED party leadership and the GDR government to a process of delegitimization and self-liquidation that caused them to expressly desire negotiations with high-ranking church representatives, which suddenly had a stabilizing effect for the SED. At first, though, Protestant Church leaders were the preferred interlocutors. Generally, leaders in both churches remained fixated on the GDR government in a centralist tradition, notwithstanding its deficient legitimacy and creeping loss of authority. On 17 October 1989 at a session of the Politburo, Honecker was forced to resign from his position as secretary general and from the Politburo. The ZK then elected Egon Krenz, who was wildly unpopular among the general populace, as the new secretary general on 18 October 1989. On 24 October he was rubber-stamped as chair of the State Council by the Volkskammer.[298]

Independently of the diplomatic discussions planned at the central level in Berlin, identical developments were taking place at the regional level of the Catholic Church, as well as in all other areas of society. Power shifted to the streets. Catholics entered into initiatives, participated in demonstrations, entered themselves in signature lists, and signed petitions with demands directed at the government posts. Several priests opened Catholic churches and institutions, usually after Protestant officials had done so, for peace prayers and open councils.

The Bishops' Conference was not able to control such acts, nor did it try: locally, every bishop, every priest, and every layperson had become autonomous. Now that central state and church organs had lost their monopolies in Kirchenpolitik, their representatives lost their custodial relevance.

Groups across the country pursued what Braun had initiated with his letter in Magdeburg on 24 September 1989: many Catholics also appointed themselves spokespersons for society-wide issues and voiced solidarity with oppositional demands. On 12 October 1989, for instance, seventy-one employees of the Berlin administrative offices of Caritas signed a letter directed to Premier Stoph "on their own authority as concerned citizens and Christians," merely "notifying" Sterzinsky and Caritas director Reinhold Janiszewski of it after the fact. The letter unambiguously called for "an open and general societal dialogue about the foundational democratization of the state," the "acknowledgment and maintenance of all human rights," and a "comprehensive and truthful report in the media on the events in recent months," as well as the "release of those arrested during the demonstrations, the cessation of investigations, and suspension of sentences." The letter, made available to church lay workers, contained drastic words: "Accustomed to remaining silent and waiting for clarifying words 'from above,' we are very concerned about the current situation in our country. As Catholic Christians and church employees, we want to speak up and no longer wait for what church authorities negotiate non-publicly with the state."[299]

In Dresden, the Catholic clergy of the parish of Johannstadt embraced the demands of the Friedenskreis Johannstadt—a group it had previously eyed with suspicion. On 15 October 1989, in an "open letter" to the SED district leadership of Dresden, they demanded punishment of violent security forces, release of those arrested, permission to demonstrate publicly and to form political groups, new election law, and an end to all travel restrictions.[300] A pastoral letter of 16 October 1989 by Bishop Reinelt, which was read publicly in all churches in the Diocese of Dresden-Meißen, hardly differed from the speeches at the street demonstrations. Reinelt had conceived it in a feeling of "solidarity with the people across denominations and worldviews": "The people now hope for true dialogue and real changes. But hardly anything has changed . . . Now is the time to talk. Hesitation and tarrying are now wrong. The truth must be brought to light. The whole truth. Truth never destroys. Truth always constructs. So let us speak it." Reinelt demanded that all borders be opened, that authorities end their contemptuousness, that "those responsible" honestly correct their mistakes, and that "a proper space for societal plurality" be established, alongside "truthful information," "absolute freedom from violence," and "more effective economic structures." Only then did he make some Catholic requests regarding questions of education. Reinelt further asked his listeners to bring all misdeeds against "peace-loving demonstrators and those who are completely uninvolved" to his attention and applauded the effect of the demonstration:

I will continue, as I have done up to now, act on behalf of human rights with all means at my disposal. However, it is an undeniable fact for us that the many negotiations of the bishops and priests in recent weeks and years past have had less impact than the unanimous demonstration of the will of tens of thousands on the street.[301]

In Erfurt, Bishop Wanke, acting as the official chair of the BBK, approved a declaration of his pastoral advisory council from 14 October 1989 that was publicly read on 22 October in all churches in the territory of the Episcopal Office of Erfurt and Meiningen. The text admitted the church had not "conveyed to all of society" nor "defended boldly enough" the dignity of human beings, "which derives from God." The necessary prerequisites for open dialogue had not existed "in the hitherto recognized structures (institutions)." For this reason, Catholics, together with other Christians, were now to "position [themselves] in all groups that let their willingness for change be credibly known."[302] The first demonstrations in the Catholic enclave in Eichsfeld began in Heiligenstadt on 23 October 1989—relatively late, compared to other developments in the GDR. They achieved a special dynamic through the petitions of numerous parishes to the SED party leadership, all the way to an unusually fast disempowerment of the SED and very early demands for German unity. In many district and regional towns, the church mediated weekly demonstrations and public "dialogues" that successively disempowered the SED and state organs. At the same time, the pressure from the people in the capital concentrated on an artists' demonstration on 4 November 1989. A million people took part in this assembly—the largest in the history of the GDR—which ultimately led to the "*Wende*" in Berlin. A participating clergyman summed it up for the Catholic Church: "Entire parishes were to be seen, but no bishop."[303]

At the Berlin Diocesan Office, Prelate Lange fought his last rearguard battles. On 23 October 1989, he had composed an extensive draft of a "Letter of the Chair of the BBK to the Priests and All Full-Time Employees in Pastoral Service, as Well as the Employees in Church Service in Leadership Positions in Pastoral and Caritas" as an "orientation." The letter never went beyond its draft status and was, in light of the developments in the country and the church, simply grotesque.[304] In it, Lange remarked that making Catholic churches available for citizens' meetings was "an extraordinary occurrence" that only an "extraordinary situation" could justify. In such situations, the bishop's approval had to be attained. "We will only permit political groups to use the spaces in our parishes in exceptional cases and in no way as a general rule; but the political and societal goals of the grouping cannot be ignored. For even here the well-known phrase applies: We are a church for everyone, but not for *everything!* . . . Even here it will be necessary to make an arrangement with the deacon or even the bishop." Lange emphasized that clerics' participation "in the demonstrations with the clear goal of immediate political engagement" was not "consonant with priestly service." A priest could only participate to avoid escalations where "the attitudes with which a priest participates" were important. All officials were to "refrain from the media at present. This especially goes for spontaneous statements to reporters and for telephone interviews." In addition, Lange doubted that a *Wende* had begun, which is why one "had to keep the political environment within the GDR under watch."

On 27 October 1989 a Minor Commission for the Preparation of Government-Level Discussions convened under the direction of the auxiliary bishop of Schwerin, Norbert Werbs. The commission decided that a subject catalogue of demands should be put together for the discussions with the GDR government. Yet, due to the government's loss of authority and the rapid developments in the country with their concomitant changes in party and state, it was not possible to negotiate any issues with the church. Bloc parties changed course, and, of course, with new political groupings, occupied and filled pluralistic functions. Eventually the entire centralist structure of the GDR dramatically shattered, rendering the government incapable of taking any concerted action or participating in substantial discussions with the authority to speak for the entire country.

When the BBK met for a special session on 7 and 8 November 1989 to elect Georg Sterzinsky as its new chair—before the Catholic bishops had to depart on a long trip to Rome—it intended, due mainly to the pressure from the Magdeburg clergy, to approve a collective public declaration. In a letter to the BBK of 6 November 1989, Magdeburg Provost Theodor Stolpe, together with eighteen other leading Catholic clergy of the city, had challenged them to make a declaration:[305] "The questions of people from Christian and non-Christian circles are becoming more and more pressing as to why the Catholic Church does not speak out in this situation." "Many Catholics who place all their bets on change and sacrifice all of their liberty" were waiting for a public position statement from the bishops. Based on his local involvement, Stolpe had concrete expectations of the BBK and expressed them unreservedly: he expected the BBK to "announce its opinion to the government of the GDR that partial reforms do not create a new society," and to demand "[f]ree elections among competing parties." The letter asked the bishops to "deploy responsible employees within their jurisdictions at the main focal points of demonstrations and political actions, who would establish ties to other denominations and groups and take note of matters and opinion statements and document them properly," including unlawful acts by the demonstrators or state representatives. The letter further suggested that such employees coordinate with one another across the GDR and provide information to the BBK, which, in turn, should provide information to local priests and "encourage [them] to make church spaces available for discussions and conversations to facilitate as broad an exchange of ideas as possible."

In a list of demands from the same day, the Magdeburg clerics suggested six points for a public declaration to the BBK: the SED should give up its leading role in all areas and disband the National Front; the bloc party system should be suspended and free elections instituted; ideology should be taken out of the educational system and required participation in civics, scouting organizations, the Free German Youth, and the Jugendweihe should be abolished; market structures should prevail rather than a planned economy; the freedoms of speech, religion, and travel should be granted; and the security organs (police, MfS, military brigades) should reduce their sphere of operations or even be dissolved.[306]

In Berlin, though, Prelate Lange formulated an opposing memo for the bishops' session entitled "The Berlin Conference of Bishops and the Present Situation, Estimation and Missions."[307] He characterized his political ideas as the guiding principles of the bishops and also described pending diplomatic missions as he saw them: the new chair of the BBK was to conduct his inaugural visit with the premier of the GDR so that he might use the opportunity to come to an agreement on a "mixed State-Church Commission." This commission would deal with church issues and prepare for a papal visit to the GDR "collectively." Referring to a resolution of the Fulda Bishops' Conference of 1937, Lange asserted that he himself should act as the church liaison to the government with his own commissariat, including a lawyer, and lobby for general Catholic interests.

On 6 November 1989 Lange also drafted a "Declaration of the Berlin Conference of Bishops on the Present Situation and the Resulting Missions" without acknowledging Stolpe's expectations. On 7 November 1989 the BBK approved the public reading of this declaration in all Catholic worship services in the GDR on 11 and 12 November 1989. In the realm of the Episcopal Office of Magdeburg, though, all the churches also read in addition the demands the Magdeburg clergy had presented to the BBK in vain on 6 November 1989.[308] These church declarations in the Magdeburg worship services occurred at the height of the historical events, for in the "meantime" the ZK had unintentionally caused the opening of the borders on 9 November 1989, initiating an irreversible development.

With the opening of the borders, it was now possible for people to travel largely uninhibited into and out of the GDR, resulting in an abundance of euphoric contacts between East and West Germans. These extended into the realm of the church, especially in light of the church-internal formation of lay initiatives in the GDR that had taken off at the end of October 1989. With the end of GDR confinement, the SED's power to control its people finally contracted once and for all. The *Wende* could not be undone; demonstrations and protests became less and less risky. Even the new government under Modrow, the reformist chair of the Council of Ministers of the GDR who had been in power since 13 November 1989, could do no more than react to developments. When the media in the GDR and the Federal Republic began to disclose compromising information from within the state and party apparatus, more and more functionaries in the Politburo and the ZK, the SED district administrations, and the state apparatus lost their positions. MfS leaders implemented actions to protect their institution under the new circumstances. In November, they began to destroy files in the main departments in Berlin and the district administrations.

During these events, some in the Catholic Church followed their own pace and continued to act largely as before. Berlin's Bishop Sterzinsky directed letters of thanks dated 9 November 1989 to already-discredited functionaries such as

Chair of the State Council Krenz, Premier Stoph, and State Secretary Löffler after they had congratulated him with three different letters of 8 November 1989 on his election as the new chair of the BBK. Sterzinsky's letters all contained reminders of truthfulness and constitutionality but declared the preparedness "of the Catholic Church to take over its share of responsibility" in the current situation. The letter to Löffler also mentioned the convenience of "controlled cooperation between the Catholic Church and the state."[309] But since no initiatives came from the dissolving state to allow "the Catholic Church" such a "share of responsibility," Lange, as the delegate of the BBK, took on the assignment. He led a first exploratory discussion on 3 November 1989 with the director of the Department of Church Affairs and the main chair of the CDU, Wulf Trende. As a result, a candidate for the CDU chairmanship, Lothar de Maizière, was personally introduced to Sterzinsky on 17 November. On 23 November Sterzinsky, following Lange's advice, congratulated Modrow on his election to chair of the Council of Ministers of the GDR and conveyed to him "the best wishes of the members of the Berlin Conference of Bishops. The hopes of many people are directed toward you and the members of your cabinet."[310] That same day, Sterzinsky petitioned Modrow for a meeting out of "concern for the common good and my responsibility for the Catholic Church in this country." He hoped they could get to know each other personally and have an "exchange of thoughts on the tasks arising from the current situation for everyone, and so also for the government and the church, each in its own way."[311]

On 24 November Peter Kraußer, director of the Department of Church Affairs at the ZK of the SED, notified Wolfgang Herger, director of the Department of Security, of an exploratory discussion Kalb had had with Lange about an inaugural visit by Sterzinsky to Krenz. Krausser reported that Lange had thought such a visit would be advantageous after the special party congress of the SED, scheduled for 15–17 December 1989. On the issue of a papal visit, Lange had stated:

> If it serves the stability of the GDR and the authority of the Chair of the State Council, there would be a willingness to organize a papal visit in the GDR—before the planned visits to Hungary and Cuba—before 1990. One would only have to give the pope a proper signal. In such a case, the variant of a pastoral visit (without visiting Berlin) could not be considered but rather a state and pastoral visit. The invitation would then be officially announced by the Chair of the State Council and the Berlin Conference of Bishops.

Krausser told Herger that he thought one would have take on the issue after the special SED party congress, whereby an "offensive position—a visit at a time beneficial to us—would surely be best."[312]

Just a few days later, Krenz, Herger, Krausser, and many others were no longer in office. Legal proceedings against leading functionaries of the SED had begun in mid November. On 18 November the Volkskammer assembled a commission to investigate the misuse of authority, as well as corruption and personal gain. On

23 November the furnishings of the Politburo settlement in Wandlitz, north of Berlin, were shown on television in the GDR for the first time. The Volkskammer commission gave its first public report on 1 December. The office of the attorney general investigated and then arrested Politburo members Günter Mittag and Harry Tisch, as well as the previous SED district secretaries Hans Albrecht of Suhl and Gerhard Müller of Erfurt. Alexander Schalck-Golodkowski eluded arrest by fleeing to West Berlin and from there to a debriefing by the Federal Intelligence Service of the Federal Republic of Germany. Also on 1 December, the Volkskammer struck the SED's leadership role from the constitution of the GDR. The SED delegate elections, held to prepare for its special party congress, resulted in several established functionaries being voted out office. People in the 2.3 million-member party began to resign their memberships in droves. A meeting of the ZK was quickly scheduled for 3 December. On this day, the remainder of the Politburo came together and resolved that they and the entire ZK should resign. Several hours later the Central Committee of the SED met for the last time and dissolved itself, never to be elected again.[313] On 3 and 4 December civic committees began to occupy MfS administrative offices. A disproportionate number of Christians of all denominations were involved in this, not without personal risks. By the first week of December 1989, the power of the SED had been irrevocably broken, and the GDR, with its open borders, found itself in a transitional phase that would lead to German unity.

On 7 December the BBK held a press conference for the first time. Now even Prelate Lange sensed the GDR's demise and provided wisdom in hindsight. When he gave a statement on the BBK's position regarding the ransoming of political prisoners in the GDR, he also put a rather grotesque revisionist spin on the historical fundamentals of the Catholic Church's relationship to the dissolving state:

> The facts made known through the party leadership of the SED on the exercise of the power monopoly and the misuse of the state as an instrument for many dark schemes and illegalities—even to the point of applying the legal system against innocent people—reveal the true character of this state more day by day. At no point in time did the Catholic Church award legitimacy to this state, which was established without free and anonymous elections—that is, constitutional means . . . Evidence of this can be found, among many other things, in the fact that Bishops Preysing, Weskamm, Döpfner, Bengsch and Meisner, who were at the top of our Conference of Bishops, consistently refused to take part in official meetings with the state leader of the GDR, [and] that the Catholic Church upheld absolutely no relationship with the SED. Regardless, the Catholic Church in this country had to accommodate the fact of this state's existence. It always did this in the sense of St. Augustine when he spoke of states that have the character of "organized bands of robbers."[314]

Notes

1. Cf. in general: Peter Przybylski, *Tatort Politbüro: Honecker, Mittag und Schalck-Golodkowski*, vol. 2.
2. See, for example, the transcripts of phone conversations between Kohl and Honecker between 1 January and 18 April 1983, in Detlef Nakath/Gerd-Rüdiger Stephan, *Von Hubertusstock nach Bonn: Eine dokumentierte Geschichte der deutsch-deutschen Beziehungen auf höchster Ebene 1980-1987* (Berlin, 1995), 114–32.
3. Heinz Heitzer, *DDR: Geschichtlicher Überblick* (East Berlin, 1979), 298.
4. Przybylski, *Tatort Politbüro: Akte Honecker* [Vol. I], 321–39.
5. Honecker told the SED district first secretaries on 15 September 1976 that a public statement about the suicide of Protestant leaders was "one of the biggest counter-revolutionary acts against the GDR." SAPMO-BA-rch, DY 30, IV B 2/14/81.
6. See Groß's eight-page minutes of his meeting with Casaroli, dated 8 February 1973. ROO, J II.
7. DAB, V/5-7-1.
8. SAPMO-BArch, DY 30, J IV 2/2/1402 (Attachment 13).
9. ROO, A VIII 6 (Aktennotiz, Memorandum).
10. See the 7 September 1972 file notes by Groß. ROO, J II.
11. ROO, A VIII 6.
12. ROO, A IV 6.
13. Lamberz presented his notes to the Politburo on 6 February 1973. SAPMO-BArch, DY 30, IV B 2/14/46, Anlage 5. The talks in Rome also established that future contacts would be handled through the GDR embassy in Rome. SAPMO-BArch, DY 30, IV B 2/14/46.
14. Notes on a conversation in the Office of the State Secretary on 15 January 1973, BStU, ZA, AIM 2716/75, Part 1, p. 71. Groß is quoted as asking, "Why is the GDR bringing a monitor from Rome to Berlin?"
15. SAPMO-BArch, DY 30, J IV 2/2/1513.
16. ROO, A IV 8.
17. See the 2 August 1976 letter of Foreign Minister Oskar Fischer to Erich Honecker. BAO, DO-4, 465.
18. SAPMO-BArch, DY 30, IV B 2/14/164.
19. SAPMO-BArch, DY 30, J IV 2/2/1643 (Anlage Nr. 5).
20. DAB, V/5-6-4.
21. Ibid.
22. BAP, DO-4, 465.
23. BStU, ZA, Z 2880, pp. 1–6.
24. BStU, ZA, ZAIG, Z 2932, pp. 1–10. See also a fifteen-page MfS report on the pope from 20 April 1979 that was clearly researched in Poland, BStU, HA XX/4, 1719, pp. 1–15.
25. BStU, ZA, ZAIG, Z 3151, pp. 1–11.
26. BStU, ZA, ZAIG, Z 3446, pp. 1–3.
27. For details, see Dieter Grande/Bernd Schäfer, *Zur Kirchenpolitik der SED: Auseinandersetzungen um das Katholikentreffen 1983-1987* (Leipzig, 1994), pp. 55–92.
28. SAPMO-BArch, DY 30, J IV 2/2/2179.
29. Notes from the Dresden SED office. LV Sachsen der PDS, LPA-Dresden, 12012. Only months before, at an election meeting in Weimar on 27 May 1986, Gysi had referred to the pope as "a dangerous man who has 'unfortunately' not retained his good sense." LV Thuringia der PDS, LPA-Erfurt, AR-BL 1500. Internal memo of 6 June 1986 from Dorothea Reschwamm, the official responsible for church affairs in the SED district leadership in Erfurt, to local First Secretary Gerhard Müller.
30. See Przybylski, *Tatort Politbüro*, vol. 2, 247ff. and 292ff.
31. See the article "Weiß der Teufel," *Der Spiegel*, 25 May 1992.

32. Norbert Pötzl, *Basar der Spione: Die geheimen Missionen des DDR-Unterhändlers Wolfgang Vogel* (Hamburg, 1997); Craig Whitney, *Advocatus Diaboli: Wolfgang Vogel, Anwalt zwischen Ost und West* (Berlin, 1993); Przybylski, *Tatort Politbüro*, vol. 2, 389.

33. Deutscher Bundestag, *Beschlußempfehlung und Bericht des 1. Untersuchungsausschusses vom 27.5.1994, [plus three volumes of appendices]*, 130ff. and 548. See also Andreas Förster, "Dubiose Geldgeschäfte bis kurz vor dem Tod: Stasi-Anwalt Manfred Wünsche starb in Berlin," *Berliner Zeitung*, 12 August 1994, 5.

34. *Berliner Zeitung*, 27 December 1993, citing a study by Barthold Witte, a member of the Protestant synod.

35. See Besier, *Der SED-Staat und die Kirche 1969–1990: Die Vision vom 'Dritten Weg,'* (Berlin and Frankfurt am Main, 1995), 517–33.

36. Deutscher Bundestag, *1. Untersuchungsausschuß* [1992].

37. Deutscher Bundestag, *Beschlußempfehlung und Bericht* [1994], 304.

38. See the 9 August 1984 letter from Werner Eberlein, SED first secretary in the Magdeburg district, to Egon Krenz, a Politburo member. It refers to the considerable number of Catholic building projects in Magdeburg. Eberlein sought to make Krenz aware "that the scope of this construction, the location of the projects, and their architectural form give rise to discussion among the population." LV S-A der PDS, LPA-Magdeburg, IV E 2/14/833.

39. SAPMO-BArch, DY 30, IV B 2/14/59.

40. SAPMO-BArch, DY 30/vorl. SED 42070.

41. SAPMO-BArch, DY 30/vorl. SED 42071.

42. SAPMO-BArch, DY 30, IV 2/14/19.

43. SAPMO-BArch, NY 281/110.

44. BAP, DO-4, 1322.

45. SAPMO-BArch, DY 30, IV B 2/14/45 ("Kirchenstudie 1979," p. 25).

46. See the 5 October 1987 letter from Klaus Gysi to Kurt Kleinert (secretariat head of the Council of Ministers) which makes clear this situation. BAP, DO-4, 712.

47. See Wolfgang Kaul, "Zu Verlauf und Resultaten des Säkularisierungsprozesses in der DDR," *Institut für vergleichende Staat-Kirche-Forschung, 3. Berliner Staat-Kirche-Kolloquium vom 19. bis 19. Januar 1995: Säkularisierung in Ost und West* (Berlin, 1995), 56–73.

48. MLHA Schwerin, Rat des Bezirkes Schwerin, 21298. I am grateful to the Heinrich Theissing Institute, Schwerin, for this reference.

49. "Maßnahmen und Hinweise für die Gespräche mit den anderen Bischöfen der katholischen Kirche in der DDR," BAP, DO, 405.

50. Notes by Rudi Bellmann from the Central Committee apparatus, 4 November 1985, entitled "Zur 'Geschäftsgrundlage' der Beziehungen der Leitung der katholischen Kirche in der DDR zum Staat unter Kardinal Bengsch." BAP, DO-4, 1258.

51. BAP, DO-4, 1296.

52. BAP, DO-4, 830.

53. See notes of the Dresden district council from 9 March 1976, on a 16 December 1975 meeting with Huhn, and 24 April 1977, notes by the Cottbus district council on another meeting on 14 April 1977. BAP, DO-4, 827. At the latter meeting, Bishop Huhn was able to add his own lecture to the council chairman's, a singular exception in these affairs.

54. BAP, DO-4, 661.

55. SED officials in Erfurt noted that the average participation in the Jugendweihe in the Heiligenstadt district was "only" 67–70 percent, exceptional in the GDR. LV Thüringen der PDS, LPA-Erfurt, AR-BL 4644.

56. According to reports from 1975 (BAP, DO-4, 844) and 1977 (BAP, DO-4, 1296).

57. BAP, DO-4, 843.

58. ROO, A VIII 10.

59. See Johannes Braun, *Volk und Kirche in der Dämmerung: Ein Einblick in die vier Jahrzehnte des Sozialismus in der DDR* (Leipzig, 1992), 61.

60. See the government notes in BAP, DO-4, 825.
61. File note of 12 November 1975 for State Secretary Seigewasser by Horst Dohle, his personal chargé at the time. BAP, DO-4, 464.
62. LV Sachsen der PDS, LPA-Dresden, IV D, 2/14/690.
63. ACDP VII-013-3149.
64. For more detail, see Bernd Schäfer, "'Um "anzukommen" muß man sich "ankömmlich" artikulieren.' Zur Berliner-Konferenz (BK) zwischen 1964 und 1993," in Michael Richter und Martin Rißmann, eds., *Die Ost-CDU* (Weimar, Cologne, Vienna, 1995), 111–25.
65. "Überlegungen zur weiteren Entwicklung und Arbeit der BK," 1 July 1978. SAPMO-BArch, DY 30, IV B 2/14/186. The original phrasing here incorporates a play on words: " 'Um "anzu-kommen" muß man sich "ankömmlich" artikulieren.'"
66. BAP, DO-4, 1264.
67. BAP, DO-4, 1264. The Modrow government nonetheless continued to finance the Berlin Conference.
68. Jens Gieseke, "Die hauptamtlichen Mitarbeiter des Ministeriums für Staatssicherheit," in Klaus-Dietmar Henke et al., eds., *Anatomie der Staatssicherheit: Geschichte, Struktur und Methoden, MfS-Handbuch,* Vol. 4 (Berlin, 1995), 1–107.
69. Clemens Vollnhals, "Die kirchenpolitische Abteilung des Ministeriums für Staatssicherheit," in Clemens Vollnhals, ed. *Die Kirchenpolitik von SED und Staatssicherheit: Eine Zwischenbilanz* (Berlin, 1997), 93ff.
70. Dissemond's MfS file was opened in 1975 and "erased" by HA XX/4 in December 1989. BStU, ZA, XV 655/75. Some of his conversations with the MfS can be reconstructed from parallel accounts in other files; certain torn documents have been restored by the BStU.
71. See Friedrich Kronenberg, "Zur Rolle des Zentalkomitees der deutschen Katholiken: Ein Bericht aufgrund eigener Kenntnisse und persönlicher Erfahrungen," in Ulrich von Hehl and Hans Günther Hockerts, eds., *Der Katholizismus – gesamtdeutsche Klammer in den Jahrzehnten der Teilung?* (Paderborn, 1996), 39–68.
72. See BStU, ZA, HA XX/4, 977, pp. 52–63.
73. BStU, Ast Dresden, XII 1590/74, especially AIM 685/85 ("Sorbe").
74. Letter from Bruno Bessau to Wolfgang Heyl on 3 November 1987. ACDP VII-013-3149.
75. BStU, ZA, XV 1647/70, IMB "Birke."
76. BStU, ZA, XV 3851/76 ("Egbert").
77. BStU, Ast Dresden, XII 590/73, AIM 4924/90, Teil I: 1 Band and BStU, Ast Dresden, XII 2079/70.
78. BStU, Ast Erfurt, IX 305/65, Teil I: 1 Band, Teil II: 6 Bände.
79. BStU, Ast Erfurt, IX 337/77.
80. BStU, Ast Halle, VIII 2046/86.
81. Ibid., VIII 120/83. No one within the Halle Action Group could ever have expected "Rechner," a member of a parish board in Halle, to be an informer. The "Helmut" file was purged in late 1989.
82. BStU Ast Neubrandenburg, III 251/82 (IMB "Tobias").
83. BStU, Ast Halle, OV "Tabernakel," VIII 1635/70, specifically AOP 2145/72; OV "Academica," VIII 757/75 AOP 1986; OV "Kanzel," VIII 644/80 AOP 1986. Separate files were opened in Halle on two female members of the Halle Action Group who joined a peace group called "Christian Women in Hohenthurm", OV "Kreis" and OV "Reigen."
84. BStU, Ast Schwerin, OV "Vereinigung," II 600/70, AOP 10/1974; BStU Ast Neubrandenburg, OV "Talar," I 1128/78, AOP III 1449/86; BStU, Ast Rostock, OPK "Stafette" (sic!), I 921/87 AOPK 337/89. I am very grateful to Anton Beer for granting me access to these piles of documents.
85. BStU, ZA, HA XX/4, 273, p. 69.
86. BStU, ZA, HA XX/4, 90, pp. 1–9.
87. BStU, ZA, HA XX/4, 2487.

88. BStU, ZA, HA XX/4,853.
89. BStU, ZA, HA XX/4,715, pp. 345–49.
90. See Grande and Schäfer, *Zur Kirchenpolitik der SED,* 14.
91. BStU, ZA, HA XX/4. 1049, p. 147.
92. BStU, Ast Chemnitz, XIV 3255/84 (IMB "Ernesto").
93. Quoted in Konrad Feiereis, "Katholische Theologie in der DDR: Chance, Grenze, Selbstver-ständnis," *hochschule ost* 4 (1995): 46–55.
94. BStU, ZA, XV 1534/74 ("Irmchen").
95. See Peter-Paul Straube, *Katholische Studentengemeinde in der DDR als Ort eines außeruniversitären Studium generale* (Leipzig, 1996), 134–45.
96. BStU, ZA, HA XX/4, 1528, pp. 1–2 and 69ff.
97. BStU, ZA, HA XX/4, 2510, pp. 207–10.
98. BStU, ZA, JHS 21234; Straube, *Katholische Studentengemeinde,* 138.
99. BStU, ZA, ZAIG, Z 2418, pp. 1–12, quotes pp. 1 and 10.
100. BStU, Ast Magdeburg, VII 918/82, AOPK 1521/87 (OPK "Patron"). I am grateful to Günter Särchen for allowing me access to files on him.
101. BStU, Ast Leipzig, XIII 720/84, AOPK 1696/86 (OPK "Missionar"), as well as XIII 1273/89 (OPK "Basel"). I am grateful to Hans-Friedrich Fischer for allowing me access to his files.
102. BStU, ZA, HA XX/4, 721, 273ff.
103. See Reinhard Meinel/Thomas Wernicke, eds., *Mit tschekistischem Gruß: Berichte der Bezirksverwaltung für Staatssicherheit 1989* (Potsdam, 1990), 34ff.
104. BStU, Ast Dresden, XII 3089/88, AOP 323/92. I am grateful to Johannes and Martina Pohl for allowing me access to files on the peace group and for a highly informative interview with members of the group.
105. For access to files relating to the following sections, I am grateful to the late Claus Herold, Willi Verstege, and Friedrich Rebbelmund.
106. ROO, A V 25.
107. Quoted by Claus Herold in a lecture in Halle, 15 May 1992.
108. Dohle's report on his travel to Poland on 18–20 November 1986. BAP, DO-4, 1034.
109. Gerhard Lange et al., *Katholische Kirche – Sozialistischer Staat DDR,* 243–46.
110. See Dieter Grande, "Die Pastoralsynode der Jurisdiktionsbezirke in der DDR – ein Zwischenbericht nach einem Jahr Synodenarbeit," *Priesterjahresheft* (1975): 25ff.
111. See Bengsch's declaration in *Herder-Korrespondenz* 27 (1973): 643.
112. MLHA Schwerin, Rat des Bezirkes Schwerin, 21298.
113. See notes by Gerald Quast, head of the CDU steering committee's church affairs section, 15 May 1972 (ACDP VII-013-2129).
114. LV S-A der PDS, LPA-Halle, IV B/2/14/824.
115. BAP, DO-4, 4999, p. 10.
116. SAPMO-BArch, DY 30, J IV 2/2/1431 (Anlage 13 zum Protokoll vom 23.1.1973).
117. SAPMO-BArch, DY 30, B 2/14/160.
118. A government report dated 26 July 1972 contained these and other detailed quotes from the preparatory documents for the synod. BStU, ZA, HA XX/4, 1262, pp. 211–33.
119. Notes by Horst Dohle, 16 June 1972. SAPMO-BArch, DY 30, IV B 2/14/160. Compare Bishop Schaffran's notes on this conversation (OAB, Akten Bischöfliche Sekretarie, Staat und Kirche), where he says: "The danger of extremists taking things too far in any direction is recognized by both sides."
120. BOK declaration of 15 September 1972. SAPMO-BArch, DY 30, IV B 2/14/161.
121. SAPMO-BArch, DY 30, IV B 2/14/161. Zobel probably thought the conversation was confidential. Dohle reported on it to the SED Central Committee on 19 January 1973.
122. See Dohle's notes on the conversations on 29 January, 28 February, and 6 March 1973. SAPMO-BArch, DY 30, IV B 2/14/160. The quotes are from the 28 February 1973 conversation.

123. BAP, DO-4, 843.
124. SAPMO-BArch, DY 30, IV B 2/14/161.
125. Compare the explanations by Zobel and Bengsch on 19 October 1973 in *Herder-Korrespondenz* 27 (1973): 642–46.
126. BAP, DO-4, 403.
127. SAPMO-BArch, DY 30, IV B 2/14/161.
128. Information on the second plenary assembly of the pastoral synod. SAPMO-BArch, DY 30, IV B 2/14/161.
129. SAPMO-BArch, DY 30, IV B 2/14/161.
130. BStU, ZA, HA XX/4, 273, Bl. 69f.
131. BStU, ZA, ZAIG, Z 2204, Bl. 1–13.
132. LV S-A of the PDS, LPA-Halle, IV C 2/14/550 and IV D 2/14/474, respectively. I am grateful to Dr. Gerhard Nachtwei of Magdeburg, director of the office of pastoral care and the director of the former Zentralarchiv des Bischöflichen Amtes Magdeburg, and the archivist Dr. Franz Schrader for documents from this archive. I would also like to thank Aloys Funke of Berlin, the clergyman who was displaced after the pilgrimage, for private documents and information.
133. SAPMO-BArch, IV B 2/14/17.
134. See copy of the letter dated 21 September 1973 (BAP, DO-4, 470). For (identical) information from 18 October 1973, see Lange et al., *Katholische Kirche*, 254ff.
135. Konrad Feiereis, "Weltanschauliche Strukturen in der DDR und die Folgen für die Existenz katholischer Christen," in: Deutscher Bundestag, *Materialien der Enquete-Kommission "Aufarbeitung von Geschichte und Folgen der SED-Diktatur in Deutschland"*, Vol. VI (Baden-Baden/Frankfurt am Main, 1995), I-602f.
136. "Information" from 15 November 1974. BStU, ZA, ZAIG, Z 2355, p. 1f.
137. See the text of the pastoral letter from 17 November 1974, Lange et al., *Katholische Kirche*, 257–62.
138. See the corresponding letter. DAB, V/5-7-2.
139. Memoranda from the Administrative Office of the State Secretary for Church Affairs from 13 and 14 November 1974. SAPMO-BArch, DY 30, IV B 2/14/156.
140. Postscriptum recapitulatory memo from 28 November 1974 by Prelate Dissemond (ROO, A IV 8).
141. Transcript by Advisor to the Ordinariate Lange from November 18, 1974 (ROO, A VIII 6).
142. Seigewasser's information from 18 November 1974. SAPMO-BArch, DY 30, IV B 2/14/156.
143. Memo of 10 December 1974 from MfS Major Helmut Wegener, on a conversation between Willi Barth from the ZK of the SED with the director of HA XX/4, Lieutenant Colonel Franz Sgraja, on 6 December 1974 where Verner's instructions were conveyed to the MfS. BStU, ZA, AP 12052/92, p. 38f.
144. Cf. the nearly identical content of the records from the Administrative Office of the State Secretary for Church Affairs, despite the different language registers (Horst Pätzke from 13 December 1974, BAP, DO-4, 470) and the Berlin Diocesan Ordinariate's version (Gerhard Lange, undated, ROO, A VIII 6).
145. Cf. Dieter Grande and Bernd Schäfer, "Interne Richtlinien und Bewertungsmaßstäbe zu kirchlichen Kontakten mit dem MfS", in Vollnhals, ed., *Kirchenpolitik von SED und Staatssicherheit*, 388-404.
146. Concerning Kalb, see esp. BStU, ZA, AP 14416/92.
147. SAPMO-BArch, DY 30, IV B 2/14/156.
148. Memo from department head Horst Hartwig of 2 March 1982. SAPMO-BArch, DY 30, IV B 2/14/158.
149. Cf. Ute Haese, "Das Protestverhalten der Katholischen Kirche in der DDR bei der Einführung des Wehrunterrichts", in *Deutschland Archiv* 26 (1993), 1049-1057.
150. See the text dated 12 June 1978 in Lange et al., *Katholische Kirche*, 294ff.

151. See the state memo from 12 June 1978, BAP, DO-4, 465, and the undated file note by Paul Dissemond on this discussion, ROO, A VIII 6.

152. Text from the Berlin Ordinariate from 28 June 1978 in Lange et al., *Katholische Kirche*, 296.

153. Quoted from information of the delegate of the Chair of Internal Affairs of the Erfurt district council from 23 July 1978. LV Thüringen der PDS, LPA-Erfurt, IV D 2/14/568. Protest of the Administrative Office of the State Secretary and the reactions of Lange in a conversation on 2 August 1978. BAP, DO-4, 465.

154. Appendix no. 7 on the minutes of the Politburo session of 4 April 1980. SAPMO-BArch, DY 30, J IV 2/2/1839.

155. On this, consider the regular meetings of representatives of the ZdK, which later included the DBK, with East German bishops and higher clerical officers in East Berlin from 1966, who were given preferred border passage. These meetings, later referred to as "Presidial Committee" and, as of 1968, "Service Meetings," were tolerated and finally even promoted by the MfS. Kronenberg, "Zur Rolle des Zentralkomitees," 53–67.

156. Günter Gaus, *Wo Deutschland liegt: Eine Ortsbestimmung* (Hamburg, 1993), 200. The applicable observation becomes more precise when one swaps positions two and three.

157. Cf. Trilling, *Kirche auf Distanz,* in Edward Schillebeeckx ed., *Mystik und Politik: Theologie im Ringen um Geschichte und Gesellschaft* (Mainz, 1988), 322-332.

158. Cf., e.g., this quotation from the final passage of an address by Bishop Wanke of Erfurt on 12 July 1987 at the Catholic convention in Dresden: "Even in Bavaria and Hesse, one can lose faith and become a materialist. No, it is not the other affairs that get to us, but rather that we have lost sight of God and have become religiously small-minded people." Karl-Heinz Ducke and Winfried Weinrich, *Joachim Wanke: Last und Chance des Christseins* (Leipzig, 1991), 284.

159. *Rheinischer Merkur,* 14 April 1989, 27.

160. Cf. in general: Grande and Schäfer, *Kirchenpolitik.*

161. Ibid., 173 (Sermon at the Celebratory Service).

162. Ibid., 175.

163. "Information on the Conclusions and Measures for the Continuation of Political Work with the Catholic Church through the State Organs in the District of Dresden." LV Sachsen der PDS, LPA-Dresden, no call number.

164. SAPMO-BArch, DY 30, IV B 2/14/162.

165. Lange et al., *Katholische Kirche,* 320–31.

166. Undated nine-page "Information und Einschätzung über das Pastoralschreiben der Berliner Bischofskonferenz (BBK) an die Priester und Diakone." ACDP VII-013-3153.

167. This is from a speech entitled "Follow-Up to the Pastoral Letter of September 8, 1986," which Wanke had given on 4 March 1987 in Berlin at an "administrative meeting" of the BBK with representatives of the DBK and the ZdK, and revised in October 1987. ROO, A VII 5.

168. Cf., e.g., Joachim Garstecki's extensive reflections from October 1984 in the Halle Action Group (AKH) circular "Living and Staying in the GDR: Thoughts on a New Old Topic." The AKH dedicated a plenary assembly to this topic in 1984, which even the Western media covered.

169. BAP, DO-4, 991.

170. BStU, ZA, ZAIG, Z 3372, pp. 1–8.

171. ROO, A III 16.

172. BStU, ZA, HA XX/4, 1528, p. 122f., and BStU, ZA, ZAIG, Z 3062, p. 5.

173. Cf. also Haese, "Katholische Kirche in der DDR: Bischof Schaffran's Honecker-Besuch 1981" in Hartmut Mehringer ed., *Von der SBZ zur DDR: Studien zum Herrschaftssystem in der Sowjetischen Besatzungszone und in der Deutschen Demokratischen Republik* (Munich, 1995), 269-289.

174. Cf. the file note by Prelate Dissemond on a conversation with State Secretary Gysi from 15 December 1980, ROO, A VIII 1, and the information from Gysi on a conversation with Lange from 13 January 1981, BAP, DO-4, 466.

175. See the documents prepared in the Administrative Office of the State Secretary for Church Affairs from September/October 1980 for the conversation between Honecker and Schaffran, which Honecker studied and signed. BAP, DO-4, 718. They contained suggestions for a state talking point, directions for the BBK, and the election of the new chairperson, as well as dossier-type, annotated "biographical sketches" of the three church interlocutors.

176. Cf. an undated file note by Prelate Dissemond as well as Prelate Lange from 19 January 1981. ROO, A VIII 1.

177. Undated file note by Prelate Dissemond. Ibid.

178. BStU, ZA, HA XX/4, 352, p. 18f.

179. Honecker's meeting with the Catholic leader had taken place on 15 January 1981, and his meeting with the Protestant leaders had occurred on 6 March 1978. After the latter, the state sought to discipline Protestants by admonishing them "not to violate the spirit of March 6, 1978." In order to avoid a Catholic parallel, the March 1981 pastoral letter debate quashed any legacy of a "spirit of 15 January 1981."

180. ROO, A III 14.

181. ROO, A VIII 8.

182. BStU, ZA, ZAIG, Z 3112, pp. 1–4.

183. Lange et al., *Katholische Kirche*, 301–305, here 302f.

184. BAP, DO-4, 466; BStU, ZA, HA XX/4, 352, p. 44f.

185. BAP, DO-4, 1252.

186. See the rather contradictory discussion notes by Kalb from 9 March 1981, BAP, DO-4, 466, and by Schaffran from 6 March 1981, OAB, Files of the Episcopal Secretary, State, and Church.

187. See the HA XX/4 summary from 9 March 1981 due to the teletype message from the administrative regions. BStU, ZA, HA XX/4, 352, p. 47f.

188. Ibid., pp. 49–52.

189. Brief from an employee of the SED regional administrative authority of Neubrandenburg to Prime Secretary Hans Chemnitzer from 17 March 1981. MLHA, BPA Neubrandenburg, IV D 2/14/381.

190. See the shredded and completely reconstituted fragmentary circular from December 1989 in HA XX/4. BStU, ZA, HA XX/4, 2505.

191. For this reason, Günter Särchen was "attended to" by the MfS-BV Magdeburg from the beginning of 1982 as an OPK "Patron."

192. "Brief" of the MfS from 7 December 1982. BStU, ZA, ZAIG, No. 628/82, pp. 1–5.

193. Cf. Kalb's post scriptum on a conversation with Prelate Lange from 17 December 1982, reacting to the comment from 15 December 1982. BAP, DO-4, 466.

194. Cf. Jürgen Selke, *Katholische Kirche im Sozialismus? Der Hirtenbrief der katholischen Bischöfe in der DDR zum Weltfriedenstag 1983* (Altenberge, 1995), 124–68.

195. Cf. "Information on the intended public reading of a 'pastoral letter' in all Catholic churches of the GDR on January 10, 1982" from 24 December 1981. BStU, ZA, ZAIG, Z 3178, pp. 1–4.

196. I would like to thank the Heinrich-Theissing-Institut in Schwerin for this information from the personal records of Bishop Heinrich Theissing.

197. Cf. Selke, *Katholische Kirche im Sozialismus?*

198. Lange et al., *Katholische Kirche*, 306–11.

199. *Neues Deutschland* from January 7, 1983.

200. Undated text from early 1983 from the Administrative Office of the State Secretary "On the situations in the Berlin Conference of Bishops of the Catholic Church in the GDR." BAP, DO-4, 1296, p. 2).

201. Undated MfS brief from the year 1983 on the "Perceptions of Adverse Activities of the Vatican against the Socialist States and the Resulting Political-Operative Challenges." BStU, ZA, HA

XX/4, 1209, p. 69. From the surviving documents, it is not possible to determine how the discussions might have been "supported operatively by the agencies."
202. Note from Department Director Pätzke from 19 January 1983, on a telephone conversation with Lange. BAP, DO-4, 716.
203. "Brief" from State Secretary Gysi of 1 January 1983, on the discussion with Meisner on 20 January 1983. BAP, DO-4, 466.
204. BStU, ZA, ZAIG, Z 3282, pp. 1–6 (quoted on p. 3).
205. Memo by Kalb from November 7, 1983, on Prelate Lange's statements in a discussion on November 7, 1983 (BAP, DO-4, 466). Lange tried to exploit this centralism to expand the sphere of responsibilities and consolidate them in his person. Thus, in a discussion with Kalb on August 29, 1989, he suggested that all copiers for all church administrative offices in the GDR pass through him in order to establish "unified criteria" and to be able to lead an "instruction session" on how to use the machines (memo from Kalb from September 11, 1989: BAP, DO-4, 1329).
206. BStU, ZA, HA XX/4, 90, p. 277f. According to Dissemond, Meisner did not inform the BBK of this declaration.
207. MfS brief from 6 June 1984 on "Background of a Declaration of Cardinal Meisner Opposite the Government of the GDR from May 25, 1984." BStU, ZA, HA XX/4, 343, pp. 77–89, quoted on p. 79.
208. Cf. Prelate Dissemond's file note from 15 December 1980. ROO, A, VIII 1.
209. Draft of the official discussion from 8 November 1982. BAP, DO-4, 418.
210. BAP, DO-4, 1258. See also Grande and Schäfer, *Kirchenpolitik,* 29f.
211. Cf., e.g., the brief of State Secretary Gysi from 1 April 1985. SAPMO-BArch, DY 30, IV B 2/14/159. Gysi thought the Catholic Church wanted to portray itself as a "holy oppositional power to the atheist state."
212. "Information on 2 Planned Events of the Catholic Church in the GDR and in West Berlin" from the ZK of the SED from 28 October 1985. SAPMO-BArch, DY 30, IV B 2/14/162.
213. Report by Gysi at the advisory meeting with the sector leaders for Church Affairs with the advisors of the districts on 17 December 1986. SAPMO-BArch, DY 30, IV B 2/14/68.
214. ROO, A VIII 5.
215. Cf. "Information" of the MfS from 12 December 1987, on "Considerations of Cardinal Meisner in Connection with the 750th Anniversary Festivities of Berlin." BStU, ZA, HA XX/4, 618-vol. 1, p. 63f.
216. Cf. Lange's comment from 15 February 1987. ROO, A VIII 5.
217. Cf. the "Kurzinformation" from Cardinal Meisner from 28 October 1987 on his participation in the act of state. ROO, A VIII 1.
218. MfS brief from 29 October 1987. BStU, ZA, HA XX/4, 276, p. 108ff.
219. Grande and Schäfer, *Kirchenpolitik,* 132–45.
220. Ibid., 144f.
221. Undated memo from June 1987. LV Sachsen der PDS, LPA-Dresden, 12011.
222. Cf. Ute Haese, "SED-Kontakte der katholischen Kirche im Bistum Dresden-Meißen" In *Kirchliche Zeitgeschichte* 8 (1995), 510-531.
223. Discussions on 27 February 1986, BAP, DO-4, 1256, and on 6 April 1987, LV Sachsen of the PDS, LPA-Dresden, 12010.
224. Wilhelm Ernst et al., *"unter kommunistischer Zensur": Theologisches Jahrbuch 1991* (Leipzig, 1992), 317ff.
225. Ibid., 357–71.
226. This was seconded via church-political channels. Thus, Feiereis's critical article "Wahrheit-Wissenschaft-Fortschritt: Philosophie in der DDR betrachtet aus christlicher Sicht" was not published by the Catholic St. Benno Press due to GDR state censorship—abetted by Prelate Lange. In contrast, Marxist lecturer Franklin Borrmann from the University of Jena, in a letter to State Secretary Gysi of 11 February 1988, advocated the publication of the article.

BAP, DO-4, 1305. It could not be published until 1991. Ernst et al., *"unter kommunistischer Zensur,"* 220–44).

227. Klohr, "Atheismus und Religion in der DDR" in Günter Heydemann and Lothar Kettenacker eds. *Kirchen in der Diktatur: Drittes Reich und SED-Staat* (Göttingen, 1993), 285. Klohr's assertion that the concept of "scientific atheism" had thus been laid to rest, however, is not accurate. At least, Klohr's research group by that name in Rostock-Warnemünde did not change its name before the end of 1989. Cf. also a "working point of view' from March 1989 from the Ministerium für Hoch- und Fachschulwesen, "zu den Aufgaben und Entwicklungsrichtungen in Lehre, Forschung und Kaderentwicklung auf dem Gebiet des wissenschaftlichen Atheismus *(sic!)* an den Universitäten und Hochschulen der DDR bis 1995." BAP, DO-4, 1031.

228. BAP, DO-4, 1378.

229. Monsignor Franz Xaver Walter of Berlin in a letter to Cardinal Meisner on 5 June 1986. ROO, old Signatur [aSig] XIV.

230. Undated file note from Cardinal Meisner (ibid.).

231. Ducke and Weinrich, *Joachim Wanke,* 249ff. This address was published only in the West: *Herder-Korrespondenz* 40 (1986): 548.

232. ROO, N 4.1, Protocol No. 4/1986.

233. See several letters to the BBK. ROO, N 19.

234. Ibid. See also Garstecki, "DDR-Ökumene mit beschränkter Haftung?" in *Orientierung* 51 (1987), 81-83.

235. See the minutes from 18 November 1987 on the session of the bishops on 15 November. ROO, N 4.1. I am grateful to Bishop Dr. Joachim Wanke, Erfurt, for a written position statement on this action from 18 October 1995.

236. ROO, aSig XIV: ÖV-Durchführung. Protocol No. 4/1987. "Powers'" mainly implied the CDU, the (Protestant) Christliche Friedenskonferenz (CFK), and the (Catholic) BK.

237. XXVII. Parteitag der KpdSU: *Politischer Bericht des Zentralkomitees der KPdSU an den XXVII. Parteitag der Kommunistischen Partei der Sowjetunion. Berichterstatter: M.S. Gorbatschow,* Moscow 1986.

238. Küchenmeister, Daniel: "Wann begann das Zerwürfnis zwischen Honecker und Gorbatschow? Erste Bemerkungen zu den Protokollen ihrer Vier-Augen-Gespräche." *Deutschland Archiv* 26 (1993), 39; Küchenmeister, Daniel (ed.): *Honecker-Gorbatschow: Vieraugengespräche,* Berlin 1993.

239. *Neues Deutschland,* 10 April 1987.

240. The joint declaration of the SPD and SED.

241. Potthoff, Heinrich: *Die "Koalition der Vernunft": Deutschlandpolitik in den 80er Jahren,* Munich 1995, 564–661.

242. "Thesen zur Arbeitsberatung mit leitenden Mitarbeitern des III. und IV. Departementes der Sicherheitsorgane der VR Polen (23.3.–31.3.1988 in Warschau)" of HA XX/4 from 23 March 1988. BStU, ZA, HA XX/4, 1257, p. 110.

243. Cf. Eisenfeld, Bernd: "Die Ausreisebewegung: eine Erscheinungsform widerständigen Verhaltens." In Poppe, Ulrike/Eckert, Rainer/Kowalczuk, Ilko-Sascha (eds.): *Zwischen Selbstbehauptung und Anpassung: Formen des Widerstandes und der Opposition in der DDR* (Berlin, 1995), 192–223; Bernd Eisenfeld, "Die Zentrale Koordinierungsgruppe: Bekämpfung von Flucht und Übersiedlung", in Henke, Klaus-Dietmar/Suckut, Siegfried/Vollnhals, Clemens/Süß, Walter/Engelmann, Roger (eds.): *Anatomie der Staatssicherheit. Geschichte, Struktur und Methoden: MfS-Handbuch,* Vol. IV (Berlin 1995), I, 1–52.

244. Brief to the Politburo as 8-page attachment 1 to protocol of Politburo meeting from 19 April 1988. SAPMO-BArch, DY 30, J IV 2/2/2269.

245. Addendum No. 1 to the minutes of the session of the Politburo from 8 March 1988. SAPMO-BArch, DY 30, J IV 2/2/2263, p. 5.

246. *ND,* 3 December 1988.

247. *ND,* 20 January 1989.

248. Working group Iustitia et Pax, *Arbeitshilfe: Der konziliare Prozeß für Gerechtigkeit, Frieden und Bewahrung der Schöpfung* (East Berlin, 1987). Manuscript in author's possession.
249. Lange et al., *Katholische Kirche,* 341ff.
250. Cf. the memo of 4 February 1988 on a conversation with Lange on 2 February. BAP, DO-4, 716.
251. Cf. a 2 February 1988 memo from Peter Kraußer, director of the Working Group for Church Affairs at the ZK, for Politburo member Werner Jarowinsky. SAPMO-BArch, DY 30, IV B 2/14/172.
252. Cf. the measures suggested by HA XX/4 from 2 February 1988 after the first plenary assembly. BStU, ZA, HA XX/4, 545, p. 77.
253. Minutes of the session from 8 March 1988. SAPMO-BArch, DY 30, J IV 2/2/2263.
254. Compare this to the text of the "Verbalnote" from 9 March 1988. SAPMO-BArch, DY 30, IV B 2/14/165.
255. Memo of the Working Group for Church Affairs at the ZK of the SED of 10 March 1988, ibid.
256. Eight-page brief by Werner Jarowinsky from 5 May 1988 on the conversation of State Secretary Gysi and Cardinal Meisner on 25 April 1988, signed by Erich Honecker. SAMPO-BArch, DY 30, IV B 2/14/19.
257. ROO, A VIII 5.
258. SAPMO-BArch, DY 30, J IV 2/2/2290.
259. See the telegram of the GDR ambassador in Rome, Wolfgang Kiesewetter, of 5 May 1988 to the MfAA in Berlin on a conversation with Cardinal Achille Silvestrini. BStU, ZA, HA XX/4, 90, p. 276.
260. Cf. Bernd Schäfer, "Verzweifelte SED-Planspiele kurz vor dem Untergang: Am Ende war der Papst Honeckers 'Chefsache'", *Der Tagesspiegel,* 21 June 1996, for an overview of the developments surrounding the papal visit to the GDR between 1988 and 1990.
261. Brief by the director of the Department of State and Law in the SED district leadership of Dresden, Andreas Graff, from 19 December 1988, on an advisory meeting in the ZK of the SED in Berlin on 16 December 1988. HStA Dresden, Bezirksleitung der SED Dresden, 14086.
262. Brief by Andreas Graff from 6 September 1988, on an advisory session in the ZK of the SED in Berlin on 28 July 1988. Ibid., quoted on p. 5.
263. Kalb's letter of 25 November 1988 to Heinrich. BAP, DO-4, 1240.
264. BStU, ZA, HA XX/4, 733, p. 164.
265. BStU, ZA, HA XX/4, 550, p. 181.
266. See the "Einsatzkonzeption" of HA XX/4 from 13 April 1989, with the listing of all IM. BStU, ZA, HA XX/4, 378, p. 164.
267. Ibid., p. 227.
268. Ibid., p. 70.
269. See the undated multilateral draft of this description from the end of 1988. BAP, DO-4, 1030.
270. SAPMO-BArch, DY 30, IV B 2/14/9.
271. Mission statement of the OLZ from 18 January 1989. BAP, DO-4, 959.
272. Brief by department head Andreas Graff from 22 March 1989 on a discussion with Peter Kraußer from the ZK of the SED. HStA Dresden, BL of the SED Dresden, 14086.
273. Cf. the state file note from 30 April 1989. Ziemer, Christof: "Der konziliare Prozeß in den Farben der DDR: Die politische Einordnung und Bedeutung der Ökumenischen Versammlung der Christen und Kirchen in der DDR für Gerechtigkeit, Frieden und Bewahrung der Schöpfung." In Deutscher Bundestag: *Materialien,* Band VI-2, 1575f.
274. For the state's aggressive postures, cf. Feiereis, *Weltanschauliche Strukturen,* 611f.
275. BStU, ZA, HA XX/4, 378, p. 100.
276. ROO, N 4.7.

277. "5. Tagesbericht" of the task force of the advisory council of the District of Dresden from 30 April 1989. HStA Dresden, Bt/RdB 47575.

278. Brief of an employee of the SED district leadership of Dresden from 26 May 1989. HStA Dresden, BL der SED Dresden, 14086.

279. Cf. also on the founding of the VdF Bernd Schäfer, "Die KPD/SED und ihr Umgang mit religiösem Brauchtum und kirchlichem Leben im Alltag von SBZ und DDR - unter besonderer Berücksichtigung Mecklenburg-Vorpommerns bzw. der ehemaligen drei Nordbezirke", in Landtag Mecklenburg-Vorpommern (ed.): *Zur Arbeit der Enquête-Kommission "Leben in der DDR, Leben nach 1989 - Aufarbeitung und Versöhnung", Volumes I-IX* (Schwerin, 1996/1997), VI-156-194.

280. BStU, ZA, HA XX/4, 1740 and 934.

281. ROO, A VIII 1. Cf. the then repeated, fundamentally opposed position of church-political abstinence under the denunciation of the Ecumenical Convocation as promoting an "ideal type of Utopian socialism" by Prelate Gerhard Lange on 19 August 1989 in the formulation "Zur politischen und kirchlichen sowie kirchenpolitischen Lage August 1989," ibid.

282. ROO, N 1.3.1.

283. ROO, N 8.1.

284. Secretary of the Berlin Conference of Bishops (BBK) press office, Documentation, Dokument 1. Author's possession.

285. Durstewitz, Heinz Josef: "Die Rolle der Kirchen, vor, während und nach dem Umbruch in der ehemaligen DDR", in Jürgen Israel ed., *Zur Freiheit berufen: Die Kirche in der DDR als Schutzraum der Opposition 1981–1989* (Berlin, 1991), 40. One day later, on 9 September 1989 at the St. Matthias Kirche in West Berlin, the new bishop spoke of leaving as being "the more comfortable way," which could be "the more dangerous." Sekretariat der BBK/Pressestelle, Dokumentation, Dokument 2. Cf. the relativization of these statements in a further sermon of Sterzinsky on 24 September 1989, in St. Hedwig's Cathedral. Ibid., Dokument 6.

286. Letter of 18 September 1989 from Löffler to Jarowinsky. BAP, DO-4, 993. Löffler wanted to draw this conclusion from the "tenor" of the bishop of Berlin's response letter, which had gone to Honecker after Honecker had congratulated Sterzinsky on his new position on 9 September 1989. Cf. both letters in BAP, DO-4, 993.

287. Secretary of the BBK, Press Office, Dokumentation, Dokument 3, quotes p. 3ff. Cf. Dokumente 4 and 5 with similar statements by Bishop Wanke on the issue of emigration.

288. Israel, *Zur Freiheit berufen*, 90–95, here 93.

289. Memo from Walter Fuchs, representative to the president of the interior at the advisory council of the district of Dresden, from 28 September 1989, on a staff meeting on 27 September 1989. HStA Dresden, BL of the SED Dresden, 14086, quotes on p. 1f.

290. On the following quotes, see Braun, *Volk und Kirche*, 229ff. On Braun's previous foray at the advisory council of the District of Magdeburg on 13 September 1989, see the letter of the representative of the president of the interior to Hermann Kalb from 15 September 1989. BAP, DO-4, 1288. His poor health kept this attempt from leading to the agreed-upon proclamation.

291. Braun, *Volk und Kirche*, 231.

292. See Eckhard Bahr, *Sieben Tage im Oktober: Aufbruch in Dresden* (Leipzig, 1990) for a graphic presentation of events in Dresden from 3–10 October 1989.

293. Ibid., 43ff.

294. BStU, ZA, HA XX 4/, 90, p. 290.

295. Cf. Bishop Wanke's text from 10 October 1989, signed as official chair of the BBK. BAP, DO-4, 993.

296. Note from Kalb from 11 October 1989 on a discussion with Lange on 9 October 1989. BAP, DO-4, 993.

297. Office of the BBK, Press Office, Dokumentation, Dokument 14. Cf., in addition, the MfS brief from 17 October 1989, which already contained a first list of church suggestions on

pertinent issues (Jugendweihe, people's education, equal professional opportunities, church kindergartens, printing permits, the right to have Catholic lay organizations, pastoral care in prisons, alternative civil service). BStU, ZA, HA XX/4, 88, p. 7f.

298. Cf. the letter of 24 October 1989 by Bishop Wanke in his capacity as official chair of the BBK to Krenz after the latter's election. BAP, DO-4, 993.

299. BAP, DO-4, 993.

300. LV Sachsen der PDS, LPA-Dresden, 14087.

301. Office of the BBK, Press Office, Dokumentation, Dokument 16.

302. See the text in *Tag des Herrn*, 5 November 1989, p. 4f.

303. Durstewitz, "Rolle der Kirchen," 43. Many teachers and students from Berlin also participated in this demonstration. The Berlin Ordinariate, though, prohibited students of the private Catholic Theresienschule from participating and mandated lessons (personal correspondence of Prof. Jens Reich, Berlin, one of the speakers at the mass demonstration whose daughter was in the Theresienschule).

304. ROO, B 8.

305. ROO, B 8.

306. Ibid.

307. ROO, A VIII 1.

308. Braun, *Volk und Kirche*, 233f.

309. Cf. the exchange of letters from 8 and 9 November 1989. BStU, ZA, HA XX/4, 88, pp. 68–72.

310. BStU, ZA, HA XX/4, 88, p. 74.

311. Ibid., p. 75.

312. SAPMO-BArch, DY 30, IV B 2/14/159.

313. Hans-Hermann Hertle/Gerd-Rüdiger Stephan eds., *Das Ende der SED: Die letzten Tage des Zentralkomitees* (Berlin, 1997). See also Gregor Gysi/Thomas Falkner, *Sturm aufs Große Haus: Der Untergang der SED*, (Berlin, 1990).

314. *KNA-Dokumentation* Nr. 212 from 7 December 1989, p. 1f.

CONCLUSION

Over a period of almost forty-five years, relationships developed between the Catholic Church in the GDR and the socialist state that shaped both sides. It was natural that, forced to exist under a dictatorship, the church was more deeply marked than the state. The supposition that the German Democratic Republic was going to last led to changes in the attitudes and behaviors of Catholic Church members and representatives that to some extent grew out of the church's institutional dynamic. Church-state relations were characterized by mutual skepticism and distance, but they also constituted an amalgamation of conflicts and pragmatic cooperation, as well as irreconcilable differences and areas of convergence. Over the course of the history of the GDR, mutual influences emerged between these two completely antithetical structures, which ultimately led to a kind of routine.

It took the SED a long time to develop a more objective way of dealing with the churches, in which Kirchenpolitik always remained subordinate to tactical calculations. It saw the church as a potential enemy that needed to be monitored with suspicion. Because religion and the churches were merely forms of "institutionalized superstition," the SED long believed that both would die out gradually in the course of building up socialism. The SED had to move away from this hope, as actual events did not conform to the deterministic vision of "scientific atheism." Communist ideologues had to modify their prognostications in the 1960s. The pressure of a hostile environment had shrunk the churches down to a hard core, it was true, but that core remained stable. The churches were able to sustain themselves and to bring up new generations, and it appeared likely that they could continue to do so for the foreseeable future. After a considerable delay, the SED openly conceded this in the late 1970s. At international conferences in the 1980s, the GDR pointed to the existence of "its" churches as proof of the state's tolerance, claiming that there was religious freedom in the GDR.

Notes from this chapter begin on page 281.

Compared with the rest of the Communist world, the GDR's repressive Kirch-enpolitik was rather moderate. No lay Catholics or priests lost their lives in the GDR due to political persecution for their religious conviction or function within the church. No more than fifteen Catholic priests were imprisoned between 1945 and 1961 for political "crimes," and church intervention saw that most of these were only detained for a short time or released before their full sentences were served, although there were some draconian exceptions. Yet the GDR's special circumstances—the fact that it lacked the true character of a nation-state through its special relationship with the Federal Republic of Germany and corresponding restraints—spared the churches from the much harsher measures of Stalinist-type repression as experienced in the Soviet Union and Eastern Europe in the late 1940s and 1950s.

Stabilization

The SED finally came to terms with the existence of the churches and no longer fundamentally challenged them once the Berlin Wall was built in 1961. Without the resulting internal stabilization of the GDR—and the official international recognition by other countries achieved a decade later—the SED leadership would likely not have found a path to a more pragmatic form of Kirchenpolitik. After 1961, the SED was often satisfied merely to contain unwanted political activities by using disguised forms of measured repression or by sending mes-sages via the state's Catholic negotiating partners. Not a single priest or leading Catholic official was arrested for political reasons between September 1961 and December 1989, although some individual Catholics were.

In this period, the "ruling party" gradually recognized the economic useful-ness of the Catholic Church and its value for foreign relations. Although all of the legal connections across the German-German border were cut off, the SED approved the influx of West German money and materials to finance and sup-ply the churches because of the GDR's growing need for hard currency, in the end even encouraging the growth of this enterprise. The SED needed to fund its ambitious economic and social programs, as well as its massive security apparatus. For GDR leaders, social stability and "law and order" were the unconditional foundation of their monopoly on power. Thus the churches simply made good business sense for the GDR's "commercial coordination" bureaucratic apparatus, which had aimed to secure hard currency on a large scale since its establishment in 1966. As of the mid 1970s, the regime sought to expand Western financial transfers even more. All this substantially undermined the "dying-out prognoses" of "scientific atheism": permanent West German financial aid for the Catholic Church in the GDR was so essential that it did much more than just preventing the church from its demise.

Finally, the SED leadership's policy vis-à-vis the Vatican contributed to a sta-bilization of the Catholic Church in the GDR and expanded its sphere of activities. In the 1960s, the GDR sought to use the Catholic Church's international character for its campaign to gain diplomatic recognition as a sovereign state in the world community; in the 1970s and 1980s, it tried to use the church to further aid its diplomatic ambitions. GDR leaders thereby saw the Vatican less as a religious institution than as a state of tremendous diplomatic potential, which did not even preclude the possibility of an official exchange of ambassadors and a papal nuncio in East Berlin as doyen of the diplomatic corps. The Soviet Union vetoed the latter, but a pope who communicated with all the other global heads of state always remained an attractive target for providing evidence of the GDR's international standing.

The state thus respected and cautiously expanded the room for maneuver of the Catholic Church in the GDR, which was much greater than that of churches in other socialist countries (except for the special case of Poland). The GDR church, for its part, was able to use this relative freedom also to the advantage of Catholics in other countries through private and official visits by bishops, or by means of discreetly organized transfers of literature or other assistance. Numerous Czechoslovakian priests, for example, were secretly ordained on GDR territory after entering the country as tourists across the visa-free border. The Vatican, too, made use of the GDR's special situation in its own policy toward the Communist world and hoped to establish the East German Catholic Church as a diplomatic bridgehead for Central and Eastern Europe. The Berlin Conference of Ordinaries (BOK) and the Berlin Bishops' Conference (BBK) were somewhat afraid of this allegedly too-accommodating Vatican policy (developed under Pope Paul VI) for reasons related to both domestic Kirchenpolitik and German-German relations. Yet this did not in any way diminish the favorable status quo that the Catholic Church in the GDR enjoyed. By the end of the 1980s, this status had finally made it possible to mutually plan for a special visit of Pope John Paul II to the GDR and Berlin, scheduled for 1991.

Neutralization

SED tolerance was calculated to stabilize the party's power. It went so far as to grant the bishop of Berlin, who resided in the East, regular and steady access to West Berlin beginning just a few weeks after the erection of the Berlin Wall. For the dictatorial regime, neutralizing the internal political threats posed by the church was the precondition for establishing informal "rules for mutual business" *(Geschäftsgrundlage)*. In August 1961, the MfS negotiated such rules with the Catholic Church's emissaries, which developed into the best possible "modus vivendi" from the perspective of Catholic leaders.

The road to this "modus vivendi" had been a long one. The inner-Catholic conflict in 1950 between West Berlin and "the zone" (i.e., the GDR) over the very existence of a Catholic Church in the GDR took place without Communist authorities monitoring or attempting to influence the discussion. The ordinaries who lived and worked in the Soviet zone/GDR prevailed in this debate; their orientation reflected what they called the "zone reality." In 1951, Wilhelm Weskamm, who strongly advocated this position, became bishop of Berlin. Although he wanted Catholics in the GDR to develop a unique church identity, the repressive period of Kirchenpolitik in 1952–1953 and the introduction of the Jugendweihe ceremony in 1955 conflicted with hopes for an orderly "modus vivendi" with the state. In 1956, Weskamm's last year in office (when he was already seriously ill), the new strongman in the East German Catholic community, Bishop Otto Spülbeck of Meißen, tried to achieve a working relationship with the state, feeling encouraged to do so by Pope Pius XII. But his unintentionally undiplomatic sermon before the Cologne Catholic Congress in September 1956, combined with the generally worsening repression in the Communist world in the wake of the bloody suppression of the Hungarian uprising, made this impossible.

Instead, beginning in 1957, the GDR's centralized political apparatus, especially the MfS, used surveillance and administrative measures to set increasingly clear boundaries regarding what public Catholic activities it would tolerate. Deploying listening devices in Catholic offices on a massive scale, the security services were able to gather comprehensive internal information in 1958–1959 and to use it to intimidate the church. The state continued an intensive campaign of atheist propaganda until about 1963 to "prove the superiority of dialectical materialism over religious superstition." In the same period, it also reconfigured the entire education system with a comprehensive socialist slant, thereby pushing the churches completely out of the schools.

In March 1960, Catholic ordinaries residing in the GDR refrained from making joint public statements when Berlin Bishop Julius Döpfner's movements were severely restricted and the state increased pressure on them. After May 1958, Döpfner was no longer allowed to visit his diocese or any other place in the GDR except the city of Berlin. Döpfner's course—a political offensive to expose the Communist regime—was rooted in his perspective from West Berlin; he clearly overestimated the potential of the Catholic Church within the GDR as a supposed counterpart of the regime. In light of the harsh realities of power relations, his efforts led nowhere. The Vatican ultimately transferred Döpfner to Munich in July 1961 to ease the situation for the church in the GDR.

The new bishop of Berlin, Alfred Bengsch, who resided in East Berlin, was elected two weeks before the building of the Berlin Wall. In a summit meeting with GDR Prime Minister Willi Stoph on 2 November 1961, Bengsch implemented a paradigm change in GDR-Catholic relations. Through his MfS contacts, which he had built up since 1958, Prelate Johannes Zinke had established, in at least three conversations in the second half of August 1961, a central long-term agreement to be ratified in the November Stoph-Bengsch meeting: the Catholic Church would be "loyal" to the state by abstaining publicly from political statements in return for the "unity of the Diocese of Berlin," which would be achieved by granting the bishop, who permanently resided in the East, regular access to the western part of the city. Despite the informal character of this mutual agreement, which was in no way guaranteed, this was the first time that the long sought-after "modus vivendi" between the state and the Catholic Church had been negotiated.

After August 1961, Bengsch repeatedly signaled to state officials that the Catholic Church would practice strict "political abstinence" regarding comments on SED politics; as a rule, this policy was upheld. For the state, this silence counted as "loyalty." In turn, leading Catholic representatives also used the term "loyalty" to describe their positions to state agencies. Up until the 1970s, the GDR state wanted political abstinence to be understood in a one-sided way, merely as refraining from critical statements. In addition, however, it also expected the church's "loyalty" to include a public affirmation of SED political positions. The Catholic bishops refused to do this, pointing to their intention to refrain from any kind of public political pronouncement, whether affirmative or critical. When state agencies realized that it was fundamentally hopeless to expect "positive" political positions from the Catholic Church, they grasped the major advantage of also having no "negative" public statements, either. In contrast to the wide and unreliable range of both positive and negative opinions coming from the majority of Protestants, the regime began to see Catholic political abstinence as the lesser evil, and ultimately as a model for the role of the churches in the public sphere. Some Catholic officials did not perceive (or did not want to perceive) how the regime changed its attitude toward political abstinence. Instead, in anticipation of the state's expectations, they expanded "loyalty" by promoting "predictability" as the measure of church actions.

The state, however, could not always completely rely upon the Catholic Church to remain politically abstinent. In rare cases, the bishops themselves broke the political silence by publicly reading pastoral letters with political implications. In January 1972, for example, a letter regarding abortion was read, in November 1974 there was one concerning the socialist educational system, and in March 1981 another on the Jugendweihe. To be sure, the bishops expressed themselves with such clarity only in those rare cases when they felt compelled to do so by their religious beliefs (to combat the general moral acceptance of abortion in the population, to shield Christian faith from the secularist school system, or to fight an attempt to replace Christian rituals with atheistic ones, respectively, in the cases just mentioned). The government knew about these letters in advance because the church handed them to the MfS a few days before their reading, yet the regime was still unable to exert an influence on their content. In two cases in November 1974 and March 1981, the state secretary for church affairs attempted to prohibit the reading of pastoral letters, threatening sanctions if the ban was not followed in formal declarations.

Such declarations, however, were not the main threat to the GDR/Catholic *Geschäftsgrundlage* (whose advantages for the church, as shown, included bishops' access to West Berlin, transfers of money and material from West Germany, and permission to communicate with the FRG and the Vatican, as well as to travel there). Political figures in both the church and the government saw the "undip-lomatic actions" of individual bishops after Cardinal Bengsch's death in 1979 as a greater danger, and were even more concerned over "potential dissent and disturbances" from individual lay Catholics and clergy dating back to the 1960s and reemerging during the late 1980s.

Indeed, this potential for dissent had unfolded after 1965 in the wake of the Second Vatican Council as a result of a pluralist and anti-authoritarian under-standing of the church. Catholic dissenters demanded critical dialogue with Marxist theory and the practical realities of life in the GDR in order to change society by means of personal "engagement." For the SED, such social activism "diverted" and "undermined" socialism. Collaborating with other state agen-cies, the MfS increased surveillance and stepped up the targeted "destruction" of Catholic groups and individuals. Because the GDR was simultaneously striving for international recognition, the SED was careful to use less overt means of repression. The state viewed the emergence of a church movement for the "criti-cal affirmation of socialism" with trepidation, as a "modernization" of the church would give it greater potential for "mass appeal." But the regime was not able to exploit this movement by means of its differentiation policy (e.g., by promoting "pro-GDR" Catholics while isolating others) or by means of controlled organiza-tions like the (East German) CDU or the Berlin Conference. Instead, state and party organs had to try to infiltrate the church in order to have influence upon these internal Catholic battles.

The Catholic leadership in Berlin, like the Catholic leadership in many other parts of the world, perceived the pluralist post–Vatican II movement within the church as damaging, particularly as a threat to papal and episcopal author-ity. However, in these internal Catholic debates in the GDR of the late 1960s, the leadership there presented political rather than theological objections to the movement: it would be especially dangerous in the GDR, they argued, because it would give the regime an opening for its "differentiation policy." Ensuing Catho-lic leaders' demands that the church "close ranks" were interpreted by some in the Catholic community as a convergence of the church with the GDR authoritarian environment. For example, Claus Herold, a priest in Magdeburg and head of a working group of youth pastors in the GDR, said on 1 November 1967 in his annual report to the bishops that "the uniform thinking in this Church is a totali-tarian response to totalitarianism, the response of a minority forced into a ghetto, behind a wall, a response to the pressure of state organizations and power."

In the final analysis, the state's successes in its policy of "differentiation" did not result from the internal Catholic movement for pluralism after Vatican II but rather from the efforts of Catholic leaders to quash this pluralism within its own ranks. In other words, those "dissidents" who were deeply rooted in the church very rarely allowed themselves to be used by the SED, whereas some representa-tives of the Catholic leadership were quite willing to cooperate with the SED powers to neutralize their own internal "dissidents."

Intersections

To achieve effects of stabilization and neutralization of the church, the GDR state used secret diplomatic avenues of negotiation as a tool of Kirchenpolitik. Talks were held with Catholic clergy authorized by the bishops. Within the capricious and unpredictable realm of GDR Kirchenpolitik, the church saw such talks as an appropriate means to negotiate and maintain its sphere of activities. The successes of secret diplomacy, which had led in 1961 to the establishment of the *Geschäftsgrundlage,* came at a price for the church, however, which depended upon the personal integrity of the given individual Catholic negotiators. If they tried to use their diplomatic power—which automatically derived from the specific conditions within the GDR—to push their own ideas and policies about the church, then these channels became a kind of church-state axis of communication or even mutual cooperation.

Based on their notion of "security policy," the MfS and the Office of the State Secretary for Church Affairs used these channels to demand that their Catholic negotiation partners discipline potentially "disruptive" critics within the church. If the Catholic officials in question happened to be motivated against specific Catholic groups or individuals, whether for ideological or personal reasons, then a de facto convergence of the interests of the state and of Catholic leaders took place. Official contacts between Catholic officials authorized by the bishops and the MfS and other GDR government branches became more intimate and pragmatic during the internal church conflicts of the 1960s and early 1970s. The state was unable to score any successes for its "differentiation" policy in public, but behind closed doors the accent was on "predictability" and a perceived common responsibility to maintain and expand the *Geschäftsgrundlage* at the expense of Catholic dissidents.

Regarding the actual content of the secret diplomacy, there was very little transparency within the Catholic Church in the GDR, or even within the BOK/BBK or between individual delegates and the bishops they reported to (the Diocese of Dresden-Meißen was an exception in this regard). When critical inquiries were raised from within church ranks, the leadership called for "discretion" and "a basic trust in church leaders." Research shows, however, that the GDR bishops did not always maintain this basic trust in one another, nor did some bishops trust the delegates who carried out negotiations. Inner-Catholic conflicts were often based on a personal dislike or an attempt by one or another person to raise his profile. These conflicts did not remain hidden from GDR government officials for long; some high-ranking Catholic negotiators liked to talk. Within the church, those talks as such were known to only a few leading figures, and hardly to their full extent.

The state's knowledge about the church was not nourished by these contacts alone. Using "operative techniques" (telephone surveillance, listening devices) and informers from all parts of the GDR, the MfS gained a wealth of information over the decades. The security services could use this knowledge to target certain groups or individual lay Catholics or clergy. Such practices not only destroyed trust and solidarity but also turned individual lives upside down. Without the information that church members—often thoughtlessly—gave, as well as the intelligence gathered by the many informers from outside the Christian milieu in GDR society, the MfS would not have been able to interfere and intervene. Remarkably, most of the information it gathered was given voluntarily, not extorted.

But at no point in the entire history of the GDR were the security services or, thus, the SED in a position to actually steer the entire Catholic Church. The ultimately small degree to which information gained by secret police could be used to political advantage in a real crisis situation was proved during the SED collapse in the autumn of 1989 (and not only concerning the Catholic Church). The mechanisms of the regime's kirchenpolitik had begun to gradually falter since 1987. The intransigent posturing of the SED leadership and its proud public refusal to engage in dialogue with the churches in 1988 and 1989 could in no way be compensated for by MfS action.

The Catholic Church in the GDR

In conclusion, it can be said that Catholic life under the totalitarian conditions in the GDR produced two characteristic features that were contradictory but parallel. On the one hand, it produced multiple spaces for exercising human freedom that people both inside and outside the church could use as an "alternative public sphere." In spite of its limitations, people found such freedom useful for dealing with life in a monotonous socialist society. The internal changes in the church in the wake of Vatican II, combined with the productive discussion in the Catholic student milieu, in Catholic professional circles, and during the Dresden synods, were especially helpful in creating such a free space within the GDR. Catholics claimed this free space as something natural; it was not first achieved through secret diplomacy.

Sometimes secret diplomacy helped protect this freedom, but only when individual Catholic negotiators cared to work for it. Many leading Catholic officials had a limited view of freedom and human rights that included only the freedom to practice one's religion in services and the freedom of conscience to live their lives in the Catholic faith. Catholic educators, students, and congregations, in contrast, often worked for fundamental human rights denied to citizens in the GDR. The Catholic Assembly in Dresden in 1987 and the Catholic participation in the Ecumenical Convocation for Peace, Justice, and the Conservation of Creation held in 1988 and 1989 in Dresden and Magdeburg rejuvenated Catholics' need for discussion and critical public debate about dealing with their socialist environment.

At the same time, some clergy—whether motivated by personal or theological concerns—saw the dictatorial conditions in which they lived as an opportunity to preserve hierarchical features and practices in their own domain. Parallel to the increasing desire for travel and emigration among GDR Catholics, a still greater sense of home and GDR identity could also be perceived, not for the "socialist homeland" but for "this country" or "our country." Catholic leaders, however, only hesitantly took up the corresponding wish to stay in the GDR while working for change in society that accompanied this sense of home. As in other socialist countries in Eastern Europe in these years, or among some in the Vatican, one could put a theological spin on the peculiarity of existence of the Catholic Church under dictatorial socialist conditions: Berlin's Cardinal Meisner was fond of saying that in contrast to Westerners, GDR Catholics "had less opportunity to sin." Seen from this perspective, the Berlin Wall and the tightly controlled German-German border shielded GDR Catholics from the kind of "permissiveness" and consumer-oriented "practical materialism" that could lead to a loss of Christian faith. In the GDR, it also must be concluded, the strict division of church and state and the stigmatization of religion unintentionally strengthened Catholic identity and thus enabled the survival of a small but stable Catholic culture.

Notes

1.   ROO, AII 22.

BIBLIOGRAPHY

Archival Abbreviations Used in References

ABAM	Archiv des Bischöflichen Amtes Magdeburg
ABAS	Archiv des Bischöflichen Amtes Schwerin
ACDP	Archiv für Christlich-Demokratische Politik
ADN	Allgemeine Deutsche Nachrichtenagentur
AP	Allgemeine Personenablage (des MfS)
Ast	Außenstelle (des BStU)
BAP	Bundesarchiv, Abteilungen Potsdam
BL	Bezirksleitung
BStU	Der Bundesbeauftragte für die Unterlagen des Staatssicherheitsdienstes der ehemaligen DDR
BV	Bezirksverwaltung
DAB	Diözesanarchiv Berlin
DEFA	Deutsche Film-Aktiengesellschaft
FAZ	*Frankfurter Allgemeine Zeitung*
HStA	Hauptstaatsarchiv
KNA	Katholische Nachrichtenagentur
LPA	Landesparteiarchiv
LV	Landesvorstand (der PDS)
MdI	Ministerium des Innern
MfAA	Ministerium für Auswärtige Angelegenheiten
MfS	Ministerium für Staatssicherheit
MLHA	Mecklenburgisches Landeshauptarchiv
NKFD	Nationalkomitee Freies Deutschland
OAB	Ordinariatsarchiv Bautzen
ÖV	Ökumenische Versammlung für Frieden, Gerechtigkeit und Bewahrung der Schöpfung
ROO	Regionalarchiv Ordinarien Ost
SAPMO-BArch	Stiftung Archiv der Parteien und Massenorganisationen der ehemaligen DDR im Bundesarchiv
VPLA	Vorpommersches Landesarchiv
VVN	Vereinigung der Verfolgten des Nazi-Regimes
ZA	Zentralarchiv
ZAIG	Zentrale Auswertungs- und Informationsgruppe (des MfS)
ZMA	Zentrale Materialablagen

Overview of Archives

Archives of Parties, State Organs, and Mass Organizations of the GDR

Der Bundesbeauftragte für die Unterlagen des Staatssicherheitsdienstes der ehemaligen
  DDR, Zentralarchiv und Außenstellen, Berlin (BStU, ZA), Chemnitz, Erfurt, Frankfurt/
  Oder, Dresden, Gera, Halle, Leipzig, Magdeburg, Neubrandenburg, Potsdam, Rostock,
  Schwerin, Suhl (BStU, Ast ...)
Stiftung Archiv der Parteien und Massenorganisation der DDR im Bundesarchiv Berlin
  (SAPMO-BArch)
Bundesarchiv Abteilungen Potsdam (BAP)
  (now in Bundesarchiv Berlin)
Archiv für Christlich-Demokratische Politik der Konrad-Adenauer-Stiftung Sankt Augustin
  (ACDP)
Landesvorstand Sachsen der PDS, Landesparteiarchiv Dresden (LV Sachsen, LPA-Dresden)
  (now in Sächsisches Hauptstaatsarchiv Dresden/HStA)
Landesvorstand Thüringen der PDS, Landesparteiarchiv Erfurt (LV Thüringen, LPA-
  Erfurt)(now in Thüringisches Hauptstaatsarchiv Weimar)
Landesvorstand Sachsen-Anhalt der PDS, Landesparteiarchiv Magdeburg (LV Sachsen-
  Anhalt, LPA-Magdeburg) (now in Landeshauptarchiv Sachsen-Anhalt in Magdeburg)
Landesvorstand Sachsen-Anhalt der PDS, Landesparteiarchiv Halle (LV Sachsen-Anhalt,
  LPA-Halle) (now in Hauptstaatsarchiv Sachsen-Anhalt in Merseburg)
Sächsisches Hauptstaatsarchiv Dresden (HStA)
Mecklenburgisches Landeshauptarchiv Schwerin (MLHA) and Vorpommersches
  Landesarchiv Greifswald (VPLA) (individual files made available by the Heinrich-
  Theissing Institute Schwerin)

Church Archives

Regionalarchiv Ordinarien Ost, Erfurt (ROO)
Diözesanarchiv des Erzbistums Berlin, Berlin (DAB)
Ordinariatsarchiv des Bistums Dresden-Meißen, Bautzen (OAB)
Archiv des Bischöflichen Amtes Magdeburg, Magdeburg (ABAM)

Monographs, Anthologies, and Scholarly Editions

Adolph, Walter: *Kardinal Preysing und zwei Diktaturen: Sein Widerstand gegen die totalitäre
  Macht,* West Berlin 1971.
Agde, Günter (ed.): *Kahlschlag: Das 11. Plenum des ZK der SED 1965,* Berlin 1991.
Badstübner, Rolf/Loth, Wilfried (eds.): Wilhelm Pieck: Aufzeichnungen zur
  Deutschlandpolitik 1945–1953, Berlin 1994.
Bahr, Eckhard: *Sieben Tage im Oktober: Aufbruch in Dresden,* Leipzig 1990.

Beckmann, Andreas/Kusch, Regina: *Gott in Bautzen: Gefangenenseelsorge in der DDR*, Berlin 1994.

Beier, Peter: *Die "Sonderkonten Kirchenfragen": Sachleistungen und Geldzuwendungen an Pfarrer und kirchliche Mitarbeiter als Mittel der DDR-Kirchenpolitik (1955–1989/90)*, Göttingen 1997.

Bennewitz, Inge/Potratz, Rainer: *Zwangsaussiedlungen an der innerdeutschen Grenze: Analysen und Dokumente*, Berlin 1994.

Beschloss, Michael R.: *Powergame. Kennedy und Chruschtschow: Die Krisenjahre 1960–1963*, Düsseldorf 1991.

Besier, Gerhard: *Der SED-Staat und die Kirche: Der Weg in die Anpassung*, Munich 1993.

————: *Der SED-Staat und die Kirche 1969–1990: Die Vision vom 'Dritten Weg'*, Berlin/Frankfurt am Main 1995.

————: *Der SED-Staat und die Kirche: Höhenflug und Absturz*, Berlin/Frankfurt am Main 1995.

Besier, Gerhard/Wolf, Stephan (eds.): *"Pfarrer, Christen und Katholiken": Das Ministerium für Staatssicherheit der ehemaligen DDR und die Kirchen*, 2nd edition, Neukirchen/Vluyn 1992.

Boese, Thomas: *Die Entwicklung des Staatskirchenrechts in der DDR von 1945 bis 1989: Unter besonderer Berücksichtigung des Verhältnisses von Staat, Schule und Kirche*, Baden-Baden 1994.

Börger, Bernd/Kröselberg, Michael (eds.): *Die Kraft wuchs im Verborgenen: Katholische Jugend zwischen Elbe und Oder 1945–1990*, Düsseldorf 1993.

Braun, Johannes: *Volk und Kirche in der Dämmerung: Ein Einblick in die vier Jahrzehnte des Sozialismus in der DDR*, Leipzig 1992.

Brodkorb, Clemens: *Bruder und Gefährte in der Bedrängnis – Hugo Aufderbeck als Seelsorgeamtsleiter in Magdeburg: Zur pastoralen Grundlegung einer "Kirche in der SBZ/DDR"*, Paderborn 2002.

Broszat, Martin/Weber, Hermann (eds.): *SBZ-Handbuch: Staatliche Verwaltungen, Parteien, gesellschaftliche Organisationen und ihre Führungskräfte in der Sowjetischen Besatzungszone Deutschlands*, Munich 1990.

Conze, Werner: *Jakob Kaiser: Politiker zwischen Ost und West 1945–1949*, Stuttgart 1969.

Coreth, Emerich/Ernst, Wilhelm/Tiefensee, Eberhard (eds.): *Von Gott reden in säkularer Gesellschaft: Festschrift für Konrad Feiereis zum 65. Geburtstag*, Leipzig 1996.

Denzinger, Heinrich/Schönmetzer, Adolf (eds.): *Enchiridion Symbolorum Definitionum et Declarationum de Rebus Fidei et Morum*, 35th edition, Freiburg 1973.

Deutscher Bundestag: *1. Untersuchungsausschuß, Drucksache 12/3462 vom 14.10.1992*.

————: *Beschlußempfehlung und Bericht des 1. Untersuchungsausschusses vom 27.5.1994 und 3 Anlagenbände, Drucksache 12/7600*.

Deutscher Bundestag (ed.): *Materialien der Enquête-Kommission "Aufarbeitung von Geschichte und Folgen der SED-Diktatur in Deutschland" (12. Wahlperiode des Deutschen Bundestages)*, Nine volumes in 18 parts, Baden-Baden/Frankfurt am Main 1995.

Diederich, Georg M.: *Aus den Augen, aus dem Sinn: Die Zerstörung der Rostocker Christuskirche 1971*, Bremen/Rostock 1997.

Drobisch, Klaus (ed.): *Christen im Nationalkomitee "Freies Deutschland"*, East Berlin 1973.

Ducke, Karl-Heinz/Weinrich, Winfried (eds.): *Joachim Wanke: Last und Chance des Christseins*, Leipzig 1991.

Ernst, Wilhelm/Feiereis, Konrad/Hübner, Siegfried/März, Claus-Peter (eds.): *"unter kommunistischer Zensur": Theologisches Jahrbuch 1991*, Leipzig 1992.

Ernst, Wilhelm/Feiereis, Konrad (eds.): *Denkender Glaube in Geschichte und Gegenwart*, Leipzig 1992.

Evangelisches Bildungswerk Berlin (ed.): *Staatliche Kirchenpolitik im "real existierenden Sozialismus" in der DDR. Wissenschaftliches Kolloquium im Adam-von-Trott-Haus vom 1. bis 3. Oktober 1992,* Berlin 1993.

van Flocken, Jan/Schulz, Michael F.: *Ernst Wollweber: Saboteur-Minister-Unperson,* Berlin 1994.

Fricke, Karl-Wilhelm: *Politik und Justiz in der DDR: Zur Geschichte der politischen Verfolgung 1945–1968,* Cologne 1990.

Gaus, Günter: *Wo Deutschland liegt: Eine Ortsbestimmung,* Hamburg 1983.

Gerth, Franz: *Josef Streb (Christ in der Welt,* 44), East Berlin 1978.

Gieseke, Jens: *Die Hauptamtlichen 1962: Zur Personalstruktur des Ministeriums für Staatssicherheit,* Berlin 1994.

Grande, Dieter/Schäfer, Bernd: *Zur Kirchenpolitik der SED: Auseinandersetzungen um das Katholikentreffen 1983–1987,* Leipzig 1994.

Grütz, Reinhard: *Katholizismus in der DDR-Gesellschaft 1960–1990,* Paderborn 2004.

Gysi, Gregor/Falkner, Thomas: *Sturm aufs Große Haus: Der Untergang der SED,* East Berlin 1990.

Hackel, Renate: *Katholische Publizistik in der DDR 1945–1984,* Mainz 1987.

Haese, Ute: *Katholische Kirche in der DDR: Geschichte einer politischen Abstinenz,* Düsseldorf 1998

Hallberg, Bo: *Die Jugendweihe: Zur deutschen Jugendweihetradition,* 2nd edition, Göttingen 1979.

Havemann, Robert: *Dialektik ohne Dogma,* Reinbek 1964.

Hehl, Ulrich von/Hockerts, Hans Günter (eds.): *Der Katholizismus – gesamtdeutsche Klammer in den Jahrzehnten der Teilung? Erinnerungen und Berichte,* Paderborn 1996.

Heimann, Siegfried/Walter, Franz: *Religiöse Sozialisten und Freidenker,* Bonn 1993.

Heitzer, Heinz: *DDR: Geschichtlicher Überblick,* East Berlin 1979.

Henke, Klaus-Dietmar/Engelmann, Roger (eds.): *Aktenlage: Die Bedeutung der Unterlagen des Staatssicherheitsdienstes für die Zeitgeschichtsforschung,* 2nd edition, Berlin 1996.

Henke, Klaus-Dietmar/Suckut, Siegfried/Vollnhals, Clemens/Süß, Walter/Engelmann, Roger (eds.): *Anatomie der Staatssicherheit. Geschichte, Struktur und Methoden: MfS-Handbuch,* Volume IV/1, Berlin 1995.

Herbst, Karl: *Jenseits aller Ansprüche: Neue ökumenische Perspektiven,* Munich 1972.

Hertle, Hans-Hermann/Stephan, Gerd-Rüdiger (eds.): *Das Ende der SED: Die letzten Tage des Zentralkomitees,* Berlin 1997.

Hoffmann, Dierk/Schmidt, Karl-Heinz/Skyba, Peter (eds.): *Die DDR vor dem Mauerbau: Dokumente zur Geschichte des anderen deutschen Staates 1949–1961,* Munich 1993.

Höllen, Martin: *Heinrich Wienken, der 'unpolitische' Kirchenpolitiker: Eine Biographie aus drei Epochen des deutschen Katholizismus,* Mainz 1981.

———: *Loyale Distanz? Katholizismus und Kirchenpolitik in SBZ und DDR: Ein historischer Überblick in Dokumenten,* Volume I: *(1945 bis 1955),* Berlin 1994.

———: *Loyale Distanz? Katholizismus und Kirchenpolitik in SBZ und DDR: Ein historischer Überblick in Dokumenten,* Volume II: *(1956 bis 1965),* Berlin 1997.

Institut für vergleichende Staat-Kirche-Forschung (ed.): *Der Weg der katholischen Kirche in verschiedenen realsozialistischen Ländern in den Jahren 1945 bis 1948/49: ein historischer Vergleich,* Berlin 1995.

———: *3. Berliner Staat-Kirche-Kolloquium vom 18. bis 19. Januar 1995: Säkularisierung in Ost und West,* Berlin 1995.

Israel, Jürgen (ed.): *Zur Freiheit berufen: Die Kirche in der DDR als Schutzraum der Opposition 1981–1989,* Berlin 1991.

Janka, Walter: *Die Unterwerfung,* Munich/Vienna 1994.

Jung, Ruth: *Ungeteilt im geteilten Berlin? Das Bistum Berlin nach dem Mauerbau* (Berlin, 2003).

Kaff, Brigitte (ed.): *"Gefährliche politische Gegner": Widerstand und Verfolgung in der sowjetischen Zone/DDR*, Düsseldorf 1995.

Kapferer, Norbert: *Das Feindbild der Marxistisch-Leninistischen Philosophie in der DDR 1945– 1988*, Darmstadt 1990.

Keiderling, Gerhard (ed.): *"Gruppe Ulbricht" in Berlin April bis Juni 1945. Von den Vorbereitungen im Sommer 1944 bis zur Wiedergründung der KPD im Juni 1945: Eine Dokumentation*, Berlin 1993.

Kirchberg, Annaliese (ed.): *Theresienschule zu Berlin: 1894–1994*, Berlin 1994.

Klohr, Olof (ed.): *Religion und Atheismus heute*, East Berlin 1966.

Köhler, Joachim/van Melis, Damian: *Siegerin in Trümmern: Die Rolle der katholischen Kirche in der deutschen Nachkriegsgesellschaft*, Stuttgart/Berlin/Cologne 1998.

Kösters, Christoph/Tischner, Wolfgang (eds.): *Katholische Kirche in SBZ und DDR*, Paderborn 2005

Kowalczuk, Ilko-Sascha/Mitter, Armin/Wolle, Stefan (eds.): *Der Tag X. 17. Juni 1953: Die "Innere Staatsgründung" der DDR als Ergebnis der Krise 1952/54*, Berlin 1995.

Krone, Heinrich: *Tagebücher. First Volume: 1945–1961*, Düsseldorf 1995.

Küchenmeister, Daniel (ed.): *Honecker-Gorbatschow: Vieraugengespräche*, Berlin 1993.

Landtag Mecklenburg-Vorpommern (ed.): *Zur Arbeit der Enquête-Kommission "Leben in der DDR, Leben nach 1989 - Aufarbeitung und Versöhnung", Volumes I - IX*, Schwerin 1996/1997.

Lange, Gerhard/Pruß, Ursula/Schrader, Franz/Seifert, Siegfried (eds.): *Katholische Kirche – Sozialistischer Staat DDR: Dokumente und öffentliche Äußerungen 1945–1990*, 2nd edition, Leipzig 1993.

Lange, Gerhard/ Pruß, Ursula (eds.): *An der Nahtstelle der Systeme: Dokumente und Texte aus dem Bistum Berlin, 1st Volume/1st Part: 1945–1961*, Leipzig 1996.

Lemke, Michael: *Die SED und die Berlinkrise 1958 bis 1963*, Berlin 1995.

Leugers, Antonia: *Gegen eine Mauer bischöflichen Schweigens: Der Ausschuß für Ordensangelegenheiten und seine Widerstandskonzeption 1941 bis 1945*, Frankfurt am Main 1996.

März, Claus-Peter (ed.): *Die ganz alltägliche Freiheit. Christsein zwischen Traum und Wirklichkeit*, Leipzig 1993.

Mayer, Tilman (ed.): *Jakob Kaiser: Gewerkschafter und Patriot*, Cologne 1988.

Mehringer, Hartmut (ed.): *Von der SBZ zur DDR: Studien zum Herrschaftssystem in der Sowjetischen Besatzungszone und in der Deutschen Demokratischen Republik*, Munich 1995.

Meier, Otto: *Partei und Kirche*, East Berlin 1947.

Meinel, Reinhard/Wernicke, Thomas (eds.): *Mit tschekistischem Gruß: Berichte der Bezirksverwaltung für Staatssicherheit Potsdam 1989*, Potsdam 1990.

Ministerium für Nationale Verteidigung (ed.): *Wehrdienstgesetz und angrenzende Bestimmungen*, 4th edition, East Berlin 1984.

Mitter, Armin/Wolle, Stefan: *Untergang auf Raten: Unbekannte Kapitel der DDR-Geschichte*, Munich 1993.

Mitzscherlich, Birgit: *Diktatur und Diaspora: Das Bistum Meißen 1932–1951*, Paderborn 2005

Möhlenbrock, Tim: *Kirche und Bodenreform in der Sowjetischen Besatzungszone Deutschlands (SBZ) 1945–1949: Eine Untersuchung über das Verhalten der Evangelischen Landeskirchen und der Katholischen Kirche während der "demokratischen Bodenreform" in der SBZ unter Berücksichtigung der Auswirkungen der Bodenreform auf das kirchliche Vermögen*, Frankfurt am Main 1997.

Mothes, Jörn/ Fienbork, Gundula/Pahnke, Rudi/Ellmenreich, Renate/Stognienko, Michael (eds.): *Beschädigte Seelen: DDR-Jugend und Staatssicherheit,* Bremen/Rostock 1996.

Müller, Silvia/Florath, Bernd (eds.): *Die Entlassung: Robert Havemann und die Akademie der Wissenschaften der DDR 1965/66,* Berlin 1996.

Müller-Enbergs, Helmut (ed.): *Inoffizielle Mitarbeiter des Ministeriums für Staatssicherheit. Richtlinien und Durchführungsbestimmungen,* 2nd edition, Berlin 1996.

Naimark, Norman M.: *The Russians in Germany: A History of the Soviet Zone of Occupation, 1945–1949,* Cambridge, MA/London 1995.

Nakath, Detlef/Stephan, Gerd-Rüdiger: *Von Hubertusstock nach Bonn: Eine dokumentierte Geschichte der deutsch-deutschen Beziehungen auf höchster Ebene 1980–1987,* Berlin 1995.

Pilvousek, Josef (ed.): *Kirchliches Leben im totalitären Staat. Seelsorge in der SBZ/DDR 1945–1976: Quellentexte aus den Ordinariaten,* Hildesheim 1994.

Poppe, Ulrike/Eckert, Rainer/Kowalczuk, Ilko-Sascha (eds.): *Zwischen Selbstbehauptung und Anpassung: Formen des Widerstandes und der Opposition in der DDR,* Berlin 1995.

Potthoff, Heinrich: *Die "Koalition der Vernunft": Deutschlandpolitik in den 80er Jahren,* Munich 1995.

———: *Bonn und Ost-Berlin 1969–1982. Dialog auf höchster Ebene und vertrauliche Kanäle: Darstellung und Dokumente,* Bonn 1997.

Pötzl, Norbert F.: *Basar der Spione: Die geheimen Missionen des DDR-Unterhändlers Wolfgang Vogel,* Hamburg 1997.

Przybylski, Peter: *Tatort Politbüro: Die Akte Honecker,* Berlin 1991.

———: *Tatort Politbüro, Band 2: Honecker, Mittag und Schalck-Golodkowski,* Berlin 1992.

Raabe, Thomas: *SED-Staat und Katholische Kirche: Politische Beziehungen 1949–1961,* Paderborn 1995.

Rahner, Karl/Vorgrimler, Herbert (eds.): *Kleines Konzilskompendium: Sämtliche Texte des Zweiten Vatikanums,* 17th edition, Freiburg i. Br. 1984.

Reinhardt, Heinrich J.F. (ed.): *Theologia et Jus Canonicum: Festgabe für Heribert Heinemann zur Vollendung seines 70. Lebensjahres,* Essen 1995.

Richter, Klemens (ed.): *Wolfgang Trilling. "Trauer gemäß Gott": Leiden in und an der Kirche in der DDR,* Altenberge 1994.

Richter, Michael/ Rißmann, Martin (eds.): *Die Ost-CDU: Beiträge zu ihrer Entstehung und Entwicklung,* Weimar/Cologne/ Vienna 1995.

Rintelen, Friedrich Maria: *Erinnerungen ohne Tagebuch,* 3rd edition, Paderborn 1988.

Rißmann, Martin: *Kaderschulung in der Ost-CDU 1949–1971: Zur geistigen Formierung einer Blockpartei,* Düsseldorf 1995.

Roesler, Jörg: *Zwischen Plan und Markt: Die Wirtschaftsreform in der DDR zwischen 1963 und 1970,* Berlin 1990.

Rühle, Jürgen/Holzweißig, Günter: *13. August 1961: Die Mauer von Berlin,* Cologne 1981.

Russig, Peter: *Wilhelm Grothaus: Dresdner Antifaschist und Aufstandsführer des 17. Juni,* Dresden 1997.

Scherstjanoj, Elke (ed.): *"Provisorium für längstens ein Jahr": Protokoll des Kolloquiums "Die Gründung der DDR",* Berlin 1993.

Schillebeeckx, Edward (ed.): *Mystik und Politik. Theologie im Ringen um Geschichte und Gesellschaft: Johann Baptist Metz zu Ehren,* Mainz 1988.

Schirdewan, Karl: *Aufstand gegen Ulbricht,* Berlin 1994.

Schulte-Umberg, Thomas (ed.): *Akten deutscher Bischöfe seit 1945: DDR 1957–1961,* Paderborn 2006.

Schroeder, Klaus (ed.): *Geschichte und Transformation des SED-Staates: Beiträge und Analysen,* Berlin 1994.

Selke, Jürgen: *Katholische Kirche im Sozialismus? Der Hirtenbrief der katholischen Bischöfe in der DDR zum Weltfriedenstag 1983,* Altenberge 1995.

Staadt, Jochen: *Die geheime Westpolitik der SED 1960–1970: Von der gesamtdeutschen Orientierung zur sozialistischen Nation,* Berlin 1993.

Stehle, Hansjakob: *Geheimdiplomatie im Vatikan: Die Päpste und die Kommunisten,* Zürich 1993.

Straube, Peter-Paul: *Katholische Studentengemeinde in der DDR als Ort eines außeruniversitären Studium generale,* Leipzig 1996.

Suckut, Siegfried: *Blockpolitik in der SBZ/DDR 1945–1949: Die Sitzungsprotokolle des zentralen Einheitsfront-Ausschusses,* Cologne 1986.

Tischner, Wolfgang: *Katholische Kirche in der SBZ/DDR 1945–1951,* Paderborn 2001.

Urban, Detlef/Weinzen, Hans Willi: *Jugend ohne Bekenntnis? 30 Jahre Konfirmation und Jugendweihe im anderen Deutschland 1954–1984,* West Berlin 1984.

Vollnhals, Clemens (ed.): *Die Kirchenpolitik von SED und Staatssicherheit: Eine Zwischenbilanz,* 2nd edition, Berlin 1997.

Wagner, Armin: *Walter Ulbricht und die geheime Sicherheitspolitik der SED: Der Nationale Verteidigungsrat der DDR und seine Vorgeschichte 1953–1971,* Berlin 2002.

Weber, Hermann (ed.): *Parteiensystem zwischen Demokratie und Volksdemokratie: Dokumente und Materialien zum Funktionswandel der Parteien und Massenorganisationen in der SBZ/ DDR 1945–1950,* Cologne 1982.

Wenzel, Otto: *Kriegsbereit: Der Nationale Verteidigungsrat der DDR 1960 bis 1989,* Cologne 1995.

Wenzke, Rüdiger: *Die NVA und der Prager Frühling 1968: Die Rolle Ulbrichts und der DDR-Streitkräfte bei der Niederschlagung der tschechoslowakischen Reformbewegung,* Berlin 1995.

Werkentin, Falco: *Politische Strafjustiz in der Ära Ulbricht,* Berlin 1995.

Whitney, Craig: *Advocatus Diaboli. Wolfgang Vogel: Anwalt zwischen Ost und West,* Berlin 1993.

Zentralkomitee der deutschen Katholiken (ed.): *Ihr sollt mir Zeugen sein: Der 76. Deutsche Katholikentag in Fulda,* Paderborn 1954.

XXVII. Parteitag der KpdSU: *Politischer Bericht des Zentralkomitees der KPdSU an den XXVII. Parteitag der Kommunistischen Partei der Sowjetunion. Berichterstatter: M.S. Gorbatschow,* Moscow 1986.

Essays and Articles

Arnold, Alfred: "'Mater et Magistra': Werkzeug der ideologischen Kriegsvorbereitung." In: *Deutsche Zeitschrift für Philosophie* 9 (1961): 1446–1460.

Barth, Willi/Bellmann, Rudi: "Die Rechtfertigung der imperialistischen Atomkriegspläne durch den politischen Klerikalismus." *Einheit* 13 (1958): 1564–1576.

Bergner, Dieter/Preuß, Gernot: "Differenzierung im politischen Klerikalismus: Zur Enzyklika 'Pacem in Terris.' In *Deutsche Zeitschrift für Philosophie* 11 (1963): 1189–1202.

Boyens, Armin: "Staatssekretariat für Kirchenfragen und Militärseelsorgevertrag: Anmerkungen zur Geschichte eines Amtes." *Kirchliche Zeitgeschichte* 6 (1993): 211–235.

———: "'Den Gegner irgendwo festhalten': 'Transfergeschäfte' der Evangelischen Kirche in Deutschland mit der DDR-Regierung 1957–1990." *Kirchliche Zeitgeschichte* 6 (1993): 379–390.

Braun, Günter: "Zur Entwicklung der Wahlen in der SBZ/DDR 1946–1950." In Weber, 545–562.

Carrillo, Elisa A.: "The Italian Catholic Church and Communism 1943–1963." *The Catholic Historical Review* 77 (1991): 644–657.

Dowidat, Christel: "Personalpolitik als Mittel der Transformation des Parteiensystems der SBZ/DDR (1945–1952)." In Weber, 484f.

Durstewitz, Heinz Josef: "Die Rolle der Kirchen, vor, während und nach dem Umbruch in der ehemaligen DDR." In Israel, 37–45.

Dusdal, Edgar: "Gesellschafts- und kirchenpolitische Positionen innerhalb des Protestantismus und der SED nach 1945." In Evangelisches Bildungswerk (Berlin, 1993), 21–33.

Eisenfeld, Bernd: "Die Ausreisebewegung: eine Erscheinungsform widerständigen Verhaltens." In Poppe/Eckert/Kowalczuk, 192–223.

———: "Die Zentrale Koordinierungsgruppe: Bekämpfung von Flucht und Übersiedlung." In Henke/Suckut/Vollnhals/Süß/Engelmann, 1–52.

Engelmann, Roger/Schumann, Silke: "Der Ausbau des Überwachungsstaates: Der Konflikt Ulbricht-Wollweber und die Neuausrichtung des Staatssicherheitsdienstes der DDR 1957." *Vierteljahreshefte für Zeitgeschichte* 43 (1995): 341–378.

Feiereis, Konrad: "Katholische Theologie in der DDR: Chance, Grenze, Selbstverständnis." *hochschule ost* 4 (1995): 46–55.

———: "Weltanschauliche Strukturen in der DDR und die Folgen für die Existenz katholischer Christen." In Deutscher Bundestag: *Materialien,* Band VI–I, 583–614.

Fischer, Alexander: "Der Einfluß der SMAD auf das Parteiensystem in der SBZ am Beispiel der CDUD." *Deutschland Archiv* 26 (1997): 265–272.

———: "Andreas Hermes und die gesamtdeutschen Anfänge der Union." In Manfred Agethen and Alexander Fischer, eds., *Die CDU in der sowjetisch besetzten Zone/DDR 1945–1952* (Sankt Augustin, 1994), 7–20.

Förster, Andreas: "Dubiose Geldgeschäfte bis kurz vor dem Tod: Stasi-Anwalt Manfred Wünsche starb in Berlin." *Berliner Zeitung,* 12 August 1994, 5.

Garstecki, Joachim: "DDR: Ökumene mit beschränkter Haftung?" *Orientierung* 51 (1987): 81–83.

Gieseke, Jens: "Die hauptamtlichen Mitarbeiter des Ministeriums für Staatssicherheit." In Henke/Suckut/Vollnhals/Süß/Engelmann, 1–107.

Grande, Dieter: "Die Pastoralsynode der Jurisdiktionsbezirke in der DDR: ein Zwischenbericht nach einem Jahr Synodenarbeit." *Priesterjahresheft* (1975): 25ff.

Grande, Dieter/Schäfer, Bernd: "Interne Richtlinien und Bewertungsmaßstäbe zu kirchlichen Kontakten mit dem MfS." In Vollnhals, 388–404.

Gülden, Josef: "Über Wesen und Aufgabe der Diaspora." In Zentralkomitee, 311–319.

Haese, Ute: "Das Protestverhalten der Katholischen Kirche in der DDR bei der Einführung des Wehrunterrichts." *Deutschland Archiv* 26 (1993): 1049–1057.

———: "Katholische Kirche in der DDR zwischen Staat und Gesellschaft." *Stimmen der Zeit* 211 (1993): 241–254.

———: "SED-Kontakte der katholischen Kirche im Bistum Dresden-Meißen." *Kirchliche Zeitgeschichte* 8 (1995): 510–531.

Hartelt, Konrad: "Die Entwicklung der Jurisdiktionsverhältnisse der katholischen Kirche in der DDR von 1945 bis zur Gegenwart." In Ernst/Feiereis, 415–440.

Haupts, Leo: "Die CDU ist die Partei, in der am stärksten der Feind arbeitet". In Kowalczuk/Mitter/Wolle, 278–310.

Hehl, Ulrich von/Tischner, Wolfgang: "Die katholische Kirche in der SBZ/DDR 1945–1989." In Deutscher Bundestag: *Materialien,* Volume VI-2, 875–949.

Heise, Joachim: "Zwischen ideologischem Dogma und politischem Pragmatismus: Kirchenpolitik der SED in den 50er Jahren." *Berliner Dialog-Hefte,* Sonderheft (1993): 1–8.

————: "Kirchenpolitik der SED zwischen ideologischem Dogmatismus und politischem Pragmatismus." In Scherstjanoj, 344–352.

Herold, Claus: "'Zwischen Elbe und Oder': Rückblicke auf die zweite Hälfte des 'anderen Weges.'" In Börger/Kröselberg, 132–136.

————: "Katholische Jugendseelsorge nach Einführung der NVA-Wehrpflicht. Dokumentation eines Reflexionsprozesses." In Börger/Kröselberg, 277–288.

Kaul, Wolfgang: "Zu Verlauf und Resultaten des Säkularisierungsprozesses in der DDR." In Institut für vergleichende Staat-Kirche-Forschung, *3. Berliner Staat-Kirche-Kolloquium,* 56–73.

Kirschke, Siegfried: "Moderne Abstammungslehre und klerikale Propaganda." *Deutsche Zeitschrift für Philosophie* 7 (1959): 603–613.

Kleineidam, Erich: "Vorgeschichte, Gründung und Aufbau des Regionalpriesterseminars Erfurt. Eine fragmentarische Chronik." In Ernst/Feiereis, 97–116.

Klohr, Olof: "Probleme des wissenschaftlichen Atheismus und der atheistischen Propaganda." *Deutsche Zeitschrift für Philosophie* 12 (1964): 133–150.

Kosing, Alfred: "Die 'gesunde Vernunft'des Jesuitenpaters Josef de Vries." *Deutsche Zeitschrift für Philosophie* 7 (1959): 65–85.

Kronenberg, Friedrich: "Zur Rolle des Zentralkomitees der deutschen Katholiken: Ein Bericht aufgrund eigener Kenntnisse und persönlicher Erfahrungen." In Hehl/Hockerts, 39–68.

Küchenmeister, Daniel: "Wann begann das Zerwürfnis zwischen Honecker und Gorbatschow? Erste Bemerkungen zu den Protokollen ihrer Vier-Augen-Gespräche." *Deutschland Archiv* 26 (1993): 30–40.

Mechtenberg, Theo: "Briefwechsel polnischer und deutscher Bischöfe 1965: Die Reaktion der Machthaber in der DDR." *Deutschland Archiv* 28 (1995): 1146–1152.

Mollnau, Karl A./Schöneburg, Karl-Heinz: "Die sozialtheoretischen Grundlagen des Klerikalfaschismus." *Deutsche Zeitschrift für Philosophie* 7 (1959): 271–289.

Oehme, Marlies: "Die Theorie der katholischen Soziallehre vom "Klassenfrieden": ein demagogisches Verwirrungsmanöver des politischen Katholizismus." *Einheit* 13 (1958): 199–210.

Pilvousek, Josef: "Flüchtlinge, Flucht und die Frage des Bleibens: Überlegungen zu einem traditionellen Problem der Katholiken im Osten Deutschlands." In März, 9–23.

————: "'Innenansichten': Von der 'Flüchtlingskirche'zur 'katholischen Kirche in der DDR.'" In Deutscher Bundestag: *Materialien,* Volume VI-2, 1134–1163.

————: "Gesamtdeutsche Wirklichkeit – Pastorale Notwendigkeit: Zur Vorgeschichte der Ostdeutschen Bischofskonferenz." In Coreth/Ernst/Tiefensee, 229–242.

Puschmann, Hellmut: "Zur Brückenfunktion des Deutschen Caritasverbandes." In Hehl/Hockerts, 127–138.

Richter, Klemens: "Aufbruch oder Resignation? Zur Situation der katholischen Kirche in der DDR," *Deutschland Archiv* 4 (1971): 972–976.

————: "Jugendweihe und katholische Kirche." *Deutschland Archiv* 20 (1987): 168–180.

Rudloff, Michael: "Das Verhältnis der SED zur weltanschaulichen Toleranz in den Jahren 1946 bis 1949." *Internationale wissenschaftliche Korrespondenz zur Geschichte der deutschen Arbeiterbewegung* 29 (1993): 490–505.

Rüstau, Hartmut: "Bemerkungen zur Enzyklika 'Mater et Magistra.'" *Deutsche Zeitschrift für Philosophie* 10 (1962): 653–656.

Schäfer, Bernd: "'Inoffizielle Mitarbeiter' und 'Mitarbeit': Zur Differenzierung von Kategorien des Ministeriums für Staatssicherheit im Bereich der katholischen Kirche." *Kirchliche Zeitgeschichte* 6 (1993): 447–466.

———: "Selbstbehauptungsstrategie und (Über)lebensmuster der katholischen Kirche in der Zeit des DDR-Staat." *Kirchliche Zeitgeschichte* 7 (1994): 264–278.

———: "'Um "anzukommen" muß man sich "ankömmlich" artikulieren.' Zur 'Berliner Konferenz' (BK) zwischen 1964 und 1993." In Richter/Rißmann, 111–125.

———: "Katholische Kirche in der DDR." *Stimmen der Zeit* 213 (1995): 212ff.

———: "Verselbständigung ohne Zugewinn: DDR, katholische Kirche und Vatikan von 1965–1972." *Stimmen der Zeit* 213 (1995): 321–332.

———: "Verzweifelte SED-Planspiele kurz vor dem Untergang/Am Ende war der Papst Honeckers 'Chefsache.'" *Der Tagesspiegel*, 21 June 1996.

———: "Die KPD/SED und ihr Umgang mit religiösem Brauchtum und kirchlichem Leben im Alltag von SBZ und DDR - unter besonderer Berücksichtigung Mecklenburg-Vorpommerns bzw. der ehemaligen drei Nordbezirke." In Landtag Mecklenburg-Vorpommern, Volume VI, 156–194.

———: "'Er wollte in Fulda Zeuge sein': Eine deutsch-deutsche Geschichte aus den fünfziger Jahren." In Köhler/van Melis, 242–259.

———: "Priester in zwei deutschen Diktaturen: Die antifaschistische Legende des Karl Fischer (1900–1972)," *Historisch-Politische Mitteilungen* 7 (2000): 49–74.

Schmitz, Theodor: "Kirchenfinanzen in der SBZ/DDR 1945–1989." Unpublished manuscript 1996 (in possession of author).

———: "Die Bischofswahlen in Berlin zwischen 1945 und 1989." In Reinhardt, 605–617.

Schrader, Franz: "Erfahrungen mit der Herausgabe einer wissenschaftlichen Festschrift zum 1000jährigen Jubiläum der Gründung des Erzbistums Magdeburg." *Wichmann-Jahrbuch des Diözesangeschichtsvereins Berlin* 32/33 (1992/1993): 147–155.

Steiner, Andre: "Politische Vorstellungen und ökonomische Probleme im Vorfeld der Errichtung der Berliner Mauer: Briefe Walter Ulbrichts an Nikita Chruschtschow." In Mehringer, 233–268.

Suckut, Siegfried: "Der Konflikt um die Bodenreformpolitik in der Ost-CDU 1945: Versuch einer Neubewertung der ersten Führungskrise der Union." *Deutschland Archiv* 15 (1982): 1080–1095.

———: "Zum Wandel von Rolle und Funktion der Christlich-Demokratischen Union Deutschlands (CDUD) im Parteisystem der SBZ/DDR (1945–1952)." In Weber, 129ff.

———: "Christlich-Demokratische Union Deutschlands: CDU(D)." In Broszat/Weber, 521.

———: "Innenpolitische Aspekte der DDR-Gründung: Konzeptionelle Differenzen, Legitimations- und Akzeptanzprobleme." *Deutschland Archiv* 25 (1992): 370–384.

Trilling, Wolfgang: "Kirche auf Distanz." In Schillebeeckx, 322–332.

Vollnhals, Clemens: "Zwischen Kooperation und Konfrontation: Zur Kirchenpolitik von KPD/SED und SMAD in der Sowjetischen Besatzungszone 1945–1949." *Deutschland Archiv* 27 (1994): 478–490.

———: "Die kirchenpolitische Abteilung des Ministeriums für Staatssicherheit." In Vollnhals, 79–119.

Volze, Armin: "Kirchliche Transferleistungen in die DDR." *Deutschland Archiv* 24 (1991): 59–66.

Wentker, Hermann: "Ost-CDU und Protestantismus 1949–1958: Die Partei der 'fortschrittlichen Christen' zwischen Repräsentationsanspruch und Transmissionsaufgabe." *Kirchliche Zeitgeschichte* 6 (1993): 349–378.

————: "'Kirchenkampf' in der DDR: Der Konflikt um die Junge Gemeinde 1950–1953." *Vierteljahreshefte für Zeitgeschichte* 42 (1994); 95–127.

————: "Die Einführung der Jugendweihe in der DDR: Hintergründe, Motive und Probleme." In Mehringer, 139–165.

Werkentin, Falco: "Zwischen Tauwetter und Nachtfrost (1955–1957): DDR-Justizfunktionäre auf Glatteis." *Deutschland Archiv* 26 (1993): 341–349.

Wetzler, Helmut: "Pater Wetter kämpft mit stumpfen Waffen," *Deutsche Zeitschrift für Philosophie* 10 (1960): 1554–57.

Wilk, Stanislaw: "Der Vatikan, die Regierung und die Kirche in Polen in den Jahren 1945–1948." In Institut für vergleichende Staat-Kirche-Forschung: Der Weg, 28–37.

Ziemer, Christof: "Der konziliare Prozeß in den Farben der DDR: Die politische Einordnung und Bedeutung der Ökumenischen Versammlung der Christen und Kirchen in der DDR für Gerechtigkeit, Frieden und Bewahrung der Schöpfung." In Deutscher Bundestag: *Materialien,* Volume VI-2, 1430–1635.

INDEX OF PERSONS AND ORGANIZATIONS